Work, Capitalism, and Democracy

AMERICAN BUSINESS, POLITICS, AND SOCIETY

Series editors: Andrew Wender Cohen, Shane Hamilton, Kimberly Phillips-Fein, and Elizabeth Tandy Shermer

Books in the series American Business, Politics, and Society explore the relationships over time between politics, society, and the creation and performance of markets, firms, and industries large and small. The central theme of this series is that culture, law, and public policy have been fundamental to the evolution of American business from the colonial era to the present. The series aims to explore, in particular, developments that have enduring consequences.

A complete list of books in the series is available from the publisher.

WORK, CAPITALISM, AND DEMOCRACY

The United States Since the New Deal

Edited by Elizabeth Tandy Shermer

PENN

UNIVERSITY OF PENNSYLVANIA PRESS

PHILADELPHIA

Published by
University of Pennsylvania Press
Philadelphia, Pennsylvania 19104–4112
www.pennpress.org

Printed in the United States of America on acid-free paper
10 9 8 7 6 5 4 3 2 1

Cataloging-in-Publication record for this book
is available from the Library of Congress

Hardback ISBN 978-1-5128-2871-9
eBook ISBN 978-1-5128-2872-6

Dedicated to Eileen Boris, Historian, Feminist, Radical

CONTENTS

Introduction 1
Elizabeth Tandy Shermer

PART I: THE NEW DEAL AND ITS CONTESTED ORDER

Chapter 1. "The Nine Judges Have Gone Home": Liberals, the 1949 "Closed Shop Cases," and the Undermining of Union Democracy 13
Jean-Christian Vinel

Chapter 2. "The Credit Problem Is Our Biggest Labor Problem": Labor and the Making of Monetary Policy 37
Samir Sonti

PART II. POSTWAR DISCONTENT

Chapter 3. "The Magnanimity of Disorder": Counterculture Intellectuals and the Rise of Anti-Statist Thought in Late Twentieth-Century America 63
Reuel Schiller

Chapter 4. Cheater in Chief: Presidential Taxpaying and Fiscal Citizenship 88
Joseph J. Thorndike

Chapter 5. McGovernites and Neocons: Michael Harrington, Max Shachtman, and the Realignment of the Democratic Party 112
Daniel Geary

Chapter 6. *Gender Gap*: Bella Abzug and Mim Kelber's Labor Feminist Critique of American Politics in the Late Twentieth Century 137
Leandra Zarnow

PART III: ADRIFT IN A NEW WORLD ORDER

Chapter 7. "We're Taking All the Risks and They're Getting All the Profits": Capitalism, Labor, and Democracy in the Wastelands of Southeastern Louisiana 163
Jennifer Klein

Chapter 8. From the "Labor Question" to the "Immigration Question": Newcomers, Politics, and Democracy in the Contemporary United States 186
Carl Bon Tempo

Chapter 9. Management and Power in Global Supply Chains: The Need for History in an Ahistorical Field 211
Shane Hamilton

PART IV: HISTORICIZING THE POLITICS AND CULTURE OF THE NEW DEAL ORDER

Chapter 10. "A Working-Class Hero Is Something to Be": Popular Culture and the Manufacture of "Labor" 237
Lauren Rebecca Sklaroff

Chapter 11. From Labor History to Political Economy: A Reassessment of Work, Capital, and Democracy 260
Meg Jacobs

Afterword 279
Nelson Lichtenstein

List of Contributors 293

Index 297

Acknowledgments 309

Introduction

"If they can do it, we can do it!" That was the mood in the breakroom of a New York City Starbucks after baristas in Buffalo voted to unionize in December 2021. That victory was at just one of the 9,000 stores that the multibillion-dollar, multinational retailer owned in the United States. That union election had, nonetheless, been two years in the making. Frustrated employees first reached out to Workers United (WU) in early 2020, a few years after that affiliate of the Service Employees International Union (SEIU) had begun organizing local coffee shops in the area. WU soon discovered interest in unionizing at almost every Starbucks in Buffalo, as well as an enormous management pushback. "There was an absolute onslaught of corporate people" after the first three stores filed for an election in August 2021, shift supervisor Gianna Reeve remembered. Managers listened in on staff headsets, threatened to take employees' health insurance away, and made significant staffing changes in the stores scheduled for National Labor Relations Board (NLRB) elections. They were also, Reeve stressed, "sweeter than pie, trying to fix grievances, trying to sow divisions."

Those "purely psychological" tactics backfired. "Shift supervisors and baristas baring their souls" in mandatory "listening sessions" just showed "corporate's lack of empathy and understanding," shift supervisor Rachel Cohen insisted. "Partners . . . recognized that partners need to trust other partners." Starbucks Workers United ended up with a decisive December 9th victory at an Elmwood Avenue store, making national headlines and energizing baristas in stores across the country. Thirty-three Starbucks in fourteen states filed for union elections by the middle of January 2022. That number rose to ninety-seven less than a month later and well into the hundreds within another couple of years.[1]

Baristas were not the only ones out organizing or on picket lines. Hollywood actors and writers, university graduate students, as well as autoworkers and other factory workers walked off the job in the early 2020s. Reporters across the country took notice. This strike wave stood in vibrant contrast to the sad memorialization that had in recent decades characterized Labor Day in the United States. The employees daring to unionize Starbucks and other retail giants did not toil in coal mines, steel mills, or auto plants. Most were young or female or queer, providing the working class with an imagery quite different from those hard-hatted men who had long symbolized American proletarianism. And even among the membership of the United Automobile Workers, whose rolling set of "Stand-Up Strikes" in the fall of 2023 caught so many executives, journalists, and politicians off guard, White men were a minority among a workforce increasingly Black, Brown, and female. Moreover, the wave of strikes by teachers, bus drivers, hotel housekeepers, retail clerks, and academics were highly visible, involving workers that were often quite well known to the larger public. Few Americans visit a coal mine, auto factory, or container port, but millions go to school, shop, watch television, or buy a cup of coffee every day.[2]

Auto workers, graduate students, actors, and writers had one thing Starbucks baristas didn't have: a signed collective bargaining contract. That difference was and remains a really big deal. Winning a union of workers' choosing remains but one step in making workplaces more equitable and democratic. Autoworkers', graduate students', actors', and writers' strikes certainly dragged on for months, but Starbucks employees still did not have an agreement years after Buffalo baristas voted for a union. CEOs could just keep stalling and ignoring labor law violations in a way that auto, university, and Hollywood executives could not; their employees had already won union contracts.[3]

Baristas' frustrations as well as the historic victories of autoworkers, graduate students, writers, and actors were reminders in the early 2020s that the nature of work, the strength of the labor movement, the structure of US capitalism, and the health of US democracy have always been intertwined. The collective bargaining agreements that coal, steel, and auto workers fought for did much to transform American capitalism during the Roosevelt era when the labor laws that are supposed to protect baristas' right to organize were first enacted. What it meant to physically toil on the docks, in a coal mine, or in a garment shop was transformed for the better when workers used the New Deal labor laws to raise wages and make unionism a living reality for millions. But beyond those unionized workplaces, a potent labor movement also compelled thousands of companies to raise wages and improve working conditions for their employees, if only to forestall organizing by an impatient and expectant working class. And, of course, during the Roosevelt era and afterward, a powerful labor movement, at its 1950s apogee representing one in three non–farm workers, prodded governments at the local, state, and federal levels to vastly expand social welfare programs that initially did the most for White working-class men and, by extension, their families.

Yet the academy and the pundit class did not highlight the deep connections between work, capitalism, and democracy after World War II. Experts instead looked back at the past and focused on the dramatic conflicts between business and organized labor. The government seemed a world apart from both, an idea befitting how New Deal labor laws had conceived of the state as a kind of independent arbitrator to ensure industrial peace. The sharp, narrow definitions of labor, business, and the state reflected how scholars of the modern United States categorized themselves as the historical profession grew during the mid-twentieth-century expansion of higher education. There were distinct journals, conferences, and professional associations for business, labor, and political history. Those distinctions could be found in other disciplines too, which shaped political and popular perceptions of business, politics, and labor as somehow separate from one another. Labor, too, seemed limited to those in the trade union movement, which never represented the majority of Americans who worked.

The deep connections between work, capitalism, and democracy again caught the public's attention in the late twentieth century.[4] Those hegemonic terms became buzzwords in an era that some scholars considered a second Gilded Age. Americans embraced, sometimes prided themselves on, gigs that supplemented what their employers paid them for full-time work in industries that once guaranteed good wages, benefits, and hours. Critics considered the new app-economy as just another symptom of unchecked capitalist greed.[5] Indeed, left-wing activists and progressive politicians eagerly threw around the term capitalism as a way of describing an entire system of laws and regulations that enabled corporations to put profits before people.[6]

Democracy hardly seemed like an antidote. A lot of those enterprises benefited from election rules that favored the rich. There were fierce battles across the country over how to make voting easier or harder while the Supreme Court continued to undermine the 1965 Voting Rights Act, to allow wealthy donors to spend a lot on campaigns, and to permit states to pass laws that made it difficult for marginalized communities to vote.[7] Judges also restricted how much power working people had on the job as large employers (most notoriously Amazon and Starbucks) undermined union elections, retaliated against employees, and delayed recognition of these new locals.[8]

Scholars also became attuned to the intersections between politics and economics in the lead-up to the Great Recession when clear academic distinctions seemed a barrier, not a conduit, to academic inquiry. A cohort of historians, many of whom came of age after the Cold War ended, proclaimed the arrival of a "new history of capitalism," which really reflected a larger political-economic turn in the academy. But historians did not forsake the social-cultural scholarship that had transformed understandings of Americans' lives on the job and at home in the 1970s and 1980s; they promised grand, sweeping narratives that would really excavate the inner workings of American politics and economics.[9]

This volume furthers that impulse by suggesting a new approach to interrogating the past and understanding the current crisis in American democracy. Focusing broadly on work (not just organized labor), capitalism (instead of only business), and democracy (as opposed to just party politics) highlights how interwoven these categories have been throughout the twentieth century. As such, these essays, individually and as a whole, do not tell a familiar, tidy story of a mid-century Democratic coalition that stood behind a liberal governing consensus felled by the conservative movements that transformed the Republican Party and then built a neoliberal order. The research presented in these pages instead reveals that the postwar prosperity that many White American families enjoyed did not stop the fights over whose work would be recognized, how corporations would be regulated, and whose democratic rights would be protected, both on the job and off. The complex struggles over which working-class rights, business regulations, economic policies, and taxes were recognized legally, politically, and culturally have continued to shape how democratic and inclusive the country and its workplaces were, are, and will be.

This collection begins with a reexamination of the Roosevelt administration, once thought a unified and powerful fount of labor-liberalism. Jean-Christian Vinel's chapter shows that the trade union movement was embattled throughout the 1930s and 1940s, the very years in which the New Deal order was being forged. His research significantly deepens the scholarship on the right-to-work laws that undermined the 1935 National Labor Relations, or Wagner, Act, the landmark legislation guaranteeing many workers a union of their choosing. While most historical research has focused on conservative efforts to erode union strength and solidarity at the state level, Vinel shows that even Democratic Senator Robert Wagner (NY) was uncomfortable with trade union power when the law bearing his name was winding its way through Congress in the 1930s. Liberal discomfort grew during World War II and shortly after when otherwise liberal Supreme Court jurists played a crucial role curbing trade union power. For example, a 1949 case, *Arizona Sash and Door*, helped unleash a wave of ballot initiatives across the US South and West that enabled states to put in place new restrictions on union organizing rights, thereby encouraging the capital flight, from North to South and East to West, that undermined shopfloor democracy, transformed the geography of US capitalism, and altered the way liberals thought about regulating the economy.

Managing that economy was central to the conflict examined in Samir Sonti's chapter, which shows how important the New Deal–era Federal Reserve was to the fate of the trade union movement and working-class living standards. The "Labor Question," as economist John Commons stressed early in the twentieth century, was inextricably linked to the "Money Question." That relationship vexed reformers before and after the era of Franklin Roosevelt. There was more public oversight of the Fed under FDR, when monetary policy kept interest rates low and consumer spending high. That dynamic benefited both the unions in and the strength of the manufacturing sector, but the fear of postwar inflation caused problems. Conservatives demanded an "independent," and therefore an anti-labor Federal Reserve, willing to discipline the working class during the periodic recessions that the Fed itself helped instigate. Thus Fed monetary policy became a venue for class struggle, even as organized labor, at the height of its postwar power, unsuccessfully sought to democratize that powerful institution.

The essays in "Postwar Discontent," the second section in this volume, emphasize how divided the country remained in the Cold War's early years, an era that historians once considered a period of liberal consensus. But conservatives were not the only ones peddling hostility toward the regulatory state. Disdain could also be found among a set of influential liberal and countercultural thinkers whom Reuel Schiller identifies. Buckminster Fuller, E. F. Schumacher, and Charles Reich were celebrated, would-be visionaries who saw the liberal state as suffocating and claustrophobic. Though they wrote on vastly different topics, they were all moving toward a political and economic posture that endorsed the market as the most effective and even democratic tool for regulating capitalism and ensuring prosperity for everyone.

Joseph Thorndike shows that at the very highest levels of government, resistance to progressive taxation, another hallmark of modern liberalism, grew apace. Several US presidents, including moderate Republicans like Dwight Eisenhower, turned to inventive ways to avoid paying their taxes in the years after the New Deal imposed a set of higher levies. Chief executives, in effect, insulated themselves from revenue policies that had made ordinary people pay a lot more taxes. The New Deal had helped make those payroll deductions the primary point of contact between citizens and the state that presidents oversaw. But President Richard Nixon, unlike his predecessors, got caught asking for an especially large deduction for the presidential papers he gave to the National Archives. Nixon also had made other questionable write-offs, which just added to the sense that he might very well be a crook. Those and other misdeeds contributed to the post-Watergate cynicism of many citizens, especially by the mid-1970s when ordinary Americans found themselves struggling in a stagnant and inflationary economy. Those hurt included the White working- and middle-class families who had benefited the most from the New Deal's once progressive tax regime.

The public's complex reaction to Nixon's chicanery opened up a set of political opportunities for Democrats during and after the Watergate scandal. Daniel Geary examines that moment to show how two radical intellectuals, Max Shachtman and Michael Harrington, came to disagree so profoundly about how the Democratic Party might serve as a vehicle for their separate versions of a transformative working-class politics. Shachtman, a former Trotskyist, and his small band of sometimes influential followers embraced the most conservative wing of the American trade union movement, arguing that support of the Vietnam War, along with hostility to feminism and Black militancy, constituted a politics that spoke to the vast bulk of American workers. By the early 1970s, Harrington, though once a leading Shachtmanite, rejected this increasingly stolid, neoconservative outlook. This fight among New York intellectuals might seem obscure but the conflict had larger consequences. As Geary points out, Harrington's vision of a much more inclusive Democratic Party, and one that includes a robust democratic socialist cohort, has come to characterize left-liberal politics in twenty-first-century America, while Shachtman's views helped birth the neoconservative politics once influential in the Republican Party.

Leandra Zarnow's chapter stresses how important women were to the Democratic Party's new direction. Bella Abzug and Mim Kelber got their political start in the 1930s as part of a Popular Front that sought to prod the Roosevelt administration to the left. Both remained politically engaged, with Abzug winning a seat in Congress in 1970 as a progressive Democrat. Both Abzug and Kelber, who served as the congresswoman's speechwriter and policy advisor, broke with Jimmy Carter's tepid liberalism in the late 1970s, emphasizing that women's liberation could only achieve success when the labor market was made more equitable, the military-industrial complex defanged, and democratic rights assured. Only then would there be justice for all Americans, not just the White working men who benefited the most from the New Deal.

Part III, "Adrift in a New World Order," highlights important connections between New Deal–era conflicts and those that have defined post-1970s America as a country of stagnant working and middle classes wages, ever increasing inequalities, and political paralysis. Who was left out of the New Deal in the 1930s still mattered at the millennium's turn. One of the largest groups was agricultural workers, including the largely Black Southerners whose travails are traced in Jennifer Klein's chapter. She shows how conservative Louisiana businessmen enticed chemical companies to move to southeastern Louisiana, where sugar planters had once used slaves to grow that cash crop. The plantations were gone but the people remained, so lawmakers could assure chemical and waste firms that labor costs would be cheap, taxes low, and regulations unenforced. That area quickly became an environmental disaster known as Chemical Corridor. Because Louisianans could do little at the state level, they looked to the federal government for help in the 1970s, which finally enabled local environmental and community groups to become a potent threat to the firms and politicians that had turned so much of the state into a chemical wasteland.

By then, immigration had dramatically changed American understandings of who did what work, as Carl Bon Tempo's essay underscores. First- and second-generation Americans had been foundational to the trade union movement that forced elite reformers to wrestle with the so-called labor question in the early twentieth century. But after passage of the 1965 Immigration and Nationality Act, an immigration question rose to the fore, dramatically expanding and problematizing who might emigrate to the United States. With more people arriving from Asia, Africa, and Latin America, immigration in the last half century has become as incendiary an issue as labor strife had been decades before. Just as unionization had once threatened the status and power of a northern European elite, so too did mass immigration seem to threaten the status of Americans whose families had come from Eastern and Southern Europe, once the chief beneficiaries of New Deal social liberalism. The immigration question thus remained unresolved in the new millennium, when social programs were stretched, good jobs were in short supply, and Americans increasingly expressed skepticism that the democratic system could resolve this pressing issue.

The resulting political paralysis suited supply chain managers and theorists just fine, argues Shane Hamilton. His chapter provides important political and cultural insights into the growth and study of the logistics networks that did so much to offshore US manufacturing and devastate the once unionized cities and towns of the Steel Belt. Most students of "supply chain management" wrote from an ahistorical perspective that put the growth of new transport and computer technologies at the heart of these global structures. But Hamilton emphasizes a historically and ideologically rooted managerial expert culture that sought to bolster retailer profits and undermine workers' power. The story taught in business schools, he emphasizes, has erased the more tangible, contingent, conflictual history of the men and women who actually "invented" the contemporary supply chain. Hamilton's study of supply chains thus helps explain why our understanding of twenty-first-century capitalism, both global and domestic, has been given an ahistorical flavor that has erased how interconnected the status of labor, the character of work, and the structures of world capitalism have always been.

Fittingly, the final section, "Historicizing the Politics and Culture of the New Deal Order," focuses on how historical scholarship has evolved to challenge the simplistic idea of a conservative backlash against the New Deal and the liberal order it ushered in. Lauren Sklaroff describes how historians have probed the way capitalism has transformed everyday life and the popular culture depicting it. Tin Pan Alley, Hollywood, and the major record labels often celebrated a particular kind of working-class icon, usually a White, straight man. Sklaroff emphasizes that there were, of course, Black, queer, and female working-class heroes, but they rarely achieved the same notoriety or cachet as their White counterparts. That began to change in the late twentieth century. Movies, reality TV shows, and scripted dramas reflected a much more diverse America whose heroes no longer had to be White, male, or heteronormative.

Meg Jacobs, in contrast, offers a critical reflection on how historians have parsed the laws and policies responsible for bolstering the working class, particularly the White men who would be idolized in song, television, and film. That scholarship both celebrated ordinary workers' demands for democracy on the job and criticized New Deal–era unions for being too big, too bureaucratic, and too subservient to the government. But Jacobs makes clear that in the years after Ronald Reagan's firing of unionized air traffic controllers, historians have begun to reconsider that New Left–inflected critique. After all, the Buffalo baristas struggling for legal recognition and a union contract needed all the help they could get from the federal government.

This volume ends with an afterword from Nelson Lichtenstein, who has been at the forefront of efforts to integrate labor history with subfields now labeled politics, policy history, business history, and the history of capitalism. He asks how intellectuals and activists, often isolated and marginal, leveraged their ideas to influence and alter the institutions—ranging all the way from the stolid Federal Reserve, and the secretive Internal Revenue Service, to the porous world of Hollywood—in an era of capitalist stability so characteristic of the middle decades of the twentieth century. Like other pioneering scholars in the New Left tradition, Lichtenstein focuses on the people who built, shaped, transformed, undermined, and brought an end to these seemingly hegemonic forces in twentieth-century American capitalism, which had a profound effect on what it meant to live and work in what many still revere as the American democratic experiment.

Notes

1. Saurav Sarkar, "Buffalo Baristas Touch Off a Starbucks Organizing Wave," *Labor Notes*, February 18, 2022, https://labornotes.org/2022/02/buffalo-baristas-touch-starbucks-organizing-wave.

2. Lauren Kaori Gurley, "UAW Strike Caps Off Long Hot Labor Summer," *Washington Post*, September 14, 2023, https://www.washingtonpost.com/business/2023/09/14/uaw-strike-labor-movement/; Nelson Lichtenstein, "Striking Workers and Actors Hold the Line Against Tech Slicing and Dicing," *Labor Notes*, August 9, 2023, https://labornotes.org/blogs/2023/08/striking-writers-and-actors-hold-line-against-tech-slicing-and-dicing.

3. Gurley, "UAW Strike Caps Off Long Hot Labor Summer"; Lichtenstein, "Striking Workers and Actors Hold the Line Against Tech Slicing and Dicing"; Michael Sainto, " 'The Law Is Finally Catching Up': The Union Contract Fight at Starbucks," *Guardian*, May 12, 2023, https://www.theguardian.com/business/2023/may/12/starbucks-union-busting-nlrb-contract; "Who Are Today's Union Workers," Economic Policy Institute Fact Sheet, April 21, 2021, https://www.epi.org/publication/who-are-todays-union-workers/; Jamie Wiggan, "From Steelworkers to Baristas," *Pennsylvania Capital-Star*, September 5, 2022, https://www.penncapital-star.com/working-the-economy/from-steelworkers-to-baristas-the-new-face-of-pittsburghs-evolving-labor-movement/; Chris Isidore, "Despite Union Wins at Starbucks, Amazon and Apple, Labor Laws Keep Cards Stacked Against Organizers," *CNN*, September 5, 2022; Megan K. Stack, "Inside Starbucks' Dirty War Against Organized Labor," *New York Times*, July 21, 2023, https://www.nytimes.com/2023/07/21/opinion/starbucks-union-strikes-labor-movement.html;

Parker Purifot, "Starbucks, Union Reach Tentative Agreements for Job Protections," *Bloomberg Law*, May 31, 2024, https://news.bloomberglaw.com/daily-labor-report/starbucks-union-reach-tentative-agreements-for-job-protections; Noam Scheiber, "Starbucks and Union Agree to Work Out Framework for Contract Talks," *New York Times*, February 27, 2024.

4. James Livingston, "The Myth of a Second Gilded Age," *Chronicle*, January 31, 2016.

5. Charles Towers Clark, "Uberization of Work: Pros and Cons of the Gig Economy," *Forbes*, July 8, 2019.

6. See *Dissent*'s September 17, 2021, series on the tenth anniversary of Occupy Wall Street, https://www.dissentmagazine.org/tag/occupy-at-ten.

7. Zach Montellaro, "The Supreme Court Has Chipped Away at the Voting Rights Act for 9 Years," *Politico*, June 27, 2022; Tim Lau, "Citizens United Explained," *Brennan Center*, December 12, 2019.

8. Ian Kullgren and Aaron Kessler, "Unions Fend Off Membership Exodus in 2 Years Since Janus Ruling," *Bloomberg Law*, June 26, 2020; Isidore, "Despite Union Wins at Starbucks, Amazon and Apple, Labor Laws Keep Cards Stacked Against Organizers."

9. Jennifer Schuessler, "In History Departments, It's Up with Capitalism," *New York Times*, April 6, 2013; "The New History of Capitalism," *Journal of American History*, online interchange, 101 (September 2014); Elizabeth Tandy Shermer, "Whither the History of Capitalism?: Reconsidering Finance's Place in the American Democratic Experiment," *Reviews in American History* 49 (2021): 452–459.

PART I

The New Deal and Its Contested Order

CHAPTER 1

"The Nine Judges Have Gone Home": Liberals, the 1949 "Closed Shop Cases," and the Undermining of Union Democracy

Jean-Christian Vinel

"The Court's liberalism is an illusion," disappointed *Los Angeles Citizen* reporters pointedly surmised after the announcement of the Supreme Court's nearly unanimous 1949 decision in *American Federation of Labor v. American Sash and Door* and its companion cases. The holding surprised liberal journalists, but even more baffling to them was the fact that the majority opinion was written by Justice Hugo Black, "one of the strongest liberals" according to the *New York Times*.[1] The first of Franklin Delano Roosevelt's nominations to the court, Black was joined by another devoted New Dealer, Justice Felix Frankfurter, whose blistering concurrence in this case liberals found equally alarming. Both liberal jurists had sided against organized labor in a ruling that upheld recent "right-to-work" legislation in Arizona, Nebraska, and North Carolina, just three of the state laws then threatening the labor rights and protections that FDR had proudly signed into law in the 1930s. Anti-union conservatives across the country celebrated that 1949 ruling because it limited what kind of membership rules unions could bargain for during contract negotiations. Many workers, by contrast, considered those so-called security or shop clauses essential for organized labor's ability to democratize workplaces. "The nine judges have gone home and the Court is where it used to be, on the conservative side of American politics," the *Los Angeles Citizen* reporters ruefully concluded. A disappointed reader actually mailed the *Citizen* article to Black, asking: "Justice Black, have you deserted the American people?"[2]

That question highlights a missing link in our understanding of the history of the right-to-work movement. Over the last decade, scholarship on the drive to pass restrictions on unions' ability to bargain for "closed shop" and "union shop" conditions has grown enormously. Studies have revealed the ideological, economic, but also racial dynamics that played out at the local and national levels as conservatives used the promise of protecting the "right to work" as a way to challenge the legitimacy of trade unions and liberal policies. Labor leaders often argued those contract stipulations were a matter of basic security because unions required 50 percent of eligible workers for federal recognition and protection. They needed even more members to bargain for better wages and benefits and exert their political power. Yet the history of the right to work has been framed almost exclusively in terms of a conservative countermobilization, with liberals appearing in the story only for their failure to deal with the tension between labor rights and civil rights.[3] On the whole, this scholarship has mostly highlighted two key moments in this anti-union challenge: the early years of right-to-work campaigns, showing how they provided the impetus for the 1947 Taft-Hartley Act, which amended the 1935 National Labor Relations (or Wagner) Act, and then the mid-1950s when several states passed these laws.[4]

American Sash and Door and the other "closed shop cases" the Supreme Court considered with it had deeper importance to American labor, capitalism, and democracy. Those rulings reflected the limits of the labor-liberalism that defined the Roosevelt era. Those decisions were vital to late-1940s debates about union security and shopfloor democracy. This time was also a turning point for the labor question that Carl Bon Tempo's chapter shows the immigration question to have eclipsed by the twentieth century's end. Unions unsuccessfully tried to organize the South and failed to generate the political impetus necessary to repeal section 14(b) of Taft-Hartley, the provision that allowed states to prohibit all forms of union security agreements.

As this chapter argues, liberal justices offered little assistance. Black's and Frankfurter's opinions reveal the ambiguous stance of liberals involved in drawing the boundaries of New Deal reform in the workplace, which shaped the late twentieth-century divides between Democrats discussed in Leandra Zarnow's and Daniel Geary's chapters. As such, the "closed shop cases" challenge the overly neat definitions of liberalism and conservatism that have grown out of recent work parsing the rise and fall of the New Deal order.

"The Closed Shop as a Weapon of Tyranny"

The labor movement's security and power were hardly guaranteed after Roosevelt signed the Wagner Act. Particularly contentious were closed shop agreements, which stipulated that employers could only hire union members, but there was also opposition to union shop clauses, which required workers to join the union (usually after a short probationary period). Since the Progressive Era, both types of membership agreements had been attacked as a threat to an individual person's right to work, which eventually became an effective label for laws prohibiting unions and employers for including them in contracts.[5] This fierce resistance was symbolized by the anti-union lawyer Walter Gordon Merritt's *The Struggle for Industrial Liberty*, an early—and influential—case for the notion that both the closed shop and the union shop favored collective solidarity in a way that "infringed upon the rights and duties of the individual." To Merritt, both were incompatible with the American dispensation, which was geared to offer limitless opportunities to citizens.[6]

The 1935 National Labor Relations Act championed the ideal and practice of industrial democracy but offered no clear guidelines on the ability of unions to restrict employment to their members. Even New York Democratic Senator Robert Wagner—the architect of the act—and his allies equivocated on the issue and refrained from fully endorsing the closed shop when they sought to build congressional support for the bill's passage. Wagner even insisted that state laws prohibiting the closed shop could remain. "[T]here is nothing in the bill which favors the closed shop." "Closed shop agreements may be made," the senator emphasized, "but only in those states where they are now legal."[7] Wagner's hesitancy captured liberals' belief that the most pressing task was to lay the legal groundwork necessary for workers to express a collective voice.

As a result, it was left to courts, state legislatures, and National Labor Relations Board (NLRB) appointees to rule on the union security issue. From 1935 onward, they increasingly confronted the difficult task of reconciling the unions' quest for security and stable labor relations on the one hand and the necessity for federal labor policy to protect access to the labor market on the other. There was a need, as NLRB member James Reynolds noted in 1947, to prevent unions from "using the closed shop contract as a weapon of tyranny."[8] Initially, the board ruled discharges under valid closed shop contracts legal and received significant support from the courts, which also put a premium on protecting incumbent unions.[9] In one revealing 1939 case, the board found no violation of the Wagner Act in a plant where—under a closed shop contract with the AFL—rival Congress of Industrial Organization (CIO) adherents were discharged even though they then constituted a new majority of workers. That in this case the employer had given assistance to the AFL local trying to secure its footing in the plant made no difference.[10] Such decisions were in fact largely in tune with the tenets of industrial pluralism, which put a premium on stable unions.[11]

Yet there was a shift in the early 1940s that presaged Black's and Frankfurter's opposition to union security. By 1942, the NLRB had decided to restrict the ability of incumbent unions to protect themselves from challenges by ruling that discharges were no longer permissible "as the life of the contract drew to a close."[12] A year later, the board ruled against a company, Wallace Corporation, with a closed shop contract. In that case, a CIO union had staged a strike to press for recognition by a recalcitrant employer, wresting from him both an agreement to hold an election and the promise that a closed shop contract would subsequently be signed. However, the election resulted in the victory of an independent union, which had been assisted by the company. The closed shop contract was subsequently signed with the independent union, which then turned down the application of forty workers who had supported the CIO, even though the employer had actually pushed the independent union to accept them as members. The board decided that the closed shop contract could not be an "instrument of discrimination against employees," meaning that the closed shop contract had been signed with the clear intent on the part of the independent union to remove CIO adherents from the plant. In 1944, the Supreme Court supported the board's decision.

But that ruling was not unanimous. Four dissenting judges, including Felix Frankfurter, argued that the closed shop was a traditional and legitimate goal of unions. It was also legal and Congress had not given the board authority "to supervise union membership" or deal with union practices.[13] There was an important catch to this defense of the closed shop, however. The dissenters noted that the company was located in a small town in West Virginia, "where opportunities for employment are not plentiful." It was therefore "not unlikely that denial of the right to work for this company will keep these men from earning a livelihood in a place they long have lived." Indeed, the power wielded by the union in this town alarmed the justices. "This and the other cases" had convinced them (the dissenters) that "the labor movement in the United States is passing into a new phase" that required the courts "to reconcile the rights of individuals and minorities with the power of those who control collective bargaining groups."[14]

By then, liberals expressing doubts about union security procedures could also be heard outside the legal world. Liberal NLRB appointees had also become uncomfortable with membership guarantees. As early as 1943, William Leiserson expressed his weariness with the wartime federal labor policies that guaranteed union security, and he openly criticized unions for using them to compel membership instead of building the organic solidarity needed to sustain themselves, let alone fend off conservative attacks.[15] His May 5, 1943, diary entry noted a Gallup poll showing that a majority of workers favored prohibiting strikes, a ban leaders opposed. "Organization of workers from the top down with compulsory membership," he tersely concluded, "has resulted in the opinion of the leaders being taken as labor opinion when the rank and file feels differently."[16]

Such polls, which indicated significant opposition to union security procedures from workers, worried organizers and intellectual allies. The magazine *Labor and Nation* even devoted an entire section to labor and public opinion, which sociologist C. Wright Mills managed. Polls were dissected and analyzed—but hardly refuted. Rather, they were taken as a sign that there was a growing disjunction between the numerical growth of labor unions and what seemed to be significant ideological divisions between the rank and file and their leaders.[17]

Socialist Will Herberg was more outspoken. As the head of the research staff of the International Ladies' Garment Workers' Union (ILGWU), Herberg likewise feared that the movement relied too much on union security guarantees. Leaders seemed to ignore that members did not like the unions' political activities. "The individual worker transfers to his union not his total rights as a man or citizen," he stressed; "such total alienation would be intolerable in a free society." A member had only given "his rights to bargain over conditions of employment. This is the case whatever be the form of recruitment, whether it be the traditional procedure of voluntary affiliation or the quasi-compulsory enrollment under the closed shop or the Wagner Act."[18] Organizers' mandate to lead was "circumscribed," not "absolute." Not understanding that distinction created divisions within unions, weakened them, and endangered democracy by concentrating too much power.[19]

"Wave of the Future"

While liberals failed to offer clear guidance on the issue, by the mid-1940s conservatives were exploiting the discomfort with federally guaranteed union security and power, thus contributing to the tensions that came to a head in the 1949 "closed shop cases." Sit-down strikes in the 1930s had stoked opposition, but critics of unions also won seats in Congress after the Roosevelt administration failed to pack the court with liberal justices before the 1938 midterms. That election provided enough seats for conservatives to band together in a coalition that frustrated liberal reforms. Those senators and representatives bedeviled the White House throughout World War II when federal labor policies, particularly maintenance of membership guarantees, strengthened the labor movement's size and power.[20] The anti-union movement then gained prominent figures beyond the corporate world, most notoriously filmmaker Cecil B. DeMille and journalist Westbrook Pegler, who made a name for himself deriding legal union activities as "rackets."[21]

Closed and union shop clauses were first challenged at the state level. In 1944, Florida, Arkansas, and California legislatures let voters decide whether to ban such agreements. Notably, the first right-to-work referenda passed in the southern states where supporters argued the right to work would protect the region's strict racial hierarchy.[22] Yet AFL leaders initially dismissed those anti-union victories as a minor threat. General counsel Joseph Padway confidently reported in August 1945 that the tide of antilabor legislation had been stemmed though a mixture of legal action, lobbying, and bargaining.[23] Padway and his peers were confident that collective bargaining had become firmly rooted and that local laws weakening it had little future.[24] Wartime rulings seemed to trump constitutional amendments in Florida and Arkansas where membership policies had been a part of contracts between unions and military contractors. The situation looked promising nationwide too. Nearly half of the nation's thirty-one million workers who were eligible for collective bargaining were employed under one form of union security or another, which suggested that union security was a natural development in collective bargaining.[25]

Yet, by 1947, the political and legal environment had been transformed. The AFL and the CIO had just concluded a frustrating campaign to organize the South that had brought small numbers of additional members at considerable financial expense. Those fragile union beachheads already seemed under siege as an increasing number of states joined the early right-to-work movement.[26] Opponents of membership guarantees seized on public anxiety about veterans' returning home to find themselves out of work, as so many World War I soldiers had. Notably, that fear shaped the 1946 right-to-work referendum in Arizona. The face of that campaign was Herbert Williams, a veteran who opened a welding business with five other nonunion returning servicemen in the Phoenix area. Williams and his co-workers chafed at the control that the AFL local exercised and blamed the area's construction trades for using the closed shop to keep out competitors like them.[27]

When challenged, those statutes were upheld in state courts although, in effect, they reasserted freedom of contract and, in North Carolina, revived the doctrines of conspiracy and combination. Jurists even suggested, ever so subtly, that the states that adopted these laws were stoking such a rebellion against the New Deal that they would likely provoke a shift in the national labor policy. "Great weight must be attached to the fact that so many separate jurisdictions have, within so short a space of time, seen fit to exercise their police power in the same manner and for the same purposes," the North Carolina Supreme Court said. "The composite will of such a broad section of our country cannot be lightly discarded as unreasonable, arbitrary or capricious or lacking in substantial relationship to its objective."[28] Right-to-work statutes, that court boldly argued, were "the wave of the future."

A Republican-controlled Congress further energized the state-level right-to-work movements. Democrats had lost control of the House and Senate in the 1946 midterms, and the coalition of conservative Republicans and southern Democrats had subsequently grown enough to challenge labor rights. Two of organized labor's fiercest opponents in Congress, Minnesota Representative Joseph Ball and Michigan Representative Clare Hoffman, brazenly pushed for an unsuccessful national right-to-work law. Their fellow Republicans, Ohio Senator Robert Taft and New Jersey Representative Fred Hartley, did not give up on the issue. They secured passage of the law that bears their name over Democratic President Harry Truman's veto. Section 14(b) of the 1947 Taft-Hartley Act did not prohibit union security agreements on a national scale, but nevertheless allowed states to pass right-to-work laws, which enabled state supreme courts to sanction right-to-work statutes as legitimate legislative endeavors.[29]

"A Declaration of War on Unions"

The AFL, not the CIO, mounted the constitutional defense of union security in the face of those potent challenges. The more progressive wing of the US labor movement was undoubtedly the prime target of many of the first anti-union laws, some of which were even drafted so as to leave the AFL mostly untouched. The CIO was nonetheless slower than the AFL in recognizing the threat that right to work represented. The organization lacked the structure and resources to mount legislative or legal challenges to laws that one observer called a "declaration of war on Unions," whether CIO or AFL.[30] The CIO only introduced an amicus brief for two of the "closed shop cases," one of which did align with the AFL's legal strategy.

These statutes were, admittedly, a bigger threat to the AFL. That older organization was better represented in the southern, western, and southwestern states that formed the perimeter of the right-to-work movement (the CIO-affiliated textile workers being an exception). The closed shop had also been central to craft traditions and practices for a long time in the small locals affiliated with the AFL, particularly their hiring halls. Their vitality was more precarious than that of the big CIO unions organizing large factories. A few members failing to pay dues or leaving the local had a bigger impact on AFL unions. The Arizona case was illustrative of this vulnerability: In 1947 the AFL boasted 2,500 closed shop contracts in the state; only about 26,000 workers were covered.[31] The AFL's decision to mount a constitutional strategy against right-to-work statutes thus reflected the pressure it faced.

The lack of coordination between the AFL and the CIO on this crucial legal battle, however, extended to other parts of the struggle against Taft-Hartley. Meetings in the spring of 1947 to devise ways to reach a united labor front largely failed, and the two federations were unable to offer any legislative alternative to Taft-Hartley. This was largely a consequence of their debilitating divisions. Not only did the two federations disagree over NLRB rulings arbitrating their rivalry, but they also held differing views on crucial topics such as prices and wages, with the AFL accusing the CIO of facilitating inflation. As a result, the two federations parted ways in the struggle against the anti-union impulse that dominated American politics. While the AFL became involved in a vigorous public relations effort through paid media to influence congressional votes, the CIO decided that the 1948 election was the true test of labor's strength, and it relied on its Political Action Committee (PAC) and grassroots political machinery to mobilize for the Democratic Party.[32]

The AFL's strategy was to cover enough ground for a landmark decision derailing the right-to-work movement reshaping state and federal policies.[33] Padway and his aides carefully selected and timed three cases that they chose to combine to bring before the Supreme Court. All of them were on appeal from supreme courts in states that had passed right-to-work statutes in the run-up to Taft-Hartley's passage. The Arizona, Nebraska, and North Carolina lawsuits nonetheless spoke to different facets of the legal struggles that these individual challenges to union security provoked. Nebraska's Supreme Court had ruled against metal workers in *Lincoln Federal Union vs. Northwestern Iron*. These workers had signed a collective bargaining contract with a scrap metal company before the adoption of the open shop amendment in November 1946. Dan Giebelhouse, one of the workers covered by the agreement, stopped paying his dues at the time the referendum was held and subsequently lost his membership. However, the employer, the Northwestern Iron Company, refused to discharge him (but still employed union men—including the president of the metal workers union). The firm had not ignored any other provisions of the contract, but now it contended that the Nebraska open shop amendment simply made the closed shop provision in the contract invalid.[34]

An employer was behind the North Carolina case defending the closed shop, *Whitaker v. North Carolina*. James Whitaker, a building contractor from Asheville, signed a closed shop contract with an AFL local in May 1947—two months after the North Carolina amendment was adopted. He then received a warrant. So did the officers of the AFL local involved in the case, the Building Trades Council, who were charged with violating the law. A subsequent trial resulted in a fifty-dollar fine for both the union and the employer, a conviction upheld by the state supreme court.[35] Given the long history of the closed shop in the craft unions, the suit brought by this employer was not surprising. In the building trades particularly, where the rate of workers covered by closed shop agreements exceeded 90 percent, the closed shop was seen as necessary both to secure the union's hold on apprenticeship programs and protect it against the high worker turnover resulting from the seasonal nature of the work.[36]

Such dynamics were also visible in Arizona where the attorney general threatened criminal prosecution for violation of the 1946 right-to-work law. The *American Sash and Door* case originated with Local 2093 of the United Brotherhood of Carpenters and Joiners of America in Maricopa County. This local signed closed shop contracts both *before* and *after* the adoption of the right-to-work law. Leaders found that the law made it impossible to enforce those agreements even if just one worker defaulted on his dues. Indeed, the case stemmed from the refusal of the Sash and Door company—which had signed a contract before the referendum held in November 1946—to discharge a worker who had left the local.

All three cases thus offered a glimpse into the limits being placed on the New Deal order just a few years after FDR's death and the Republican takeover of Congress. The timing of these cases also mattered. The Supreme Court heard arguments in early November 1948, the week before an Election Day, when both the White House and Congress were at stake. These cases also came before the court when unions and their liberal allies were pushing for a repeal of Taft-Hartley and as right-to-work laws were being considered in a number of states. Some statutes passed but voters elected Truman and defeated right-to-work propositions in Massachusetts, Maine, and New Mexico a week later. Prevailing when the Supreme Court announced its rulings a few months later would still be a much larger victory.[37]

A Constitutional Right to Organize and Bargain Collectively?

AFL general counsel Joseph Padway worked out a bold strategy but died before he could make it before the court himself. Padway, who immigrated from Leeds in 1905, came of age politically in the yeasty environment of Wisconsin's progressive politics, which combined political action, expertise, and legal reform in favor of labor. After graduating from Marquette University's law school, he made a name in political, legal, and union circles, helping to draft the Wisconsin Labor Act before becoming the AFL's general counsel in 1938. Importantly, Padway was also a member of the American Bar Association Committee on the Bill of Rights, and he interacted with a loose group of activists who sought to ground labor rights in a refurbished vision of civil liberty including the right to organize, picket, and strike.[38] One of his main achievements was convincing the Supreme Court to uphold picketing rights twice (in 1937, *Senn v. Tile* and in 1940, *Thornhill v. Alabama*), and he hoped to build on that basis as he confronted the challenge of right-to-work laws.[39] Indeed, Padway now wanted to establish that right-to-work laws deprived the workers of their First Amendment freedom to assemble and denied them the due process and equal protection that the Fourteenth Amendment guaranteed.[40]

This was a daring argument, for it meant asking the Supreme Court to reenter a political debate over substantive economic rights it had left ten years earlier when it upheld the Wagner Act and other key pieces of New Deal legislation. But Padway was asking justices to do it amid a political crisis that threatened to undermine the union security and power that had been central to making the still fledgling New Deal order. This constitutional approach seemed vital to protect the labor movement from right-to-work legislation but also to establish that there was a necessary and indispensable synergy between labor organizations and union security procedures.[41] To make the argument that all forms of union security fell under the purview of the Bill of Rights, the AFL submitted both a legal brief and an economic brief written by Boris Shishkin. Together, these briefs boldly argued that union security was good for individual and collective rights, democracy, and the public's interest. Union security in general and the closed shop in particular were vital to the New Deal's premise that the "policy of our society is that labor be free."[42]

The legal brief asserted that the right to organize and collectively bargain was not just an economic right. It should be afforded the same preferred position that the court had granted other First Amendment rights like freedom of worship or the right to a free press.[43] The brief thus looked back to the 1937 *Jones & Laughlin* decision, which had upheld the Wagner Act, contending that the court's observation in that case that organizing was a "fundamental right" clearly derived from the freedom of assembly protected by the First Amendment.[44] "Workingmen exercise their right to assembly in a very real and practical sense when they form unions and participate in their affairs," the brief noted.[45] Having established that constitutional basis, the brief moved on to argue that history, particularly early cases such as *Commonwealth vs. Hunt* (1842), showed that the right to organize implied "unanimous group action." Shishkin's economic brief expanded that argument at length, using the work of historians Selig Perlman and Philip Taft to show that only union security arrangements allowed unions to develop labor standards that would protect all workers. It was precisely this history, the economic brief argued, that would allow unions to meet New Dealers' expectation for federally protected trade unionism: stabilizing labor relations, preventing strikes, and safeguarding the purchasing power that Samir Sonti's chapter shows to be important to the fights over combating inflation after World War II.[46]

Both briefs thus reaffirmed a collective vision of democracy. That argument was anchored in the Wisconsin politics that had shaped Padway's thinking and that of other labor leaders and intellectuals. Shishkin's economic brief asked the court to consider that individual workers did not have the power to negotiate working conditions (thus denying the existence of untrammeled economic opportunities lauded by the likes of Walter Gordon Merritt). When they take up employment, the brief argued, "they enter an economic society"—a labor market. This economic society would be either arbitrary if it was premised on rules imposed by managers, or it would be democratic if unions negotiated working rules. This negotiation of rules—a staple of labor economist John R. Commons's vision of labor relations—could not be done efficiently if all workers were not unionized.[47] Union security arrangements thus could not be said to violate the right to work—membership guarantees actually helped workers exercise their right to work in a democratic way. Accordingly, the AFL argued in its legal brief, the state laws being passed could be said to threaten the equal protection clause of the Fourteenth Amendment because they weakened unions by preventing workers from pooling their bargaining power together without reducing the power of management. That danger was particularly visible in the Arizona law, which prohibited discrimination against nonunion workers but contained no provision prohibiting employers from discriminating against union members.[48]

The AFL's arguments for workplace democracy were thus actually bolder than New Dealers' conception of them had been. Liberals had insisted on a *process-oriented* definition, which stressed the need for union elections free from employer pressure. Under the influence of Padway, the AFL instead championed a *results-oriented* conception of workplace democracy grounded in collective constitutional rights. That interpretation equated a democratic workplace with union security arrangements much more forcefully than the Roosevelt administration had. Still, the AFL brief insisted that there was precedent for its reading of the Constitution, pointing particularly to cases such as *Hague* and *Thornhill*, where the court had held that states could not impair the workers' ability to exercise their First Amendment rights. Other cases, according to the AFL, suggested that individual contracts could not stand in the way of collective bargaining.[49] This included *Senn v. Tile* (which Padway had argued himself), where the court had ruled that a "hoped for job is not property guaranteed by the constitution and the diversion of it to a competitor is not an invasion of a constitutional right."[50]

Surprisingly, however, the AFL's brief suggested that the court might alternatively revisit late nineteenth-century freedom of contract cases and the Fourteenth Amendment's due process clause to bolster union rights. For years, labor progressives had decried how that amendment had been used against the trade union movement. But to the AFL, which was still steeped in the culture of voluntarism, the Fourteenth Amendment seemed a failsafe as the court might reject its First Amendment arguments. Notably, the brief did not argue for an individual person's right to sign a contract. Instead it insisted that the due process clause protected workers' collective freedom to sign closed shop agreements. In doing so, the brief contended that right-to-work laws deprived workers of the right to obtain the best value possible for their labor. It also pushed the court to reject clearly the notion that right-to-work laws served a public interest by preventing labor monopolies and other abuses. That attempt was a clear effort to address debates in the media at the time about legal union activities, which conservative reporters like Westbrook Pegler called "rackets."[51]

The AFL was thus getting as close to asking the court to recognize the right of unions to exist and maintain themselves as one could get. Doing so, the union's arguments forced liberals to confront the question of security arrangements and workplace democracy head on. Progressives had in fact been uncomfortable with that question for decades. Some had argued since 1902 that the loss of individual freedom in the collective bargaining process was a problem of much less significance than the economic coercion exercised by employers. The loss of personal freedom was conceded, but it was considered to be a necessary trade-off for the greater gain of a strong collective voice. The logic of industrial democracy enshrined in the Wagner Act had thus been for workers to come together and present a united front that in turn made bargaining possible. But even Senator Wagner had equivocated on the closed shop question a decade before the first state right-to-work referenda had been passed.[52]

By contrast, the AFL's conservative opponents were not ambivalent about the closed shop. Padway's and Shishkin's defense of union security struck many of them as proof of the danger unions posed to American democracy. Donald Richberg, one of the state of Arizona's counsels, was particularly concerned about the AFL's claim that taking a job meant entering an "economic society," which, as he explained in a private letter, seemed to "create within the formal structure of our political government a private government by labor unions, which is independent of the political government." That idea seemed the real threat to democracy because it would "make the government established by all the people subordinate to a private government established by some of the people."[53] Richberg's brief subsequently denounced the AFL's argument as a challenge to the Constitution's "promise of individual liberty and freedom from every form of private tyranny."[54]

A former labor progressive, Richberg's evolution captured how much public, even worker, opinion had changed on unionism since 1935. Richberg, the drafter of the 1925 Railway Labor Act—which did not include the closed shop—had soured on the New Deal, arguing that unions had moved away from a struggle for economic justice and now staged strikes that constituted a threat to the public order and workers themselves. True to his growing anti-union persuasion, Richberg now asked the court to rule that the right to work was a constitutional right that needed as much protection as other individual rights. He did not call unions and their leaders Communists but did warn that their vision of democracy would lead to the emergence of a "dictatorship of the proletariat" in every industry. Protecting union security as a basic right would give unions tremendous power over individual lives that only governments should be granted, and with serious checks at that. There would be no such protections against unions, Richberg warned.[55]

The AFL's opponents also made timely arguments about the challenge union security might pose to racial equality on the job. Noting that the court had recently ruled that restrictive covenants keeping Black Americans out of White neighborhoods were unenforceable,[56] Richberg and his colleagues argued that the justices must deem closed shop contracts based on racist practices equally void. Although the AFL had claimed its locals were open to all workers and imposed "no arbitrary and unreasonable requirements as a condition of membership," the brief pointed out that many AFL locals did discriminate against citizens of color, which showed that labor unions were undemocratic monopolies that hoarded economic resources at the expense of workers who were left out. Richberg's brief for the state of Arizona thus noted that thirty unions in the United States barred Black Americans from membership, thus offering a privileged entry into the job market to millions of workers. The building trades involved in the Arizona case were prime examples of these exclusionary practices—their apprenticeship programs' high entry fees and competency exams kept Black members out of well-paying jobs.[57]

The conservatives' decision to rely on racial exclusions to attack union security procedures was no doubt cynical and opportunistic but such exclusions were becoming an important part of liberals' discomfort with union security. Historian Reuel Schiller has shown that unions' duty to provide fair representation created significant challenges to protecting group rights and individual rights in nonracial cases in the 1960s. Yet tensions were also present in the 1940s debates over the closed shop and union security, which undercut the AFL's arguments about the link between the closed shop and a healthy democracy.[58]

Such tensions were visible in Gunnar Myrdal's widely read *An American Dilemma*, a book that made powerful arguments about US race relations during World War II when many Black war production workers rallied around the idea of a Double V, a victory against fascism abroad and racism at home. A social democrat, Myrdal was a supporter of labor unions who, very early on, had interacted with advocates of industrial democracy such as John R. Commons. Unions were no doubt a part of the dilemma that Myrdal analyzed, but he believed that federal regulation would lead to a decline of exclusionary practices. "We foresee that the trend of unionization, social legislation, and national planning will tend to break down economic discrimination," he explained. Because the labor movement could not afford to reject government support, it would have to adapt to governmental guidelines in racial relations. Even the most recalcitrant unions would have to fall in line with the progressive policies of the CIO.[59]

Yet Myrdal would not have supported the AFL's case that the union shop should be a constitutional right. Labor unions, he added, were "a weak movement getting strong powers."[60] As they matured and became established, they would have to discard some of the practices that they had developed to overcome the staunch opposition of American businessmen. Among these were "a readiness to take the law into their own hands" and the "insistence on the rule of the union shop." "A strong union movement," Myrdal continued, "does not need to be provided with such measures."[61]

Judicial Restraint and Liberal Retreat

The Supreme Court agreed in a notably short opinion. Handed down on January 3, 1949, the court's ruling was a significant defeat for the AFL, one that suggested that it had seriously misread the logic of the constitutional evolution that the New Deal had set in motion. While the main holding—that states were free to sanction or prohibit union security arrangements—was no doubt a disappointment to the AFL, the language was also unmistakably harsh. Black's majority opinion read like a sharp rebuke of the constitutional strategy that Padway had sought to build before his untimely death in 1947. Black chided AFL lawyers for an "expansive construction of the right to speak, assemble, and petition," the basis of which was "not entirely clear." "There cannot be wrung from a constitutional right to assemble," Black concluded, "a further right to drive from remunerative employment all other persons who will not or cannot participate in union assemblies." Worse, Black did not really engage with the AFL's argument. There was no need, Black wrote dismissively, "to appraise or analyze with particularity the startling ideas" that the brief put forth in support of its contention that both freedom of speech and freedom of assembly extended to the right to organize and contract for a closed shop.[62]

Black really only addressed the AFL's claims about the Fourteenth Amendment's due process clause, upon which the union had rested its final argument. There again he found no compelling logic. A due process argument for the closed shop was an invitation to "return, at least in part, to the due process philosophy" that had been "deliberately discarded" during the New Deal. Yet Black was not content with suggesting that the AFL's argumentation had actually jeopardized, not cemented, the constitutional basis of labor rights. He also intimated that the AFL's claim of the right to discriminate against nonunion members was comparable to the right employers once claimed to sign yellow dog contracts, thus divesting the union of any moral superiority.

Black offered an equally harsh reprise to the notion that right-to-work laws were a violation of the Fourteenth Amendment's equal protection clause. He conceded that such laws indeed tipped the scales in favor of employers but added that their value rested in the fact that they protected the "employment opportunities" of independent unions—a phrase that came quite close to the "right to work" formulation. Black's reasoning actually reached back to the 1944 case that had required an employer to reinstate unfairly dismissed CIO workers, *Wallace Corp. v. NLRB*, but he now suggested that the closed shop was incompatible with the rights of workers who were not members of the union.[63] Equal protection lay in fact with the right-to-work laws. "Just as we have held that the due process clause erects no obstacle to block legislative protection of union members," Black concluded, "we now hold that legislative protection can be afforded non-union workers."[64]

Frankfurter's concurrence in one of the three cases, *American Sash and Door*, ceded even more ground to conservatives pushing for the right to work, for it seemed to plant the court squarely on the side of those who opposed the closed shop. In this case, judicial restraint rhymed with liberal retreat. Unlike Black, Frankfurter took exception to the notion that substantive rights were involved in union security clauses. He noted that before the New Deal, activist judges had often prevented the legislatures from adopting social legislation. "When the tide had turned," Frankfurter argued, it had not left in its wake a fresh vision of substantive economic rights impervious to regulation.[65] Rather, the court had decided to leave the legislature the latitude they needed to pass economic legislation. Frankfurter suggested that right-to-work laws were part of a process of governmental regulation that had nothing to do with the fundamental rights that the First Amendment protected. Hinting at the court's recent effort to establish a hierarchy between political and economic rights—the latter deserving less judicial scrutiny—Frankfurter added that the open shop and union security "are not matters, like censorship of the press or separation of Church and State, on which history, through the Constitution, speaks so decisively as to forbid legislative experiments."[66]

Frankfurter even invoked liberal legal icon Louis Brandeis to attack the closed shop as un-American. Brandeis was in many ways Frankfurter's mentor; the two had a long friendship that went back to the early days of the Progressive Era. They had exchanged letters over this subject, and, as Frankfurter knew, Brandeis believed that the closed shop was an "abridgement of liberty."[67] Channeling Brandeis to add weight to his disagreement with the AFL's constitutional claims, Frankfurter cobbled together two letters from Brandeis who argued that the closed shop was "antagonistic to the American spirit." "The objections, legal, economic, and social, against the closed shop are so strong," Frankfurter thus asserted, "that the insistence upon it has been a serious obstacle to union progress. (. . .) The American people should not and will not accept unionism if it involves the closed shop. They will not consent to the exchange of the tyranny of the employer for the tyranny of the employees."[68]

Frankfurter conceded that labor unions "must be strong and stable," to have the capacity to preserve their members' "industrial liberty," but he nonetheless considered that membership guarantees thwarted industrial democracy. Unlike leaders who considered organizing, not the open shop, the key to solidarity, Frankfurter argued—again quoting Brandeis's words—"It is not true that the 'success of a labor union' necessarily means a 'perfect monopoly,'" for such "absolute power leads to excesses and to weakness." "In any free community," Frankfurter thus argued, "the diversity of character, of beliefs, of taste—indeed, mere selfishness—will insure such a supply if the enjoyment of this privilege of individualism is protected by law." Nonunion workers would be "a nucleus of unorganized labor," which "will check oppression by the union as the union checks oppression by the employer."[69] At this stage, it was clear that Frankfurter's faith in judicial restraint had taken the shape of a liberal retreat—while Brandeis had mostly assailed the excesses of the closed shop rather than the union shop that the CIO favored, the ruling in the "closed shop cases" failed to differentiate between them and left states free to prohibit both types of union security arrangements.

Ambiguous Legacy

Black's and Frankfurter's judicial opinions highlighted how tenuous union security, shopfloor democracy, and the New Deal's labor liberalism were a mere decade after the Wagner Act's passage. Yet the two judges' correspondence reveals that they also received praise for their ruling. Ella Kristensen, a seventy-three-year-old former teacher from Nebraska, wrote to Black to tell him the decision "made me feel like waving our flag and shouting 'We are still free.' " Kristensen explained that a meatpacking strike the previous year had alarmed her for the violence and intimidation that wives and children had faced. She also found no redeeming virtues in the social wage that the CIO union sought to offer its members. "A monopoly by unions is still a monopoly," she insisted; "rackets are rackets."[70] New Yorker D. Rodriguez also wrote to Black to declare: "Your judgement on the closed shop was fine." "If we as wage earners are forced into these unions in order to work," Rodriguez insisted, "we are no better than slaves. And I am sure the Republic was not founded to give union racketeers rights."[71] Samuel Richardson likewise appreciated the ruling. A fifty-four-year-old carpenter from Philadelphia, he had never been in a union, but he had once been forced to give up a job because of his refusal to join. He still resented what he saw as an illegitimate infringement of his rights. "This is a free country. No group of radical reds, union bosses should be able to force a man to join a union," he noted contentiously.[72] Brandeis's daughter, Elizabeth, agreed with that sentiment. "Personally," she admitted in a letter to Frankfurter, "I think father was right as to the dangers of the closed shop in the long run. The individual worker or minority union member needs some protection." The decision, she insisted, was "a beauty." "I don't doubt some of the labor boys will talk about the reactionary court," she added. "But if they are honest to themselves they will have to admit that you are right."[73]

Others, however, took a dismal view of the court's opinion. Since the New Dealers had thrown the weight of the federal government behind collective bargaining in the mid-1930s, millions more had joined labor organizations. They used the union card to seize on the language of Americanism, claim a social wage, and redefine their relationship to Washington, D.C.[74] Even foremen and supervisors, once a reliable bulwark of management, had shown an increasing appreciation for the collective benefits of unionism—an appreciation the Taft-Hartley Act now thwarted by removing them from the purview of the law.[75] The court's ruling on right-to-work laws was thus another check on the labor impulse. That was why the ruling was such a disappointment and shock to the *Los Angeles Citizens'* reporters. "Black's record is so good it is hard to believe he has turned," that AFL newspaper explained. "The language he used to uphold the ban on the closed shop could have been used by the National Association of Manufacturers."[76]

In a long article analyzing the decision, Irving Dilliard—a well-known liberal columnist with the *Saint Louis Post-Dispatch*—likewise worried that the court had not simply upheld the right of states to prohibit union security arrangements, it had taken sides in the debate. The ruling seemed to have "thrown a judicial cloud" over the closed shop. Wasn't the court suggesting, he asked, that the closed shop was in fact unconstitutional?[77] Justice Wiley Rutledge, another Roosevelt appointee, wrote to law professor Joseph Klammon of his disappointment that "no one took the trouble to speak a good word concerning the merits of the closed shop." Rutledge took pains in his letter to distance himself from Frankfurter's harsh words. "Certainly I did not sign with Black on any idea that he was condemning the closed shop or doing anything more than saying that the whole subject matter was in lying with the legislative field and not the judicial one."[78]

Rutledge's caveat captured how ambiguous the legacy of the court's closed shop decision was. Indeed, as their failure to distinguish between the union and the closed shop revealed, the justices had not fleshed out precisely the constitutional contours of the workers' right to organize and bargain collectively in the post–Taft-Hartley era. Quite beyond the New Deal judges' preference for judicial restraint, this refusal reflected recent cracks in the liberal faith that union security procedures naturally produced a democratic workplace. These fissures had appeared because federal protections for recognition and collective bargaining had relied much more clearly on the constitutional recognition of the right of the federal government to intervene in labor relations than on fully-fledged individual or collective rights to join a union, about which AFL lawyers had hoped to convince the court.

The ruling's focus on the abuses and excesses of labor unions also contributed to its murky consequences. Fear about union power had predated the Wagner Act, but anxiety had increased during World War II when Westbrook Pegler and other muckraking journalists had made legal activities out to be corrupt, the supposed rackets that angered the Americans writing to Black and Frankfurter. Those aspersions had also been a part of the early right-to-work referenda, which increased in number after this ruling effectively upheld states' right to pass such restrictions, a key component of the Taft-Hartley Act. More Southern and Western states passed those laws in the 1950s when a lot of businesses began investing in those once impoverished regions. There were more jobs as a result, but ordinary people had lower wages and fewer workplace protections in states where it was also hard for a lot of people, especially citizens of color, to vote.[79] Those inequities raise questions about the cost of liberal ambiguity about union security, which mattered to the complex, changing dynamics of work, capitalism, and democracy in America.

Notes

1. "Closed Shop Ban in States Upheld by Supreme Court," *New York Times*, January 4, 1949, 1, 7. The "closed shop cases" were cases bearing on the constitutionality of state right-to-work laws, namely Nebraska, North Carolina, and Arizona, that resulted in two Supreme Court decisions: *Lincoln Federal Labor Union v. Northwestern Iron & Metal Co., ante,* 335 U.S. 525 (on the Nebraska and North Carolina statutes, the North Carolina case on appeal being *Whitaker v. North Carolina*) and *AFL v. American Sash and Door Co*, 335 U.S. 538 (on the Arizona statute).

2. See "The High Court Goes Home," *Los Angeles Citizen*, January 21, 1949, 4, in Hugo L. Black Papers, box 299, folder #3, Library of Congress. This newspaper was an AFL supporter.

3. See Elizabeth Tandy Shermer, *Sunbelt Capitalism: Phoenix and the Transformation of American Politics* (Philadelphia: University of Pennsylvania Press, 2013); Elizabeth Tandy Shermer, "Counter-Organizing the Sunbelt: Right-to-Work Campaigns and Anti-Union Conservatism," *Pacific Historical Review* 78, no. 1 (February 2009): 81–118; Marc Dixon, "Movements, Counter-Movements, and Policy Adoption: The Case of Right-to-Work Activism," *Social Forces*, vol. 87:473–500; Marc Dixon, "Limiting Labor: Business Political Mobilization and Union Setback in the States," *Journal of Policy History*, vol. 19:313–344; Andrew Kersten, *Labor's Home Front: The American Federation of Labor During World War II* (New York: NYU Press, 2006).

4. Kersten, *Labor's Home Front* is illustrative. It ends its fine analysis of the right-to-work movement in 1947, with the Taft-Hartley Act being the main defeat for Joseph Padway, the AFL's general counsel. On the history of right to work from the 1950s onward, see Gilbert Gall, *The Politics of Right to Work: The Labor Federations as Special Interests 1943–1979* (New York: Greenwood, 1988).

5. Shermer, "Counter-Organizing the Sunbelt," 83–84.

6. Walter Gordon Merritt, *The Struggle for Industrial Liberty* (New York: League for Industrial Rights, 1922), 97.

7. National Labor Relations Board, *Legislative History of the National Labor Relations Act, 1935* (Washington, DC: Government Printing Office, 1949), vol. I, 3234. Tellingly, the Senate and House reports also emphasized that Congress did not mean the NLRA law to affect state laws prohibiting the closed shop. See Senate Report No. 573, in *Legislative History*, I, 2311, and House Report No. 969, *Legislative History*, I, 2927.

8. James Reynolds as quoted in Harry Millis and Emily Clark Brown, *From the Wagner Act to Taft-Hartley: A Study of National Policy and Labor Relations* (Chicago: University of Chicago Press, 1950), 215. See for example *In the Matter of Mill B. Inc.*, 40 NLRB 346 (1942), where the board openly talked of "weighing and resolving the conflicting interests." See the Testimony of Paul Herzog, Amendments to the National Labor Relations Act: Hearings Before the Committee

on Education and Labor, House of Representatives, Eightieth Congress, first session, vol. 5, 3155. Herzog was responding to a classic argumentation against the closed shop by Almond E. Roth (National Federation of American Shipping, Inc.) as being incompatible with freedom of association.

9. Christopher L. Tomlins, *The State and the Unions* (New York: Cambridge, 1985), 238–239.

10. Ansley Radio Corporation, 18 NLRB 1028 (1939).

11. On industrial pluralism see Tomlins, *State and the Unions* and H. Harris and N. Lichtenstein, eds., *Industrial Democracy: The Ambiguous Promise* (New York: Cambridge, 1991), 87–205.

12. Rutland Court Owners 44 NLRB 587 (1942).

13. *Wallace Corp*, 323 U.S. 248, 258.

14. *Wallace Corp*, 271.

15. William Leiserson, "The Growing Pains of Organized Labor," *Annals of the American Academy of Political and Social Science*, 1943.

16. William Leiserson Diary, May 5, 1943, vol. 4 (Dec 1, 1942–May 11, 1944), William Leiserson Papers, Box 48.

17. *Labor and Nation*, "Public Attitudes Towards Unions," October 1945, 34–47 (polls taken by Elmo Roper); "What the People Think," November–December 1946, 11–14; "What the People Think," January–February 1947, 28–32; "What the People Think," March–April 1947, 25–29; "What the People Think," November–December, 8–12.

18. Will Herberg, "For 'Limited' as Against 'Total Unionism,'" *Labor and Nation*, April–May 1946, 52.

19. Herberg, "For 'Limited' as Against 'Total Unionism,'" 52–54.

20. Maintenance of membership guarantees required all businesses with a government contract to enroll every worker into unions. This principle was formulated and adopted by the National War Labor Board in July 1942 as a way to buttress labor unions, which had taken a no-strike pledge, and ensure their stability during the war effort.

21. Nelson Lichtenstein, *State of the Union* (Princeton, NJ: Princeton UP, 2002, 2nd ed. in 2013), 20–97; David Witwer, *Shadow of the Racketeer: Scandal in Organized Labor* (Urbana: University of Illinois Press, 2009), 188–205.

22. Shermer, "Counter-Organizing the Sunbelt."

23. See Ray Marshall, *Labor in the South* (Cambridge: Harvard University Press, 1966), 244; David Witwer, "Westbrook Pegler and the Anti-Union Movement," *Journal of American History* 92, no. 2 (September 2005): 527–552.

24. On this point, see Kersten, *Labor's Home Front*, chapter 2.

25. This was also one of the points made by Boris Shishkin in the economic brief submitted alongside the appellants' brief in the "Closed Shop Cases." Yet one might have been forgiven for reading these figures differently—they suggested that one half of all workers were not in unions, and that a large number of workers employed under union security agreements were in fact in the largest industrial states.

26. On the Southern campaigns, see Elizabeth Fones Wolf and Ken Fones Wolf, *Struggle for the Soul of the Postwar South: White Evangelical Protestants and the Struggle for Operation Dixie* (Urbana, Chicago, and Springfield: University of Illinois Press, 2015); Barbara Griffiths, *The Crisis of Labor, Operation Dixie and the Defeat of the CIO* (Philadelphia: Temple University Press, 1998); and Marshall, *Labor in the South*, 246–269.

27. On the controversy over the seniority of veterans, see Glenn Altschuler and Stuart Blumin, *The GI Bill: The New Deal for Veterans* (New York: Oxford, 2009), 176. There was also, of course, an important racial subset to this question, as Black Americans were the first to bear the brunt of the veterans' hope to regain a secure job. See Karen Tucker Anderson, "Last Hired, First Fired: Black Women Workers During World War II," *Journal of American History* 69, no. 1 (1982): 82–97. On the case of Herbert Williams, see Shermer, *Sunbelt Capitalism*, 106–107.

28. *Whitaker v. State*, 228 N.C. 352, 367, 45 S.E.2d 860, 87, as quoted in William F. Swindler, "The Right to Work: A Decade of Development," 36 Neb. L. Rev. 276 (1957) at 315.

29. There is, as yet, no definitive history of Taft-Hartley; however, see Melvyn Dubofsky, *The State and Labor in Modern America* (Chapel Hill: University of North Carolina Press, 1994), 169–195.

30. See Gall, *The Politics of Right to Work*, 27–33.

31. *American Sash and Door*, "Abstract of Record," Appellate Case Files, 25 O.T. 1948, box # 5431, Supreme Court Records, RG 267, National Archives, 10. For an example of the history of the closed shop and its prevalence at the beginning of the twentieth century in some skilled trades see Walter Galenson, *The United Brotherhood of Carpenters* (Cambridge: Harvard University Press, 1983), 135–136.

32. This paragraph relies on Rachel Burstein's PhD dissertation, "The Fight over John Q: How Labor Won and Lost the Public in Postwar America, 1947–1959," CUNY, 2014, 11–36.

33. *AFL vs. American Sash Door*, n° 27, 335 U.S. 538 (1949), *Lincoln Federal Union vs. Northwestern Iron*, n° 47, 335 U.S. 525 (1949), *Whittaker v. North Carolina*, n° 34, 335 U.S. 525 (1949). Remarks by Joseph Padway, General Counsel of the AFL, *Proceedings of the 66th Annual Convention*, 1947, p. 99. Padway died of a stroke on October 9, 1947, before the annual convention was concluded.

34. Nebraska Constitution, Art 15, §13. Adopted November 5, 1946. Although the amendment was self-executing, an enabling legislation, J. 1706, was passed in 1947. See Swindler, "A Decade of Development," 304. *Lincoln Federal Union vs. Northwestern Iron*, n° 47, Appellate Case Files, 46 O.T. 1948, box #5431, Supreme Court Records, RG 267, National Archives.

35. *AFL vs. American Sash Door*, n° 27, *Whittaker v. North Carolina*, n° 34, "Brief for Appellants," Appellate Case Files, 25 O.T. 1948, box #5431, Supreme Court Records, RG 267, National Archives, p. 25.

36. Grace Palladino, *Skilled Hands, Strong Spirits: A Century of Building Trades History* (Ithaca: Cornell University Press, 2005), 122–144.

37. On the 1948 victories see Gall, *The Politics of Right to Work*, 43.

38. On this committee, see Laura Weinrib, *The Taming of Free Speech* (Cambridge: Harvard University Press, 2016), 226–269.

39. This biographical sketch is derived from Kersten, *Labor's Home Front*; Laura Weinrib, "The Right to Work and the Right to Strike," *University of Chicago Legal Forum*, Vol. 2017, Article 20. Available at: https://chicagounbound.uchicago.edu/uclf/vol2017/iss1/20.

40. See infra, p. 19, note 83. Padway had tried that approach before in *AFL v. Watson*, a suit in which he and the AFL had won a qualified victory, as the court issued a mixed ruling remanding the case back to the state courts so they might assess whether the Florida statute was in keeping with the Florida constitution. *American Federation of Labor v. Watson*, 327 U.S. 582, 1946.

41. This brief was published. See Boris Shishkin/AFL, *The Closed Shop and Union Security: Economic Brief of the American Federation of Labor* (Washington, DC: Judd and Detweiler, 1947).

42. *American Sash Door*, Appellant's brief, 118.

43. Brief for Appellants, 34. To make this point the brief relied on *West Virginia v. Barnette*, 319 U.S. 624 (1942) and *Thomas v. Collins*, 323 U.S. 516 (1945). It was in the latter that the "preferred position" doctrine was enunciated. See "Brief for Appellants," 32–34, 79–81.

44. *AFL vs. American Sash Door*, n° 27, *Lincoln Federal Union vs. Northwestern Iron*, n° 47, *Whittaker v. North Carolina*, n° 34, October Term, 1948, Brief for Appellants, 22, 32.

45. Brief for Appellants, 32–34, 71–81.

46. Boris Shishkin/AFL, *The Closed Shop and Union Security: Economic Brief of the American Federation of Labor*, 24–37, 56–66.

47. *American Sash Door*, Brief for Appellants, 47.

48. Brief for Appellants, 23, 25.

49. *J. I Case* (321 U.S. 332).

50. 301 U.S. 468, p. 482. This case involved Paul Senn, a nonunion tile layer hiring nonunion workmen. Senn complained that union pickets deprived him of jobs, thus violating his individual rights.

51. Brief for Appellants, 82–109.

52. *Final Report of the Industrial Commission*, vol. 19 (Washington: GPO, 1902), 804–809, esp. 807. See also Charles O'Gregory, *Labor and the Law* (New York: Norton, 1946), 117.

53. Donald Richberg to David B. Robertson and Bert M. Jewell, February 25, 1949, 4.

54. *American Sash Door*, Appellees' brief, 47. RG 267, National Archives.

55. *American Sash Door*, Appellees' brief, 45–50.

56. See *Shelley v. Kramer*, 344 U.S. 1 (1948).

57. *American Sash Door*, Appellees' brief, 45–50.

58. Reuel Schiller, "From Group Rights to Individual Liberties: Post-War Labor Law, Liberalism, and the Waning of Union Strength," *Berkeley Journal of Employment and Labor Law* 20, no. 1 (1999): 1–73.

59. Gunnar Myrdal, *An American Dilemma* (New York: Carnegie Foundation), 1944, chapter 18, 407–408. On the history of this book see Thomas Sugrue, *Sweet Land of Liberty: The Forgotten Struggle for Civil Rights in the North* (New York: Random House, 2009), 81.

60. Myrdal, *An American Dilemma*, 404.

61. Myrdal, *An American Dilemma*, 405.

62. *Lincoln Union v. Northwestern Co*, 335 U.S. 525 (1949), 530–531.

63. *Lincoln Union v. Northwestern Co*, 532.

64. *Lincoln Union v. Northwestern Co*, 537.

65. Felix Frankfurter, Concurring Opinion, *American Sash Door and Co.*, 335 U.S. 538 (1949), 543–545.

66. *American Sash Door and Co*, 550.

67. Louis Brandeis to Felix Frankfurter, November 26, 1920, in David Levy and Melvyn Urofsky, eds., *Half Brother, Half Son: The Letters of Louis D. Brandeis to Felix Frankfurter* (Norman, OK: University of Oklahoma Press, 1991), 48.

68. *American Sash Door and Co*, 335 U.S. 538 at 551, quoting a letter from Louis Brandeis, Letter of Sept. 6, 1910, to Lawrence F. Abbott of the *Outlook* and a Letter of Feb. 26, 1912, to Lincoln Steffens.

69. Quoted from Louis D. Brandeis's contribution to a discussion entitled Peace with Liberty and Justice in 2 Nat. Civic Federation Rev. No. 2, pp. 1, 16 (May 15, 1905).

70. Ella Kristensen to Hugo L. Black, January 3, 1949. Hugo L. Black Papers, box 299, folder #3, Library of Congress.

71. D. Rodriguez to Hugo L. Black, undated, Hugo L. Black Papers, box 299, folder #3, Library of Congress. Rodriguez's first name is not mentioned in the letter, and I was unable to find him in the 1940 census.

72. Samuel Richardson to Hugo L. Black, January 4, 1949, Hugo L. Black Papers, box 299, folder #3, Library of Congress. Like workers in the other letters cited here, Richardson said nothing in his letter about the type of job he held or the company he worked with. However, I was able to find additional information about them by using the 1940 US census, which is available online.

73. Elizabeth Brandeis to Felix Frankfurter, January 18, 1949, Felix Frankfurter Papers, Library of Congress, "Closed Shop Cases," reel 66.

74. On industrial workers and the political impact of the New Deal, see the classic works by Lizabeth Cohen, *Making a New Deal* (New York: Cambridge University Press, 1990), Gary Gerstle, *Working Class Americanism: The Politics of a Textile City* (Princeton: Princeton University Press, 1992), and Nelson Lichtenstein, *State of the Union* (Princeton: Princeton University Press, 2002, 2nd ed. in 2013), chapter 1. Since the adoption of the Taft-Hartley Act, which mandated a vote before a union security agreement could be signed, the unions had won 90 percent of these elections.

75. On foremen's unionism see my *The Employee: A Political History* (Philadelphia: University of Pennsylvania Press, 2020), 89–124.

76. See "The High Court Goes Home," *Los Angeles Citizen*, January 21, 1949, 4, in Hugo L. Black Papers, box 299, folder #3, Library of Congress.

77. Irving Dilliard, "The Closed Shop Decision," *Saint Louis Post-Dispatch*, January 9, 1949, p. 50.

78. Wiley Rutledge to Joseph Klammon, January 17, 1949, Wiley B. Rutledge Papers, Library of Congress, box 167.

79. Shermer, "Counter-Organizing the Sunbelt."

CHAPTER 2

"The Credit Problem Is Our Biggest Labor Problem": Labor and the Making of Monetary Policy

Samir Sonti

"The credit problem," progressive University of Wisconsin labor economist John R. Commons insisted in 1921, "is our biggest labor problem."[1] A century later, one could mount a credible case that it remains so. Nevertheless, it is notable that the labor scholars who came after Commons paid little attention to this relationship between the realm of finance and the world of work. The half century of relative financial stability ushered in by New Deal reforms had something to do with this, but after the 2008 banking crisis, students of class relations have become more attuned to the ways in which financialization affects the conditions of work itself.[2] That catastrophe exposed just how much basic economic security, a central New Deal promise, has hinged on the power of the Federal Reserve, an institution whose independence from democratic accountability has bedeviled unionists and left-liberals since the 1950s.

This chapter examines how and why the Federal Reserve attained that independence and then used it to pursue a restrictive monetary policy inimical to the interests of organized labor and working Americans. Debates over the conduct of monetary policy during the 1950s, an era of relatively low inflation, revealed just how charged politics surrounding the Federal Reserve could be even before the 1970s stagflation crisis. Political economists have argued the "holy trinity" of modern central banking began to take shape—independence, inflation control, and short-term interest rate manipulation.[3] All contributed to a restrictive monetary policy then widely believed to have contributed to three recessions that occurred between the mid-1950s and early 1960s.

Union economists like Donald Montgomery, Stanley Ruttenberg, and Nat Goldfinger, along with public figures like Leon Keyserling, mounted a sustained campaign against this restrictive monetary policy. They elaborated an analysis of the ways in which an independent central bank committed to fighting inflation with general monetary policy would prove incompatible with the federal government's responsibility to pursue full employment. First, they contended that central bank independence posed a threat to the *coordination* of national economic policy and set the Federal Reserve on a collision course with other economic agencies. Second, they stressed that general monetary policy would prove an *ineffective* way of addressing key drivers of postwar inflation—namely, nondemand factors like corporate pricing power. Finally, they called for a demonstration of greater *flexibility* in the central bank's approach to economic stabilization. These labor intellectuals advocated for a "selective credit policy" through which financial authorities could regulate the flow of credit to different ends—making it readily available for productive purposes and restricting the supply that enabled speculative uses.[4]

The analysis that follows builds on a large and growing body of work that sees the politics of inflation as a central front of social struggle. Institutionally minded social scientists have outlined a sociological interpretation of inflation that locates its origins in interest group conflicts.[5] Historians have traced how those very conflicts sowed the seeds of the disintegration of the New Deal order well before the 1970s.[6] And many scholars have examined how the political response to stagflation, above all dramatic interest rate increases (like the so-called Volcker Shock), inaugurated the neoliberal era.[7] Meanwhile, heterodox economists have analyzed how monetary policy has functioned as an instrument of class power.[8] Others, including modern monetary theory (MMT) adherents, have suggested that a democratized Federal Reserve could play a valuable role in facilitating a green energy transition and other laudable public investment programs. Modern central banks in advanced capitalist economies, they contend, face few limits in their ability to underwrite ambitious fiscal policies.[9] The return of inflation in the early 2020s spurred progressives to advocate for alternative means of managing the price level. Price controls, excess profit taxes, and antitrust measures, for example, could achieve price stability without austerity.[10]

Yet there remains a need for a longer view on the relationship between class politics and the governance of the Federal Reserve. Historians have shown how the late nineteenth-century money question was inseparable from the labor question, a perspective also advanced by more recent scholars investigating the impact of neoliberal financialization on working-class life. Postwar arguments for a more democratic and accountable Federal Reserve ought to be understood as a bridge between those two ideas and eras. Purposeful and democratic management of credit, according to these union economists, was one important piece of a comprehensive economic strategy to achieve full employment *and* control inflation. Accomplishing this required making Federal Reserve operations a subject of public deliberation, because, as a 1953 CIO statement put it, "decisions made in the remote chambers of American finance are of concern to all the people, not just a mere handful."[11] Or, as the UAW's Donald Montgomery argued, the fate of working people in the postwar era would hinge on the question of whether the Federal Reserve would be "a part of Government" or "a Government apart."[12]

Reforming the Fed

The Federal Reserve underwent a profound transformation in the 1930s as part of the broader New Deal overhaul of the national financial system. Key to this process was Republican Marriner Eccles, Franklin Roosevelt's pick to lead the central bank. This successful Mormon banker hailed from historically credit-starved Utah and lamented how the Federal Reserve had been "profoundly influenced by a narrow banking rather than a broad social point of view."[13] The only path out of the Great Depression was through substantial deficit spending geared toward job creation. "You have got to take care of the unemployed," Eccles insisted to a 1935 Senate committee, "or you are going to have a revolution in this country."[14]

If fiscal policy was to be in charge, then monetary policy belonged, as one leading scholar of the Federal Reserve has put it, "in the backseat."[15] Or in the words of Eccles advisor Lauchlin Currie, "the actions of the monetary authority . . . must be subject to the control of the [Roosevelt] administration."[16] The "most important role of monetary control," Currie added, "is assuring that adequate support is available whenever needed for the emergency financing involved in the recovery program."[17] The Federal Reserve, in this vision, acted not as an independent entity but rather coordinated its policy with the borrowing needs of the New Deal. The Banking Act of 1935 reformed the Federal Reserve toward this end by centralizing policymaking authority in the presidentially appointed Board of Governors, thereby shifting the system's center of gravity from the Federal Reserve Bank of New York (FRBNY) to the more publicly accountable Washington headquarters.[18]

The White House had the most control over the Federal Reserve during and immediately after World War II. Financing the war effort required an unprecedented increase in borrowing. Federal debt climbed by $200 billion between 1941 and 1945—almost half again as much of GNP in that initial year. To ensure that this proceeded smoothly, and above all to keep manageable the cost of servicing the growing public debt, Eccles doubled down on the subordination of central bank autonomy to Treasury Department imperatives. Starting in April 1942, the Federal Reserve committed to fixing the interest rates on government securities through a set of "pegs"—from 0.375 percent for the shortest-term Treasury bills to 2.5 percent for long-term bonds.[19] Two political economists argued this arrangement represented an "unprecedented experiment in democratic, rather than banker, control of monetary policy," which provided a glimpse into how a social democratic central bank might function.[20]

The pegs might be seen as a kind of price control for credit to the government. Maintaining them required active intervention by the Federal Reserve to shape the market for government securities. Under ordinary circumstances, should investor appetite for these assets fall, the rate on offer would have to rise—and with it the cost of public debt service would climb. To avoid this, the Federal Reserve stood ready to buy Treasury bills from banks as needed so as to sustain a volume of demand that kept rates at the target level—that is, at the pegs.[21]

But there was a catch. The minimal yield on short-term government debt together with the Federal Reserve guarantee incentivized bankers to exchange Treasury bills for cash. That money could then be put to other uses—like loans to private borrowers at higher rates. Each successive central bank purchase of Treasury bills placed that much more liquidity in the hands of the banks. And with every increase in banks' reserves, their lending ability increased several times over, for such is the nature of a fractional-reserve system.[22] That much more loan-making carried real inflationary risks—for, all else equal, households and businesses awash in credit could not help but bid up the prices of a limited supply of goods.

All else was not equal. During the war, the Office of Price Administration (OPA) strictly regulated what businesses could charge, and an excess-profits tax disincentivized price gouging. At the same time, production controls, materials allocation requirements, and consumer rationing limited the ends to which investment and consumer spending was directed. In addition to the pegs, the Federal Reserve also maintained a range of selective credit controls and restricted lending for the purchase of various consumer goods, financial assets, and, for a time, real estate, thus containing demand in those areas. These measures kept the price level relatively stable for the duration of the conflict, even as output and employment reached extraordinary heights.[23]

The War at Home over Monetary Policy

What would happen after the war? "If left uncontrolled," Eccles told a congressional committee in 1945, "the vast and rising war-created liquid funds could overwhelm the markets."[24] His warning proved prescient. The twelve months after V-J Day were marked by a successful business campaign to dismantle the wartime stabilization machinery, while the largest strike wave in US history secured substantial wage increases across every industry. By mid-1946, both the excess profits tax and OPA price controls had been terminated, unleashing an inflationary wave that pushed the price level up by some 20 percent. This paved the way to a Republican landslide in the 1946 midterm elections that year, which enabled congressional conservatives to pass the Taft-Hartley Act and agitate against any further government regulation of the economy.[25]

The Federal Reserve's autonomy and public accountability became a part of that political maelstrom. Prominent members of the financial community, led by FRBNY President Allan Sproul, seized the opportunity to call for a restoration of central bank independence to combat the troublesome inflation by means of higher interest rates, thus ending the wartime pegs. "[T]he need for a rigid structure [of interest rates], in order to facilitate Government borrowing," Sproul argued, had been rendered moot by the end of the war, and it was time "to introduce some flexibility into the interest rate structure."[26] To "sail the narrow channel between Scylla and Charybdis, between inflation and deflation," J. P. Morgan Chairman Russell Leffingwell added in a widely circulated *Fortune* article, the Federal Reserve must buy and sell government securities in accordance with their own good judgment about the money market's needs, not in abject obedience to long-ago decisions of the Treasury for the proper level of interest rates. He concluded, "The peg ties the hands of the Federal Reserve and may make inflation control impossible."[27]

Sproul and Leffingwell faced potent opposition from the Truman administration. Treasury Secretaries Fred Vinson and John Snyder firmly opposed any change to the wartime arrangement, whereas the Council of Economic Advisers, the body created by the 1946 Employment Act, held that any such disruption would be "dangerous beyond description."[28] The principal reason for their opposition was the issue of "debt management." The federal budget had indeed moved from deficit to surplus soon after the war, but the Treasury remained responsible for dealing with the large debt that had been accrued during the conflict. Short-term obligations—about one-third of the total stock—would need to be rolled over, and long-term servicing costs had to be kept at predictable levels. Higher interest rates could make all of this much more expensive.

Eccles also opposed abandoning the pegs. He warned that the government would be left "entirely at the mercy of uncontrolled factors in the market." Eccles asked, "How high would interest rates have to rise to deter business and individuals from borrowing from banks?" "I doubt if anybody knows."[29] Eccles nonetheless worried that in the absence of price controls, the pegs would force the Federal Reserve to act as an "engine of inflation." Every action on behalf of Treasury securities injected additional liquidity into the banking system and served as the basis for so much more private lending.[30]

To solve this problem, Eccles devised an innovative solution. If the banks could be made legally obligated to hold on to a certain amount of short-term government securities in a "special reserve," the Federal Reserve would gain the ability to tackle the problem of bank credit expansion without affecting the cost of public borrowing.[31] Banks would no longer be able to freely convert Treasury bills into lendable cash, and their loan-making ability would shrink in equal proportion. This "Special Reserve Plan," Eccles explained, "would divorce the market for private debt from the market for Government securities."[32] As he later clarified, "the low rates from government financing would not determine the rates on all other types of lending."[33] The plan was a selective policy that differentially managed the flow of credit to public and private ends. It would function, claimed Eccles, by "putting the restraint on lenders, that is, banks," instead of on the federal government.[34]

However, the Special Reserve Plan faced tall legislative odds after the 1946 midterms. Bankers correctly saw the Eccles proposal as a threat. The Federal Advisory Council (FAC), a body of financial interests that consulted with the central bank, charged that the proposal would "substitute the edicts of a board in Washington for the judgments of the boards of directors of 15,000 banks throughout the country." The FAC called it "a step towards the socialization of banking."[35] Indeed, the financial community had long considered even traditional reserve requirements—the ratio of cash to loans they were mandated to hold—as, in the words of Russell Leffingwell, "one of the most dangerous weapons in the armory of the Federal Reserve Board."[36] It was a demand, Leffingwell insisted, for "effective nationalization."[37]

With any legislative path toward reform of the Fed now blocked, the political forces in favor of central bank independence gained momentum. In 1949, Democratic Senator Paul Douglas, formerly an academic economist, used his position as chair of the JEC's Subcommittee on Monetary, Credit, and Fiscal Policies to undertake high-profile hearings on the question of Federal Reserve independence and anti-inflation monetary policy. The Douglas Committee's final report echoed the arguments that Sproul, Leffingwell, and others had been making: "We believe that the advantages of avoiding inflation are so great and that a restrictive monetary policy can contribute so much to this end that the freedom of the Federal Reserve to restrict credit and raise interest rates for general stabilization purposes should be restored."[38] Some months later, a group of Douglas's old colleagues at the University of Chicago Department of Economics put an even finer point on it: "Monetary policy cannot serve two masters at once."[39]

The onset of the Korean War set the stage for Federal Reserve officials, now led by the more conservative Thomas McCabe, to make the final break and establish who the sole master would be.[40] After a series of dramatic confrontations with the Truman White House early in the Korean War, McCabe's Fed and the US Treasury issued a joint statement on March 4, 1951, asserting that the Federal Reserve would no longer commit to intervening in securities markets on behalf of government borrowing. In Federal Reserve history, this date occupies a most important place. There is a time before the Fed-Treasury Accord and a time after.[41]

To contemporary observers, however, the matter seemed hardly settled. The full Joint Committee had refused to endorse the Douglas report and handed the problem to a House committee chaired by the acerbic Federal Reserve critic, Rep. Wright Patman of Texas. Speaking before the Patman Committee, Truman's CEA Chair Leon Keyserling later insisted that the accord amounted to nothing but a "mild modification in policy." "I cannot accept the viewpoint that the main key to future economic stability," he added, "consists in pushing monetary manipulation as far as it seemingly would be pushed by those who regard it as a panacea." Such an approach, Keyserling concluded, would bring highly "undesirable consequences."[42]

Labor's Vision for Monetary Policy

Labor intellectuals responded to the new policy by elaborating an alternative, more democratic, labor-oriented vision of central bank policy. Rather than relying on the "broad ax" of general monetary policy, the CIO sought a "selective credit approach" that discouraged speculation and encouraged growth in the real economy.[43] Direct controls over lending toward "nonessential business activity or speculation," the CIO held, could prevent dangerous activities in the commodity markets—where investors bet on everything from lard to oats to cotton—that "fed into the pipeline and were translated into price boosts all the way from the processor to the wholesaler to the retailer."[44] These union-oriented economists also touted the value of reserve requirements—including Eccles's Special Reserve Plan—as a tool for moderating private credit expansion. Higher reserve requirements, Keyserling explained to Truman, "could be used to absorb excessive bank lending power" and thereby would "reconcile the objective of checking inflationary credit expansion with policies of sound debt management."[45] "Such practical and feasible methods of restraining credit inflation," the UAW's Donald Montgomery added, would "at the same time [permit] support for the market for Government securities."[46]

Such a selective, flexible credit policy, the union economists held, would animate the 1946 Employment Act, reconciling the full employment goal with price stability. An independent central bank committed to fighting inflation with the "broad ax" of general monetary policy, on the other hand, threatened such coordination. As Donald Montgomery insisted to the Patman Committee, the Employment Act "contemplates no independent action by any part of Government." The Federal Reserve, Montgomery continued, was "a special type of agency, and it is a very special type of independence it claims for itself," but "we find no provision in the Constitution for a fourth branch of Government."[47] Likewise, Keyserling held that "in no event can any realistic concept of 'independence' mean that there is no relationship or interdependence" between the Federal Reserve and the rest of the federal government. Should there ever be a "collision" of objectives—say between fiscal policy directed toward economic expansion and restrictive monetary policy—Keyserling stressed that the central bank "must recognize the ultimate and decisive authority of the Congress."[48]

This specter of a "collision" between Federal Reserve decisions and the broader economic aims of the federal government—above all the maintenance of full employment—raised serious questions about the compatibility of central bank independence with a democratic process. It would be "both naïve and shortsighted," a 1953 CIO report concluded, to believe "that the Federal Reserve bankers, left to their own devices, can automatically be trusted to act in the public interest." Because of the "far-reaching implications for the entire Nation" resulting from central bank decisions, "they should not be left outside of the general area of coordinated Government decision-making."[49] Or as Boris Shiskin of the AFL put it rather more bluntly to the Patman Committee, the Federal Reserve, "which is now just above the angels [must] be brought down to earth, in order to find out and take into account the interest and necessities of the public they serve, beyond those of the select fraternity of bankers."[50]

Protecting the Dollar and the Country from Disaster

That select fraternity of bankers gained a friend in the Dwight Eisenhower administration. During his presidency, the "independence" that central bankers had won became, as one observer put it, "a rallying cry for conservatives," ranking in their value system right alongside "budget balancing and motherhood." In the words of another contemporary, the institution quickly secured a reputation as "the last citadel protecting the dollar and the country from disaster."[51] During those years, no one cut a more powerful figure in that world of financial respectability than Federal Reserve Chair William McChesney Martin. He was the son of a Missouri banker who had helped draft the 1913 Federal Reserve Act before taking on the presidency of the system's St. Louis branch. After graduating from Yale, the younger Martin picked up the family craft, and by the age of thirty-two headed the New York Stock Exchange. After the war, Martin assumed the directorship of the influential Export-Import Bank, a post he held for three years before transitioning in 1949 to the Treasury Department, where he served as assistant secretary charged with overseeing monetary affairs. From the Treasury, Martin played a key role in brokering the Fed-Treasury Accord, earning enough trust from Truman that the president tapped his fellow Missourian as the first post-Accord leader of the Federal Reserve. Truman came to regret the appointment. Legend has it that when the two encountered one another at an event many years later Truman had one word for his former associate: "traitor."[52]

Truman had reason to feel betrayed. Despite relative price stability during his first years in office, Martin relentlessly warned that "inflationary seeds may be germinating." That particular remark came in January 1955, when the price level was actually falling. Martin nonetheless impressed upon his colleagues how important it was to "nip inflation in the bud." "Inflation," he continued a few months later, "is a thief in the night." "If we don't act promptly and decisively we will always be behind." Over the years to come, Martin returned to the same theme—about an alarming "inflationary psychosis," how "inflation dominated the economy," a "very serious inflation atmosphere." As the economic historians Christina Romer and David Romer have argued, this "discussion [among Federal Reserve officials] was often so fervent and the predictions so dire that it is hard to believe that inflation was actually very low."[53]

Martin practiced what he preached, describing his approach to managing inflation expectations with a simple phrase: "leaning against the wind." The wind, in this formulation, meant total demand, and the force that did the leaning was the short-term interest rate. This could seem innocuous enough—a kind of counter-cyclical monetary management intended to prevent both bubbles and busts. But as Martin admitted, "It's pretty hard to know which way the wind is blowing," and for one who saw price stability as *the* ticket to economic success, the gusts could frequently seem too strong.[54] Martin's default position through those years was to raise short-term interest rates early in economic upswings—so as to get in front of any potential "inflationary psychology"—and to refrain from lowering them for as long as possible.[55] What counted was not simply that prices remained stable but also that everyone *expected* them to stay put, especially important for the industrial unions, whose bargaining power had the capacity to ratchet up national wage patterns.[56]

This doctrine came to be called "Bills Only"—a reference to Treasury Bills, or the shortest-term government securities. Under this framework, the price and yield of long-term government securities would be left to the "principles of the free market." Because long-term government bonds accounted for three-quarters of all long-term borrowing—public and private—by decade's end, this policy influenced the entire structure of long-term interest rates. Indeed, Bills Only proved the definitive rebuke to what Martin called the "dictated money rates" of the World War II pegs. Purposeful intervention into the government securities market of that sort, he declared in a widely heralded 1953 speech to the Economic Club of Detroit, "breed[s] dictated prices across the board." "This is characteristic of dictatorships. It is regimentation. It is not compatible with our institutions."[57] With the Federal Reserve on the sidelines, demand for long-term government bonds softened and interest rates thus began a steady, decades-long ascent.

The unionists who had opposed the Fed-Treasury Accord saw in Bills Only proof of everything they had feared, blaming Martin for the rather underwhelming economic performance of the late 1950s. From the end of the Korean War boom in 1954 through the end of the Eisenhower presidency, the average national unemployment rate consistently stood above 5 percent. In certain places, like Detroit, it was much higher. "Incredible as it may seem," UAW economist Donald Montgomery wrote to UAW President Walter Reuther in February 1955 (just when Martin worried that "inflationary seeds may be germinating"), the Federal Reserve had demonstrated a willingness "to bring an economic expansion to an end when there is no inflation and they only fear inflation may be coming." What this amounted to, Montgomery told Reuther, was "a deliberate attempt to keep the unemployed unemployed."[58] Central bankers' "reactionary and outmoded financial theories," a CIO *Economic Outlook* article stated in 1953, "spoke of a 'little less employment—and a 'little more unemployment,'" as if it were possible to "touch off just a little atomic explosion!" or "experiment with a small dose of the bubonic plague."[59] Indeed, as AFL-CIO Research Director Stanley Ruttenberg told a meeting of central bankers, that Federal Reserve decisions "'tilting at the windmill' of inflation" have been "hampering the healthy expansion of our economy."[60]

The most powerful argument against the Martin Federal Reserve's monetary policy, however, was that it simply did not work. Despite the program of tightening begun by 1955, prices on average continued to rise. Viewed in historical perspective, the rate was not high—some 5 percent between early 1956 and mid-1957—but it was sufficiently serious for one reporter to call it "possibly the steepest inflation in history not directly associated with a war."[61] The price level kept climbing even as the Federal Reserve's monetary restraint helped push the US economy into the 1957–58 recession. Unemployment reached 7.5 percent in what was to that point the sharpest contraction since 1937. All throughout that downturn, however, the annualized rate of inflation remained stuck above 3 percent—high, by 1950s standards.

Contemporary observers, like the *New York Times*'s chief financial correspondent, considered this simultaneous incidence of rising prices and worsening economic performance to be "baffling," flying in the face of prevailing orthodoxy. Economist J. M. Clark called it "a new kind of inflation," the taming of which threatened to make a bad unemployment situation worse. Conversely, how could the Fed and the rest of the government revitalize economic growth without stoking an already troubling inflation? No fewer than four congressional probes inquired into that question, bringing to Washington some of the most influential figures from the corporate world and academe. Dwight Eisenhower did his part in establishing a Cabinet Committee on Price Stability, led by Vice President Richard Nixon, to complete an investigation of its own.[62]

Many came to blame organized labor. Business leaders and conservative officials had long raised alarm about the structural consequences of industrial unionism, highlighting the dangers of the "wage-price spiral" that workplace militancy threatened to ignite. If unions raised wages in excess of productivity growth, business conservatives argued, firms would have to raise prices or else see their profits squeezed. Union economists, for their part, insisted that the upward creep in the consumer price level was "not due to general inflation" but rather was "the result of selective price pressures—price boosts by large-leading corporations in key basic industries that are being passed on."[63] This issue had been at the center of the epic 1945–46 strike wave, when the UAW demanded that General Motors provide a hefty wage increase while committing to refrain from raising the price of its cars. The new inflation of the late 1950s provided an opportunity to politicize the wage-price relation yet again, and once more the autoworkers took the lead. Reading the tea leaves in early 1957, Walter Reuther urged the liberal Tennessee Senator Estes Kefauver to use his Subcommittee on Antitrust and Monopoly to undertake a study of "the root causes of the creeping inflation," so as to determine "where the fault really lies so that the innocent will not be condemned for the sins of the guilty."[64]

After U.S. Steel used the occasion of a contractual wage increase to hike tonnage rates in July 1957, Kefauver's subcommittee announced plans to investigate the existence of "administered prices" in key industry sectors.[65] In the hearings that followed—which *New York Times* columnist Edwin Dale considered "among the most stimulating in recent memory"—Kefauver's team scrutinized price trends from steel and automotives to pharmaceuticals and sliced bread. The administered price framework on which the subcommittee drew had been developed more than twenty years earlier by the institutional economist Gardiner Means as an explanation for the intractability of the Great Depression. Before the late 1950s Kefauver subcommittee, Means began, as he had in the mid-1930s, with the straightforward observation that under modern corporate capitalism, price setting bore little resemblance to the idealized depictions of laissez-faire. Large firms in concentrated industries, he argued, did not adjust prices in response to demand as orthodox theory predicted they would. Instead, they set prices administratively, based on a host of internal calculations and varied output levels in accordance with movements in demand. Corporate managers might respond to sluggish economic conditions by cutting output while keeping prices stable—or even increasing them. This dynamic, Means noted, could very well feed on itself, with one round of production cuts and price increases spurring another, and another, and another—crunching demand and throwing people out of work all while generating inflation. Viewed this way, recession with inflation was not a puzzle at all but rather a predictable outcome in a system with concentrated economic power.[66]

To Means, the Federal Reserve was not equipped to manage this new "administrative inflation."[67] Such corporate pricing, he argued, had nothing to do with demand, so restraints like monetary tightening could not address it. The Federal Reserve "cannot control administrative inflation without creating excessive unemployment," Means emphasized, and therefore its efforts "to aim at both high employment and price stability involves some measure of contradiction." The central bank should instead "adopt policies which bring about the expansion in demand required for full employment without demand inflation, while other measures were adopted to prevent serious administrative inflation."[68]

By 1959, even Federal Reserve officials had to concede that there was something to the administered price argument. That March, Woodlief Thomas, a senior economist at the Fed, published a piece in the *Washington Post* which acknowledged that Gardiner Means had "made a significant contribution to a better understanding of the problems of inflation and fluctuations in economic activity." Administered prices produced "distortions and inflexibilities in the price and income structure," he concluded, which "cannot be avoided by monetary and fiscal policies." Here, the *New York Times* noted, was "the unusual spectacle of a high-raking representative of the Federal Reserve Board joining actively, and even vigorously, in the criticism that has been leveled at the steel and automotive industries for raising prices in a time of business recession."[69]

The Federal Reserve nonetheless tightened policy once again in 1959, even as criticism of the Fed became more widespread. An influential JEC report reiterated Means's conclusions during the 1960 election year, while the Democratic platform promised an "end to the present high interest, tight money policy." Because inflation "has its roots in a variety of causes," the Democrats continued, "its cure lies in a variety of remedies"—like "action to restrain 'administered price' increases in industries where economic power rests in the hands of a few."[70] Richard Nixon, meanwhile, went to his grave holding a grudge against Martin for having precipitated the recession that cost him the 1960 election.

"Monetary Policy for All Americans"

The AFL-CIO felt particularly aggrieved, publishing in August 1959 a blistering denunciation of the Fed in *Labor's Economic Review.* "The choice for the American people seems to be either tight money or runaway inflation," charged the labor federation. "The facts don't jibe with this choice. Neither does the law."[71] What George Meany called a "phantom 'inflation,'" and what Senator Paul Douglas—himself the Democrat who had pushed for the accord in the first place—labeled "scare talk" was in their view being used to justify "one of the tightest credit squeezes most Americans have ever seen." In the name of fighting inflation, the Federal Reserve was waging "an intensive campaign against economic growth and full employment." The result was "a shocking state of stagnation."[72] "America," the labor federation stressed, "cannot afford to sacrifice the needs of its citizens in the fight against inflation."[73] The AFL-CIO analysis concluded that central bank independence had meant "independence from the American people." The Fed was able to "tell the head of its own government to go fly a kite."[74]

Union leaders imagined reforms that would transform the Federal Reserve into "a public system representative of American life," an institution that would be "flexible enough to permit selective credit controls if and when actual inflationary shortages exist or . . . ease credit for certain types of activities declared to be essential."[75] And that included the public sector. The "hardships caused by hard-money," another AFL-CIO statement on monetary policy stressed, have included the "delay of worthwhile social programs"—things like "Federal Aid to Education, an expanded public housing program and a program for middle-income housing."[76]

State and local governments struggled to compete for capital on the open market. The higher rates these public bodies were forced to offer, Stanley Ruttenberg complained, "hampers the development of needed public facilities."[77] Because the existing system "permit[s] the banking institutions to allocate the loan resources of the country," rather than subjecting those decisions to the democratic process, "important social developments in the fields of housing, small business, schools and roads, and distressed areas are prohibited."[78]

Why not, the AFL-CIO proposed, provide central bankers with a program of public priorities—say education, health, and housing? Private financial institutions could then "borrow from the Federal Reserve Banks only for these specific purposes at interest rates substantially below the current levels of discount rates." With such investments being made with low-cost capital, "restrictive measures should be taken against other types of borrowing" toward speculative ends. "In this way," concluded an AFL-CIO research memo on the subject, a "better balanced relationship" between "socially needed objectives" and private sector objectives could be achieved.[79]

One way to move toward that kind of monetary policy would be to change the way the Federal Reserve managed long-term government debt. Union economists thought it high time that "the 'bills only' policy is reversed." Since the accord, when the Martin Federal Reserve began operating in accordance with the Bills Only doctrine, rates on long-term government debt had climbed, swelling into one of the largest items in the federal budget. Public investment was thereby constrained, and to the degree that the government bond market conditioned the overall structure of long-term interest rates, so too was productive private investment. AFL-CIO economists thus called for Congress to instruct the Federal Reserve that "the U.S. and U.S. Treasury are not ordinary 'competitors' in a 'free' business market." Instead, government bonds must be "managed positively as part of national economic policy, instead of managing them as if they were the securities of a private corporation."[80] To do so, the Federal Reserve would have to "judiciously buy all types of government securities" so as to achieve moderate and sustainable long-term interest rates.[81]

These ideas were not on the periphery of American politics. The Joint Economic Committee echoed these laborite arguments in an influential 1960 study, *Employment, Growth, and Price Levels*. "More monetary tools rather than less," the report concluded, "are necessary for the simultaneous achievement of all of our economic goals." Bills Only needed to be "abandoned," and a top priority of credit policy should be "reducing the long-term interest rate" through regular central bank intervention in the long-term government securities market.[82]

However, Bills Only had become, in the words of Allan Sproul, a "high church" gospel within the Fed, part and parcel of central bank independence.[83] William McChesney Martin's most trusted staff counsel felt that departing from Bills Only would "result in something pretty close to, if not actually, a peg," thereby jeopardizing everything the Federal Reserve had accomplished since its showdown with Truman years earlier.[84] Returning to anything like that relationship, Martin said before the JEC in 1959, would make the central bank "the price and yield administrator of the long-term Government securities market."[85] He hoped that "the Treasury of the United States will never be so weak that it has to rely on the central bank to justify its existence."[86] Doing so, Martin concluded, would signal to everyone around the world a central bank willingness to turn to the "printing press" on behalf of the government's spending desires.[87] Nothing, one perceptive observer commented, "scares the central bankers from New Delhi to The Hague [like the word] 'printing press.'"[88]

Martin's remarks were indeed "inflammatory," as the Federal Reserve critic Rep. Henry Reuss complained, but central bankers did have reason to be concerned about the global standing of the US currency.[89] Through the latter half of the 1950s, the national balance of payments had trended downward. It moved into negative territory for the first time in 1959. Under the Bretton Woods international monetary regime, which had become fully operational only in 1958, international investors could freely convert dollars into gold, and thus deficits in the balance of payments could spell problems for Fort Knox. Martin feared that steps to ease monetary policy at home—with respect to long-term securities or anything else—would only encourage speculators to take their dollars elsewhere and thereby worsen the balance of payments problem and imperil the US gold stock.[90]

Such concerns created a real "dilemma," Martin told the JEC in early 1961.[91] In the words of economist Paul Samuelson, then an advisor to President-elect Kennedy, "The days are gone when America could shape her domestic stabilization policies taking no thought for their international repercussions." At the same time, however, Samuelson stressed that "it would be unthinkable for a present-day American Government to deliberately countenance high unemployment as a mechanism for adjusting to the balance-of-payments deficit"—"only a cynic would counsel its acceptance."[92] Walter Heller, President Kennedy's CEA chair, added that the "'gold outflow' problem will be used to oppose all bold expansionary measures by people who oppose them anyway." Major economic policy decisions, he urged, "can and should be made in Washington, not by bankers in Zurich or Frankfurt or London or even New York."[93] Kennedy remained worried—to the point of an "almost phobia," according to Douglas Dillon, his Treasury secretary—about the power those foreign bankers had over the US balance of payments. "If there's ever a run on the bank, and I have to devalue the dollar or bring home our troops," Kennedy is reported to have privately remarked, "I'm the one who will take the heat."[94]

Just weeks after the 1960 election, the AFL-CIO began lobbying for a proposal to meet both sides of the dilemma simultaneously. The key, in labor's view, was to develop a two-pronged strategy for dealing with short- and long-term interest rates. Because long-term rates were most important for encouraging investment and job creation, "action by the Federal Reserve System to bring down interest rates on long-term securities" was urgently needed. Having acted on that front, the central bank could then afford to bump short-term rates upward without causing too much collateral damage. The latter "would increase the ability of the U.S. to keep [dollars] in the United States" since it was the gravitational pull of short-term rates that induced cross-border capital flows.[95] Around the same time, Paul Samuelson's transition taskforce raised the same idea: Because "long-term rates [are] most decisive for investment spending" and "short-term rates [are] most decisive for foreign balances," the Federal Reserve could get around the dilemma by "bring[ing] long-term rates down relative to short-term rates."[96] By breaking with Bills Only, labor and Kennedy administration officials suggested that the central bank could thus "twist" the interest rate structure in a way that would enable them to achieve two goals at once.[97]

Twisting, Not Democratizing, Monetary Policy

William Martin blinked.[98] In January 1961, the Federal Reserve chair told his colleagues that they could no longer ignore "the very heavy barrage both from within and outside Government . . . for the uncompromising position they allegedly took" in years past. It was incumbent upon monetary authorities, Martin added, "to give some further tangible indication of open-mindedness and willingness to experiment"—for should they fail to adapt, there might be no "escape from the charge of doctrinaire commitment to a laissez faire, free private market position."[99] While he "was not going to give an inch" on the idea that the Federal Reserve adopt a policy of "easier money" to achieve employment goals, the dilemma had made it "more difficult to espouse the theory that Bills Only was something on which the System ought to stand or die."[100] Martin now thought the Fed would have to "lean against crosswinds, and lean against them simultaneously."[101]

The next month, the Federal Reserve's policymaking body voted to begin a "period of experiment" with open market operations in longer-term government securities designed to push those rates downward.[102] Contemporary observers understood the significance of this trial, which monetary officials first named "Operation Nudge" and later took to calling "Operation Twist"—for the twist in the interest rate structure it sought to achieve. To one leading economic analyst, it marked the end of the institution's "spirited and all but intractable allegiance to an extremely limited concept of central banking."[103]

Operation Twist represented only one small step toward the kind of selective credit policy union economists had envisioned. As Walter Heller explained to Kennedy, "it takes more than a nudge to budge the market."[104] Some four months into the experiment, actual Federal Reserve purchases of longer-term bonds had been, in Heller's telling, "minute." "The massive power of the Fed has yet to move into action," the CEA chair complained, and its leadership continued to be "too passive" and "too unimaginative."[105] An AFL-CIO report the next month lamented how "the end of 'bills only' was more in words than deeds," as Martin's "failure to drive down long-terms shows little will to move them." "New policies," the federation added, "require new attitudes" in place of "old fears, old problems, and timorous actions"—and it was incumbent upon the central bank to "vigorously buy long-term bonds in the open market, help stabilize short term rates and spur credit availability in a nation that needs rapid recovery."[106]

The complex, politically fraught end to Bills Only presaged the complicated policy and political battles covered in the essays in this volume's next two sections. Organized labor remained engaged and influential in monetary policy debates in the 1960s and 1970s, continuing to fight for selective measures rather than "reliance on the blunderbuss approach."[107] They enjoyed some real successes. Both the Kennedy and Johnson administrations pieced together various capital controls, and in 1969 Congress passed the Credit Control Act, which authorized the president and Federal Reserve to regulate any and all extensions of credit.[108] That law, labor officials celebrated, would enable the kind of targeted policies that "allocate the flow of bank credit to where it is most needed, while restraining the extension of credit to low-priority purposes."[109] Unions stood firm in their support for those measures during the 1970s stagflation era and played a key role in securing important legislative reforms that prodded the Federal Reserve to prioritize moderate long-term interest rates, increase transparency, and mandate that the institution pursue both maximum employment and price stability.

This was the context in which Federal Reserve Chair Paul Volcker—a Jimmy Carter appointee—shocked the economy with an unprecedented interest rate hike, thus initiating the deep recession that helped usher in the neoliberal era. The Volcker Shock was an assertion of Fed authority in the face of a credible challenge from below. And it had its intended effect. Over the next several decades, central banks grew into the most powerful economic institutions on the planet. As the world became ever more financialized, the management of that system ceased to be a subject of social struggle. With the specter of inflation once again affecting our politics, it would be well to remember Nat Goldfinger's assertion that "no one should be misled by the pretense of the Federal Reserve . . . that the mysteries of monetary policy are too complicated for ordinary people to understand."[110] Indeed, just as John Commons put it more than a century ago, the credit problem may still be among our most grave of labor problems.

Notes

1. John R. Commons, "Unemployment: Compensation and Prevention," *The Survey* (October 1, 1921), reprinted in *John R. Commons: Selected Essays, Vol. 1*, ed. Malcolm Rutherford and Warren J. Samuels (New York: Routledge, 1996).

2. Melanie Sheehan, "The AFL-CIO, the U.S. Balance of Payments, and the End of the Post–World War II Liberal Order, 1965–1973," *Enterprise and Society* (2023): 1–24; Jeffrey Sklansky, "Labor, Money, and the Financial Turn in the History of Capitalism," *Labor: Studies in Working-Class History* 11, no. 1 (2014): 23–46.

3. Benjamin Braun and Leah Downing, "Against Amnesia: Re-Imagining Central Banking," Council on Economic Policies Discussion Note, Jan. 2020: https://www.cepweb.org/wp-content/uploads/2020/01/CEP-DN-Against-Amnesia.-Re-Imagining-Central-Banking.pdf.

4. Douglas J. Elliott, Greg Feldberg, and Anderas Lehnert, "The History of Cyclical Macroprudential Policy," Board of Governors of the Federal Reserve System, Finance and Discussion Series, May 2013; Daniel Monnet, *Controlling Credit: Central Banking and the Planned Economy in Postwar France, 1948–1973* (Cambridge: Cambridge University Press, 2018).

5. John Goldthorpe and Fred Hirsch, eds., *The Political Economy of Inflation* (Cambridge: Harvard University Press, 1979).

6. Meg Jacobs, *Pocketbook Politics: Economic Citizenship in Twentieth Century America* (Princeton: Princeton University Press, 2004); Charles Maier, "The Politics of Inflation in the United States," in *In Search of Stability: Explorations in Historical Political Economy* (Cambridge: Cambridge University Press, 1987).

7. David Harvey, *A Brief History of Neoliberalism* (Oxford: Oxford University Press, 2005); Judith Stein, *Pivotal Decade: How the U.S. Traded Factories for Finance in the 1970s* (New Haven: Yale University Press, 2010).

8. Edwin Dickens, *The Political Economy of U.S. Monetary Policy: How the Federal Reserved Gained Control and Uses It* (London: Routledge, 2016); Gerald Epstein and Juliet Schor, "The

Federal Reserve–Treasury Accord and the Construction of the Post-War Monetary Regime in the United States," Political Economic Research Institute, Working Paper No. 273 (2011), 11.

9. Stephanie Kelton, *The Deficit Myth: Modern Monetary Theory and the Birth of the People's Economy* (New York: Public Affairs, 2021).

10. Andrew Elrod, "Stabilization Politics in the Twentieth Century United States: Corporatism, Democracy, and Economic Planning, 1945–1980," PhD diss., University of California Santa Barbara, 2021.

11. "Higher Interest Rates Help Banks—Hit You," *CIO Economic Outlook*, May 1953.

12. U.S. Congress, Joint Committee on the Economic Report [hereafter "JCER"], *Monetary Policy and the Management of the Public Debt: Hearings Before the Subcommittee on General Credit Control and Debt Management*, 82nd Cong., 2nd sess., 1952 [hereafter "1952 General Credit Control"], 819.

13. Quoted in Donald Kettl, *Leadership at the Fed* (New Haven: Yale University Press, 1986), 48.

14. Quoted in Dwight L. Israelsen, "Marriner S. Eccles, Chairman of the Federal Reserve Board," *American Economic Review* 75, no. 2 (1985), 361.

15. Allan Meltzer, *History of the Federal Reserve, Volume 1: 1913–1955* (Chicago: University of Chicago Press), 415.

16. Lauchlin Currie, "The Relation of Government to Monetary Control (1935)," reprinted in *Journal of Economic Studies* 31, no. 3/4 (2004): 270–279.

17. Lauchlin Currie, "Desirable Changes in the Administration of the Federal Reserve System (1934)," reprinted in *Journal of Economic Studies* 31, no. 3/4 (2004): 267–269.

18. Ronnie Phillips, "An End to Private Banking: Early New Deal Proposals to Alter the Role of the Federal Government in Credit Allocation," *Journal of Money, Credit, and Banking* 26, no. 3 (1994): 552–568.

19. Meltzer, *History of the Federal Reserve*, 580–581. I use "Treasury bills" interchangeably with short-term securities and "Treasury bonds" interchangeably with long-term securities. In practice, there were a number of securities of intermediate maturity and related instruments that follow a similar pattern.

20. Epstein and Schor, "The Federal Reserve–Treasury Accord," 7.

21. Elmus R. Wicker, "The World War II Policy of Fixing a Pattern of Interest Rates," *Journal of Finance* 24, no. 3 (1969): 447–458.

22. Herbert Stein, *The Fiscal Revolution* (Washington, DC: AEI Press, 1990), 241–282, passim.

23. Hugh Rockoff, *Drastic Measures: A History of Wage and Price Controls in the United States* (Cambridge: Cambridge University Press, 1984), 85–126.

24. Quoted in Kettl, *Leadership at the Fed*, 62.

25. See Jacobs, *Pocketbook Politics*, 221–231.

26. Allan Sproul, "How Long Will Government 'Peg' Prices of Its Securities?" Nov. 12, 1948, Federal Reserve Bank of New York and Sproul, *Statements and Speeches of Allan Sproul*, 1946–1963, https://fraser.stlouisfed.org/title/6743; Meltzer, *History of the Federal Reserve*, 629–645.

27. Russell C. Leffingwell, "How to Control Inflation," *Fortune*, Oct. 1948.

28. John Clark to Truman, July 31, 1948, Box 123, CEA General, President's Secretary's Files, Harry S. Truman Presidential Library, Independence, MO.

29. JCER. *Anti-Inflation Program as Recommended in the President's Message of November 17, 1947: Hearings Before the Joint Committee on the Economic Report*, 79th Cong., 1st sess., 1947 [hereafter "JCER 1947"], 139–140.

30. Marriner Eccles and Sidney Hyman, *Beckoning Frontiers: Public and Personal Recollections* (New York: Knopf, 1951), 398.

31. Board of Governors of the Federal Reserve System, *Thirty-Second Annual Report of the Board of Governors of the Federal Reserve System Covering Operations for the Year 1945* (Washington, DC: Board of Governors of the Federal Reserve System, 1946), 8.

32. JCER 1947, 143.

33. Eccles and Hyman, *Beckoning Frontiers*, 427–428.

34. JCER 1947, 143.

35. "Statement of Federal Advisory Council Addressed to the FRB," Nov. 18, 1947, reprinted in JEC 1947, 146–148.

36. Leffingwell to Snyder, Jan. 26, 1948, Box 7, Folder 156, Leffingwell Family Papers, Manuscripts and Archives, Yale University, New Haven, CT.

37. Leffingwell, "How to Control Inflation."

38. U.S. Congress, Senate, JCER, Subcommittee on Monetary Credit, and Fiscal Policies, *Monetary, Credit, and Fiscal Policies: Report (Pursuant to S. Con. Res. 26)*, 81st Cong., 2nd sess., 1950, Doc. 129, 2.

39. Theodore Schultz et al., "The Failure of the Present Monetary Policy," Jan. 30, 1951, 61/2/1, Marriner S. Eccles Papers, University of Utah, https://fraser.stlouisfed.org/archival/1343.

40. Truman surprised observers by replacing Eccles, with whom personal and political tensions had long existed, with McCabe in 1948.

41. For different perspectives, see Stein, *Fiscal Revolution*, 241–282 and Epstein and Schor, "The Federal Reserve–Treasury Accord."

42. 1952 General Credit Control, 159–161.

43. Ibid., 808–809.

44. CIO, "Fed Policy and the Control of Inflation in a War or Defense Emergency," reprinted in U.S. Congress, Senate, *Standby Economic Controls: Hearings Before the Committee on Banking and Currency*, 83rd Cong., 1st sess., 1953, 793–798; Nat Goldfinger, "Memo on Commodity Market Trading," June 12, 1952, Box 2, Folder 3, Stanley H. Ruttenberg Papers, Special Collections and University Archives, University of Maryland, College Park, MD [hereafter SR]; 1952 General Credit Control, 819.

45. CEA to Truman, Feb. 7. 1952, Box 2, Monetary Policy and Reserve Requirements, Leon H. Keyserling Papers, Harry S. Truman Presidential Library [hereafter LHK].

46. 1952 General Credit Control, 819.

47. Ibid., 818–822.

48. Ibid., 162–163.

49. CIO, "Fed Policy and the Control of Inflation in a War or Defense Emergency."

50. 1952 General Credit Control, 830.

51. Hobart Rowen, *The Free Enterprisers: Kennedy, Johnson, and the Business Establishment* (New York: Putman, 1964), 25.

52. Robert M. Bremner, *Chairman of the Fed: William McChesney Martin and the Creation of the Modern Financial System* (New Haven: Yale University Press, 2004); Robert L. Hetzel and Ralph F. Leach, "The Treasury–Fed Accord: A New Narrative Account," Federal Reserve Bank of Richmond, *Economic Quarterly* 87, no. 1 (2001): 52.

53. Federal Open Market Committee [hereafter FOMC] Minutes, Jan. 11, 1955, 7–8; FOMC Minutes, August 18, 1958, 54; Christina D. Romer and David H. Romer, "A Rehabilitation of Monetary Policy in the 1950s," *American Economic Review* 92, no. 2 (2002): 3; U.S. Congress, Joint Economic Committee [hereafter JEC], *Employment, Growth, and Price Levels Part 6A—The*

Government's Management of Its Monetary, Fiscal, and Debt Operations: Hearings Before the Joint Economic Committee, 86th Cong., 1st sess., 1959 [hereafter "1959 JEC Part 6A], 1243.

54. Edwin L. Dale Jr., "Reserve System 'Feeling Its Way,'" *New York Times*, Feb. 8, 1956.

55. Robert L. Hetzel, *The Monetary Policy of the Federal Reserve: A History* (Cambridge: Cambridge University Press, 2008), 49–59.

56. James Forder, *Macroeconomics and the Phillips Curve Myth* (Oxford: Oxford University Press, 2014).

57. William McChesney Martin, "The Transition to Free Markets: An Address by William McChesney Martin Jr. at the Economic Club of Detroit, April 13, 1953," reprinted in *Monthly Business Review: Federal Reserve Bank of Dallas* 38, no. 5 (1953): 1–4, https://fraser.stlouisfed.org/title/5730/item/575600/toc/524980; JEC, *Employment, Growth, and Price Levels: Report*, 86th Cong., 1st sess., 1960, S. Con. Res. 13, 37.

58. Montgomery to Reuther, Feb. 5, 1955, Box 2, Folder 39, SR.

59. "Higher Interest Rates Help Banks—Hit You," *CIO Economic Outlook*, May 1953.

60. Stanley Ruttenberg, "A Different Look at Monetary Policy," Statement before Federal Reserve Board, Monetary Policy Meeting, Fall 1956, reprinted in *AFL-CIO Economic Trends and Outlook*, Jan. 1957.

61. Edwin L. Dale Jr., "Basic Inquiry into a Baffling Inflation," *New York Times*, August 25, 1957.

62. Norikazu Takami, "The Baffling New Inflation: How Cost-Push Inflation Theories Influenced Policy Debate in the Late-1950s United States," *History of Political Economy* 47, no. 4 (2015): 605–629.

63. AFL-CIO, *Economic Trends and Outlook*, Feb. 1957.

64. Walter Reuther to Estes Kefauver, Jan. 11, 1957, Box 201, Folder 3, Estes Kefauver Papers, Modern Political Archives, University of Tennessee, Knoxville, TN.

65. On the Kefauver Committee, see Robert Bud, "Antibiotics, Big Business, and Consumers: The Context of Government Investigations into the Postwar American Drug Industry," *Technology and Culture* 46, no. 2 (2005): 329–349; Daniel Scroop, "A Faded Passion?: Estes Kefauver and the Senate Subcommittee on Antitrust and Monopoly," *Business and Economic History On-Line*, 5 (2005): https://thebhc.org/sites/default/files/scroop.pdf; Jacobs, *Pocketbook Politics*, 256–261.

66. See U.S. Congress, Senate, *Industrial Prices and Their Relative Inflexibility*, 74th Cong., 1st sess., 1935, S. Doc. 13-E-7; Gardiner C. Means, *Administrative Inflation and Public Policy* (Washington, DC: A. Kramer Associates, 1959). See also Theodore Rosenof, *Economics in the Long Run: New Deal Theorists and Their Legacies* (Chapel Hill: UNC Press, 1997), 128–144; Richard Goode, "Gardiner Means on Administered Prices and Administrative Inflation," *Journal of Economic Issues* 28, no. 1 (1994): 173–186.

67. U.S. Congress, Senate, *Administered Prices: Hearings Before the Subcommittee on Antitrust and Monopoly of the Senate Committee on the Judiciary, Part 1*, 85th Cong., 1st sess., 1957, 88–89.

68. Means, *Administrative Inflation and Public Policy*, 42–43.

69. "An Aroused Reserve Board," *New York Times*, March 14, 1959; Edwin L. Dale Jr., "U.S. Aides Uneasy on Price Policies," *New York Times*, March 15, 1959.

70. JEC, *Employment, Growth, and Price Levels*, 30–31; Charles L. Schultze, *Recent Inflation in the United States* (Washington, D.C.: Government Printing Office, 1959), 2. Democratic Party Platforms, 1960 Democratic Party Platform Online by Gerhard Peters and John T. Woolley, The American Presidency Project, https://www.presidency.ucsb.edu/node/273234.

71. "Monetary Policy for All Americans," *Labor's Economic Review*, August 1959.

72. "Money and Credit: Tighter and Tighter"; JEC, *Employment, Growth, and Price Levels Part 9B: Constructive Suggestions for Reconciling and Simultaneously Obtaining the Three Objectives of Maximum Employment, an Adequate Rate of Growth, and Substantial Stability of the Price Level (Materials Submitted by 12 Organizations at the Invitation of the Joint Economic Committee): Hearings Before the Joint Economic Committee on Employment, Growth, and Price Levels*, 86th Cong., 1st sess., 1959 [hereafter "1959 JEC Part 9B], 3090, 3094.

73. "AFL-CIO Executive Council Resolution on Monetary Policy," Feb. 1, 1957, Box 2, Folder 38, SR.

74. A. H. Raskin, "Labor Asks Seat on Reserve Board," *New York Times*, Feb. 25, 1959; "Remarks as Presented to the Board of Governors, Federal Reserve Board," Nov. 28, 1956, Box 2, Folder 38, SR.

75. *NYT*, Feb. 25, 1959; 1959 JEC Part 9B, 3110.

76. "AFL-CIO Executive Council Resolution on Monetary Policy," Feb. 1, 1957, Box 2, Folder 39, SR.

77. "A Different Look at Monetary Policy," Box 2, Folder 38, SR.

78. "Points for Discussion in Developing AFL-CIO Policy Relating to Monetary Policy," Jan. 8. 1957, Box 1, Folder 8, SR.

79. "Points for Discussion in Developing AFL-CIO Policy Relating to Monetary Policy."

80. 1959 JEC Part 9B, 3110.

81. "Monetary Policy for All Americans."

82. JEC, *Employment, Growth, and Price Levels*, 32–42.

83. Allan Sproul, "The Sickness of Inflation," *Fortune*, July 1959, 118.

84. Quoted in Bremner, *Chairman of the Fed*, 154. See also Kenneth Garbade, *Treasury Debt Management Under the Rubric of Regular and Predictable Issue, 1983–2012* (New York: Federal Reserve Bank of New York, 2021), 22–26.

85. 1959 JEC Part 6A, 1235.

86. 1959 JEC Part 6A, 1318.

87. Martin to Rep. Richard Simpson, July 14, 1959 printed in 1959 JEC Part 6A, 1287–1288.

88. 1959 JEC Part 6A, 1292.

89. 1959 JEC Part 6A, 1292.

90. Francis Gavin, "The Gold Battles Within the Cold War: American Monetary Policy and the Defense of Europe, 1960–1963," *Diplomatic History* 26, no. 1 (2002): 61–94.

91. U.S. Congress, Joint Economic Committee. *January 1961 Economic Report of the President and the Economic Situation and Outlook: Hearings Before the Joint Economic Committee.* 87th Cong., 1st sess., 1951 [hereafter "January 1961 Hearings"], 468.

92. Paul A. Samuelson, "Prospects and Policies for the 1961 American Economy: A Report to President-Elect Kennedy," reprinted in "January 1961 Hearings," 705.

93. CEA, "A Second Look at Economic Policy in 1961," March 17, 1961, Box 5, Heller Papers.

94. Quoted in Irving Bernstein, *Promises Kept: John F. Kennedy's New Frontier* (Oxford: Oxford University Press), 121.

95. *AFL-CIO News*, Nov. 26, 1960.

96. Paul A. Samuelson, "Prospects and Policies," 709.

97. See also Sheehan, "The AFL-CIO."

98. Bremner, *Chairman of the Fed*, 176, 183; FOMC Minutes, Feb. 7, 1961, 45.

99. FOMC Minutes, Feb. 7, 1961, 45. On break with bills only, see Bremner, *Chairman of the Fed*, 152–155.

100. FOMC Minutes, July 11, 1961, 56; FOMC Minutes, Nov. 14, 1961, 34.

101. "January 1961 Hearings," 464.

102. FOMC Minutes, Feb. 7, 1961, 46; Bremner, *Chairman of the Fed*, 152–155.

103. M. J. Rossant, "Mr. Martin and the Winds of Change," *Challenge* 12, no. 4 (1964): 11.

104. Heller to JFK, April 6, 1961, Heller Papers, Box 5.

105. Heller to JFK, April 6, 1961, Heller Papers, Box 5; Heller to JFK, June 6, 1961, Heller Papers, Box 5.

106. Meany to Kennedy, May 8, 1961; AFL-CIO Research Department, "Steps Necessary to Implement Monetary Policies to Spur Recovery," Box 1, Folder 45, Nat Goldfinger Papers, Special Collections and University Archives, University of Maryland, College Park, MD.

107. U.S. Congress, House, *Investigation of Increase in Prime Rate: Hearings Before the Committee on Banking and Currency*, 91st Cong., 1st sess., 1969, 227.

108. Stacy Schreft, "Credit Controls: 1980," *Federal Reserve Bank of Richmond Economic Review* 76: 25–55.

109. U.S. Congress, Senate, Committee on Banking, Housing, and Urban Affairs, *Selective Credit Policies and Wage-Price Stabilization*, 88. See also Lester Thurow, Peter Temin, Alan Blinder, Joseph Quinn, and Ernesto Tironi, *Activities by Various Central Banks to Promote Economic and Social Welfare Policies*, report prepared for the use of the House Committee on Banking and Currency, 91st Cong., 1st sess., 1971, Committee Print.

110. U.S. Congress, House of Representatives, Committee on Banking, Currency and Housing. *Federal Reserve Consultations on the Conduct of Monetary Policy: Hearings before the Committee on Banking, Currency, and Housing*, 94th Cong., 1st sess., July 22, 23, and 24, 1975, 5–6.

PART II

Postwar Discontent

CHAPTER 3

"The Magnanimity of Disorder": Counterculture Intellectuals and the Rise of Anti-Statist Thought in Late Twentieth-Century America

Reuel Schiller

Academics, journalists, and political pundits frequently identify something called "The End of the Sixties."[1] "The Sixties," in this instance, is not an actual decade, but a period of social, political, and cultural reform. It represents the apogee of postwar political liberalism, the flowering of participatory activism around contentious social issues, and the dramatic explosion of youth culture into the mainstream of American consciousness. Its end is marked by signature events, often tragic, in the realms of politics and culture: the assassinations of Martin Luther King Jr. and Bobby Kennedy, the self-immolation of Students for a Democratic Society, the election of Richard Nixon, or the murder at the Altamont music festival. In the words of Todd Gitlin, both a participant in "The Sixties" and one of its most perceptive chroniclers, what started as "Years of Hope" ended with "Days of Rage." According to this narrative, conservative forces in American society reasserted themselves, crushing the remnants of the progressive reform movements that survived the fratricidal self-destruction and centrifugal fragmentation of the political and cultural left that occurred at the end of the decade.

For many historians of twentieth-century America, "The End of the Sixties" has come to represent the end of a form of liberalism of a longer duration as well. Forged during the Great Depression and the New Deal, this type of liberal politics reflected a commitment to economic egalitarianism and political and cultural pluralism, a central theme in the essays in this volume's first section. The federal government was to act as a force to further these goals by regulating business, relieving economic insecurity through wealth redistribution, and implementing policies aimed at abolishing distinctions among races, religions, and ethnicities. These aspirational goals were achieved with varying degrees of success, but historians have argued that the widespread desire to implement them shaped the politics of the middle decades of the twentieth century. In this narrative, "The End of the Sixties" was the end of the political era discussed in the chapters of this book's second section. New Deal liberalism was replaced by something else: hostility toward government, demands to curtail commitments to racial egalitarianism, and the rebirth of political conservatism.

The collapse of liberal politics at "The End of the Sixties" was also marked by changes both in beliefs about the administrative state and in actual regulatory policy.[2] The political successes of twentieth-century liberalism had created a substantial administrative state to implement the policies it generated. These policies often stemmed from a skepticism about the ability of the free market to fairly order society. They also reflected a deep commitment to expertise and a belief that large, centralized bureaucracies could efficiently implement policies furthering the public interest. By the 1970s, these ideas had fallen out of favor, as had many of the regulatory policies that were animated by them. Skepticism about the ability of government to effectively regulate replaced skepticism about markets. Faith in expertise and the effectiveness of large bureaucracies and top-down administrative regulation receded. Instead, theories of regulation that favored decentralized planning and governance emerged. In many circumstances, policymakers simply rejected regulation altogether, advocating deregulation of entire sectors of the economy. "The End of the Sixties" thus marked a retreat from the regulatory policies and institutions that midcentury liberalism had created. Novel regulatory thought and practice emerged as part of a new period of American political and legal history.

Periodizing history in this fashion is, of course, a tricky business. At every point of rupture—"liberalism's collapse," for example—continuities exist. As many historians have noted, politically conservative, anti-statist thought hardly disappeared during liberalism's ascendence. Furthermore, right-wing intellectuals and policymakers made a concerted effort to boost its fortunes just as liberalism weakened at the end of the 1960s.[3] This chapter, however, argues that the anti-statist political culture that typified this new period of American politics was as much the product of a very different source: a particular strand of left-wing and countercultural thought that flourished during the 1960s and 1970s. This thinking reflected a dramatic shift away from a vision of a state that advanced humanist, democratic values and promoted stable governance through representative interest groups and the application of expertise. Instead, it promoted a robust, sometimes utopian commitment to libertarian principles as an antidote to an administrative state that had become corrupt, oppressive, and dehumanizing.

Historians have recognized that liberal conceptions of politics, governance, and the state were rooted in the thinking of so-called "pluralist" intellectuals like Daniel Bell, Robert Dahl, David Truman, and John Kenneth Galbraith who imagined that the stability and prosperity of postwar America stemmed from the clash of powerful interest groups representing various segments of society.[4] This vision of politics was harshly critiqued by radical thinkers in the 1950s and 1960s. These thinkers—C. Wright Mills, Dwight Macdonald, Gabriel Kolko, Theodore Lowi, Grant McConnell, and Henry Kariel, for example—rejected the pluralists' vision of a benign state efficiently producing policy in the public interest by facilitating interest group compromise.[5] Instead, they described a society run by intertwined corporations and government bureaucracies, acting in the interests of a rarified "power elite." Indeed, business and government were barely distinct institutions at all. They were a single entity, run by an elite class bound together by economic interests, as well as social and psychological affinities nurtured in a wide variety of elite institutions. The American public's ability to resist this leviathan had been destroyed by a deadening mass culture and an oppressive bureaucracy that turned the people into passive consumers of elite opinion. It rendered them, in Mills's words, "inactionary"—unable to assert their own opinions, let alone any political power.[6]

To get a sense of how pervasive this anti-statist thought had become by the beginning of the 1970s, this chapter looks at thinkers who had a wider audience than academics like Kolko and Lowi, or even public intellectuals like Mills and Macdonald. I have picked three such people: R. Buckminster Fuller, E. F. Schumacher, and Charles Reich. All three were quite famous in the late 1960s and early 1970s. Fuller, best described as an architect and inventor, was cover-of-*Time*-magazine famous. Reich, whose early professional life was that of a conventional, if accomplished, academic, became wildly popular in the first years of the 1970s when his book, *The Greening of America*, sat atop the *New York Times* bestseller list for twenty weeks.[7] Schumacher, who spent the bulk of his life as a British bureaucrat, was the least well-known of the three. Nonetheless, his book, *Small Is Beautiful*, was an international bestseller, and his standing-room-only tours of the United States in the 1970s caught the imagination of the public at large, as well as a number of significant policy-makers and activists including Stewart Brand, Ralph Nader, Jerry Brown, and Jimmy Carter.

None of these authors were particularly popular in the New Left circles that erected much of their political thought on the intellectual scaffolding built by Mills, Kolko, and Lowi.[8] Instead, at the time, all three were more closely associated with the counterculture, as odd a fit as that was for each of them, generationally and, for Fuller at least, aesthetically. Yet the work of all three reflected an important shift in American political culture that occurred in the 1970s. Political scientists such as Martha Derthick, Paul Quirk, and Anthony Brown have noted that there emerged in the 1970s "widely shared desires, sentiments and values" that reflected a "widely diffused disaffection with government" and a "deep cynicism about government institutions."[9] Historians of the 1960s have noticed this change as well. As Maurice Isserman and Michael Kazin have noted, though many political and cultural radicals "survey[ed] the ruins of their successive . . . failures" at the end of the 1960s, "it is striking that while 'nothing' was accomplished . . . everything was different afterwards."[10] "The ambiance of our lives," they wrote, was affected by the emergence of a new culture that included "a vigorous libertarian spirit."[11]

Central to these observations is the argument that attitudes held by people at the political and cultural periphery in the 1960s had moved into the mainstream by the 1970s. While it is easy to see this phenomenon with respect to politics (environmentalism, opposition to the war in Vietnam, an acceptance of an increasingly pluralist society) or culture (music, clothing, and beliefs about sex and drug use), it also occurred with respect to attitudes toward the state. Hostility toward the state did not remain cabined in the barely comprehensible tomes of Marcuse, far-out counterculture newspapers, or dull journals of public administration. Instead, some of the most popular public intellectuals of this period generated and promulgated these ideas. They climbed to the top of the bestseller lists and appeared on the covers of the most popular news magazines. The popularity of Fuller, Schumacher, and Reich illustrates this fact. Their ubiquitous presence in the culture acted as a conduit by which ideas hostile to an active state made their way into the thinking of the public at large. Indeed, the fact that the culture was so receptive to these ideas demonstrates that they had made their way from the oppositional culture of the 1960s left and counterculture into the mainstream.

R. Buckminster Fuller: Comprehensive Designers Play the World Game

For the first fifty years of his life, R. Buckminster Fuller was an unsuccessful inventor, barely scraping by as a consultant for Marshall Field, Phelps-Dodge, and various Luce publications.[12] In 1954, however, he struck it rich, receiving a patent for the geodesic dome—a cheap, strong, easily built structure with numerous military and civilian applications. The resources and notoriety generated by the dome allowed Fuller to convert himself into a public intellectual. He landed a no-show academic appointment at Southern Illinois University that freed him to tour the world, lecturing on the state of society and how mass production, mobility, and the use of technology to control nature could create a peaceful, just society. In the late 1950s and early 1960s, he developed his ideas in greater detail, returning from a myriad of speaking engagements to his blue and white dome home in Carbondale to write furiously, publishing five books in 1962 and 1963 alone. In 1964, he commenced a lecture tour that would last a decade.[13] The lectures he gave were often entitled "Spaceship Earth" and "Utopia or Oblivion" and, in 1969, he published two books based on these talks. One, aimed at a popular audience, was entitled *Operating Manual for Spaceship Earth*.[14] The other, *Utopia or Oblivion: The Prospects for Humanity*, was more of a mixed bag, containing eleven essays, some based on lectures to the general public, others with a more academic bent.[15]

At the center of each book was the idea that humanity was at a perilous moment. It was destroying the Earth through war, environmental degradation, and rapacious capitalism. Yet, at the same time, it had the capability to alleviate these problems. Humans possessed the technology and scientific know-how to eliminate all material scarcity. A world without scarcity would be a place where the dismal forecasts of Malthus, the bitter conflicts predicted by Darwin and Marx, and the brutal competitive ethos of capitalism should all disappear. "Because science now finds there can be ample for all . . . the basic you-or-me-not enough-for-both-ergo-someone-must die-tenets of class warfare are extinct."[16] Fuller's central concern was explaining why conflict and destruction existed in a world where scarcity should have been eliminated.

Fuller's explanation for this dismal situation was exceedingly eccentric. In many of his books, including *Utopia or Oblivion* and *Operating Manual*, he recounted a narrative of world history that laid the foundation for the contemporary crisis. It suggested that, until the early twentieth century, the world was controlled by brilliant "comprehensively anticipatory design scientists"[17]—evil

DaVincis who were able to anticipate and plan for future events in a manner that "enabled them to become masters of the world and of all its people and wealth."[18] These rulers, whom Fuller called "The Great Pirates" (or "G.P.'s"), acted in complete secrecy, using visible world leaders ("their local-stooge sovereigns"[19]) to implement polices that enriched themselves and kept others weak and impoverished. They were able to do this, Fuller believed, because they invented the strategy of "divide and conquer" for this purpose.[20] The most significant divisions they created to prevent the rise of rival "comprehensive thinkers" were expertise and specialization. The G.P.'s would seek out the most brilliant members of society who might challenge them and channel these young geniuses into specific academic disciplines. Such specialization would prevent people from developing the comprehensive skills necessary to truly shape the world, thus protecting the G.P.'s from potential rivals. Even worse, these specialized experts developed further atomizing ideas (religion, class struggle, racism) and institutions (the nation state, bureaucracies, universities), thereby creating a world of "fragmented dominions" that the G.P.'s enthusiastically maintained to keep themselves in power.[21]

This world domination, however, ended during the first decades of the twentieth century. Science and technology had become so complicated that even the G.P.'s could no longer understand them. Technology also became so expensive that only the G.P.'s creations—nation states—could afford to deploy it. Consequently, technology broke loose from their exclusive control. The puppets freed themselves from the puppet masters. Science and technology were now wielded, in an uncontrolled fashion, by the ignorant, parochial "stooges" the G.P.'s had set up as political leaders. The results were obvious: economic collapse in 1929, followed by a world war that ended with nuclear destruction. The world was poised on the edge of oblivion. The G.P.'s may have been evil and self-aggrandizing, but, as comprehensive planners, at least they were able to maintain some degree of social stability, even if it was only for their own benefit. With their disappearance, no one was left to guide civilization. Instead, the world was reaping what the G.P.'s had sown: fragmented struggles for power based on "meaningless" ideologies, uncoordinated scientific and technological advancements made with no thought to their effect, environmental degradation, and the ever-increasing potential for nuclear apocalypse.[22]

After describing this alarming situation, Fuller proposed a way to prevent "man's spin-dive towards oblivion."[23] Humans must become new comprehensive designers who, this time, were inculcated with virtuous values.

Fortunately, the time was ripe for just such an occurrence. The computer, Fuller argued, would soon take over all the specialized tasks that had "enslaved" most humans under the thrall of the G.P.'s. "*Automation* displaces *automatons*."[24] Accordingly, "man himself is being forced to reestablish, employ, and enjoy his innate 'comprehensivity.'"[25] Humans could abandon specialization and embrace "systems theory" and "synergy" in a manner that would allow the type of innovative, coordinated, long-term planning that would create a "regenerative landscape" on Earth—a landscape without poverty, war, or environmental degradation. Humankind will have chosen utopia over oblivion.[26]

On its face, this remedy—the creation of benign comprehensive designers to replace the "Great Pirates"—would seem to necessitate a powerful state apparatus. But Fuller emphatically rejected this conception of the state. Indeed, it would not be too strong to suggest that Fuller hated the state. Both *Spaceship Earth* and *Utopia or Oblivion* were permeated with disdain for government, politics, and bureaucracy. Such institutions were the quintessential creation of the Great Pirates in their efforts to divide and conquer humanity. Having outlived the G.P.'s, politicians and bureaucrats now continued to wield power, under the illusion that they had been in charge all along.[27] Fuller frequently referred to policymakers and bureaucracies, both public and private, as "patrons," who subjected society to their "supine concessions to nonsynergetical thinking."[28] This type of thinking—siloed, short-term, and reactive—typified bureaucratic governance. Because the G.P.'s conditioned state actors to think in this manner, they would always favor short-term Band-Aids over long-term solutions to social ills. Thus, they only mobilized the state to respond to "lethal emergencies," which, according to Fuller, were usually "solved" by war or violence.[29]

The key to utopia was to find new comprehensive designers who would ignore politics and the state and develop solutions to the world's problems in a radically decentralized fashion. Fuller's vision for this was, frankly, anarchistic. "World coordination of design-systems development is to be administered . . . by spontaneously self-organized university students whose world-around design science coordinating authority . . . will progressively displace the sovereign nation's political authority."[30] Thus, the plans for the "omni-regeneration" of humanity would occur in an essentially stateless environment—what Fuller called "world-around patronless conditions."[31] In Fuller's vision, these plans would be so self-evidently superior to the status quo that nation states would be forced to capitulate to the sheer intellectual power of comprehensivity, and ultimately disappear. "The political leaders will be forced by their engineers and science educated public to choose to integrate [i.e., eliminate themselves] and all the ideological difference will vanish."[32] Between the end of the nation state and the disappearance of ideological cleavages, "almost all obstacles to man's comprehensive physical success will be removed."[33] Fuller believed that the marketplace of ideas was so powerful that it would destroy the pathological remnants of the Great Pirates' order and replace it with a utopia.

Nor was Fuller content to allow this marketplace to develop on its own. Instead, he conceived of this form of bottom-up policymaking as a competitive game. This was not a metaphor. In order to avoid the crippling obstacles to comprehensive policymaking imposed by national political systems, Fuller proposed creating a "World Game."[34] "Comprehensive logistical information" about the earth—resources, population, pollution, trade—would be loaded, in real time, into a computer. Then players, or teams of players, would compete to maximize human health and happiness by implementing "grand world strategies" on a football field-sized, computer-enabled game board. These competitions would be televised. As the public became aware that actual solutions to the world's problems had been developed, politicians would respond by implementing them. "Ultimately [the World Game's] most successful winning techniques will become well known around the world and as the game's solutions gain world favor they will be spontaneously resorted to as political emergencies accelerate."[35] Once the public learned of the power of synergetic, comprehensive policymaking, they would demand its implementation. Politicians would not be able to resist.

It is not hard to see the appeal of Fuller's thinking to a broad range of people, particularly younger folks coming of age in the 1960s. He identified problems that had become increasingly salient—war, environmental degradation, ideological conflict, nuclear apocalypse—and solved them with a combination of gee-whiz technology and game play. As Fred Turner has argued, Fuller allowed the young people to whom he appealed with enormous success to embrace technology while erasing its origins in the military industrial complex. They could "escape industrial bureaucracy while enjoying its fruits."[36] Moreover, all it took to solve the world's problems was for individuals to come up with good ideas, not through advanced study, but by becoming "comprehensive designers," jacks-of-all-trades, but masters of none. What was *not* required was difficult political organizing, contentious debates about ideology, or violence in the streets. You could think and play your way to utopia.

E. F. Schumacher: Unleashing the Policy Entrepreneur

E. F. Schumacher's life was as conventional as Fuller's was improvised.[37] A German-trained economist, Schumacher fled Germany in 1936 and settled in the United Kingdom. There he worked as an economic planner, first for the wartime government, then with the British forces occupying Germany, and finally with the National Coal Board, the administrative entity created by the postwar labor government to manage the recently nationalized coal industry. It was a job he held for twenty years.

Though this career path suggested the conventional economic views of a man of the left in midcentury Britain, Schumacher became an increasingly heterodox thinker over the course of his life. By the 1960s, his commitments to the twin drivers of postwar British economic policy—socialism and Keynesianism—had been discarded in favor of a view of political economy shaped by his increasing interests in environmentalism, Catholic social thought, Buddhism, and the problems of "Third World" economic development. These ideas animated his 1973 book *Small Is Beautiful*, in which he combined previously published essays, adapted speeches, and newly composed text to lay out a coherent, humanist approach to economic planning for both developing and developed nations.

Published in 1973, the success of *Small Is Beautiful* transformed Schumacher from an anonymous, retired bureaucrat into a celebrity and public intellectual. Schumacher was surprised at the appeal of his work, particularly to people forty years younger than he.[38] Yet, people within the counterculture had known of his work for almost a decade. *Small Is Beautiful*'s most famous chapter, "Buddhist Economics," was based on an article of the same name that had been circulating in counterculture circles in the United States since it was first published in 1966.[39] In it, Schumacher suggested that economics and technology needed to reject the "ego-centeredness" of its traditional goals: promoting consumption and leisure.[40] Instead, humanity should work toward an economic system that created emotionally satisfying work, environmental sustainability, small-scale communities, and individual liberation and self-actualization. Schumacher's surprise aside, it is easy to see how these subjects appealed to young adults in the 1960s. Other chapters of *Small Is Beautiful* addressed similar subjects. They offered systematic critiques of contemporary economic theory, suggested economic development strategies for the "Third World," and demonstrated how environmentally sustainable economic growth would benefit humankind more than the Keynesian economic goals of consumption and wealth generation that Schumacher had come to disdain. The book's most famous legacy was its discussion of "intermediate technology"—the use of small-scale, low-capital technologies that encouraged local, community-focused, sustainable economic growth.

Despite this eclectic collection of subjects, Schumacher returned to a few themes again and again. The most prominent one was obvious from the title of the book—Schumacher disliked large institutions. Throughout the book he condemned them, be they businesses or governmental bureaucracies. Modern societies were obsessed with "pathological growth" and "an almost universal idolatry of giantism."[41] When institutions grew beyond the "human scale," they became disconnected from humanist values and individual oversight.[42] Accordingly, they became oppressive, imposing "rigid organization and totalitarian control."[43] No wonder, Schumacher suggested, that such institutions oppressed workers and poisoned the environment. They also crushed individual initiative and creativity, subjugating it to the need to control from above. So long as society valued the "trend towards vastness,"[44] it would neglect the things that should be society's goals: individual happiness, meaningful work, and a healthy relationship with the environment.

Though Schumacher had little nice to say about any large organizations, he was most hostile to governmental institutions. They were, after all, likely to be the largest institutions in society. Government planners had a particular "addiction to over-centralization."[45] Government planning and public management substituted "bureaucratic ponderousness for private flexibility."[46] State bureaucracies also evidenced an overreliance on expertise. Indeed, according to Schumacher, one of the most frightening attributes of bureaucracies was the way they deployed expertise to assert power over individuals, limiting their freedom.[47] Expert predictions about human behavior, Schumacher believed, led bureaucracies to deny individuals agency and suppress it when it was exercised. Even worse, expertise was often simply an illusion, the "spurious verisimilitude" of planners who believed that the social sciences could predict human behavior with a degree of precision that was inconsistent with the freedom that individuals exercised in their lives.[48]

Schumacher's desire to preserve individual autonomy in a world of increasingly oppressive institutions was not simply a moral preference. He also articulated an overtly instrumentalist rationale for promoting it. Some individuals, when released from the yoke of large institutions, were the driving, creative force in society. Schumacher called such people "entrepreneurs." They were his version of Fuller's "comprehensive designers"—people who moved society forward by generating "new developments, new creative ideas . . . and progress, the *entrepreneurial* activity *par excellence*."[49] "The man of creative freedom is the *entrepreneur* . . . [whose] freedom calls for, and opens the door to, intuition and leads to innovation."[50] (Schumacher frequently italicized the word *entrepreneur* and its cognates, as if to emphasize their importance.) Like Fuller, Schumacher viewed these entrepreneurs as the natural antagonists of planners and experts, who tried to control their creative, innovative judgment by deploying "bogus" "figures" and "calculations."[51] Thus, Schumacher's ideal society was one in which public and private institutions were kept small in order to allow for the social progress that would be brought about by individual creativity. Such creativity would only flourish if people's actions were left unconstrained by overbearing institutions. It was nourished by "the magnanimity of disorder."[52]

Not surprisingly, when Schumacher turned his attention from society in general to the state in particular, his prescriptions were infused with the basic themes that animated much of *Small Is Beautiful*—a suspicion of large institutions, a love of decentralization, hostility toward expertise, and lionization of individual entrepreneurialism. Like Fuller, Schumacher started his discussion of the state with a visceral hostility. Bureaucracy disrupted "the integrity of the individual" by transforming him into "a cog in a vast machine." This made "the human relationships of his daily working life . . . increasingly dehumanized."[53] People working within large institutions, Schumacher suggested, were necessarily "divided between *us* and *them*, torn by mutual suspicion, with a hatred of authority from below and contempt of people from above."[54] The obvious analogies were Kafka's terrifying dystopias—worlds of people compelled to do work they do not understand by authorities they never meet.[55] Schumacher did not believe it was possible to have a humane bureaucracy in a society that required vast public and private institutions: "Nobody really likes large-scale organizations; nobody likes to take orders from a superior who takes orders from a superior who takes orders . . . [elision in the original] Even if the rules devised by bureaucracy are outstandingly humane, nobody likes to be ruled by rules."[56]

Being of a more practical bent than Fuller, Schumacher acknowledged that in a modern, complex society, some large institutions were inevitable. Every such organization had to have some degree of centralized control or it would collapse into anarchy. The regimentation that came with this type of control, however, stifled creativity. Order was "static and lifeless."[57] Creativity and innovation would only occur if actors within a bureaucracy were given freedom. Accordingly, there was tension within every organization between "the administrator" (or "the accountant") and Schumacher's beloved "*entrepreneur*," the man of "creative intuition" and innovation.[58] The ideal organization must somehow balance the need for order with the equally powerful need for freedom.

Schumacher's method of creating this balance was to require that every bureaucratic entity be divided into small "quasi-firms"—small, autonomous "*entrepreneurial* unit[s]" within the bureaucracy that carried out the basic functions of the institution. (The British Coal Board, Schumacher told his readers, had seventeen such units.[59]) The administrators who ran the bureaucracy were prohibited from interfering with the operations of these units except under specific circumstances. In an ideal world, each subsidiary unit would only be judged on a single criterion related to the central mission of the organization. For a private business, for example, that criterion would be profitability. For a public agency it might be whether people entitled to a government benefit received it.[60]

Schumacher combined this idea of minimizing the number of criteria upon which each unit was judged with a self-regulating system of incentives. When a subsidiary unit succeeded, it should be given more autonomy. On the other hand, when it failed, its autonomy should be diminished. This practice would create the proper incentives for individual units. It would also have the effect of finding the ideal degree of decentralization within a given organization. Each assessment cycle would move each unit toward more and more autonomy, until it reached a degree of autonomy where the need for order outweighed the benefits of autonomy. At that point, the center could reassert its control, but only up to the point where the unit began succeeding again. Implemented correctly, the process would keep each unit hovering at an equilibrium that maximized the benefits of both autonomy and control. The result, Schumacher told his readers, was not simply the efficient governance of large institutions but, consistent with *Small Is Beautiful*'s repeated emphasis on nonmaterial values, "freedom and happiness" within the organization.[61]

Charles Reich: The Market Power of "Consciousness III" Man

Born in New York City in 1928, Charles Reich was the youngest of these three authors.[62] The son of a doctor and a private school administrator, he received an elite, progressive education that took him through a series of experimental primary and secondary schools, and then on to Oberlin College and Yale Law School. Having excelled at every step of his education, he clerked for United States Supreme Court Justice Hugo Black and then worked at two elite law firms, Cravath, Swaine and Moore, and Arnold, Fortas, and Porter. After five years in practice, Reich returned to Yale Law School in 1960 as a thirty-two-year-old professor.

Reich's time at the law school began in a conventional manner. His scholarship was progressive and brilliant, but traditional, with an emphasis on doctrinal issues related to constitutional law, property law, and administrative law. It focused on the threat to individual liberties posed by the increasingly expansive administrative state. By the middle of the 1960s, however, the path of Reich's career began to diverge from that of his law school colleagues. His interests shifted away from examinations of legal and doctrinal matters to a more general, sociological critique of American society. In 1966, he started teaching undergraduates. His course—"The Individual in America"—used literature (Normal Mailer, Ken Kesey) and critical social theory (David Reisman, Herbert Marcuse) to describe an enormous, overbearing state that fused public and private power to oppress individuals. Taught in the shadow of the war in Vietnam, the course's appeal to Yale's all-male student body was obvious. By 1970, six hundred students were enrolling each year. That same year, he brought the ideas he had incubated in the class to a national audience. Random House published *The Greening of America*, a 430-page book that molded an amalgamation of the Frankfurt School, eastern philosophy, civil libertarianism, counterculture mysticism, and sex/drugs/rock 'n' roll evangelism into a product that tapped into a deeply libertarian, antibureaucratic zeitgeist.[63] It sat atop the *New York Times* bestseller list for twenty weeks, going through five printings in less than two weeks and eventually selling two million copies.[64] The 39,000-word excerpt that appeared in the *New Yorker* in September of that year generated more letters to the magazine than any other article in its history.

The Greening of America was a profoundly optimistic book. Reich believed that the emergent counterculture would transform America's debased society for the better. In order to make such an argument, however, he had to first describe the pathologies of contemporary America, and his description was harrowing. Heavily influenced by C. Wright Mills, Frankfurt School thinkers like Marcuse, and other heterodox leftists from Jacques Ellul to Eldridge Cleaver, Reich's America was a totalitarian amalgam of enormous corporate bureaucracies and a massive, overbearing state. According to Reich, there was no longer a distinction between the state and private industry. Instead, markets, free enterprise, and the entrepreneurial spirit had been replaced by the "American Corporate State," in which government regulation had "rationalize[d]" and "stabilize[d]" economic transactions for the benefit of large corporations.[65]

Yet the goal of regulation was not simply the furtherance of corporate power. Its goal, Reich argued, was the violent destruction of individual autonomy. Thus, while the New Deal administrative state might be a product of reform impulses, it was evil—"an inhuman structure."[66] "The lasting product of the New Deal era was not its humanism or its idealism, but a new consciousness that believed primarily in domination and the necessity of living under domination."[67] The administrative state's primary task was to "impose order" under the illusion of "the public interest," defined, according to Reich, as a homogenizing impulse designed to stamp out individual autonomy:

> The tendency of administration, while it may appear to be benign and peaceful . . . is actually violent. For the very idea of imposed order is violent. It demands compliance; nothing less than compliance will do; and it must obtain compliance, by persuasion or management if possible, by repression if necessary. It is convinced that it has the "best way" and that all others are wrong.[68]

This was a government of total domination made up of administrative entities with no goal other than the assertion of complete control. "We have turned over everything, rendered ourselves powerless, and thus allowed mindless machinery to become our master."[69]

The Greening of America did not lack for specific examples of such administrative totalitarianism. It touched, of course, on the obvious candidates: the war in Vietnam[70] and acts of police oppression against African Americans and youth.[71] Reich, however, was encyclopedic in his cataloguing of abusive[72] bureaucratic power. From the Federal Trade Commission to local boxing commissions, all were part of the unyielding machine. Indeed, he reserved his most trenchant attacks on the state not for its obviously oppressive actions, but for the way it enforced conformity through the creation of the welfare state, a theme he first touched on in his more conventional, legal scholarship. Be they occupational licenses, government jobs, public education, or welfare payments, government benefits bound people to the state, fostering complete dependence. Americans were so dependent on such government goodies that they were willing to give up their autonomy to get them: the hippie who was forced to cut his hair to go to school, the Peace Corps volunteer who took a loyalty oath, or the welfare recipient who allowed the state to police her morality in exchange for money to feed her children.[73]

Like Fuller and Schumacher, Reich proposed a solution to these pathologies. "Solution," in Reich's case, however, is not quite the right word. Reich believed that the United States was beginning to eliminate the autocratic machine state not through any institutional changes, but through an earth-shattering change in culture and, to use his word, "consciousness." When Reich started the project that would become *The Greening of America* in the early 1960s, he believed he would be telling a dismal story. The original title for the book was "The Coming of the Closed Society." Reich's outlook changed dramatically, however, after he spent the summer of 1967 in Berkeley, California. Experiencing the Summer of Love in the Bay Area epicenter of the emergent counterculture introduced Reich to a "consciousness" that infused him with optimism. When he returned to New Haven, he looked for, and found, this perspective in his students as well. Countercultural youth consciousness would bring down the Corporate State.

Reich named this countercultural outlook "Consciousness III." ("Consciousness I" was the outdated laissez-faire individualism of the nineteenth century. "Consciousness II" was the appalling commitment to managing society through giant, technocratic bureaucracies typified by the New Deal.) Youth, it appeared to Reich, were simply refusing to participate in the "Closed Society." At its core, this was a "life-style" choice, but when Reich used the phrase "life-style" he did not do so in order to minimize its importance.[74] To the contrary, personal choices about appearance, consumption, employment, and political participation were at the very center of the reform that Reich believed was going on about him. Young people were spontaneously engaging in a massive boycott of the straight world of Consciousness II oppression. The most obvious manifestations of this were the countercultural communards who dropped out of contemporary society. But Reich saw this impulse everywhere: replacing staid, traditional clothes with bell-bottoms, tie-dye shirts, and beads; replacing classical music listened to in a hushed concert hall with rock music danced to in Golden Gate Park; replacing traditional intoxicants with marijuana and LSD; replacing traditional family structures with loose agglomerations of roommates, friends, and lovers; replacing traditional careers as a cog in a giant corporation with informal gigs, service to the underprivileged, and jobs defined by personal fulfillment rather than financial reward.

Revolution was thus happening through the mechanisms of the market. "If culture changes . . . the machine is forced to obey."[75] The "machine is controlled by the consumer."[76] Accordingly, as the consumer imbued his purchases with Consciousness III values, society would be transformed—"the machine is his slave."[77] It had to "turn out Beatles records, bell-bottom pants, or better hospitals." "Businessmen," regardless of their own consciousness, "have discovered that they must alter their production and selling efforts in *response* to changes in the values of youth: nonmaterialism, concern for the environment, a renewed interest in bicycles instead of expensive automobiles."[78] The master was hoist on his own petard.

Nor did Reich limit his market-based revolution to the act of consumption. Consciousness III attitudes toward work would transform institutions. When employers hired at the entry-level, they were forced to employ a generation of people with Consciousness III values. "Our society needs its young people, and particularly its best educated young people, in its workforce; it depends on the willing worker as much as on the willing consumer."[79] Once hired, these employees would transform institutions from the inside. Young teachers would not tolerate the dress code in a high school. Young lawyers force the "largest and most conservative law firms" to create pro bono programs, not because they politely ask, but because "they refuse to work for firms that will not spend time on public interest matters."[80] The force of Consciousness III, when released onto the labor market, was irresistible. "Already bell bottoms and beads are being hired by the Post Office, perhaps because no other workers can be found; how long will it be before hippies man the FBI?"[81]

Consciousness III was so potent, according to Reich, that even the institutions of the state could not resist it. The logic of the political marketplace was as powerful as that of the economic one. Like businessmen who needed to sell corn flakes, politicians would respond to voters possessed of new, revolutionary values. "Elected officials show a remarkable ability to change when their constituencies change; New York's Senator Goodell, a backward looking man when he represented an upstate constituency, grew sideburns and became a vocal liberal as he became the representative of the entire state."[82] If government ignored the increasing number of Consciousness III voters, they would ignore the government right back, until "it became completely isolated from the people of the nation, and had no choice but to change. At that point, the President would have to don bell bottoms and a dirty T-shirt and go looking for his constituents."[83] (A remarkable image, considering that the occupant of the White House at the time was famous for wearing a suit jacket and wingtips when he went for a walk on the beach.)

Having explained the inevitability of its triumph, Reich then described how society would be restructured according to Consciousness III values. The substance of these values were easy to define: "Respect for each individual. . . . Abstention from coercion or violence. Respect for beauty in all its forms. Honesty in all personal relations. Equality of status between all individuals. . . . Genuine democracy in the making of decisions, freedom of expression, and conscience."[84] These values, Reich believed, would not be implemented by institutions.[85] Instead, it was the absence of institutions that would allow the flourishing of individual autonomy and the localized decision-making that would, in turn, bring these values to life. The key, according to Reich, was individual autonomy and experimentation: "no leadership, no organization, a dislike of theory, and a doctrine of 'do your own thing,' the new generation, in the tradition of American inventiveness, and ingenuity, began to experiment."[86] Reich's example of how this would work was the spontaneous creation of People's Park in Berkeley. "Self-constituted local groups whose legitimacy came only from their proximity and concern" simply ignored Consciousness II institutions (the City of Berkeley, "private property") and created "nothing less than a new social order," albeit on a small scale. They placed "human needs and ecology (as they saw them) ahead of 'law' and proposed a society in which aesthetics, ecology, and human requirements would be paramount."[87]

Reich's emphasis on local, atomized experimentation strongly echoed both Fuller and Schumacher. Creativity would come from the ground up if individuals were freed from Consciousness II bureaucracies and allowed to flourish. Release from these crippling institutions would allow people to "despecialize"—escape the narrow disciplines that society forced people into. (Clearly, the Great Pirates were Consciousness II individuals.) In doing so, they would "make connections and see relationships where the attempt had been made to keep them separate."[88] Reich was suggesting that Consciousness III was the perfect medium for the creation of comprehensive designers and *entrepreneurs* who "insist upon being open to all experience" and who "will experiment with anything."[89] Tearing down bureaucracy and extracting people from narrow disciplines would allow for liberation and innovation. That, in turn, would generate thousands of local institutions across the United States that would continue the spread of Consciousness III values.

Fuller, Schumacher, Reich, and the Ubiquity of Anti-Statist Thought in the 1970s

The writings of Fuller, Schumacher, and Reich were the widely read tip of an iceberg of social thought that has a lot to tell us about the erosion of faith in government in the last three decades of the twentieth century. They suggest that a widespread fear of and hostility toward the state permeated society at the end of the 1960s and the beginning of the 1970s. This is hardly surprising. These authors were writing (and their audiences were reading) in the context of monumental abuses of governmental power: the war in Vietnam; violent state reprisals against civil rights activists and student protesters; illegal governmental infiltration of political organizations; Watergate.

Beyond the obvious, but significant, observation that political culture in the late 1960s and early 1970s had an anti-statist, libertarian bent, these authors illustrate some of the salient details of that culture. First of all, they demonstrate that plenty of this anti-statist thought had its origins on the left. For at least a generation, US historians have been showing the relationship between conservative politics and thought and the rise of neoliberal governance.[90] The pervasiveness of anti-statist thought within the work of authors like Fuller, Schumacher, and Reich (as well as their less famous fellow travelers) suggests that understanding the origins of contemporary political culture requires casting a wider net.

Second, an examination of these authors demonstrates that the "vigorous libertarian spirit" of the time was unusually even handed. Often, the libertarian strands of American political culture are deployed instrumentally. "Left libertarianism" emphasizes government infringement of noneconomic rights, while "right libertarianism" focuses its ire on the states' restrictions of economic liberties. This was not the case for these writers and, perhaps, for many in their audience. Their hostility toward the state was total. Fuller and Reich were anarchistic in their libertarianism. While Schumacher was more practical in his approach to governance, he nonetheless believed that government, like all bureaucracies, manifested itself as a Kafkaesque dystopia that crushed people's creativity and humanity.

Third, these authors illustrate how hostility toward expertise was central to the anti-statist political culture of the time. For Fuller, expertise was an evil without measure. It was the opposite of comprehensive thinking, the mode of human consciousness that was necessary to avoid the "spin-dive towards oblivion."[91] The Great Pirates fooled people into valuing expertise to prevent the emergence of new comprehensive designers who would challenge their world domination. Reich also endorsed "de-specialization" as an element of Consciousness III thinking.[92] The spontaneous, instinctual policymaking episodes that he imagined necessitated broad realms of knowledge and experience. Indeed, Reich believed that, in a Consciousness III society, people would have a variety of careers and avocations. Being locked into one job requiring one set of knowledge was nothing more than the oppressive machine of Consciousness II constraining freedom and individuality.[93]

Schumacher also disdained expertise, though his objections to it differed from those of Fuller and Reich. He attributed the characteristics of contemporary society that he hated—gigantism, materialism, consumerism—to the death of spiritual, noneconomic values. He was quite clear about who the murderers were: Darwin, Marx, and Freud.[94] These thinkers created a world in which relativism, materialism, and "narrow empiricism"[95] dominated human thought. They rejected any notion that philosophical, artistic, or religious values should shape society. According to Schumacher, when we valorized experts, it was precisely this debased mode of thought that we were praising. "If we adopt—as the experts have adopted—the metaphysical position of the crudest materialism, for which money costs and money incomes are the ultimate criteria and determinants of human action . . . [then] *the living world has no significance beyond that or a quarry for exploitation*."[96] That it took modern expertise to develop pesticides and nuclear power plants told Schumacher all he needed to know about its dubious benefits.

The final element of declining faith in the state that is evident in the works of these authors was a commitment to market mechanisms as a replacement for governmental action. This renewed commitment to market fundamentalism has long been recognized by historians of American conservatism as one of the foundational attributes of the right's political offensive against the New Deal state in the 1960s and 1970s.[97] What an examination of these authors suggests is that thinkers not associated with right-wing intellectuals and policymakers and their corporate sponsors adopted the idea that markets were an effective way of allocating goods in a society. All three authors believed that a collection of decisions by genuinely autonomous individuals would yield optimal social outcomes. Indeed, this sort of thinking infused much left-leaning and countercultural thought in the 1960s. Few beliefs were more central to the culture of the 1960s than a deep commitment to preserving individual autonomy in a society controlled by oppressive, enormous institutions. As historians are only now beginning to understand, this focus on maximizing individual liberty led to a robust embrace of free markets by the counterculture and many left-thinking people.[98] Obviously, there were pockets of genuine anticapitalism in the political culture of the 1960s left. However, the popularity of Fuller, Schumacher, and Reich suggests that many people believed the problem with contemporary capitalism was not inherent in market mechanisms themselves, but was instead the result of the failure of these mechanisms. Contemporary American capitalism was corrupt because its markets were not free. They were dominated by enormous, corrupt institutions: the military-industrial complex, captured administrative agencies, and cartels of giant corporations that plotted to avoid competition.

Accordingly, it is not surprising that a vision of uncorrupted markets that maximized individual autonomy while spontaneously producing positive social outcomes appeared in the works of all three of these authors. This was most obvious in Reich's work. Consciousness III society would come into being because of market mechanisms. Large companies would sell Consciousness III products (bell bottoms, organic produce) and hire Consciousness III individuals (bead-wearing FBI agents, lawyers who do pro bono work) because the logic of the market left them no choice. In essence, Reich argued that Consciousness III would become so dominant that it would triumph in markets that were previously dominated by Consciousness II institutions. Fuller's embrace of market mechanisms is similarly delusional, but no less heartfelt. The World Game fused the marketplace of ideas with political and economic markets. The spontaneous propagation of comprehensively designed ideas would allow for political and economic systems that avoided planning and maximized individual autonomy.

Characteristically, Schumacher's arguments were more subtle than Fuller's or Reich's, but they ended up in a similar place. So long as markets could be kept small, individual action and initiative would lead to positive social outcomes. Schumacher's constant lauding of *entrepreneurs* and *entrepreneurialism* demonstrated his commitment to the idea that bigness, not markets, was the problem with capitalism. Indeed, Schumacher's plan for managing decentralized "sub-firms" in large corporations and bureaucracies was entirely market-based. Decentralization allowed entrepreneurs to flourish at the periphery, while the center staved off institutional anarchy by measuring performance indicators in a manner that led to a natural equilibrium of just the right balance between autonomy and control. Central to Schumacher's plan was the belief that neither the center nor the periphery could identify what the correct balance should be. Instead, the perfect balance could only be achieved by rewarding individual entrepreneurs when they succeeded and punishing them when they failed. Milton Friedman could not have said it better.

A recognition of this widespread embrace of anti-statism and the power of private action in the market—"the magnanimity of disorder"—helps explain what happened when the American political landscape became populated by people and institutions bathed in this political culture. The most obvious of these actors were the politicians and policymakers in the 1970s and 1980s who turned anti-statist ideas into attacks on actual state institutions. Some of these people were the traditional conservative enemies of the state: Republican President Ronald Reagan; his appointee to head the Federal Reserve, Alan Greenspan; and their accomplices. Others were actors associated with the emergent "New Democrats."[99] Still others were the state and quasi-state institutions that emerged to dismantle the New Deal state: the Office of Information and Regulatory Affairs, a federal judiciary committed to textualist interpretation of regulatory statutes, charter schools, health insurance exchanges, economic improvement zones, and public-private partnerships. Understanding these institutions and the political impulses that generated them thus requires casting our eyes to places we might not expect to find the intellectual foundations of the neoliberal order: the counterculture thought that had permeated the United States by the early 1970s.

Notes

1. For a particularly vivid account of the end of "The Sixties," see the last two chapters of Todd Gitlin, *The Sixties: Years of Hope, Days of Rage* (New York: Bantam, 1987).

2. For a detailed description of administrative law and policy from the New Deal through the late 1960s and how they changed in the post–New Deal political order, see Reuel Schiller, "Enlarging the Administrative Polity," 53 *Vand. L. Rev.* 1390 (2000); Reuel Schiller, "Reining in the Administrative State: World War II and the Decline of Expert Administration," in Daniel R. Ernst and Victor Jew, eds., *Total War and the Law: The American Home Front in World War II*, 185 (London: Bloomsbury, 2002); Reuel Schiller, "The Era of Deference: Courts, Expertise, and the Emergence of New Deal Administrative Law," 106 *Mich. L. Rev.* 399 (2007); Reuel Schiller, "Regulation and the Collapse of the New Deal Order, or How I Learned to Stop Worrying and Love the Market," in Gary Gerstle, Nelson Lichtenstein, and Alice O'Connor, eds., *Beyond the New Deal Order: U.S. Politics from the Great Depression to the Great Recession*, 168 (Philadelphia: University of Pennsylvania Press, 2019); Reuel Schiller, "The Curious Origins of Airline Deregulation: Economic Deregulation and the American Left," 93 *Bus. Hist. Rev.* 729 (2019); and Sarah Milov and Reuel Schiller, "Creating 'Initiatory Democracy': Ralph Nader and the Shaping of Liberalism in the 1970s," in Brent Cebul and Lily Geismer, eds., *Mastery and Drift: Professional-Class Liberals Since the 1960s* (Chicago, Il.: University of Chicago Press, 2025).

3. For an excellent discussion of the historical literature on the nature of postwar conservatism and its political resurgence, see Kim Phillips-Fein, "Conservatism: A State of the Field," *Journal of American History* (2011) 98 (3): 723–43. The canonical texts of this literature are Philips-Fein's own *Invisible Hands: The Businessmen's Crusade Against the New Deal* (New York, 2009) and Lisa McGirr, *Suburban Warriors: The Origins of the New American Right* (Princeton, N.J.: Princeton University Press, 2001). For the story of the rise of the intellectual right, see Angus Burgin, *The Great Persuasion: Reinventing Free Markets Since the Depression* (Cambridge, Mass.: Harvard University Press, 2012); Daniel Rodgers, *The Age of Fracture* (Cambridge, Mass., 2011), chapters 2 and 7; and Binyamin Appelbaum, *The Economists' Hour: False Prophets, Free Markets, and the Fracture of Society* (Boston: Little, Brown, 2019).

4. See, for example, Nelson Lichtenstein, *The State of the Union* (Princeton, N.J.: Princeton University Press, 2002), 148–56; Schiller, "Enlarging the Administrative Polity," 1399–1409.

5. Lichtenstein, *The State of the Union*, 156–62; Schiller, "Enlarging," 1410–16; Schiller, "Curious Origins," 732–39.

6. Quoted in Schiller, "Curious Origins," 733.

7. Another measure of Fuller's and Reich's popularity was their presence in the popular culture. Fuller's biographer, Alec Nevala-Lee, noted that, in its June 1971 issue, *National Lampoon* magazine published a mock comic book called the "Utopia Four," satirizing Fuller ("Super-Bucky") and Reich ("Mr. Mulch"), joined by Marshall McLuhan ("Media Man") and Kate Millett ("Karate Kate"), as four superheroes saving society from urban unrest and decay. *National Lampoon* later parodied Fuller's neologisms and overheated prose in "Buckminster Fuller's Repair Manual for the Entire Universe," *National Lampoon*, Jan. 1972, 43–46. Nevala-Lee, *Inventor of the Future: The Visionary Life of Buckminster Fuller* (New York: Dey Street, 2022), 386. Reich was the subject of a series of Doonesbury comic strips in 1971. See the series of strips starting on March 11, 1971. https://www.washingtonpost.com/doonesbury/strip. (Last visited January 31, 2023.)

8. Reich was particularly disliked by SDS types and others on the left with a more materialist bent. See Philip Nobile, ed., *The Con III Controversy: The Critics Look at the Greening of America* (New York: Pocket, 1971).

9. Anthony E. Brown, *The Politics of Airline Deregulation* (Knoxville, Tenn.: University of Tennessee Press, 1987), 138; Martha Derthick and Paul J. Quirk, *The Politics of Deregulation* (Brookings: Washington, D.C.: 1985), 35, 52–53, 56. Historians have also started to examine this change. See, for example, Schiller, "Curious Origins"; Reuel Schiller, "Regulation and the Collapse of the New Deal Order"; Paul Sabin, *Public Citizens: The Attack on Big Government and the Remaking of American Liberalism* (New York: Norton, 2021); Lily Geismer, *Left Behind: The Democrats' Failed Attempt to Solve Inequality* (New York: Public Affairs, 2022); Gary Gerstle, *The Rise and Fall of the Neoliberal Order: America and the World in the Free Market Era* (New York: Oxford University Press, 2022).

10. Maurice Isserman and Michael Kazin, "The Failure and Success of the New Radicalism," in Steve Fraser and Gary Gerstle, eds., *The Rise and Fall of the New Deal Order, 1930–1980* (Princeton, N.J.: Princeton University Press, 1989), 214.

11. Id., 229.

12. This biographical sketch draws from Nevala-Lee, *Inventor of the Future*; "Design: The Dymaxion American," *Time*, Jan. 10, 1964, 46–51; Calvin Thompkins, "In the Outlaw Area," *New Yorker*, Jan. 8, 1966, 35–68; Elizabeth Kolbert, "Dymaxion Man," *New Yorker*, June 2, 2008, 64; Fred Turner, "R. Buckminster Fuller: A Technocrat for the Counterculture," in Hsiao-Yun

Chu and Roberto G. Trujillo, eds., *New Views on R. Buckminster Fuller* (Stanford, Calif.: Stanford University Press, 2009), 148–59; Peder Anker, "Buckminster Fuller as Captain of Spaceship Earth," 45 *Minerva* 417–43 (Dec. 2007).

13. Anker, "Buckminster Fuller," 425–26.

14. R. Buckminster Fuller, *Operating Manual for Spaceship Earth* (Carbondale, Ill.: Southern Illinois University Press, 1969).

15. R. Buckminster Fuller, *Utopia or Oblivion: Prospects for Humanity* (Zurich: Lars Muller Publishers, 2019, reprint. Original publication date: 1969).

16. *Operating Manual*, 38–39.

17. Id., 24.

18. Id., 25.

19. Id., 26.

20. *Operating Manual*, 27.

21. Id., 27–31, 35.

22. Id., 33–47; *Utopia or Oblivion*, 341–46.

23. *Operating Manual*, 125.

24. Id., 44.

25. Id.

26. *Operating Manual*, 115–33.

27. Id., 35.

28. Id., 77.

29. Id., 77–80.

30. *Utopia or Oblivion*, 225.

31. *Operating Manual*, 128.

32. *Utopia or Oblivion*, 173.

33. Id.

34. Id., 203–208.

35. Id., 206.

36. Turner, "R. Buckminster Fuller: A Technocrat for the Counterculture," 157.

37. Schumacher has yet to attract a professional biographer. The details of his life discussed here are drawn from his daughter's detailed, affectionate biography. Barbara Wood, *E. F. Schumacher: His Life and Thought* (New York: Harper and Row, 1984). See also, Hendrik Opdebeeck, "The Role of the Charismatic Economist: E. F. Schumacher in Economic and Civil Life," in Luigino Bruni and Barbara Sena, eds., *The Charismatic Principle in Social Life* (London: Routledge, 2013).

38. Wood, *E. F. Schumacher*, 353–55.

39. E. F. Schumacher, *Small Is Beautiful: Economics as if People Mattered* (New York: Harper Perennial, 2010, reprint of 1973 edition), 56–66. According to the counterculture's first chronicler, Theodore Roszak, "'Buddhist Economics' had become a much-read and often reprinted staple of the underground press." *Small Is Beautiful*, 5.

40. Id., 58.

41. Id., 70, 72.

42. Id., 70.

43. Id., 65, quoting Harrison Brown, *The Challenge of Man's Future*.

44. Id., 257.

45. Id., 288.

46. Id., 311.
47. Id., 249–50.
48. Id., 255.
49. Id., 267.
50. Id., 260.
51. Id., 132. See also, 195–97.
52. Id., 267.
53. Id., 257.
54. Id., 257–58.
55. Id., 258.
56. Id.
57. Id., 259.
58. Id., 260.
59. Id., 262.
60. Id., 264.
61. Id., 270.
62. Reich's biographical information is drawn from Rodger D. Citron, "Charles Reich's Journey from the Yale Law Journal to the New York Times Best-Seller List: The Personal History of The Greening of America," *New York Law School Law Review* 52 (2007–2008). Less useful is Reich's autobiography, *The Sorcerer of Bolinas Reef* (New York: Random House, 1976).
63. Charles A. Reich, *The Greening of America* (New York: Crown, 1970).
64. Citron, "Charles Reich's Journey," at 387; Jesse Kornbluth, "'The Greening of America,' a #1 Best Seller, Has Been Out of Print. Now It's Back, Just as Relevant as It Was in 1970," *Huffington Post*, March 12, 2012. https://www.huffingtonpost.com/jesse-kornbluth/the-greening-of-america-a_b_1378727.html. (Last visited January 11, 2019.)
65. Reich, *The Greening of America*, 89, 119.
66. Id., 58.
67. Id.
68. Id., 101.
69. Id., 89.
70. Id., 212–16.
71. Id., 208–12.
72. According to Reich, all power was abusive: "It is not that the misuse of power is the evil; the very *existence* of power is an evil." Id., 125.
73. Id., 107–117.
74. Id., 380.
75. Id., 329.
76. Id., 344.
77. Id., 330.
78. Id., 344.
79. Id., 340.
80. Id., 345–46.
81. Id., 331.
82. Id., 331.
83. Id.
84. Id., 418.

85. Id., 388.

86. Id., 350–51.

87. Id., 396.

88. Id., 392.

89. Id., 393.

90. See note 6, supra.

91. *Operating Manual*, 125.

92. Reich, *Greening*, 405.

93. Id., 405–408.

94. *Small Is Beautiful*, 92–94.

95. Id., 94.

96. Id., 119. Emphasis in the original.

97. See the source cited in note 6, supra.

98. See, for example, Schiller, "Curious Origins"; Schiller, "Regulation and Collapse"; Andrew N. Case, *Rodale and the Making of Marketplace Environmentalism* (Seattle, Wash.: University of Washington Press, 2018); Joshua Clark Davis, *From Head Shops to Whole Foods: The Rise and Fall of Activist Entrepreneurs* (New York: Columbia University Press, 2017); Joseph Heath and Andrew Potter, *Nation of Rebels: Why Counterculture Became Consumer Culture* (New York: Harper Business, 2004); and Arthur Marwick, *The Sixties: Cultural Revolution in Britain, France, Italy, and the United States, c. 1958–c. 1974* (New York: Oxford University Press, 1998).

99. Geismer, *Left Behind*; Schiller, "Regulation and Collapse."

CHAPTER 4

Cheater in Chief: Presidential Taxpaying and Fiscal Citizenship

Joseph J. Thorndike

"Make sure you pay your taxes," Richard Nixon told journalist David Frost during one of their famous interviews. "Otherwise you can get in a lot of trouble."[1] Nixon had reason to know. Three years earlier, he had been forced from the White House by his role in the Watergate break-in. But Nixon had tax troubles, too—serious enough to prompt talk of resignation even before Watergate doomed his presidency.

In the summer and fall of 1973, Nixon was engulfed by a controversy over his personal taxes. An outsize charitable donation was the proximate cause, but the scandal included numerous other issues with the tax returns Nixon and his wife Patricia had filed between 1968 and 1972. The returns were private, of course, just like the returns filed by any taxpayer. But a series of leaks, combined with informed speculation, gave critics plenty of ammunition. Nixon, it seemed, had played fast and loose with the revenue laws, exploiting his position to minimize taxes and avoid scrutiny from the Internal Revenue Service (IRS).

Nixon's tax scandal actually prompted one of his most famous public statements, generally (and mistakenly) thought to refer to Watergate. "People have got to know whether or not their President is a crook," he told reporters in November 1973. "Well, I am not a crook."[2]

This claim to innocence, which came at the end of a detailed discussion of Nixon's personal finances, did little to quell the brewing tax scandal. Three weeks later, the president took a further, extraordinary step, releasing his personal tax returns to the public and inviting the congressional Joint Committee on Internal Revenue Taxation (JCIRT) to examine them.

After a four-month investigation, the professional staff of the JCIRT concluded that Nixon had failed to meet his legal obligations as a taxpayer—to the tune of nearly half a million dollars in back taxes and interest. That was real money, equal to roughly $2.5 million in 2022 dollars and totaling almost half of Nixon's net worth at the time.[3]

Nixon's transgression, however, was never just about the sums involved. What made the president's behavior so scandalous—and its public investigation so crucial—was the damage done to the nation's tax system. Taxes were one of the many aspects of American democratic capitalism transformed during the Roosevelt era discussed in this volume's first section. In reporting on Nixon's taxes, the JCIRT stressed the danger to this crucial institution, including its centerpiece: the individual income tax. "The general public can only be satisfied by a thorough examination of the President's taxes," the staff contended. "From the standpoint of the tax system alone, this confidence of the general public is essential since ours is basically a voluntary assessment system which has maintained its high level of effectiveness only because the general public has confidence in the basic fairness of the collection system."[4]

In other words, the future of the tax system—and the government that it funded—hung in the balance. Committee staff weren't the only ones making this argument; other critics worried that presidential malfeasance posed an existential threat to the nation's fiscal health. Indeed, flagging public confidence in federal taxation might have even broader implications. A presidential scofflaw threatened to corrode the vital bonds of fiscal citizenship: that web of reciprocal rights and responsibilities that bind individuals to the state—and the state to the individual.[5]

Taxes and the State

Americans have been linking taxes to citizenship and democratic governance for centuries. When colonial leaders insisted on "No Taxation Without Representation," they put the power to tax—and the responsibility to pay—at the center of political legitimacy.[6] And it stayed there for centuries, a fixture of national debate and the engine of institutional growth for the nation's central government.

Benjamin Franklin seemed to anticipate this staying power in a 1789 letter to the French physicist Jean Baptiste Le Roy. "Our new Constitution is now established, and has an appearance that promises permanency," Franklin wrote. "But in this world nothing can be said to be certain, except death and taxes."[7] As Nicolette Makovicky and Robin Smith have observed, this was more than a rhetorical flourish: Franklin was trying to make a point about modern states. "It is no coincidence that Franklin mentioned taxes in the same breath as the Constitution," they wrote. "Not only are taxation and the management of tax revenue commonly understood as the cornerstones of the modern state, but paying taxes is usually considered a ritual of citizenship."

The rituals of taxpaying bolster the social and cultural bonds that give meaning to citizenship. Taxes, not just the workplace rights that Jean-Christian Vinel's chapter shows to have been under threat after World War II, express and shape the way that citizens conceptualize their relationship to the state, including their roles, rights, and responsibilities.[8]

Fiscal citizenship is the reason that presidential taxpaying matters. As Nichole M. Flores and Charles Mathewes have pointed out, "From its beginnings the presidency has had a unique function as representative of the entire nation." Not only is the president the military's commander in chief and the government's top law enforcement officer; he or she is also "the First Citizen of the nation as well, representing all of us in that role, embodying the determinate will of the American people as they constitute a political community."[9]

By extension, then, the First Citizen is also the First Taxpayer. As the living embodiment of the social contract that underpins revenue collection, the president's personal tax behavior is freighted with the norms and responsibilities of fiscal citizenship writ large. When the First Citizen is caught shirking the duties of fiscal citizenship, it weakens the bonds of that citizenship for other taxpayers. And to a fiscal regime dependent on voluntary self-assessment, impaired citizenship poses an existential threat.

The Tax System in the Nixon Era

As it happens, Nixon alluded to Franklin's famous "death and taxes" remark during a 1969 message on tax reform. "Taxes, often bewailed as inevitable as death, actually give life to the people's purpose in having a Government: To provide protection, service and stimulus to progress," Nixon said. "We shall never make taxation popular, but we can make taxation fair."[10]

Nixon's statement on taxation—his endorsement of its value and importance—was striking, given the state of tax politics in 1969. At both the national and the state level, the subject had become increasingly fraught since the mid-1960s; as Reuel Schiller notes in his chapter, this was a period when faith in the administrative state, having grown substantially during the New Deal and World War II, was faltering across the political spectrum.[11] Fiscal systems were straining under the twin pressures of faster inflation and slower economic growth. And in Washington, policymakers had been struggling to balance competing, often overlapping goals: collect adequate revenue to avoid embarrassing deficits, stimulate business investment, promote consumption, avoid stoking inflation, and provide tax relief to struggling consumers (a.k.a. voters).

The tax system itself, meanwhile, was suffering from all the flaws that follow from sustained congressional attention. In the decades after World War II, lawmakers had loaded the system with special provisions for favored constituents. They had also left statutory tax rates artificially high—partly to make those special provisions more valuable and partly to bolster the appearance (if not always the reality) of progressivity. The result was a system riddled with both favoritism and inefficiency—and ripe for high-minded reform.

For most people in the late 1960s, taxes were linked tightly to employment. The individual income tax functioned as a wage tax for people without significant investments. The IRS collected taxes on earned income using a system of paycheck withholding (another legacy of the Roosevelt administration); payroll taxes dedicated to Social Security and Medicare were collected in the same fashion. The Social Security tax was capped, leaving the wage and salary income of highly compensated employees only partially taxed. In 1973, the 4.85 percent payroll tax applied to wages up to $10,800 (about $78,741 in 2024 dollars); any wages above that amount were untaxed.[12]

By the early 1970s, Americans were losing faith in these and other elements of the federal tax system. Special interest provisions (popularly known as loopholes) had eroded the notion that everyone was paying their "fair share." And no one understood the resulting sense of grievance better than Richard Nixon. During his 1968 campaign for the White House, Nixon had begun developing his Silent Majority trope. "Beyond the disorders, there's another rebellion going on today," he asserted in June 1968. "This other is a quiet revolution. It's a rebellion by the great, quiet majority—those who pay their taxes, go to their jobs, perform their civic duties, send their children to school or college. I'm sure it includes many of you listening tonight."[13]

In this Nixonian world, taxpaying wasn't pleasant, but it was something that decent, respectable people were willing to do. Nixon understood that his Silent Majority had no patience for wealthy elites who exploited loopholes. While not quite a tax populist, he brought populist elements to his fiscal rhetoric. "The rising winds of inflation pose no grave threat to the economic bastions of big business and industry and organized labor," Nixon told the Republican National Convention. "But those winds do imperil the economic security and future of those individuals who can find no shelter from the storm in the safe harbors of the real estate market or the stock exchange."[14]

Tax avoiders who moored in those safe harbors would find themselves the target of uncomfortable reforms after Nixon's victory in the presidential election. In his 1969 message on tax reform, the new president took aim at wealthy tax avoiders, using terms that even Democrats could applaud. "Special preferences in the law permit far too many Americans to pay less than their fair share of taxes," Nixon said. "Too many other Americans bear too much of the tax burden." Nixon urged people to be thoughtful, noting that one person's "loophole" was another person's "incentive." But he promised to end the free ride for anyone trying to shirk their fiscal responsibilities. "We must not permit our wealthiest citizens to be 100% successful at tax avoidance," he said.[15]

Strong words—and ones that would haunt Nixon when his own tax avoidance surfaced four years later.

A President and His Papers

Nixon's tax scandal began with a charitable donation. After winning the 1968 election, the president-elect had donated a collection of personal and official records to the National Archives. On its face, the gift was unremarkable; other presidents had made similar gifts. But questions about the timing and valuation of Nixon's gift created serious problems.

Today, presidential records are treated as public property, but at the start of Nixon's presidency, they were still considered personal property. Congress had implicitly endorsed this view in the Presidential Libraries Act of 1955,[16] which facilitated the private donation of official papers.[17]

Presidents had sound financial reason to be generous. Prior to 1969, gifts to the government of official papers qualified as charitable contributions. Sitting and former presidents could deduct the full, appreciated value of donated papers, using it to offset other forms of income. The president, moreover, was not required to report the value of the papers—either at the time of their creation or afterward—as an element of taxable income.[18] This fact, combined with the value of the deduction, created an enormous incentive for presidents to give away their papers.[19]

The tax treatment of presidential papers, however, was increasingly controversial. The papers were official records, asserted Delaware's Republican Senator John Williams in a typical complaint, and they should be treated like public property. "They were developed by government officials on government time with the aid of government staff personnel, were typed by government secretaries on government paper and were even stored in government files."[20]

Swayed by such arguments, Congress began drafting legislation in 1969 to sharply limit the tax break that came from donating papers. Attorneys for both Nixon and his predecessor, Lyndon Johnson, urged lawmakers to leave the window open just a bit longer, and the two presidents discussed the possibility of making last-minute donations.[21] But ultimately, the Tax Reform Act of 1969 (passed in late December of that year) nearly eliminated the deduction. The law stipulated that any deduction for papers donated after July 25, 1969, would be limited to the cost of the paper on which the documents were produced.[22]

With a deadline in place, Nixon rushed through a final gift to the National Archives. According to "a high White House official" speaking with the *Washington Post*, the president donated 1,176 boxes of papers on March 27, 1969. He subsequently claimed a deduction for that gift of "somewhat over $500,000" on his 1969 tax return.[23]

Nixon's gift remained private for several years. Eventually, however, it came to light as part of a civil damage suit stemming from the Watergate break-in, *Democratic National Committee, et al. v. James W. McCord, et al.* A deposition taken in that case included reference to Nixon's gift of papers in 1969,[24] and *Washington Post* reporter Nick Kotz followed up. He published the details in a series of articles beginning in June 1973.

Kotz asked many of the right questions, especially about the timing of the donation, as well as the deed of gift used to actually transfer ownership of the papers.[25] On June 16, the *Post* published an interview with Nixon's personal tax attorney, Frank DeMarco Jr., who confirmed many of the details in Kotz's reporting, including the valuation of the gift at more than $500,000. Even lacking access to the president's complete returns, reporters could do the math: The president's donation had probably saved him at least $250,000, maybe more.

Seeking an Independent Auditor

In July 1973, Tax Analysts and Advocates, a public interest law firm, published an article in *Tax Notes* concluding that Nixon's deduction was unjustified. The organization urged the IRS to consider appointing an outside auditor, suggesting that agency personnel were incapable of auditing the head of the executive branch.

The IRS has long enjoyed certain legal protections designed to insulate it from political pressures. Some were established in the wake of serious scandals in the early 1950s, when dozens of Internal Revenue officials—including a former commissioner—were indicted or convicted of tax evasion, bribery, extortion, and other serious crimes. In 1952, Congress had tried to clean the slate, restructuring and rebranding the agency: the rebuilt *Bureau* of Internal Revenue became the modernized Internal Revenue *Service.*

Even with its new, eager-to-please moniker, the agency remained at the service of one person: the president. While sometimes described as an "independent agency" like the Securities and Exchange Commission or the National Labor Relations Board, the IRS was not then and is not now actually independent; it remains a part of the Treasury Department, where it was first placed when it was established in 1862. The commissioner of Internal Revenue, moreover, remains a political appointee. Since 1998, the commissioner has served a fixed, five-year term, providing some insulation from the political vicissitudes of the presidential election cycle. But only a little: The commissioner still serves at the pleasure of whichever president currently occupies the Oval Office and can be removed at will.

As Reuel Schiller's chapter points out, Americans of the 1960s and 1970s were already questioning the power and expertise of federal bureaucracies. In the case of the IRS, institutional structures did not bolster confidence. "It is obvious that Internal Revenue Service agents and their superiors throughout the Internal Revenue Service would be extremely reluctant to audit the tax returns of the President of the United States as if he were an ordinary taxpayer," wrote Ira Tannenbaum, a Tax Analysts employee. "Or even if the IRS were willing to conduct such an audit, in view of the fact that the IRS

Commissioner is responsible to the President, the results of such an IRS audit would be questioned as to whether they were reached in the proper disinterested manner."

High Stakes and Solutions

The stakes were higher than any unpaid taxes Nixon might owe to the government. "There is an important need to make clear to the American public that income taxes of Americans in positions of power and high visibility are being assessed correctly, and that the tax laws are being applied fairly to them," Tannenbaum wrote. Indeed, the viability of the modern tax system hinged on perceptions of fairness and shared responsibility. "American taxpayers are willing to pay their fair share under our self-assessment tax system only if they believe other more visible taxpayers are also paying their legal share," he declared.[26]

Earnest arguments about the importance and fragility of tax morale—the willingness of regular people to pay up, even when the tax collector is not looking over their shoulder—got a cool reception from Nixon's White House. "The allegations are unfounded," an administration spokesman declared. "The suggested procedure [of an independent auditor] would be inappropriate."[27] The IRS took a similar line, rejecting the call for an independent auditor.[28]

James Byrne, a spokesman for Tax Analysts, responded by proposing an alternative: The IRS could ask the JCIRT and its staff to conduct the examination. Byrne's idea had several points in its favor. In practical terms, the JCIRT already enjoyed statutory authority to view tax returns, including the president's.[29] More important, the panel could hold Nixon accountable in ways that executive branch officials never could; the committee did not work for the president in any fashion. Elected officials could also imbue the investigation with the authority of democratic governance—and shield it from the president's interference.

There was one serious problem with Byrne's suggestion: Congressional committees have no power to enforce the law. Congress could investigate but not compel the president to comply with the law. Still, investigation (and public exposure, should Congress deem it appropriate) would provide a partial solution to a nettlesome problem: holding the president to account.

The Leak

For months, the debate over Nixon's taxes remained an issue for experts (and tedium-tolerant readers of the *Washington Post*). But in early October, someone at the IRS service center in Martinsburg, West Virginia, leaked key information about the president's returns.[30] On October 4, the *Providence Journal-Bulletin* published an article asserting that Nixon and his wife had paid only $792.81 in federal income taxes for 1970 ($7,281 in 2024 dollars) and $878.03 in 1971 ($7,438 in 2024), despite having a joint income of more than $200,000 (roughly $1.7 million in 2024) in each year. The revelation, which the White House eventually confirmed, gave a stark populist cast to the presidential tax debate.

The *New York Times* observed that Nixon's payments were "about the same tax as would have been paid by a family of three with an income between $7,500 and $7,550 in 1970 ($68,874 and $69,333 in 2024 dollars) and a family of three with an income between $8,450 and $8,500 in 1971 ($71,587 and $72,011 in 2024 dollars)."[31] It was a politically toxic comparison, given the economic pressures facing so many working and middle-class families at the time. Just two years earlier, the combination of rising inflation and slower economic growth had prompted Nixon to adopt a range of draconian policies, including wage and price controls. But it was also the kind of tax disparity that Nixon had used to justify tax reform in 1969, when he had denounced aggressive tax avoidance by the rich. Now he found himself on the wrong side of his own rhetoric.

The Providence paper acknowledged that its reporters had not seen the president's actual returns, which were stored (along with the returns of every other president dating back to Woodrow Wilson) in a safe located just outside the IRS commissioner's office.[32] Information from the returns would also have been stored in the agency's computer systems, accessible in various locations. But as the *New York Times* observed, "any Internal Revenue employee who disclosed the information would be violating the law and subject to a jail sentence of one year and a fine of $1,000."[33]

Media reports on the Nixon tax payments often noted that that the president had been audited by the IRS for both years in question. That information came from the president himself, who apparently hoped it would bolster his claim to being a law-abiding taxpayer. In a September 5 news conference, Nixon said the "full field review" of his returns had been comprehensive; it had also specifically evaluated real estate transactions connected with his estate in San Clemente, California. Ultimately, the IRS didn't order any change to his returns. "This is good news for people who wonder if presidents are exempt from what the IRS does," Nixon said.[34]

After the Providence paper leaked Nixon's tax data, pressure mounted on the president to make a full disclosure of his personal returns. In a scathing editorial, the *New York Times* offered a litany of possible wrongdoing by the president. "Only full financial disclosure could lay these questions to rest," the editors concluded. "The release of the president's tax returns is the essential first step in this process."[35]

The Committee Gets the Job

The White House gradually accepted the need for a public release. By late November, Nixon aides were promising an imminent disclosure of financial data, although they were vague about the president's tax returns.[36] On December 4, they went a step further, notifying congressional leaders that Nixon would ask the JCIRT to examine his tax returns. Nixon asked the JCIRT to examine two transactions in particular: (1) his gift of official papers to the National Archives, and (2) the sale of twenty-three acres at the president's San Clemente estate.[37]

On December 8, the White House released voluminous financial records, including tax returns for every year from 1968 to 1972.[38] In making the tax release, Nixon promised that he would make good on any past deficiencies. "In the event that the committee determines that the items were incorrectly reported, I will pay whatever tax may be due," he wrote.[39] That promise would eventually cost Nixon about half his net worth. Assuming he actually made good on the promise.

The JCIRT agreed to undertake the investigation but insisted on conducting a comprehensive examination. A narrow focus on just two items might produce a distorted result, the panel insisted: "So many questions have been raised about the tax returns of the President for these years that the committee believed the general public can only be satisfied by a thorough examination of the President's taxes."[40]

Wilbur Mills, chair of the House Ways and Means Committee, was notably candid in his initial assessment of the president's tax behavior. "I think a public official who files a tax return has to be holier-than-thou," he told reporters shortly after the committee began its review. "Frankly, had I been the President's attorney, I would have advised him not to take the deduction [for his National Archives donation]."[41]

Other insiders were similarly blunt, although usually only on background. The president, said one tax lawyer speaking to the *Baltimore Sun*, had "played it close to the line for every last dime." An unnamed congressman was even more incredulous: "How insensitive and how stupid can you get?" he fumed.[42]

Nixon's request to the JCIRT was a gamble. The committee had "a singular reputation for expertise and integrity," as one newspaper observed, making any sort of preferential treatment unlikely.[43] At the same time, however, the committee's deeply nonpartisan ethos seemed to guarantee Nixon a fair hearing—no small thing in such a heated political environment. News coverage of the JCIRT investigation stressed the committee's professionalism and independence. The *Los Angeles Times* called the panel "the most professional and nonpartisan on Capitol Hill." The *New York Times* made the same point in more elaborate fashion, describing the committee as "a highly unusual gear in the Congressional machinery that normally runs on politics." Indeed, the *Times* noted, the JCIRT had the lowest of low profiles: "Its very existence is not much known outside of Congress and those who carefully follow tax legislation."[44] But that obscurity imparted a degree of independence, making the committee well suited for a high-profile investigation of a politically charged topic.

Perhaps even more important, the politicians who actually served on the JCIRT were famously hands-off. At the start of the Nixon investigation, committee leaders had reportedly instructed their staff to work in secret, limiting disclosures even to members of the panel itself. "The reason the committee did not want to be fully informed was to insure that the investigation be as independent and non-political as possible," reported the *Los Angeles Times*.[45]

What Did Nixon Know?

As the JCIRT got to work, public debate over Nixon's taxes grew more intense. With the returns now publicly available, focus turned to the president's role in their preparation. The White House was keen to portray the president as a passive consumer of expert advice when it came to filing his returns. But news reports suggested otherwise.

Syndicated columnist Jack Anderson reported on White House documents casting Nixon as an active participant in his tax planning.[46] In a 1969 memo from Nixon aide John D. Ehrlichman to his deputy, Edward L. Morgan (signer of the disputed deed of gift), Nixon came across as anything but passive. "The President holds the view," Ehrlichman wrote, "that a public man does very little of a personal nature. Virtually all of his entertainment and activity is related to his 'business.'" Accordingly, Nixon was keen to identify every possible tax deduction, including such things as "wedding gifts to congressmen's daughters, flowers at funerals, etc."[47] Nixon even raised the possibility of looking to history for inspiration. "He suggests that we might review the returns of one or more previous Presidents for guidance," Ehrlichman wrote.[48]

A variety of tax experts also weighed in on Nixon's personal role in the tax scandal. In a highly publicized interview, former IRS commissioner Mortimer Caplin raised doubts about the legitimacy of Nixon's charitable deduction, as well as other aspects of his tax returns. But Caplin, like many other tax professionals, emphasized the broader issues at stake. "A President is a moral leader," Caplin said. "He helps establish the values in our society. He's an example."[49]

Some commentators mused that the president might face fraud charges, either civil or criminal. But Sen. Russell Long, D-La., who had assumed the chair of the JCIRT in January, said the committee was unlikely to address the issue. Other members of the panel agreed, pointing out that the nature of the investigation did not allow for consideration of fraud charges, since witnesses had not testified under oath; the committee had concluded that a staff inquiry did not have the authority to swear in witnesses.[50]

As the JCIRT study neared its conclusion, some officials began telegraphing its likely conclusions. Mills was especially forthcoming, suggesting that Nixon's tax misdeeds might force him from office.[51] Critics assailed Mills's comment, but he stuck to his guns, arguing that the tax situation would prove bigger than Watergate. "People understand taxes," he said.[52]

Damage to the IRS

The JCIRT investigation prompted much discussion of the IRS and its abilities. The need for a congressional inquiry into Nixon's tax returns was itself a vote of no-confidence in the agency. Likewise, Nixon's repeated insistence that his returns had already been audited did little to encourage faith in the agency, especially as more details emerged about the president's wrongdoing.

Perhaps most embarrassing, Nixon's December financial release had included an obsequious note from IRS Baltimore district director William D.

Walters to the president. "Our examination of your income tax returns for the year 1971 and 1972 reveal that they are correct," he wrote in June 1973. "Accordingly, these returns are accepted as filed. I want to compliment you on the care shown in the preparation of the returns."[53]

IRS critics thought the JCIRT study might serve as a useful prod to the agency. "When the President turned to the Joint Committee, the IRS roused itself at last and decided to have another look at those returns," one editorial stated. "It realized, belatedly, that more than Mr. Nixon's net worth was at stake. The crucial question here was the integrity of the IRS itself."[54]

But according to then-Commissioner Donald Alexander, the service had begun a new audit even before Nixon turned to the JCIRT. "On November 28, 1973, before the Joint Committee commenced its audit, I told George Shultz, then Secretary of the Treasury, that we were going to reopen the audit of former President Nixon's 1971 and 1972 returns," he later recalled. Apparently, Alexander had been moved to action by the same "I am not a crook" press conference that had sparked so much public debate earlier in the month.[55]

Alexander was also on the receiving end of repeated suggestions by Tax Analysts and Advocates that he find some way to effectively audit the president. Indeed, when he later explained to the House Judiciary Committee why he had initiated the second audit, Alexander used wording lifted almost verbatim from Thomas Field's letter to the IRS in July. As the Judiciary Committee reported Alexander's testimony: "He said he decided to have the IRS examine the President's tax returns because the information which had been reported would have caused the examination of the returns of any other taxpayer."[56]

Alexander looked over Nixon's returns personally on December 3, five days before Nixon sent copies to the JCIRT, along with Deputy Commissioner Raymond F. Harless. The following day, Alexander met with a full in-house audit team and the Baltimore district director, and on December 7, the IRS hand-delivered letters to the White House notifying Nixon of the new audit for his 1970, 1971, and 1972 returns.[57] In January 1974, the agency made a public announcement of its new audit; while generally unable to comment on matters involving a particular taxpayer, the agency had been authorized by President Nixon to confirm the existence of the audit.[58]

Critics welcomed the IRS move, but it did little to quiet complaints that the agency had been too credulous during its first examination. Alexander himself seemed to agree with that assessment. "Insiders say the commissioner believes the agency goofed the first time around," noted the *Wall Street Journal.*[59] More broadly, the IRS failure to effectively audit Nixon's returns contributed to a broader crisis at the agency. "Not since the early 1950s when major scandals engulfed the IRS and a former commissioner was imprisoned for fraud has the agency fallen under such a cloud of distrust," concluded one reporter.[60]

The failures surrounding Nixon's audit unfolded at the same time that other, even more lurid scandals were engulfing the IRS. Throughout Nixon's presidency, White House officials had been pressing the agency to investigate and harass Nixon's enemies. For the most part, agency officials had resisted this pressure. "We have been unable to obtain information in the possession of the IRS regarding our political enemies," complained White House counsel John Dean in a memo to Chief of Staff Bob Haldeman. "We have been unable to stimulate audits of persons who should be audited."[61]

Eventually, the first two IRS commissioners appointed by Nixon resigned rather than accede to this White House pressure campaign. But the public disclosure of Nixon's Enemies List, which occurred during the same summer when reporters were uncovering problems with Nixon's tax returns, served to further embarrass the IRS—and to shake public confidence in its independence and objectivity.

Failures at the IRS were serious not simply because the agency performed crucial tasks of revenue collection and economic regulation. They were also emblematic of government more generally. The IRS touched the lives of more people more directly than any other federal agency, except the Post Office. The IRS was known to Americans. And in the summer of 1973, it was known to be failing.

The Investigation and Report

The JCIRT had hoped to complete its review of Nixon's returns quickly, but it took four months for the panel to issue a final report. The process was thorough and time consuming, involving approximately thirty interviews with people involved in preparing Nixon's returns. Committee staff also traveled to both California and New York to investigate transactions reported on the returns.

The resulting document, released on April 4, 1974, was more than 1,000 pages long, including appendices. It considered numerous issues surrounding Nixon's returns, some large, others quite small. It would be fair to describe the report as exhaustive but the committee preferred to call it simply "extensive."

Table 4.1. Proposed Deficiencies in President Nixon's Tax Payments

Year	*Proposed Deficiency*	*Interest*	*Deficiency Plus Interest*
1969	$171,055	*	$171,055
1970	93,410	$16,638	110,048
1971	89,667	10,547	100,214
1972	89,890	5,224	95,114
Total	$444,022	$32,409	$476,431

* The committee did not include interest for the 1969 deficiency since it was a closed tax year and any payment by the president would have been purely voluntary.

Either way, the report's central finding was succinct: Nixon owed the government $476,431 in unpaid taxes and accrued interest. The sum included a deficiency of $171,055 for 1969; technically, Nixon was not obligated to pay this amount, since the 1969 tax year was already closed. As a result, the committee did not include interest on this amount in its recommended adjustment to the president's taxes. And in any case, the committee emphasized that its finding did not constitute a demand for payment of taxes, since JCIRT had no authority to issue such a demand. But given Nixon's promise to accept the committee's findings, the proposed adjustment carried substantial weight, both political and moral.

The shortfall in Nixon's tax payments stemmed from several issues, but three stood out: his charitable deduction for the donation of papers to the National Archives; his failure to report a capital gain on the sale of acreage at San Clemente; and the deferral of his capital gain recognition on the sale of his New York City apartment.

Papers Donation

On his 1969 return, Nixon had claimed a deduction for the charitable contribution of his personal papers to the National Archives. The president claimed to have made the gift on March 27, 1969, nearly four months before the July 25, 1969, effective date set by the Tax Reform Act of 1969 for new, less generous treatment of such donations. The gift was valued by an independent appraiser at $576,000, and the return indicated that there "were no restrictions on the gift and that the gift was free and clear, with no rights remaining in the taxpayer."

A deed of gift, dated March 27, 1969, had been delivered to the General Services Administration (parent agency of the National Archives) "shortly after" April 10, 1970. That deed was signed by Edward L. Morgan, deputy counsel to the president, rather than Nixon himself.

As a result of this gift, Nixon had claimed a deduction of $95,298 on his 1969 return, consistent with limits on the annual deduction relative to income. In subsequent years, Nixon carried over the remainder, taking deductions of $123,959 (1970), $128,668 (1971) and $134,093 (1972); $93,982 was still available for later deductions.

After an extensive review of this donation—including numerous interviews with Nixon's aides, lawyers, and accountants—JCIRT staff concluded that the president had not made a valid gift before the July 25, 1969 deadline. The committee identified numerous problems with the deed of gift—dated March 27, 1969, signed by presidential assistant Edward Morgan, and delivered to the National Archives in April 1970. In fact, the deed had not been signed by all parties until April 10, 1970, and was not delivered to the National Archives until after that date. Since delivery of the deed was necessary to convey title, the gift had been made after July 25, 1969, the JCIRT concluded.

There were other problems, too. First, Morgan was not authorized to sign the deed on the president's behalf. Second, the deed imposed numerous restrictions on the gift, rendering it (in the committee's judgment) a gift of future interest in tangible property, which would only be deductible once the restrictions had expired. And third, the report concluded that a similar gift of papers made in 1968 had imposed the same restrictions, making the charitable deduction in Nixon's 1968 return also improper and barring the possibility of carrying over any portion of the deduction to future tax years.

San Clemente Real Estate Sale

The JCIRT found that Nixon had failed to report a capital gain of $117,836 on the sale of land included in his San Clemente estate. The committee rejected Nixon's assertion that he had made no profit on the sale, suggesting that he had erroneously allocated costs and depreciation between various parcels. A capital gain of $117,836 should have been reported on the president's 1970 return.

Sale of New York Apartment

The committee found that Nixon had improperly deferred the reporting of his capital gain on the sale of his New York cooperative apartment. Nixon had claimed that deferral was justified, since he had reinvested the gain in the purchase of a new principal residence (San Clemente), but the JCIRT concluded that Nixon's actual principal residence was not the San Clemente estate but the White House.

Staff concluded that the president owed tax on a capital gain of $142,912. They also contended that Nixon's cost basis in the apartment should be reduced by the depreciation and amortization allowable on the apartment for its use as a place of business. That adjustment would increase the total gain to $151,848, which should have been reported on Nixon's 1969 tax return.

Reaction to the JCIRT Report

Members of the JCIRT endorsed the staff report by a vote of 9–1, with only Sen. Carl T. Curtis, R-Neb., in dissent. The members released it, along with all supporting documents, on April 4—the same day that the IRS announced it had concluded its second audit of Nixon's tax returns.

Although the figures were not disclosed at the time, the IRS had found that Nixon owed a similar but smaller amount than the one suggested by the JCIRT: $432,787. Nixon agreed quickly to pay the IRS figure but chose not to pay interest on his 1969 deficiency, arguing (as the JCIRT had itself suggested) that the payment was voluntary since the statute of limitations had run out on the 1969 return. (For the same reason, Nixon might also have avoided paying any part of the 1969 deficiency.)[62]

JCIRT members commended Nixon for agreeing to pay so readily. But not everyone was impressed. In comments to the *New York Times*, Tax Analysts and Advocates pointed out that any voluntary payment on Nixon's 1969 taxes would be deductible on his 1974 tax return as a charitable contribution to the federal government.[63] Editors at the *Washington Post*, meanwhile, observed that Nixon really had no choice, at least regarding his 1970 and 1971 returns. "Is it necessary to point out that, under American law, paying income taxes is not a voluntary matter?" the paper asked.[64]

For its part, the White House was not exactly gracious. Presidential aides complained that the JCIRT had released its report before allowing the president to respond. They insisted that Nixon's original positions were still "valid and compelling," and prerelease news reports had suggested that Nixon might challenge the JCIRT findings. Ultimately, however, Nixon was bound, at least politically, by his promise in December to abide by the committee's findings.

Administration officials were at pains to point out that neither the JCIRT nor the IRS had leveled fraud charges against the president. In fact, the IRS had announced that it "did not believe any such assertion was warranted." The House Judiciary Committee, however, did consider tax fraud during its impeachment proceedings, including an article of impeachment stating that Nixon "knowingly and fraudulently failed to report certain income and claimed deductions in the year 1969, 1970, 1971, and 1972 on his Federal income tax returns which were not authorized by law." Eventually, the committee rejected that article.

Meanwhile, White House officials worked feverishly to shift blame for Nixon's tax troubles from the president to his subordinates. "Any errors which may have been made in the preparation of the President's returns were made by those to whom he delegated the responsibility for preparing his return and were made without his knowledge and without his approval," the White House announced.

The *Washington Post* felt compelled to challenge that statement, even in its news coverage. "A person who signs a tax return is responsible for it regardless of who else works on it," the paper noted in its coverage of the White House statement. The editorial page was even more scathing. "We have never had a President who confessed himself so sublimely unaware of the activities of his closest associates," the paper argued. "Citizens are left to reflect that, whatever the pressures of their own business, they are required by law to take responsibility for the tax returns that they sign."

Did He Really Pay?

It is not entirely clear how much Nixon actually paid to settle his tax bill. Immediately after the JCIRT made its report public, the White House promised the president would pay everything he owed. Many Nixon critics were determined to hold him to that promise. "The integrity of the national tax system urgently required Mr. Nixon to pay the full and accurate assessment of his taxes down to the last dime," the *Washington Post* editorialized in April 1974.

Later that spring, the White House announced that Nixon had paid his deficiencies for 1970, 1971, and 1972. But the president dragged his feet on the 1969 deficiency. The statute of limitations on nonfraudulent deficiencies had already expired for 1969 returns. (The IRS had declined to charge Nixon with fraud, instead assessing him a 5 percent negligence penalty. Commissioner Donald Alexander, however, referred the question of possible fraud to the Watergate special prosecutor, Leon Jaworski, for later consideration.)

Nixon continued to insist publicly that he would pay the 1969 deficiency. But on the day of his resignation, he still hadn't paid up. Addressing White House staff on August 9, 1974, he wished aloud that he could reward them financially for their loyal service. "I only wish that I were a wealthy man," he said. "At the present time, I've got to find a way to pay my taxes."

On September 8, 1974, President Ford pardoned Nixon "for all offenses against the United States"—which put to rest any lingering questions about tax fraud. In doing so, however, Ford may also have closed the books on Nixon's outstanding 1969 tax bill.

Conclusion

Nixon's tax scandal is barely a footnote in most historical treatments of his presidency. Watergate was so lurid as to obscure more pedestrian (and more tedious) misdeeds, like the papers donation. To the extent that the episode is remembered at all, the outrage is usually directed at the notion that a president would try to claim a deduction for donating his official papers to a government archive in the first place. But of course, such donations and associated deductions were perfectly legal—and entirely routine—until the middle of 1969.

Nixon's tax wrongdoing, on the other hand, was anything but legal or routine. The president and his advisers had filed returns based on outright falsehoods, especially surrounding the timing of key events. Several presidential aides involved in preparing the returns were indicted or convicted for their roles in the episode. Edward L. Morgan, who played a key role, served four months after pleading guilty to falsifying documents related to the papers donation.[65]

The tax scandal was headline news in the latter half of 1973. After the JCIRT issued its report in April 1974, many observers continued to speculate that it would prove Nixon's undoing. After interviewing Wilbur Mills, *People* magazine passed along his prediction: "When an analysis of the President's returns is made public," Mills said, "Mr. Nixon will surely resign."[66]

The most serious issue, for Mills and many others, was the message that Nixon's tax avoidance was sending to American taxpayers. "There are many, many people with a lot less income that have paid more taxes during these four years than he has, and it galls them a lot," Mills said. "A lot of people say they'd already be in the penitentiary had they paid no more on their incomes than he barely paid on his."[67]

The failure of the IRS to catch the president was also troubling. Since its creation during the Civil War, the agency has been the focus of recurring complaints about its honesty, integrity, and capacity. But the Nixon episode posed a particularly serious threat to the agency—and by extension the tax system that it administered. The scandal underscored the agency's susceptibility to political influence, and in doing so, threatened the integrity of the tax system it was charged with administering.

Ultimately, the Nixon scandal was important not because one politician shortchanged the government on his tax payments. It was important because it exposed an obvious but uncomfortable truth: American presidents have a dual relationship with the tax system. On the one hand, they serve as the nation's chief tax collector, supervising the only federal agency empowered to enforce the federal tax law. But at the same time, presidents are also themselves taxpayers, subject to all the same legal, tax-filing responsibilities as anyone else. This dual role creates complex tensions, but in the most practical terms, it means that presidents are responsible for policing their own tax behavior. Or not policing it, as the case may be.

To be sure, there are safeguards and legal barriers designed to prevent political meddling with the IRS. Many were adopted in the immediate wake of the Nixon scandal. But most of these guardrails are grounded in tradition rather than law. For instance, presidents after Nixon embraced a tradition of voluntary tax disclosure, releasing a tax return during every year in which they have held office.[68] Most major party presidential candidates have also followed this tradition while campaigning for the Oval Office.

Voluntary public disclosures allowed for a crowd-sourced audit regime; if Americans had concerns about presidential taxpaying (or the IRS's ability to audit presidents), then people could do the checking for themselves. That solution worked reasonably well—until it didn't. Forty years after Carter began the tradition, Donald Trump ended it. By simply refusing to participate, he underscored its fragility. Since 2020, Joe Biden has tried to revive the tradition. But during the 2024 campaign, few Republicans joined him in making voluntary disclosures. And with Trump having won a second term, further disclosures seem vanishingly unlikely.

In the latter half of Trump's first term, the House Ways and Means Committee tried to compel release of Trump's returns, using a century-old law that permits certain congressional committees to request, examine, and release taxpayer information when lawmakers find it necessary. But the process proved agonizingly slow, extending well beyond the end of Trump's first term.[69]

Even worse, the Ways and Means Committee discovered that voluntary disclosure wasn't the only guardrail to have given way during the Trump presidency. The IRS had failed to complete annual audits of Trump's tax returns throughout his first term, thereby flouting the agency's own internal regulations, which require audits for every sitting president and vice president.

The upshot of the Trump experience—especially when viewed in light of the Nixon scandal and its myriad institutional failures—is disquieting: America's Taxpayer in Chief remains effectively above the law.

Notes

Some elements of this chapter were originally published in the Tax Notes Federal article "JCT Investigation of Nixon Tax Returns," June 13, 2016. © Tax Analysts. Reprinted with permission from Tax Notes.

1. David Frost, *Frost/Nixon* (HarperCollins, 2014), 14.

2. Carroll Kilpatrick, "Nixon Tells Editors, 'I'm Not a Crook,'" *The Washington Post*, November 18, 1973.

3. United States Congress Joint Committee on Internal Revenue Taxation, *Examination of President Nixon's Tax Returns for 1969–72: Report from Joint Committee on Internal Revenue Taxation*, 1974, https://books.google.com/books?id=_iZeAQAACAAJ. Inflation adjustment from Samuel H. Williamson, "Seven Ways to Compute the Relative Value of a U.S. Dollar Amount, 1790 to Present," MeasuringWorth, 2022.

4. Ibid.

5. The literature on fiscal citizenship has grown briskly over the past two decades. For a useful start, see: Ajay K. Mehrotra, "Fiscal Forearms: Taxation as the Lifeblood of the Modern Liberal State," in *The Many Hands of the State*, ed. Kimberly J. Morgan and Ann Shola Orloff (Cambridge University Press, 2017), 284–305, accessed October 4, 2019, https://www.cambridge.org/core/product/identifier/9781316471586%23CT-bp-12/type/book_part; Lawrence Zelenak, *Learning to Love Form 1040: Two Cheers for the Return-Based Mass Income Tax* (University of Chicago Press, 2013); Ajay K. Mehrotra, "Reviving Fiscal Citizenship," *Michigan Law Review* 113 (n.d.): 31; Nicolette Makovicky and Robin Smith, "Introduction: Tax Beyond the Social Contract," *Social Analysis* 64, no. 2 (2020): 1–17, https://www.berghahnjournals.com/view/journals/social-analysis/64/2/sa640201.xml; Vanessa S. Williamson, *Read My Lips: Why*

Americans Are Proud to Pay Taxes (Princeton University Press, 2019); Sven H. Steinmo, *The Leap of Faith: The Fiscal Foundations of Successful Government in Europe and America* (Oxford University Press, 2018); Romain Huret, *The Not-So-Infernal Revenue Service?: Tax Collection, Citizens, and Compliance in the United States from the Eighteenth to the Twentieth Centuries* (Oxford University Press, 2018), accessed October 4, 2019, https://www.oxfordscholarship.com/view/10.1093/oso/9780198796817.001.0001/oso-9780198796817-chapter-8; James T. Sparrow, "'Buying Our Boys Back': The Mass Foundations of Fiscal Citizenship in World War II," *Journal of Policy History* 20, no. 2 (April 2008): 263–286, accessed October 4, 2019, https://www.cambridge.org/core/product/identifier/S0898030600002232/type/journal_article.

6. On the origins of this famous phrase, see "'No Taxation Without Representation' (Part 1)," *Journal of the American Revolution*, last modified May 21, 2013, accessed February 28, 2023, https://allthingsliberty.com/2013/05/no-taxation-without-representation-part-1/; "'No Taxation Without Representation' (Part 2)," *Journal of the American Revolution*, last modified May 22, 2013, accessed February 28, 2023, https://allthingsliberty.com/2013/05/no-taxation-without-representation-part-2/.

7. Franklin, *The Writings of Benjamin Franklin* (Whittemore, Niles, and Hall, 1856), 10: 410.

8. Makovicky and Smith, "Introduction: Tax Beyond the Social Contract," 1.

9. Nichole M. Flores and Charles Mathewes, "The First Citizen," last modified 2017, accessed April 25, 2022, http://firstyear2017.org/essay/the-first-citizen.

10. Richard Nixon, "Special Message to the Congress on Reform of the Federal Tax System," The American Presidency Project, Gerhard Peters and John T. Woolley, eds. https://www.presidency.ucsb.edu/node/238893.

11. On national-level tax debates, see Thomas Byrne Edsall and Mary D. Edsall, *Chain Reaction: The Impact of Race, Rights, and Taxes on American Politics* (W. W. Norton, 1992).On state-level tax revolts, see Isaac William Martin, *The Permanent Tax Revolt: How the Property Tax Transformed American Politics* (Stanford University Press, 2008).

12. The actual statutory cap in 2024 was $168,600, due to subsequent changes in the law. The existence of the cap is typically justified on the grounds that benefits are capped as well; the tax cap maintains a linkage between taxes collected and benefits paid.

13. Richard Nixon, "Remarks on the CBS Radio Network: 'Toward an Expanded Democracy,'" The American Presidency Project, Gerhard Peters and John T. Woolley, eds., https://www.presidency.ucsb.edu/node/326733.

14. Richard Nixon, Statement Submitted to Republican National Convention Committee on Resolutions: "The Threat to the American Economy." Online by Gerhard Peters and John T. Woolley, The American Presidency Project, https://www.presidency.ucsb.edu/node/326768

15. Nixon, "Special Message."

16. "Presidential Libraries Act of 1955," *National Archives*, last modified August 15, 2016, accessed April 11, 2022, https://www.archives.gov/presidential-libraries/laws/1955-act.html.

17. Taxation, *Examination of President Nixon's Tax Returns for 1969–72: Report from Joint Committee on Internal Revenue Taxation*, 28. See also, William Greider, "Who Owns the Papers of a President?," *The Washington Post*, December 18, 1973, 2.

18. Ira L. Tannenbaum, "Income Tax Treatment of Donation of Nixon Pre-Presidential Papers," *Tax Notes*, July 30, 1973.

19. Nick Kotz, "Nixon Gift Raises Questions," *The Washington Post*, June 10, 1973, 2.

20. Ibid.

21. Walter Pincus, "Mr. Nixon's Papers: The Tax Question," *The Washington Post*, January 7, 1974, 1.

22. Tannenbaum, "Income Tax Treatment of Donation of Nixon Pre-Presidential Papers." See Greider, "Who Owns the Papers of a President?."

23. Nick Kotz, "Nixon Gift Raises Questions." *The Washington Post*, June 10, 1973, 2.

24. Donald C. Alexander, "IRS Audits of High Officials," *Tax Notes*, July 17, 1977.

25. Kotz, "Nixon Gift Raises Questions."

26. Tannenbaum, "Income Tax Treatment of Donation of Nixon Pre-Presidential Papers."

27. "Tax Returns Audit of President Asked," *New York Times*, July 30, 1973, 54.

28. Cathe Wolhowe, "IRS Won't Name Nixon Auditor," *The Washington Post*, October 31, 1973, 1.

29. Dean Mills, "Tax Law Firm Bids IRS Probe Nixon 'Gift' to U.S. Archives," *The Sun*, October 31, 1973, 1.

30. "IRS Aide Quits; Leaked Nixon Tax Data," *The Washington Post*, January 17, 1974, 1.

31. Eileen Shanahan, "White House Is Silent on a Report Nixon Paid $1,670 Tax in '70–'71," *New York Times*, October 4, 1973, 1. Other papers also made such comparisons, presumably in an effort to make the Nixon numbers meaningful to readers. See, for example, "Nixon Taxes Reportedly Equal to Those on $7000," *Boston Globe (1960–1984)*, October 5, 1973, 19.

32. Shanahan, "White House Is Silent on a Report Nixon Paid $1,670 Tax in '70'71."

33. Ibid.

34. "President Says IRS Audited His Returns, Didn't Raise Taxes," *Wall Street Journal*, September 6, 1973, 3.

35. "Still a Mystery," *New York Times*, November 17, 1973, 34.

36. Don Irwin, "Nixon to Give Data on Finances Next Week," *Los Angeles Times*, November 30, 1973, 5.

37. United States Congress, Senate, Joint Committee on Internal Revenue Taxation, *Examination of President Nixon's Tax Returns for 1969 through 1972*, 1.

38. Adam Clymer, "Nixon Puts Gift Issue up to Congress," *The Sun*, December 4, 1973, 2; John Herbers, "Nixon Counsel Hints Tax Data Release," *New York Times*, December 5, 1973, 28; John Herbers, "Voluminous Data," *New York Times*, December 9, 1973, 1; Nixon letter to Wilbur Mills, quoted in United States Congress, Senate, Joint Committee on Internal Revenue Taxation, *Examination of President Nixon's Tax Returns for 1969 through 1972*, 1.

39. Ibid.

40. United States Congress, Senate, Joint Committee on Internal Revenue Taxation, *Examination of President Nixon's Tax Returns for 1969 through 1972*, 2.

41. Eileen Shanahan, "Tax Panel Plans Complete Review of Nixon Returns," *New York Times*, December 13, 1973, 1.

42. Adam Clymer, "Paying Taxes Is Hard for Nixon, Too," *The Sun (1837–1990)*, December 9, 1973, 2.

43. Ibid.

44. Richard L. Madden, "Committee Staff: Nonpartisan Professionals," *New York Times*, April 4, 1974, 29.

45. Thomas J. Foley, "1970 Date Key Issue in Nixon Tax Inquiry," *Los Angeles Times*, March 21, 1974, 2-a1.

46. Jack Anderson, "Nixon Had Checked His Tax Return," *The Washington Post*, March 8, 1974, 1.

47. Ibid.

48. Thomas J. Foley, "Nixon Look at Ex-Presidents' Taxes Denied," *Los Angeles Times*, March 13, 1974, 1-a6; P. MacKenzie John, "Nixon Role Denied on Tax Memo," *The Washington Post*, March 13, 1974, 1.

49. "Nixon's Taxes: An Interview with Mortimer Caplin," *The Washington Post*, December 16, 1973, 2.

50. Eileen Shanahan, "Joint Tax Panel Expected to Ask What Nixon Knew About Claims," *New York Times*, March 6, 1974, 22.

51. Foley, "1970 Date Key Issue in Nixon Tax Inquiry." Rep. James A. Burke, D-Mass., another member of the committee, backed Mills in this assessment of the seriousness.

52. "Mr. Mills on Mr. Nixon," *New York Times*, March 12, 1974, 36; Foley, "Nixon Look at Ex-Presidents' Taxes Denied."

53. Taxation, *Examination of President Nixon's Tax Returns for 1969–72: Report from Joint Committee on Internal Revenue Taxation.*

54. "Mr. Nixon's Taxes," *The Washington Post*, April 4, 1974, 1.

55. Alexander, "IRS Audits of High Officials."

56. Reprinted in ibid.

57. Ibid.

58. Paul Houston, "IRS Checking Two Nixon Tax Returns It Praised Last June," *Los Angeles Times (1923–Current File)*, January 3, 1974, 2–3a.

59. Timothy D. Schellhardt, "Taxing Job," *Wall Street Journal*, January 24, 1974, 1.

60. Ibid.

61. Joseph Thorndike, "Timelines in Tax History: Nixon Aide Tried to Weaponize the IRS by Pressuring the Commissioner," *Forbes*, accessed March 13, 2023, https://www.forbes.com/sites/taxnotes/2023/03/13/timelines-in-tax-history-nixon-aide-tried-to-weaponize-the-irs-by-pressuring-the-commissioner/.

62. Eileen Shanahan, "Nixon Tax Inquiry Is Closed by I.R.S. and Congress Unit," *New York Times*, April 5, 1974, 1.

63. Ibid.

64. "Taxes, Morality and Mr. Nixon," *The Washington Post*, April 7, 1974, 1.

65. Samson, "President Nixon's Troublesome Tax Returns," *Tax Notes Today Federal*, May 2, 2005, accessed March 30, 2025, available at https://www.taxnotes.com/tax-notes-today-federal/tax-history/president-nixons-troublesome-tax-returns/2005/05/03/yh5g.

66. Clare Crawford, "Wilbur Mills: Taxes Will Be Nixon's Downfall," *People*, April 15, 1974, available at http://www.people.com/people/archive/article/0,,20063956,00.html.

67. Ibid.

68. For the rather complicated and messy details of this tradition, see "Voluntary Tax Return Disclosure by U.S. Presidents, Vice Presidents, and Major Party Nominees; Testimony Before the Subcommittee on Oversight, Committee on Ways and Means, U.S. House of Representatives," February 7, 2019, accessed April 25, 2022, https://www.congress.gov/116/meeting/house/108922/witnesses/HHRG-116-WM06-Wstate-ThorndikeJ-20190207.pdf.

69. On the statutory authority, see George K. Yin, "Congressional Authority to Obtain and Release Tax Returns," *Tax Notes* 154, no. 8 (February 20, 2017): 1013–1015.

CHAPTER 5

McGovernites and Neocons: Michael Harrington, Max Shachtman, and the Realignment of the Democratic Party

Daniel Geary

In 2015, socialism seemed to be a marginal ideology in American politics. But then came the surprising success of Bernie Sanders in the 2016 Democratic presidential primary. The self-proclaimed "democratic socialist" rallied millions of supporters in a robust challenge to presumptive nominee Hillary Clinton. In subsequent years, socialists gained a small but significant foothold in American government by working within the Democratic Party. Most notably, Alexandria Ocasio-Cortez was elected to Congress in 2018 after unseating a senior Democratic leader in that year's primary. The Democratic Socialists of America (DSA), of which Ocasio-Cortez is the most prominent member, rapidly expanded its membership from 6,500 in 2015 to 95,000 in 2021.[1]

Though it appeared to come out of nowhere, the roots of this socialist revival stretch back decades. The very term "democratic socialism"—and its connotation of working within the existing American political system—is a legacy of an earlier generation of socialists. In fact, the DSA traces its origins to the Democratic Socialist Organizing Committee (DSOC), founded by Michael Harrington in 1973. The recent successes of democratic socialists owe much to Harrington's pragmatic insistence on seeking a "left wing of the possible" by working within the Democratic Party.

DSOC's strategy of realigning the Democratic Party along left-wing lines was rooted in the earlier work of a small group whose most prominent members were Harrington and the venerable one-time Trotskyist, Max Shachtman.

Beginning in the late 1950s, these self-designated "democratic socialists" operated within the liberal wing of the Democratic Party. By the time of the 1963 March on Washington, their realignment strategy seemed to be working. Democratic socialists worked with Bayard Rustin and other civil rights leaders to form a "coalition of conscience" to achieve racial equality and basic living standards for all Americans. Though small in number, the democratic socialists gathered around Harrington and Shachtman played key roles as ideologists, strategists, and organizers within a broader progressive movement. They thus participated in the broader revival of left-liberalism that began in the early 1960s and culminated with the 1972 candidacy of antiwar liberal Senator George McGovern as the Democrats' presidential nominee.

However, as fractures began to emerge within the Democratic Party in the mid-1960s—especially over the Vietnam War—democratic socialists were pulled in opposite directions as they now advanced competing visions of realignment. Harrington wed himself to the antiwar "New Politics" wing of the Democratic Party epitomized by McGovern. He hailed left-liberal reformers as a "conscience constituency" and a necessary part of any left coalition.

Shachtman and his followers (collectively known as "Shachtmanites"), however, hitched themselves to George Meany and the leadership of the AFL-CIO. By embracing McGovern, Shachtmanites claimed, Harrington had sided with a "fashionable liberal elite" against the "interests of the organized working class."[2] Reasoning that organized labor was central to pushing social-democratic policies, they allied with one of the most conservative factions of the Democratic Party. The AFL-CIO leadership ardently supported the Cold War, resisted the advances of the new social movements of the era such as feminism, and resented efforts by liberal Democrats led by McGovern to make the Democratic Party more open to democratic participation. In defending the interests of the AFL-CIO leadership, Shachtmanites contributed to the growth of "neoconservatism": the ideology of a predominantly Jewish group of intellectuals who moved rightward in revulsion to left-liberalism. The distinct contribution Shachtman and his followers made to neoconservatism was their concept of a "new class" of middle-class professionals whose ostensible embrace of liberal reforms masked a self-interested power grab.

The conflict between Shachtman and Harrington came to a head during the 1972 general election. A few days before the vote and the day before he suffered a fatal heart attack, Shachtman was visited by his protégé Tom Kahn, who had spent the campaign writing speeches for Meany. Shachtman praised Meany for having the "guts" not to endorse McGovern.[3] It was the

Shachtmanites' failure to support McGovern against Nixon that prompted Harrington to form DSOC. DSOC was based not simply on the realignment strategy but on Harrington's plan to recruit McGovern supporters into a broader coalition including progressive trade unionists, African Americans, and feminists. His original vision of DSOC of creating a cross-class coalition of "workers, reformers, the minorities, the woman's movement and other partisans of social change" still resonates among democratic socialists today.[4]

The Roots of Realignment

Born in Warsaw, Poland, in 1904, Max Shachtman reflected the experience of European migration to the United States that first defined the immigration question in Carl Bon Tempo's chapter. Shachtman emigrated to New York City with his parents when he was just a baby. He grew up in a working-class Jewish neighborhood in Harlem and was active in socialist politics from a young age. An opponent of Joseph Stalin, Shachtman was expelled from the Communist Party in 1928. He emerged as one of the leaders of American Trotskyism and formed a close relationship with Leon Trotsky himself. In 1940, Shachtman formed his own party, the Workers Party. While others, including Trotsky, claimed that the Soviet Union was a "degenerated workers' state" that required unconditional defense, Shachtman disagreed. He saw the USSR as a novel "bureaucratic collectivism" controlled by a class of party functionaries. Instead of siding with the capitalist West or Stalinist communism, Shachtman advocated the formation of a "third camp" beholden to neither.[5]

By the end of the 1940s, Shachtman was moving toward the realignment strategy. He now advanced "democratic socialism," a phrase that he played a crucial role in popularizing through his influence on a younger generation. In 1950, he dissolved the Workers Party into the Independent Socialist League (ISL). He continued to advance third camp politics: Visitors to the ISL headquarters in New York were greeted with a banner bearing the slogan "Neither Washington Nor Moscow." Yet Shachtman's new goal was the formation of a labor party in the United States modeled on the British Labor Party and other European social-democratic parties. He placed his hopes in leaders of the most progressive non-Communist labor unions, especially the United Automobile Workers (UAW). Whereas once Shachtman had urged his followers to agitate among the rank and file, he now instructed them to take union staff jobs, leading some to joke that "the best way to become a union bureaucrat was to join the Shachtmanites."[6] Shachtman's accommodation with the mainstream of American politics was mirrored in his personal life when in 1954 he surprised his comrades by moving with his wife to the suburb of Floral Park, Long Island. There he began a part-time business repairing radios and cultivated rare orchids in his garden.[7]

Shachtman was a skilled factional fighter, a brilliant thinker, and a charismatic leader. No dogmatist, he often reconsidered his positions. But he could be vindictive against comrades who disagreed with him. His organizations could never claim more than a few hundred members, but they had an outsized influence. What they lacked in numbers, they made up for in commitment, organization, and strategic thinking. Among those who passed through Shachtman's orbit were Saul Bellow, Grace Lee Boggs, Irving Howe, C. L. R. James, Dwight Macdonald, Irving Kristol, and several labor union officials. Shachtman appealed especially to young followers, for whom he often served as a father figure.[8]

Michael Harrington became the most famous of Shachtman's followers. Born in 1928, Harrington grew up in a middle-class Catholic family in St. Louis, Missouri. After graduating from the Jesuit college Holy Cross in 1951, Harrington joined Dorothy Day's Catholic Worker movement, a group of radical pacifists who ministered to the poor on New York's Lower East Side.[9] One root of Harrington's later dispute with Shachtman on the politics of the "conscience constituency" may have come from their different paths to politics. For it was precisely conscience that motivated Harrington's entry into radical politics. In contrast, Shachtman's politics were rooted in the immigrant working-class neighborhood of his youth; he was always suspicious of middle-class moralism.

After a few years with the Catholic Worker, Harrington lost his faith in God and sought another outlet for his leftism. He became close to Shachtman in the mid-1950s as chair of the Socialist Youth League, which was closely aligned with the ISL (though not formally affiliated with it). Harrington recalled the appeal of Shachtman at the time: "What Max communicated . . . even though we were pathetically small and marginal, was a sense of movement, of tradition."[10] The issue that cemented their relationship was realignment. Harrington sat as the youth representative on the ISL political committee where he lined up with Shachtman's contentious position that socialists should seek change within existing democratic institutions.

In 1958, the ISL merged with the Socialist Party (SP), once the party of Eugene Debs but then in a state of decline under the leadership of an aging

Norman Thomas. Though Shachtman had previously denounced the SP as too reformist, he was now attracted to its focus on democratic politics. By 1960, he, Harrington, and others formed the Realignment faction within the SP. Arguing against those who wanted to run their own candidates in the 1960 election, they claimed that by working within the Democratic Party socialists could "function more meaningfully than we have in the past." The Democrats, they argued, already contained "most of those Americans who sincerely favor liberal, forward-looking policies" and to whom socialists could "offer long-range ideals to serve as a yardstick while vigorously pursuing everyday actions consistent with those ideals." The Democratic Party, however, would have to purge its reactionary elements. Socialists, therefore, should exploit divisions within the party: "Let the forces of conservatism and big business, the militarists and nationalists . . . come together in a political party of their own and let labor, the farmers, the Negro people and other racial minorities, the liberal and peace forces, come together in a party of our own."[11]

The idea of realignment was hardly invented by socialists. It was common in the political science discourse of the time where it was often hoped that the two parties might more consistently develop their ideological differences, thereby allowing American voters a clearer choice. Shachtman's circle was familiar with some of this work, but they applied in a clearly left-wing direction. As Harrington explained in 1959, their goal was the creation "not of a 'third' party of protest, but . . . a real, second party of the people."[12]

Other socialists were coming to the same conclusion. The journal *Dissent*, founded in 1954 by Irving Howe and Lewis Coser, sought to join liberalism with socialism. In 1959, Howe wrote that "the decisive political struggles during the next few years will occur in the Democratic party . . . [we] would prefer, no doubt, some American version of the British labor party; but there it is: take it or leave it, a fact." The Democrats, Howe thought, reflected a "crowded variety of opinions and pressures," which gave socialists an opportunity to bolster its most liberal elements and push them in a more socialist direction.[13]

For much of the 1950s, when the second Red Scare peaked, it would have been absurd to think that a tiny band of socialists could influence American politics. But by 1960, realignment seemed a genuine possibility because of three related developments: the revival of liberalism, the growth in youth activism, and especially the rise of the civil rights movement. Democratic socialists played a role in these developments, Harrington most of all.

In 1962, Harrington published *The Other America*, a powerful exposé of poverty in the United States that became a surprise bestseller. *The Other*

America exemplified the newfound determination of socialists to influence liberals. Seeking to awaken Americans' consciences, Harrington strategically omitted any mention of socialism. Yet his primary aim was to remind Americans of the persistence of material want. He argued against those liberals such as John Kenneth Galbraith who had focused their attention instead on the problems of an "affluent society." Moreover, Harrington proposed party realignment as a necessary condition for eradicating poverty. He speculated that one reason why poverty had become "invisible" to many Americans was the "irrationalities of the American party system," which prevented Democrats from becoming a consistent champion of the poor in alliance with liberals and labor.[14]

Harrington's book proved a crucial spur for the Kennedy and Johnson administrations to launch the War on Poverty. Harrington was even recruited to work for the President's Taskforce on the War on Poverty. He was under no illusion that poverty could be adequately addressed by the policies that emerged, which were woefully underfunded and focused on job training and community building at the expense of full employment and structural change. Nevertheless, in acknowledging that poverty was a problem, liberals had opened a space for socialists to push more thoroughgoing solutions.[15]

Harrington also played a central role in the reemergence of left-wing youth activism. During the 1950s, he organized socialist youth groups at universities, a role that eventually led him to joke that he had become "America's oldest young socialist." The 1958 merger of the Socialist Party with Shachtman's ISL and the Harrington-led Socialist Youth League allowed for the revival of the Young People's Socialist League (YPSL, pronounced "Yipsel"). Though Harrington did not officially chair YPSL, everyone knew he effectively ran it. He traveled the country to college campuses to nurture the nascent student New Left. YPSL membership rose from 300 to 800 during an eighteen-month period beginning in 1960. While still small, YPSL played an important role in Berkeley, California, where it contributed to the climate of activism leading up to the 1964 Free Speech Movement and at the University of Chicago, where YPSL members, including a young Bernie Sanders, became involved with civil rights protests.[16]

Democratic socialists also influenced the Students for a Democratic Society (SDS), which became the principal organization of the student New Left. At the organization's 1962 Port Huron conference, Harrington notoriously clashed with Tom Hayden and others on what Harrington saw as the SDS manifesto's softness on communism.[17] However, along with other SDS members such as Steve Max, Harrington successfully pushed the manifesto to adopt the realignment position alongside Hayden's more expansive commitment to "participatory democracy."[18] The Port Huron Statement's final draft declared that a "real two-party system" was an "immediate necessity" even if realigned parties still wouldn't "provide adequate outlets for popular involvement."[19]

Jobs and Freedom

Democratic socialists realized the transformative potential of the civil rights movement before most White liberals did. Shachtman understood that it was the "catalytic agent capable of forcing realignment."[20] The movement's demands went well beyond formal equality to include economic equality, which could only be brought about by social democratic policies. But meeting even the movement's elementary demands would split the Democratic Party and drive out its most reactionary element, the Southern Dixiecrats. For democratic socialists, this was an opportunity to realign the Democratic Party along social-democratic lines.

Bayard Rustin, one of the leading strategists of the civil rights movement and a close adviser to Martin Luther King Jr., forged a tight relationship with democratic socialists. Rustin met Harrington in 1951 at a demonstration against the Korean War. In 1956, Rustin sought help to support the Montgomery bus boycott. Harrington introduced him to two young socialists from Brooklyn College: Rachelle Horowitz and Tom Kahn. Several years younger than Harrington, they looked up to him as a kind of older brother. They became so close to Shachtman that he referred to them as "my children." Rustin quickly became their mentor as well. For a time, Kahn also became Rustin's lover—the two lived together in the late 1950s—though their political relationship outlived their romantic one. Horowitz and Kahn provided crucial organizational support to Rustin, who lacked a secure institutional base. For them, the experience was life-changing: Two new recruits to socialism were suddenly answering phone calls from King and other leaders of the Montgomery movement.[21]

Starting during the Montgomery boycott, Rustin sometimes joined Harrington, Horowitz, and Kahn for strategy sessions at Shachtman's home. For Shachtman's circle, Rustin was a powerful recruit to their realignment strategy. As Harrington recalled, the main purpose of the discussions in Floral

Park was to push Rustin to become "more political" and to talk him out of an excessive commitment to Gandhian methods of nonviolence.[22] Additionally, Kahn enrolled at Howard University in the late 1950s and formed several connections to leaders of the militant Student Nonviolent Coordinating Committee (SNCC), including Stokely Carmichael whom he helped recruit to YPSL.

The 1963 March on Washington marked the high point of both civil rights struggle and of socialist hopes for realignment. Rustin organized the march along with A. Philip Randolph, the venerable African American labor leader and lifelong socialist for whom racial and economic justice were inseparable. Randolph asked Rustin to draw up a proposal aimed at civil rights, labor, and religious leaders for a mass march on the nation's capital to demand not only the dismantling of Jim Crow but also a public works program to provide jobs to the unemployed as well as a substantial raise in the minimum wage. Rustin did so with the assistance of Kahn and another young democratic socialist, Norman Hill. King was enthusiastic about the proposal, and all the major civil rights organizations eventually supported it. George Meany and the AFL-CIO declined to endorse it, but other labor leaders did, especially Reuther, whose UAW provided crucial backing.[23]

Horowitz and Kahn provided crucial assistance to Rustin in organizing the march. Horowitz organized transportation for thousands of marchers. Bob Dylan, who sang at the march, was a frequent guest in the apartment Horowitz shared with SNCC activist Joyce Ladner.[24] Kahn served as Rustin's chief aide and helped write speeches for Randolph and SNCC leader John Lewis. Even though the demand for economic justice was watered down by moderate civil rights leaders under pressure from the Kennedy administration, it remained a fundamental aspect of the March for Jobs and Freedom. The march also proved a pivotal moment in organizing what King and Randolph called a "Coalition of Conscience," which provided the pivotal pressure needed for Congress to pass the landmark Civil Rights Act of 1964 and Voting Rights Act of 1965.

The prospects for realignment never seemed better. A previously marginal group of socialists had been instrumental in organizing one of the largest and most successful demonstrations in American history. The day after hundreds of thousands marched to the Lincoln Memorial, the Socialist Party organized a two-day conference with speeches by King, Lewis, and Randolph. Left-liberal journalist I. F. Stone was so impressed by the conference that he concluded, "Socialism took on fresh meaning and revived urgency."[25]

A jubilant Shachtman delivered a speech, "Drive Out Dixiecrats for Jobs and Freedom." For Shachtman, the achievements of the civil rights movement were "milestone[s] on the road to . . . complete socialist democracy." Attaining the economic justice needed to make freedom a reality required breaking the power of the Republican-Dixiecrat coalition—"one of the most poisonous roots of the evil in this country"—that had blocked not just civil rights but all efforts to extend the New Deal.[26]

In a widely debated 1965 article in *Commentary*, Rustin wondered what the March on Washington coalition of "Negroes, trade unionists, liberals, and religious groups" might achieve if they engaged in a longer struggle to wrest control of the Democratic Party. Together they might effect a "qualitative transformation of fundamental institutions." Since the African American freedom struggle, which could not succeed "in the absence of radical programs for full employment, abolition of slums, [and] the reconstruction of our education system," such political change was necessary. Now advocating realignment along democratic socialist lines, Rustin advocated that the civil rights movement should move "From Protest to Politics." Rustin did not call for an end to mass demonstrations. But he did argue that the civil rights movement should focus on coalitional politics within the Democratic Party.[27]

The coalition that democratic socialists and Rustin advocated required an alliance between the civil rights movement and organized labor. After the March on Washington, Shachtman reasoned that, despite its "wretched" record on civil rights and failure to endorse the march, the AFL-CIO was the major social force pushing for jobs creation and the ally the civil rights movement most needed to promote social democratic policies.[28] Rustin sought to cement this coalition by creating the A. Philip Randolph Institute in 1965. Its main funding came from the AFL-CIO.

In 1966, Randolph and Rustin set forth an ambitious "Freedom Budget" that called for billions of federal dollars to be spent to provide a guaranteed job to anyone able to work and a guaranteed minimum income to anyone who could not. Shachtman suggested the document's name and Harrington worked on it along with AFL-CIO economists and liberal economist Leon Keyserling. Unlike Lyndon Johnson's overhyped and underfunded War on Poverty, the Freedom Budget would actually have ended poverty in the United States. The budget would have provided all Americans with medical care, decent housing, and a clean environment. African Americans would have especially benefited, but the policies were universal in scope, enabling alliances with other groups.

The Freedom Budget was strategically designed so that it might have a chance of being adopted if the Coalition of Conscience could keep the pressure on. To satisfy possible objections, it did not require raising taxes, but would be funded instead from the "growth dividend" of increasing prosperity. A wide range of civil rights, religious, liberal, and labor leaders endorsed it from Martin Luther King to the Americans for Democratic Action (ADA). The League for Industrial Democracy (LID), directed by Kahn, and the AFL-CIO Industrial Union Department printed and distributed nearly 200,000 copies of it. Randolph, Rustin, and Harrington made speaking tours to explain its principles.[29]

Fractured Coalition

The Freedom Budget demonstrated democratic socialists' newfound ability to influence the national agenda. Yet the prospect of its becoming national policy was always slim. The realignment strategy overestimated the forces available for a progressive majority. Even were the AFL-CIO fully on board, it had been unable to pass its top legislative priority—the repeal of the 1947 Taft-Hartley Act—with a Democratic supermajority in Congress. Also, even after Dixiecrats were driven out of the Democratic Party, they remained a powerful force for political reaction. Realignment proponents had wrongly predicted that after civil rights a new progressivism would emerge in the former states of the Confederacy. In 1960 Shachtman had claimed that a multiracial "true heir to the once flourishing Populist forces" would emerge in the South while in 1965 Rustin envisioned that even Mississippi might elect liberal or at least moderate congresspeople in significant numbers.[30]

The realignment strategy also overestimated the willingness of many White voters outside the South to support racial equality. In 1964, when the Democrats had won their congressional supermajority, a California fair housing law designed to eliminate racial discrimination was defeated by a 2 to 1 margin. It had been passed by a bipartisan legislature and signed by a liberal governor. In addition, even if the Freedom Budget did not call for increased taxes, it obviously redistributed economic and political power in a way that threatened the interests of economic elites.

In the short term, Democrats' disastrous performance in the 1966 midterm elections eroded any chance of passing even a scaled-down version of the Freedom Budget. In the longer term, the prospects for social-democratic policies were undermined by divisions within the liberal coalition precipitated by the escalation of the Vietnam War and the fractures that emerged within the African American Freedom Movement. The Freedom Budget sought to neutralize the war issue by claiming that the federal government had the resources to fund it regardless of whether the war continued. But this proved untenable. In a harsh yet prescient rejoinder to Rustin's "From Protest to Politics," his erstwhile pacifist comrade Staughton Lynd warned that working within the Democratic Party meant forming a "coalition with the marines."[31] So long as bombs kept falling on Hanoi, the New Left and the peace movement would remain alienated from the Democrats. Also, much of the energy of mass protest needed to push the Freedom Budget forward were siphoned away to the antiwar cause.

Two of the major civil rights organizations, SNCC and the Congress of Racial Equality (CORE), opposed the Vietnam War from the outset and starting in 1965 began advocating Black Power. Questioning the extent to which White liberals and organized labor really supported racial equality, they rejected coalitional politics in favor of organizing separate bases of power in African American communities. CORE's James Farmer dismissed the argument of "From Protest to Politics," claiming that Rustin "has no credibility in the black community . . . [his] commitment is to labor, not to the black man."[32]

Divisions among democratic socialists were a microcosm of the broader fractures emerging among American liberals. Democratic socialists had achieved their power through influence. They were important strategists, organizers, and intellectuals, but they were not leaders with any mass following. With the decline of the Coalition of Conscience, they needed to decide which social forces to attach themselves to. Committed to working within the Democratic Party, they could identify with one of its warring liberal factions: the AFL-CIO or its growing antiwar wing.

Rustin, Shachtman, Kahn, and Horowitz attached themselves to the AFL-CIO. From backing the more progressive wing of the labor leadership identified with Reuther, Shachtman's group moved toward an alliance with its more conservative wing as represented by Meany. In 1964, Don Slaiman, the most important union leader in Shachtman's circle, moved from the UAW to become the AFL-CIO's civil rights director. Rustin's Randolph Institute was financially reliant on AFL-CIO support. Several Shachtmanites took staff positions under Meany or his allies. Horowitz, for example, became political director at the American Federation of Teachers in the late 1960s, which was then fighting a bitter war against advocates of "community control" in African American neighborhoods in New York City.

The strategy of turning the AFL-CIO toward progressive ends had some early successes, as with Slaiman's role in helping push the 1964 Civil Rights Act through Congress. And the AFL-CIO leadership did back many social-democratic policies. However, it had little interest in building a mass movement of any kind. Meany once bragged that he had never walked a picket line. By allying with the AFL-CIO leadership, Shachtmanites cut themselves off from progressive stirrings within organized labor during the 1960s. They became captives of an AFL-CIO hierarchy that supported the Vietnam War and jealously guarded its influence in the Democratic Party against that of middle-class reformers and the new social movements.

Harrington, on the other hand, aligned himself with liberal intellectuals who revered him as the author of *The Other America*. He wrote frequently for liberal journals and served on the editorial board of *Dissent*, which continued to stake out a position on the socialist edge of the liberal movement. In 1966, Harrington joined the board of the ADA, the leading liberal organization. Thus, Harrington positioned himself within that part of the liberal coalition moving leftward.

Within the liberal milieu in which they operated, differences over the Vietnam War emerged slowly among democratic socialists. Shachtman supported the war. He abandoned his earlier third camp politics for a stance that backed capitalist democracies against Communists. In 1961, Shachtman shocked many of his comrades in Berkeley, California, when he declined to condemn the CIA-backed invasion of the Bay of Pigs at a meeting held the day after the event. Hal Draper, a leader of the Berkeley group, denounced Shachtman as a "State department socialist."[33] At a 1966 discussion among democratic socialists, Shachtman adamantly opposed American withdrawal from Vietnam and disparaged Harrington and Howe as "pacifists."[34]

Other democratic socialists opposed the war but silenced their views in the cause of coalitional politics. Rustin, for example, was surely one of the few Americans who became *less* outspoken against the war as it progressed. Having opposed it at the outset, Rustin grew increasingly fearful of alienating allies needed to pass his Freedom Budget. As he privately explained, he was "for peace but . . . did not want to make any enemies over Vietnam."[35] Even Harrington at first supported negotiated settlement rather than withdrawal, a position commonly adopted by liberal intellectuals who were uneasy about the war but did not want to alienate the Johnson administration. However, unlike his comrades, Harrington insisted from the outset that the realignment project was undermined not by the antiwar movement, but by the war itself. In 1965, he predicted that "the fate of Appalachia may well be determined in the jungles of Viet Nam": that the War on Poverty would be halted by the escalation of war.[36]

The realignment strategy had initially positioned democratic socialists on the leftmost edge of the liberal coalition. But now democratic socialists began attacking those on their left. They criticized the antiwar movement for tolerating a "totalitarian" element that supported Vietnamese Communists (an element they greatly exaggerated and miscast as "Stalinist").[37] But democratic socialists mainly faulted the antiwar movement for wrecking coalitional politics. In 1967, Kahn pleaded: "Let us, for God's sake, stop using the Negro as a political football—more accurately as a footnote to theses on Vietnam. How many more cities must explode before certain friends in the peace movement will abandon their deprecation of every economic proposal that does not simultaneously call for an end to the war in Vietnam?"[38] Similarly, Rustin criticized Black Power advocates for "divert[ing] the entire civil-rights movement from the hard task of developing strategies to realign the major parties of this country."[39] In policing the left, democratic socialists performed a useful service to more conservative elements of the Democratic Party such as the AFL-CIO leadership. Instead of nudging liberals to the left, they were being pushed rightward.

The contentious 1968 Democratic Party primary brought growing differences among liberals and democratic socialists to the surface. ADA liberals launched a "dump Johnson" movement to challenge the president's leadership over the war, leading some of its union backers to leave the organization. Senator Eugene McCarthy agreed to run, and his call for a negotiated settlement in Vietnam rallied antiwar Democrats. His surprising result in the New Hampshire primary led a beleaguered Johnson to drop out of the race, leaving Vice President Hubert Humphrey as the establishment candidate. At the Democratic convention that year in Chicago, police under the control of Democratic mayor and party powerbroker Richard Daley brutally beat antiwar protesters while party leaders attacked one another inside the convention hall.

Like the AFL-CIO, Shachtman and his followers lined up behind Humphrey. Harrington, however, endorsed McCarthy before switching to Robert F. Kennedy. Harrington contended that ending the war was a necessary precondition for building any liberal coalition. He observed that the Johnson administration had "de-escalated the struggle against poverty and racism every time it has escalated the attack in Southeast Asia." Most important, the war drove a wedge through the coalition of forces needed for progressive social change, separating the labor movement from "the Negroes, the liberal middle class, and others." Harrington maintained that building such a coalition within the Democratic Party remained "the only chance for humane transformations of America and, eventually, of America's role in the world."[40]

The growing rift between Harrington and his comrades resulted not just from the war itself but from Harrington's insistence on the political potential of what he called the "conscience constituency" and which he saw evident among antiwar Democrats. He introduced the phrase in his book *Toward a Democratic Majority*, published in June 1968 as struggles within the Democratic Party came to a head. The phrase echoed the "Coalition of Conscience," which Harrington sought to recreate under new conditions, while the change from "coalition" to "constituency" indicated his growing preoccupation with electoral politics.[41]

Harrington still insisted on the centrality of the organized working class to any left movement. And he shared comrades' concern that the "elitism" of the conscience constituency might lead it to scorn the working class. But unlike his comrades, he welcomed "educated people . . . who are driven to change the society not out of material need alone, but out of a spiritual and intellectual need as well." He concluded that "one who looks for a proletariat to save us from our sins in this country is going to wait until hell freezes over." Instead, change would have to come from a coalition that included both organized labor and the conscience constituency working together where the "real political struggle in the United States is taking place": within the Democratic Party.[42]

Harrington also argued that advanced capitalism produced contradictions that pushed the middle class toward democratic socialism. Here Harrington drew on *The New Industrial State*, a 1967 book by John Kenneth Galbraith, a liberal economist and ADA leader who had played a central early role in the McCarthy campaign. Galbraith theorized that the American economy was increasingly dominated by a "technostructure" that had replaced the traditional bourgeoisie with a managerial elite dedicated to long-term planning reliant on scientists and technicians. As Harrington saw it, this lent strategic power to intellectual workers who could not "be beaten like a serf or threatened with unemployment and hunger like a proletarian" and were "prone to critical thought and moved by non-material incentives."[43] Harrington hailed the political potential of this "new class" of "scientists, technicians, teachers and professionals in the public sector of the society."[44]

For Harrington, the 1968 election confirmed his analysis. Organized labor demonstrated its political strength, nearly bringing Humphrey an unlikely victory. The loyalty of working-class voters and racial minorities to the Democratic Party demonstrated the wisdom of the realignment strategy since "the Left must go where people are actually struggling to resolve the problems of their lives."[45] But the missing ingredient in 1968 was the conscience constituency, which had been demobilized by the Vietnam War and the Chicago convention. After 1968, Harrington devoted himself to achieving a coalition between organized labor and the conscience constituency that could produce a winning majority. Harrington admitted, "There are reason to fear that these different groups, all with a practical interest in the transformation of society, will war with one another rather than coalesce in a new radical majority eventually into a socialist movement. They have profound differences among themselves in style, tradition, and even in politics." But, he concluded, "they do share common interests, and it is the job of socialists in America to persuade them to act upon these interests."[46] With his links to both groups, Harrington was as well placed as anyone to foster this alliance. But his efforts were undermined by his closest comrades.

Socialists Divided

In 1968, Harrington was elected chair of the Socialist Party. Though he was the candidate of the party's Realignment faction, he already had irreconcilable differences with Shachtman and his followers. While Shachtmanites sought to capitalize on Harrington's national prominence, many also resented it. Some complained, for example, about how difficult it was to reach Harrington by telephone. More seriously, they charged Harrington with unaccountability when he voiced political views in the mainstream press that differed from those of the party.[47] Harrington no longer agreed with Shachtman, Horowitz, Kahn, and Rustin on how the Democratic Party should be realigned. While Harrington embraced the conscience constituency, his opponents blamed the New Politics wing of the Democratic Party for Humphrey's 1968 defeat. Tensions surfaced in 1969 when Kahn, as head of LID, decided to give its yearly award to Humphrey without consulting Harrington, LID's chair. Harrington boycotted the ceremony.[48]

Vietnam was the main issue in dispute. In 1969, Harrington came out in favor of unilateral withdrawal, breaking with the SP's continued stance in favor of negotiations.[49] The demand for a negotiated settlement had never accounted for the realities of the war in Vietnam: There was no reason for Vietnamese Communists to back down from their goal of national reunification if American troops withdrew. In supporting unilateral withdrawal, Harrington was years behind the New Left. But he was in step with liberals such as ADA leaders John Kenneth Galbraith and Arthur Schlesinger Jr. who like Harrington now concluded that they should have supported unilateral withdrawal from the outset.[50] In this context, Shachtmanites' continued insistence on a negotiated settlement meant continuation of the war. Nevertheless, Harrington continued to align himself with Shachtman's faction against those on the SP's left, such as David McReynolds, who shared his antiwar views.[51] At the 1970 party convention, Harrington supported a compromise resolution calling not for unilateral withdrawal but for a "just and viable political settlement."[52]

But differences over Vietnam could not be papered over. At that same party convention, a "Statement on Vietnam" circulated that was endorsed by Kahn, Shachtman, and others. It asserted that socialists were duty bound to support any regime fighting against communism. Anticipating the later argument of neoconservative Jeane Kirkpatrick, it claimed that the United States should support authoritarian but non-Communist governments such as the South Vietnamese one where democratic change would be more possible in the future. The statement concluded that unilateral withdrawal was "unwarranted and dangerous." Other than advocating democratic reforms in South Vietnam, this position was little different from Richard Nixon's.[53]

Harrington circulated a response, "Socialists and Reactionary Anti-Communism." Harrington argued that Shachtman's position was a "prescription for a savage, unwinnable, indeterminate war."[54] Privately, Harrington was outraged by his comrades' duplicity. Pushing for negotiations was actually "a way to fight the peace movement under the guise of being part of the peace movement."[55] As Harrington recalled, Shachtman was "for as many [negotiating] conditions as to make it impossible" for Vietnamese Communists "to cut a deal."[56]

After reading "Socialists and Reactionary Anti-Communism," Shachtman never spoke to Harrington again.[57] In retrospect, it seems incredible that it took Harrington two more years to publicly break with the Shachtmanites. Every year he stuck with them, he lost influence among young members of the conscience constituency. Harrington later concluded simply, "My organizational commitment overwhelmed my good sense for a while." Clearly, it was a painful personal choice for Harrington to break with comrades who had been not just political allies, but close friends. Yet perhaps the main reason why both Harrington and Shachtman delayed a factional split was because they hoped that even while disagreeing on foreign policy they could remain united in realigning the Democratic Party to support social-democratic policies at home.

The 1972 McGovern campaign finally forced a break. By the spring of 1972, Harrington had become an enthusiastic supporter of the McGovern primary campaign as demonstrating the conscience constituency's political power: "Some of us—myself most emphatically included—enormously *underestimated* the potential of the new strata as the McGovern campaign now so clearly shows."[58] Shachtman's faction, however, lined up with the AFL-CIO hierarchy who refused to endorse McGovern.

The Socialist Party's Shachtmanite-controlled national committee belatedly endorsed McGovern less than two months before the general election, though it did so while decrying his "neo-isolationist" foreign policy. Yet Harrington thought the party's leadership was actually "split between those who are straightforwardly for McGovern's defeat—and therefore for Nixon's victory—and those who privately share that attitude but, for tactical reasons, are unwilling to state it publicly."[59] Harrington's suspicion was justified. As Shachtman explained privately, he backed the McGovern endorsement to maintain party unity. But he saw no reason to actually support a "pathetic joker of a candidate" whom he "need[ed] like a double hernia."[60] While the SP's endorsement had zero impact on its own, Shachtmanites worked actively to justify Meany's consequential nonendorsement of McGovern.

Behind the debate over Vietnam was the larger question of what kind of a coalitional realignment democratic socialists should support. Harrington argued that opposition to the war was necessary to appeal to "the mass constituency of middle class liberalism and radicalism." But his opponents didn't think this conscience constituency was worth courting. In 1971, Shachtman and Rustin released a statement accusing Harrington of equating organized labor's power with that of "a group of intellectuals . . . [a] department of college professors."

For Shachtman's faction, "McGovernite" became a favorite term of abuse. Penn Kemble and Paul Feldman called for purging middle-class left-liberal reformers from the Democratic Party "because their disdain for the common man . . . [has] driven countless workers and lower-middle-class voters into political apathy or worse, into the arms of Nixon and Wallace."[61] In a 1972 article in the neoconservative magazine *Commentary*, Kemble criticized the McGovern-Fraser Commission's reforms of the Democratic Party as designed to "favor the affluent liberals within the party" as against organized labor.

Disdain for the "liberal intelligentsia" was rooted in decades of Shachtmanite thinking. In Shachtman's theory of "bureaucratic collectivism," the Bolshevik Revolution had been usurped by a new class of party leaders and intellectuals who took control of the state to serve their own interests. Now a new class threatened to take over the Democratic Party. New Politics liberals also reminded Shachtmanites of deluded fellow travelers of the Popular Front period who had misunderstood the true nature of the Soviet Union. Here Shachtmanites seized upon McGovern's previous support for Henry Wallace's 1948 Popular Front campaign for president.

Yet Shachtmanites' critique of McGovern supporters as a bureaucratic new class was deeply ironic. For by 1972, the Shachtmanites were financially dependent on the AFL-CIO leadership. Rustin directed the A. Philip Randolph Institute. Horowitz was on the staff of the American Federation of Teachers. Kemble directed the AFL-CIO's Frontlash program. Kahn began working for the AFL-CIO during the 1972 presidential campaign, after which he became Lane Kirkland's top adviser in its International Affairs division. In their attack on new class liberals, there may have been some psychological displacement for Shachtmanites seeking to reconcile their identity as tribunes of the working class with their actual positions as labor bureaucrats.

At the beginning of the 1960s, realignment had meant allying with the most progressive union leaders such as Reuther. In 1963 Shachtman had publicly attacked Meany as a coward for failing to endorse the March on Washington. Over time, though, Shacthmanites became prisoners of their belief that the AFL-CIO leadership was indispensable to any progressive realignment of the Democratic Party. Though they continued to speak of supporting a labor *movement*, they were now engaged not in the mass mobilization that characterizes a social movement but in the backroom politicking in which the AFL-CIO leadership specialized. They had now allied themselves with the most conservative elements of organized labor. The UAW split with the AFL-CIO in 1968, insurgency movements for internal democracy were growing within other established industrial unions, and public sector unions representing disproportionately female and nonwhite workers were growing in strength. This emerging, more progressive wing of organized labor enthusiastically supported McGovern when the AFL-CIO leadership declined to endorse him.

By attacking "McGovernites," Shachtmanites provided an important ideological service for Meany's AFL-CIO. McGovern's policies were actually the most pro-labor of any major presidential party candidate in American history. The author of a PhD dissertation on the Colorado coal strike that culminated in the infamous 1914 Ludlow Massacre, McGovern received top marks as a senator from the AFL-CIO's own political action wing.[62] McGovern couldn't be fairly attacked for his positions, though that didn't stop the AFL-CIO from trying. Still, the Shachtmanites' attack on McGovern supporters as a "new class" justified the AFL-CIO leadership's opposition to them. It allowed them to attack McGovern from the right while appearing to challenge him from the left, appearing to defend working-class interests rather than their own entrenched power.

The Shachtmanites' critique of the liberal "new class" also jibed with the emerging analysis of many neoconservative intellectuals such as the one-time Shachtmanite Irving Kristol. Shachtmanites played a key role in the formation of the Committee for a Democratic Majority (CDM), a key neoconservative organization founded in 1972 to wrest control of the Democratic Party back from the McGovern forces. Its founder, Ben Wattenberg, had developed an analysis similar to that of the Shachtmanites: that the party should back class-based New Deal–style social policies while avoiding "social issues" such as racism and sexism. Treating such "social issues" as noneconomic implicitly cast the real "working class" as the unionized older White workers represented by the AFL-CIO hierarchy.[63]

By misrepresenting the McGovern candidacy as a middle-class takeover of the Democratic Party, Shachtmanites also aided Meany's resistance to the party's efforts to accommodate the new social movements, especially feminism and gay rights. According to Harrington, Kahn wrote Meany's infamous speech after the Democratic Party convention in which he complained of convention delegates who "look like Jacks, acted like Jills, and had the odor of johns."[64] Shachtmanites' attack on middle-class "McGovernites" implicitly defended the overrepresentation of older White men such as AFL-CIO leaders within the Democratic Party. Their critique of the party reforms of the McGovern-Fraser Commission overlooked that the explicit impetus behind many of the reforms had been to better represent women and racial minorities.

Shachtmanites' critique of the new class allowed White men to displace their rage at being challenged by women and sexual and racial minorities onto upper-middle-class elitists. Shachtmanites, like other neoconservatives, were mostly Jewish. And, like the AFL-CIO leadership, they were overwhelmingly male. One female member of YPSL recalled the organization's "hard, masculine" style and its fear of "softness."[65] Shachtman's praise of Meany for having the "guts" not to support McGovern was telling. And though two of their leaders, Kahn and Rustin, were gay, Shachtmanites saw the gay rights movement as at best a distraction from class politics.

The Shachtmanites' style of factional warfare also jibed well with Meany's strategy in 1972. While ostensibly advocating a broad-based coalition, Shachtmanites actually prioritized their faction's control of the party. Shachtman was a brilliant in-fighter who had spent decades forming, splitting, and merging political parties to ensure that his own viewpoint prevailed. He naturally approved of Meany's strategy of ensuring a decisive McGovern defeat in 1972 in order to take back control of the Democratic Party. As an anonymous labor leader explained to the press: "If Nixon wins big against McGovern, if he makes McGovern the landslide victim of the seventies like Barry Goldwater in 1964, labor will be back on top in '76. And the left of the Democratic Party will again be centered around the labor movement."[66]

Conclusion

As the Shachtmanites hoped, McGovern lost big, but organized labor never recovered its status within the Democratic Party. In 1976, the Democrats nominated a candidate who came from neither the New Politics nor labor wings of the party. Instead of a willing ally of organized labor in George McGovern, the AFL-CIO got Jimmy Carter. Carter began a shift away from New Deal economic policies of the kind discussed in Samir Sonti's and Jean-Christian Vinel's chapters for this volume. That move would accelerate with a vengeance under his successor, Ronald Reagan. The AFL-CIO missed an opportunity to make key allies it needed in the 1970s in the face of deindustrialization and a business assault on unions. The AFL-CIO would in time seek allies in the liberal wing of the Democratic Party, especially after the 1995 election of a slate of insurgents led by John Sweeney. However, by this point the power of organized labor was substantially weakened. Shachtmanites had initially advanced the realignment strategy as a way to advance social-democratic policies. But aiding the AFL-CIO's sabotage of the McGovern campaign proved self-defeating. While Shachtmanite rhetoric about defending a traditional

White male working class from an elitist liberal professional-managerial class echoed widely in the twenty-first century, it did so not on the left but on the populist right that rallied around Donald Trump.

The version of realignment Harrington promoted following his break with the Shactmanites over the McGovern campaign was more promising. In his public letter of resignation as SP chair, Harrington denounced his former comrades' "obsessive anti-Communism" that had perversely led them to see "the main enemy, not in the multi-national corporations and the Nixon Administration, but in the 'New Politics' constituency."[67] Harrington's break with his comrades was a liberating one that allowed him to "get out of the factional closet and into the mass movement."[68] He wasted little time in forming the Democratic Socialist Organizing Committee (DSOC) in 1973.

DSOC was founded on the principle that "the left wing of realism is today found in the Democratic Party," as Harrington put it in the first *Newsletter* in a formulation that anticipated his more felicitous and better known phrase, "left wing of the possible."[69] This was but a restatement of the realignment strategy. DSOC's initial membership reflected the coalition Harrington sought to build: the group that split with Harrington from the SP, "veterans of the McGovern campaign," and progressive trade unionists. DSOC sought to unite the followers of what its leaders called "the three Georges": McGovern, Meany, and Wallace. Despite McGovern's loss, Harrington remained enthusiastic about the continued growth of a progressive conscience constituency. But any winning coalition would require healing "the split between anti-war liberals and Meany laborites" on the basis of the common economic programs of the ADA and AFL-CIO.[70]

DSOC sought to appeal to "trade unionists who fought for McGovern last fall, and trade unionists whom Richard Nixon is now teaching that they should have fought for McGovern last fall."[71] But, no longer concerned about upsetting Meany, Harrington was now free to support the more progressive elements within organized labor. Indeed, DSOC attracted a range of unionists including David Selden who challenged Albert Shanker's leadership of the American Federation of Teachers as well as a range of veteran progressive unionists including long-time UAW leaders Emil Mazey, Brendon Sexton, and Nat Weinberg. One of the vice chairs of DSOC was Victor Reuther, Walter's more radical brother who had organized labor opposition to the Vietnam War and chaired "Labor for McGovern" during the 1972 general election.

DSOC also appealed to feminists, whom Harrington now recognized had to figure in any future progressive coalition. Harrington had a long friendship with feminist Gloria Steinem and had (much to the chagrin of the Shachtmanites) endorsed Bella Abzug's Democratic campaign for Congress (discussed in Leandra Zarnow's chapter). However, Harrington's lack of working experience with feminists was evident at the DSOC founding convention in which all of the featured speakers were men. A Women's Caucus subsequently organized within DSOC raised this issue as well as the related one of the lack of women associated with *Dissent*. Yet, unlike the Shachtmanites who responded to the feminist challenge with defensiveness, Harrington was willing to learn and there was a place for feminists within DSOC.[72]

In the short term, DSOC's strategy of working within the Democratic Party bore little fruit. As the party shifted to the right, Harrington, like many of the other left-liberals who had been impressed with its possibilities for progressive change in the 1960s and early 1970s, was increasingly trapped within its structures. Harrington's contemporary heirs have rightly been more wary of such entrapment; Sanders, for example, remains formally independent of the Democratic Party though he operates within its structures. But DSOC left an institutional legacy that was strengthened in 1981 when it formed the Democratic Socialists of America (DSA) in a merger with the New America Movement made up of New Left veterans who had moved into electoral politics. But the realignment strategy's greatest successes would have to wait until the Sanders campaign.

The mass base of democratic socialism's revival in the 2010s was a strata of younger members of the professional-managerial class of the kind whose potential Harrington had once sensed among McGovern supporters. But they were not motivated purely by "conscience" as Harrington had once supposed but rather by how they had been proletarianized by the structural economic changes of neoliberalism. Some in DSA viewed Harrington's strategy of realignment as insufficiently radical, but the organization still won its greatest influence when it worked within the Democratic Party. Though socialists became important in Democratic Party politics for reasons Harrington had not foreseen, their success owed a debt to the realignment strategy he had honed along with other democratic socialists.

Notes

1. Roger Kerson, "Democratic Socialists of America Make a Strategy for the Biden Era," *In These Times*, Sept. 21, 2021. Accessed on Mar. 7, 2023 at https://inthesetimes.com/article/democratic-socialism-politics-election-dsa-convention-aoc.

2. *For the Record: The Report by the Social Democrats USA on the Resignation of Michael Harrington and His Attempt to Split the American Socialist Movement* (New York: Social Democrats USA, 1973), accessed at https://archive.org/details/ForTheRecord1973 on Sept. 24, 2021, p. 36.

3. Tom Kahn, "Max Shachtman: His Ideas and Movement," *Democratiya* 11 (Winter 2007): 258.

4. Michael Harrington, "Dear Comrades," n.d. [1973], Box 1, Democratic Socialists of America Records, Tamiment Library, New York University. The quote comes from Harrington's letter of resignation from Social Democrats, U.S.A., the organization controlled by Shachtmanites.

5. Peter Drucker, *Max Shachtman and His Left: A Socialist's Odyssey Through the "American Century"* (Atlantic Highlands, NJ: Humanities Press International, 1994).

6. Ibid., 190.

7. Ibid., 252.

8. Drucker, *Max Shachtman and His Left*; Julius Jacobson, "The Two Deaths of Max Shachtman," *New Politics* 10 (1973): 96–9.

9. Maurice Isserman, *The Other American: The Life of Michael Harrington* (New York: Public Affairs, 2000), 1–104.

10. Michael Harrington interviewed by David Hacker and Patricia Friend (August 19, 1988), Box 1, Folder 32, Maurice Isserman Research Files, Tamiment Library.

11. [Max Shachtman], "Toward a Political Realignment in America: A Socialist Declaration," Box 16, Folder 34, Max Shachtman Papers, Tamiment Library, p. 5.

12. Michael Harrington, "The New Left: The Relevance of Democratic Socialism," 1959.

13. Irving Howe, "A New Political Atmosphere in America," *Dissent* (Winter 1959), 8, 9.

14. Michael Harrington, *The Other America* (New York: Macmillan, 1962), 174. See John Kenneth Galbraith, *The Affluent Society* (Boston: Houghton Mifflin, 1958).

15. Isserman, *The Other American*, 208–20.

16. Isserman, *The Other American*, 223–25; Bernie Sanders, *Our Revolution* (New York: St. Martin's Press, 2016), 18–19.

17. Isserman, *The Other American*, 236–40.

18. Harrington, "Interview with Hacker and Friend," 14.

19. "The Port Huron Statement" (1962), reprinted in Richard Flacks and Nelson Lichtenstein, *The Port Huron Statement: Sources and Legacies of the New Left's Founding Manifesto* (Philadelphia: University of Pennsylvania Press, 2015), 271.

20. Shachtman, "Toward Political Realignment," Max Shachtman Papers, Box 16, Folder 34, p. 10.

21. Drucker, *Max Shachtman*, 269; John D'Emilio, *Lost Prophet: The Life and Times of Bayard Rustin* (Chicago: University of Chicago Press: 2004), 277–78.

22. Harrington, "Interview with Hacker and Friend," 9.

23. William P. Jones, *The March on Washington: Jobs, Freedom, and the Forgotten History of Civil Rights* (New York: W. W. Norton, 1963), 160–61.

24. Rachelle Horowitz, "Tom Kahn and the Fight for Democracy: A Political Portrait and Personal Recollection," *Democratiya* 11 (2007): 204.

25. As quoted in Paul Le Blanc and Michael D. Yates, *A Freedom Budget for All Americans: Recapturing the Promise of the Civil Rights Movement in the Struggle for Economic Justice* (New York: Monthly Review Press, 2013), 82.

26. Max Shachtman, "Drive Out Dixiecrats for Jobs and Freedom," *New America*, Sept. 24, 1963, p. 16.

27. Bayard Rustin, "From Protest to Politics," *Commentary* 39 (February 1965): 29, 28.

28. Shachtman, "Drive Out Dixiecrats," 16.

29. Le Blanc and Yates, *Freedom Budget*, 96–97.

30. Shachtman, "Toward Political Realignment," 5; Rustin, "From Protest to Politics," 30.

31. Staughton Lynd, "Coalition Politics or Nonviolent Revolution?," *Liberation* (1965).

32. Farmer as quoted in D'Emilio, *Lost Prophet*, 285.

33. Drucker, *Max Shachtman*, 279–81, Draper as quoted on 281.

34. Harrington, "Interview with Hacker and Friend," 17.

35. Le Blanc and Yates, *Freedom Budget*, 123.

36. Michael Harrington, "Poverty and Viet Nam," *New York Herald Tribune*, April 4, 1965, p. 16.

37. Isserman, *The Other American*, 158.

38. Tom Kahn, "The Riots and the Radicals," *Dissent*, Sept.–Oct. 1967, 525.

39. Bayard Rustin, "Black Power and Coalitional Politics," *Commentary* (Sept. 1966).

40. Michael Harrington, "Voting the Lesser Evil," *Commentary*, April 1968.

41. Michael Harrington, *Toward a Democratic Left* (New York: Macmillan, 1968), 290–92.

42. Michael Harrington, *Why I Am a Democratic Socialist* (New York: Young People's Socialist League), 13, 14.

43. Michael Harrington, "Liberalism According to Galbraith," *Commentary* 45 (Oct. 1967).

44. Harrington, *Toward a Democratic Left*, 290.

45. Michael Harrington, "The Road to 1972," *Dissent* (Jan. 1969), 12.

46. Michael Harrington, "Why We Need Socialism," *Dissent* (1970), 280.

47. *For the Record.*

48. Isserman, *The Other American*, 287–8.

49. Michael Harrington, "Getting Out of Vietnam," *Dissent* 17 (January–February 1970), 6–8.

50. Scott Kamen, "Making Room for Liberals in the Antiwar Movement: The Americans for Democratic Action and the Dilemma of Liberal Opposition to the Vietnam War," *Peace & Change* 44 (2019): 375–76, 384.

51. "Resolution on Vietnam (defeated)," Max Shachtman Papers, Box 18, Folder 14.

52. "Resolution on Vietnam (Accepted as amended)," Max Shachtman Papers, Box 18, Folder 14.

53. "Statement on Vietnam," Max Shachtman Papers, Box 18, Folder 14.

54. Michael Harrington, "Socialists and Reactionary Anti-Communism," Max Shachtman Papers, Box 18, Folder 18.

55. Harrington, "Interview with William Chafe," 28, Michael Harrington Papers, Box 7.

56. Harrington, "Interview with David Hacker and Patricia Friend," 19.

57. Harrington, "Interview with David Hacker and Patricia Friend," 20.

58. Harrington to "Comrades," June 29, 1972, Democratic Socialists of America, Box 1.

59. Harrington to Bayard and Sasha, Oct. 14, 1972, Democratic Socialists of America, Box 1.

60. Shachman to Ian McIntire, Sept. 28, 1972, Box 31, Folder 19, Max Shachtman Papers.

61. *For the Record.*

62. Jefferson Cowie, *Stayin' Alive: The 1970s and the Last Days of the Working Class* (New York: New Press, 2010), 106.

63. Richard M. Scammon and Ben J. Wattenberg, *The Real Majority* (New York: Coward-McCann, 1970).

64. Isserman, *The Other American*, 298.

65. Maurice Isserman, *If I Had a Hammer: The Death of the Old Left and the Birth of the New Left* (New York: Basic, 1987), 190.

66. Michael Kramer, "Early Warnings," *New York*, June 12, 1972, 10.

67. "Dear Comrades," Democratic Socialists of America Records, Tamiment Library, Box 1.

68. Harrington to "Comrades," June 29, 1972.

69. Harrington, "The Left Wing of Realism," *Newsletter of the Democratic Left*, Mar., 1973, 5.

70. Harrrington, "A Way Forward for Liberals," *Newsletter of the Democratic Left*, May, 1973, 1.

71. Harrington, "The New Shape of Our Politics," *Newsletter of the Democratic Left*, Mar., 1973, 1.

72. "Memo to the Women's Caucus of the DSOC," Box 1, DSOC Records.

CHAPTER 6

Gender Gap: Bella Abzug and Mim Kelber's Labor Feminist Critique of American Politics in the Late Twentieth Century

Leandra Zarnow

"As in other nations, the United States, throughout its history, has been marked by conflict between classes and social groups, between male rule and female subordination, between those who would reserve power only for a moneyed elite and those who say democracy must be shared by all the people," wrote Bella Abzug and Mim Kelber.[1] They delivered this incisive intersectional assessment of the structural inequities embedded in the US capitalist democratic system in the most unlikely of places: their 1984 book *Gender Gap: Bella Abzug's Guide to Political Power for American Women.*

Gender Gap provided one of the first participant accounts of feminist organizing in politics during the 1970s and helped introduce—as its title proclaimed—the concept of a gender gap in voting preferences. Determined to tell their version of "the born-again women's movement," Abzug and Kelber retraced a "long seeding process" in which women moved from the "drudgery of inter-party chores" to take on "the values and practices imposed by a male power structure that controlled both the economy and government." If women could further harness their voting power and gain more electoral offices, they imagined, the "possible dream" of a "women-ruled nation" might be achievable.[2] At the heart of this utopian vision lay a labor feminist critique of US global capitalism during what many historians now consider the neoliberal turn.[3]

Abzug and Kelber's incisive analysis in *Gender Gap* highlights just how much understandings of work, capitalism, and democracy had evolved since the bitter Roosevelt era battles covered in this volume's earlier sections. Coming into US Popular Front politics in their youth, Abzug and Kelber became important bridge organizers who helped position 1960s and 1970s protest movement politics to become a critical insurgent faction within the Democratic Party.[4] In the 1980s, they remained committed to the socialist-inflected feminist ideology they had earlier contributed to Democratic New Politics when Abzug served in the House of Representatives between 1971 and 1976. The congresswoman's role is more known than that of her Marxist sidekick and longtime speechwriter and advisor Kelber, who often pushed Abzug from pragmatism to radicalism. *Gender Gap* is a joint treatise in which they projected a shaky future for US democracy, but also a way out. Their answer reflected both their radical past and fresh research.

Abzug and Kelber believed that harnessing women's voting gender gap favoring Democrats could be useful not only for moderates, but leftists too. Analyzing exit polls from 1980 and 1982, they joined a chorus of journalists, political scientists, and organizers that noticed how women—a majority minority of the US population—were using their vote to reject President Ronald Reagan's agenda.[5] Seeing this credibility gap as positive, Abzug and Kelber argued women's vote must be harnessed to combat two negative gaps women faced in equal representation and economic parity. Progressive feminists, they contended, were the most primed to lead the effort to organize women to expand their political clout and achieve greater equity and justice in the United States and globally. The Reagan administration, with its family values politics and supply-side economics, was an obvious target. No less veiled, Abzug and Kelber delivered a simultaneous critique of Democrats touting austerity, corporatism, and privatization over economic security and social responsibility.

Gender Gap challenged Democrats' abandonment of values and commitments attached to the New Deal and Great Society. Abzug and Kelber found these earlier efforts to be inadequate, grounded especially in patriarchal, White-centric, and heteronormative belief systems. They were troubled by the consequential turn to rights talk void of analysis of entrenched structural inequities and the heightened feminization of work and poverty. These economic wrongs, they stressed, could only be righted with a gendered redistribution of power. For Abzug and Kelber, labor and feminism was not an either/or focus, and accordingly, labor and political historians should not treat identity politics as void of economic concerns.[6]

As I have argued elsewhere and Daniel Geary highlights in this volume, the New Politics wing of the Democratic Party lost its footing in the late twentieth century. Still, this period is more than an "age of fracture" in which conservative ascendancy pushed progressive ideas and organizing to the margins.[7] Rather, these transitional years should be considered as ones of sustained contestation. In the late twentieth century, longtime activists like Abzug and Kelber remained committed to actualizing a social democratic vision for change in the political arena as a noticeable counterpoint to Republican and neoliberal Democratic dominance. Accordingly, revisiting *Gender Gap* offers lessons for how to respond to difficult times of retrenchment with a posture that is equal parts sober and optimistic.

We Have to Continue That Struggle

It is unclear who came up with the idea of writing *Gender Gap* first. Working closely in the early 1980s, Kelber and Abzug entered a highly active period of reflection, reorganization, and public engagement. Closed out of insider channels in federal government, feminists created new institutions, established a foothold in the academy, and used the media as a platform. On January 12, 1979, Abzug lost considerable influence when unceremoniously fired by President Jimmy Carter from her position as co-director of his National Advisory Committee for Women (NACW). This group had publicly criticized the president's proposed budget for prioritizing military over social spending, arguing that it would hurt poor women and women of color most. As a result, White House aides decided Abzug, at the helm, had to go. She never got over this dismissal, but took advantage of public opinion being on her side. In February, March, and April, her appointment calendars reveal a packed schedule crisscrossing the nation to address colleges, clubs, and community groups.[8] This pattern of activity would continue into the 1980s. In March 1982, for instance, when the US-backed Contras attacked the Soviet-supported Sandinistas in Nicaragua, Abzug spoke at disarmament rallies and teach-ins at the Union Theological Seminary, Barnard College, University of Missouri, and New York University in the span of a week.[9] She drove home the argument in wide-ranging speeches that women, largely closed out of power and thus least responsible for globalization and militarization, could be a corrective force in global governance. Coming out of Abzug's shadow during this time, Mim Kelber increasingly penned her own editorials and delivered solo speeches while still drafting remarks for her friend. In 1979, Kelber outlined in *Ms.* how the "economy is a woman's issue," critiquing Carter's austerity politics and Cold War posturing.[10] Likewise in *Redbook*, Kelber determined a lack of money was the answer to the question, "Why has it been so difficult for them [women] to break into politics?"[11]

In *Gender Gap*, Abzug and Kelber provided readers with a sense of history that went beyond the prior decade. They deliberately connected recent rights-based struggles to a longer, continuous story of women's political engagement linked to the suffrage, peace, and abolitionist movements of the nineteenth and early twentieth centuries. Similarly, they compared the opening salvo of the 1980s to the political repression and policy conservatism of the 1920s. What they skipped over was their own coming of age story, one marked by shared engagement in anti-imperialist, pro-labor, and pacifist organizing at Walton High School in the Bronx and tuition-free, all-women Hunter College during the mid-1930s and early 1940s. Knowing this history is key to understanding how deeply their labor feminist analysis on display in *Gender Gap* is rooted in the intersectional class analysis they acquired as participants in the US Popular Front.

Abzug and Kelber—then Bella Savitzky and Miriam Kolkin—helped lead an interracial, left-liberal coalition at Hunter with Abzug as student body president and Kelber as managing editor of the *Hunter Bulletin*. Both were active in the American Student Union, where they organized to promote unionism, peace, and academic freedom while combating fascism and Jim Crow. "We had tremendous political battles in the student council over all the political issues of the day," Kelber recalled, "and we wrote about those things in the college paper."[12] These years also solidified their belief that women were capable decision-makers who should govern at every level.

Little historical attention has been devoted to Kelber, an important contributor to the feminist movement. Like Abzug, Kelber grew up in the South Bronx, where "radicalism was just part of the general atmosphere." A self-identified "red diaper baby," she read the radical press, Upton Sinclair's *The Jungle*, and Michael Gold's *Jews Without Money* at an early age. She did not see much of her father, a Communist Party and union organizer, especially after her parents divorced. Her mother worked long hours as a sewing machine operator, but the work was unstable, causing her to seek welfare. This impoverished upbringing solidified Kelber's radicalism. She did not hesitate to join the Young Communist League at Hunter, recalling, "By the time I got to college I was pretty clear in my political views."[13] She also identified as an atheist

Jew. Abzug, in contrast, was deeply religious and an ardent Zionist, attending the Jewish Theological Seminary alongside Hunter. Her early engagement in the socialist Zionist scouting movement Hashomer Hatzair nurtured her class consciousness. Likewise, her pacifist father's family business, the Live and Let Live Meat Market, provided an example of independent thinking. Abzug's Zionism never squared with Kelber, but she remained appreciative that her friend was "our broad element" on Hunter's campus.[14] Likewise, Abzug exhibited willingness to work with Communists despite finding the party's secularism and sectarianism off-putting.

After Hunter, Abzug and Kelber continued to participate in New York's Popular Front, a community increasingly beleaguered as the Cold War and domestic Red Scare set in. While Abzug attended Columbia Law School, one of nine women in her class, Kelber worked in the Washington bureau of Federated Press. In 1944, the year Abzug graduated, Kelber returned to New York as the national editor. In this position, she covered the United Nations founding convention in San Francisco in 1945, and labor actions such as the American Communications Association strike against Western Union in 1946.[15] Overseeing Betty Goldstein (the young Betty Friedan), Kelber commiserated with her about being the only women on their beat. Meanwhile, Abzug bailed out striking unionists in night court and appeared at National Labor Relations Board hearings, where labor leader clients were convinced being represented by "the *maidel*" would harm their negotiations.[16] Kelber devoted time to the Labor Press Unit of the Newspaper Guild as Abzug became active in the National Lawyers Guild. Both leftist professional organizations came under attack, and in turn, Abzug and Kelber were called before grand juries and placed under surveillance.[17]

In these years, Kelber and Abzug each raised two daughters. This shared experience brought them closer together when reconnecting as early members of Women Strike for Peace (WSP), a nuclear disarmament group founded in 1961. Advocating "women's vote is a peace vote," Abzug helped WSP become a national lobbying powerhouse that pushed for gender parity in politics alongside peace.[18] Kelber supported this political focus when some in the group leaned toward civil disobedience. At the onset of the Vietnam War, Abzug turned toward the Democratic Party after the American Labor Party fizzled, backing male antiwar politicians she calculated would move WSP's message forward. Kelber, in contrast, advocated forming a women's Lysistrata group (withholding sex) in protest of the war, a difference that reflected her separatist instincts.[19] In the late 1960s, both women increasingly expressed solidarity for and engaged in antipoverty, ethnic nationalist, and social liberationist movements. These currents came together in Abzug's 1970 campaign, which Kelber actively supported. Leading her New York congressional office, "Mimi" grounded Bella's big ideas and rounded out her words. The writer did not, however, speak for the orator. They hashed out particulars in heated conversations calmed by their shared ideology and common goals.

In the summer of 1979, Kelber helped Abzug pick up the pieces after being fired by President Carter. Their next venture, Women USA, introduced a feminist hotline delivering weekly commentary with the aim of reaching "the woman who is not a joiner, but wants to do something" and "be kept informed."[20] Abzug recruited former Hawaii Representative Patsy Takemoto Mink as vice president, former California Representative Yvonne Burke as treasurer, and journalist Gloria Steinem as secretary to bring weight to Women USA. Brownie Ledbetter, an Arkansas feminist whom Abzug met in the National Women's Political Caucus (NWPC), served as assistant treasurer, which amounted to funding the operation. At a high point, over 10,000 callers a month dialed in to 1-800-221-4945 to listen to Shirley MacLaine or Representative Barbara Mikulski addressing issues from domestic violence to the national budget. Women USA tried to make the leap from being a communication vehicle for feminism to a full-scale pressure group, with early actions including an antidraft lobbying effort on Capitol Hill and an anti-Carter "fed up with inflation" direct mailing campaign.[21] However, the fledgling organization proved unsustainable. Stalling its shuttering, the operation moved to Abzug's home with Kelber running day-to-day activities when they could no longer pay for office space or staff.

Women USA provided Kelber and Abzug with a venue to try out ideas and remain in public view. This effort was reinforced by Abzug's presence on the Cable News Network (CNN) as one of twenty-three inaugural commentators. For three years on most Mondays she offered her quick political takes on air.[22] Her first spot, naturally, took on Carter, telling viewers that the president "can't be certain of having a majority of the votes until the convention takes place—and that's still 10 weeks away."[23]

To no one's surprise, Abzug attended the DNC in August 1980 as a surrogate of longtime ally Senator Ted Kennedy, who had a strong showing in early primaries but no chance by the convention. Foremost on Abzug's mind was how to "best use" the presidential race "to advance the major goals of the women's movement" outlined at the National Women's Conference held in Houston in 1977.[24] She and Mink had shepherded through Congress

$5 million in appropriations to host this federal conference that served as the US corollary to the United Nations International Women's Year (IWY) initiative. After *The Spirit of Houston* report was delivered to Carter in 1978, Abzug co-led the National Advisory Committee for Women to keep the National Plan of Action moving forward, or so its members thought.[25] Carter, in contrast, treated the NWC as an endpoint and saw the NACW as a symbolic continuation group without real power.

Abzug and Kelber devoted considerable energy in *Gender Gap* to retelling the back-and-forth of this relationship of political disregard. Still reeling from disappointment in Carter, Abzug helped Kennedy draft his Economic Bill of Rights for Women.[26] Being a Kennedy surrogate meant less once at the DNC. Still, Abzug enjoyed considerable clout as a founder of the NWPC. She helped rally support for a plank to withhold funds from Democratic candidates who did not back the Equal Rights Amendment (ERA) and another to advocate for government funding of abortions. Both passed, demonstrating the continued influence of a feminist bloc within the Democratic Party she helped solidify. However, as Abzug and Kelber acknowledged, the planks also "helped sharpen the distinctions" between Republicans and Democrats going forward. And although women were "changing not only the face, but the structures and policies of the Democratic Party," the introduction of superdelegates at the 1984 DNC signaled the rebuff of this democratizing trend.[27]

As the general election progressed, Abzug increasingly feared that Carter would lose. "Yes, we have been" hard on "Carter & we will continue to press him, but the Carter admin's open to women's petitions and Reagan and the radical right are not," she wrote on a legal pad she carried around to draft speeches and collect her thoughts. Reagan's "defeat will be women's votes," she predicted incorrectly. More on point, she worried that "in 1960, 1968 & 1970, one more vote per precinct could have elect a dif. pres. & this vote could be even closer."[28] Abzug knew from her years analyzing women as swing voters for WSP that they could make a decisive difference. Her reading of women's increased voting strength was accurate, as was her expectation that they would lean toward Democrats. But this did not mean that Reagan would lose the election or that his following among women was weak. Quite the opposite. Abzug had been tracking conservative women's grassroots organizing since the Goldwater Coalition and spent much of the 1970s attempting to check Phyllis Schlafly's STOP ERA and anti-IWY acolytes.[29] This history made Abzug cautious even if hopeful.

Kelber was less optimistic. Days after the 1980 election, she told the Mid-Atlantic Association of Radical Historians that Reagan's presidency was "a very ominous development" and "we are in deep, deep trouble."[30] Her overlooked speech reveals the dark place many leftists inhabited after Reagan's sweeping win. Kelber predicted "major attacks on women's programs and a widening, tougher attempt to drive women out of the labor force." She expected "cuts in health, education, welfare, child care, the whole range of programs that affect women, the minorities, the poor, the elderly, and of course, the cities." She believed it inevitable that the ERA would fail "barring some miracle" and advocacy of Medicaid-funded abortions would end. Take note as well, she cautioned, how "Moynihan and other opportunists" in the Democratic Party were capitalizing on this rightward turn "to make the Democrats even more indistinguishable from the Republicans." As a result, leftists needed to refocus their energy "in ways more meaningful to the millions of women who are struggling for equal pay, for more job benefits, for economic justice." Feminists must also work at the heart of a global labor movement, "confronting the corporations and economic interests that profit from the direct exploitation of women." In closing, she encouraged, "We have to continue that struggle."[31]

Defining the Gender Gap

Mim Kelber believed this continued resistance should happen in intellectual spaces as much as the streets. She preferred deliberative analytical work, more comfortable with writing than delivering speeches. She read Adam Clymer's decisive analysis of election returns in the *New York Times* with keen interest, seeing it as a silver lining in the 1980 election. He saw Reagan's win as a vote against Carter and found it significant that 8 percent fewer women than men voted for Reagan. "Both fear about war and his opposition to the equal rights amendment handicapped Mr. Reagan's bid for their support," Clymer characterized of women voters.[32] Clearly pleased, Kelber shared these findings at the Mid-Atlantic Association of Radical Historians conference, expanding his analysis to show how women made a difference in federal elections since 1952.

Kelber also relayed what she learned to Abzug, who had been tracking election returns as well. Their back-and-forth is captured in the robust marginalia overlaid on polling data that Kelber collected and Abzug thought significant enough to save, adding comments like "explain this please."[33] These figures confirmed that women continued to make a district-level difference swinging election outcomes, an observation Abzug first had tracking voter behavior for WSP in the early 1960s. Convinced by the data, Kelber and

Abzug decided to refocus Women USA's program on voter education and registration, testing the waters with a national lobbying day.

In February 1982, around 3,000 people representing over eighty labor, civil rights, feminist, religious, and educational groups participated in this action on Women's Rights Day. Mary Tyler Moore and Gloria Steinem joined Abzug in a House call with Speaker Thomas P. "Tip" O'Neill, a celebrity sit-down reporters made sure to cover. Yet, it was the range of groups from Catholics for a Free Choice to the United Auto Workers that gained the most attention. "There are those who say that the women's movement is dead," commented Republican Representative Margaret Heckler. "We are here to prove that the women's movement is very much alive," she assured.[34] Tying together bodily rights and economic security, lobbyists joined sympathetic legislators in hearings on the Hill challenging a proposed Human Life Amendment and defending Social Security.

Women USA collaborated with the National Organization for Women (NOW) in this lobbying day effort. NOW President Eleanor Smeal, who had a master's degree in political science, had also been persuaded by Clymer's article. With the ERA campaign stalling three states short of ratification, Smeal determined, "we needed a strategy to give women more direct political clout."[35] She enlisted her political director Molly Yard and Yard's assistant Betsy Dunn to compile the report "Women Can Make the Difference." This pamphlet was the first to use the term "gender gap," popularized after journalist Judy Mann cited NOW noting the "gender gap has steadily increased" since the election.[36]

Abzug and Kelber thought NOW's singular focus on the ERA missed the mark. Instead, they believed the voting gender gap reflected in part diverse women voters' economic concerns, which the ERA alone did not adequately address. As a result, only a comprehensive, localized organizing effort would activate this voter power. As the 1982 midterms approached, Women USA employed "A Woman's Vote Counts" campaign in six states—California, Iowa, Missouri, Ohio, Oregon, and Texas—to cultivate grassroots coalitions and recruit more women candidates. Organizers surveyed voters in targeted areas and immediately publicized the results to help stimulate interracial, cross-class partnerships as a "model for mobilizing the majority."[37]

Alongside this ground-level activism, Kelber and Abzug prioritized connecting with academics doing cutting-edge research in women and politics, a field just coming into form.[38] Abzug, known for late night strategy phone calls, reveled in this opportunity to talk with smart women doing innovative research. Some brainstorming sessions were so impactful they received mention in *Gender Gap.* In a section titled "Coalitions and Collective Efforts," Abzug and Kelber recounted how invigorating it was to spend "a weekend at Frances Lear's Vermont home, discussing our next steps for advancing women's role in the political process" in the summer of 1982. Little record exists of who gathered at this retreat hosted by Lear (and those to follow at her New York City apartment), a prominent feminist booster and soon-to-be ex-wife of *All in the Family* producer Norman Lear. This "small group of leaders in the women's rights movement, academics who have studied the role of women in politics, and women who now hold or have held elective office" likely closely aligned with the names on Women USA's letterhead.[39] Abzug and Kelber retold this story of collaboration in *Gender Gap* because they understood intellectual production to be a key facet of movement development. They also saw a link between their unrealized ideas—developing a feminist think tank—and tangible action—organizing to get out the vote during the 1982 midterms.

After returns came in, Abzug and Kelber decided that a book explaining how and why a voting gender gap mattered in the last two national elections would help boost the prospects of defeating President Reagan in 1984. Yet, more than Reagan occupied their thoughts when they were writing *Gender Gap*. They retraced a string of disappointments feminists faced when trying to compel male Democratic leaders to seriously consider women's economic and social needs alongside their political rights and ambitions. The wounds still fresh, they faulted Carter most. His economic program, they told *Gender Gap* readers, was "hardly more palatable" than Reagan's. However, Carter's credibility gap with these feminists resulted from more than economics. In his 1982 memoir, *Keeping the Faith*, Carter, "alone with his word processor in his Plains, Georgia home, far away from the pressure groups and pesty feminists . . . drew a blank on women." "They are not in the book. Nowhere," Abzug and Kelber reported, their annoyance unguarded.[40] This erasure fueled their determination to write *Gender Gap*, while participation in a network of activists and academics kindled their spirits.

Studying Gender and Politics

Abzug and Kelber approached the 1982 midterm results much as they had before: sifting through raw data with the help of interpretive works by political scientists, reporters, and advocacy groups.[41] Once they determined to write *Gender Gap*, they enlisted political scientist Carol F. Casey to help forecast the 1984 election results. This was a natural fit. They had first worked with Casey in the 1970s when she served as a staff analyst at the Congressional Research Service.[42] A meticulous practitioner, she paired up with Kelber again under the auspices of Women USA. At a meeting the group sponsored in September 1981, Casey offered a state-by-state report of voters' partisan leanings and highlighted the need for a targeted voter registration campaign to shift individual precincts.

Building on prior research, Casey developed three models that could result in Reagan's defeat that Abzug and Kelber highlighted in their book. Plan one focused on securing a male Democratic candidate that could excite women, while attracting minority and White male working-class voters; here Casey predicted a 5.8 percent win over Reagan with a 10.7 percent gender gap. The next path determined that if another Republican candidate besides Reagan ran, the margin narrowed to a 2.2 percent lead for Democrats and 7.4 percent gender gap. The final "real squeaker" projected a male Democratic nominee could beat a Republican candidate besides Reagan by "a mere 1.4 percent, with a gender gap of 4.1 percent" if that Republican selected a woman vice president. Yet, if Reagan dropped George H. W. Bush for a woman, "the gesture in itself would not be enough to compensate for his antiwoman record," and if this switch happened and a Democrat also ran with a woman, this Republican gesture "would be canceled out."[43] This prediction buoyed Kelber and Abzug to make the case for a woman vice president while promoting *Gender Gap.*

Their ongoing conversations with Ruth B. Mandel further cemented their sense of purpose in *Gender Gap* to provide an organizing guide directed at potential voters and candidates alike. A Jewish refugee with a PhD in English, Mandel shifted focus after volunteering at the Eagleton Institute's Center for the American Woman and Politics (CAWP) at Rutgers University, founded in 1971. Two years later, she became the director, a position she held until 1994. Mandel found the divide between candidates and the scholars who studied them to be artificial. Public-minded academics, she believed, should tell prospective candidates, "We need you."[44] In this spirit, she published *In the Running* in 1981, the first book to analyze the representation and experience of women in politics that used Eagleton Institute data collected since the mid-1970s. Mandel had interviewed Abzug for the book, who appreciated her sympathetic rendering of the obstacles she had faced when campaigning and serving in Congress. This back-and-forth, in turn, shaped Abzug and

Kelber's articulation of who "Ms. Supercandidate" might be and what she faced in the 1980s.[45]

Mandel led Abzug and Kelber toward the conclusion that the American public harbored unconscious resistance to more women in office. Yet, it was data they collected from a "Survey of Elected Women Officials" Abzug developed and administered in June 1983 that shaped their analysis most. These results were not a sound sample, for Abzug only sent the survey to thirteen women politicians she knew well such as Barbara Boxer and Ann Richards.[46] Abzug's qualitative questions brought forward expected anecdotal responses. To a query about campaign obstacles, Dianne Feinstein, then mayor of San Francisco, wrote, "Getting people to take my candidacy seriously."[47] Similarly, Pat Schroeder quipped, "Everything was an obstacle!"[48] On voting tendencies, Barbara Mikulski reflected that the gender gap in politics is about "not only fighting for women's rights, it's for fighting for women's values."[49] Abzug's accompanying handwritten notes show how she studied the backgrounds of respondents and looked for patterns across their experience. While not a wide sampling, her survey reveals that she instinctively understood part of the gender gap story should be the impediments women faced as candidates and legislators.

For quantitative data, Abzug and Kelber called on academics connected to two emergent centers of gender and politics research. Sociologist Alice Rossi led a team of graduate students at the Social and Demographic Research Institute at the University of Massachusetts, Amherst. While Rossi studied and published on the gender gap, her work analyzing the participants of the 1977 National Women's Conference influenced Abzug and Kelber more. A Carter-appointed commissioner, Rossi immediately saw the value in completing a "systematic study of the impact of the conference" as she wished the same kind of research had been done on suffragists.[50] Before, during, and after the conference, she surveyed delegates on their view of politics, their range of community-based and national activity, and their political aspirations. This form of demographic analysis at this scale was truly pathbreaking. Rossi's resulting book, *Feminists in Politics: A Panel Analysis of the First National Women's Conference*, came out in 1982, just as Kelber and Abzug were beginning research for *Gender Gap*. "The Spirit of Houston" chapter in their book highlights Rossi's major findings, giving intellectual weight to their personal account of the NWC as a historic gathering.

Abzug and Kelber also kept abreast of work done at the University of Michigan's Survey Research Center, where innovative feminist researchers used a controlled survey approach to isolate analysis of gendered practices in voting behavior. Marjorie Lansing and Sandra Baxter modeled how this could be done in their 1980 book, *Women and Politics: The Invisible Majority*, drawing on Lansing's dissertation research. Lansing taught the first women's studies course at Eastern Michigan University and Baxter forged a career as a government statistician. Abzug and Kelber believed their conclusion in *Women and Politics* was on point and quoted it at length: "Elizabeth Cady Stanton was right: the real obstacle to equality was not the vote but the division of lifestyles between men and women—and it was only as women became 'self-supporting equal partners with men'" that they could be a political force.[51]

Finally, Abzug and Kelber worked with political scientist Ethel Klein, who taught at Harvard University and authored the 1982 book *Gender Politics: From Consciousness to Mass Politics*. Women USA commissioned Klein to conduct postelection polling with Barbara Farah, an affiliate of the Russell Sage Foundation who also taught at the University of Michigan.[52] Significantly, Klein and Farah shared that their polling revealed the majority of respondents saw economic concerns as the most important issue in the election. While job security was foremost on voters' minds, "they were more concerned with the specifics of economic survival than the more broadly defined aspects of economic health that include inflation and interest rates."[53]

These findings squared with what CBS News pollster Dotty Lynch had also reported. Women and men had different opinions on social policy, but "almost no difference in partisan orientation or support until 1980." The biggest difference that created a divide was not the ERA or Reagan's hawkish foreign policy, but rather his "competence in handling the economy."[54] Besides academic studies, Abzug and Kelber drew on research by advocacy groups including those they helped form such as the Coalition of Women on the Budget that brought together organizations from NOW to the Girl Scouts. In March 1983, they issued a report concluding the "reason for the 'gender gap' . . . should no longer be a mystery." Echoing the controversial point made by the NACW in 1979, the report asserted, "Women understand that the cumulative effects of the budget cut on women . . . are unfair and place an unconscionable burden on them."[55]

By spring 1983, Abzug and Kelber were far along in their research and ready to preview their *Gender Gap* argument. Abzug did so in a CNN spot that aired in March 1983. In it, she predicted that women voters would hold President Reagan accountable for his economic and foreign policies that hurt them most, for "American women are finally becoming a vocal majority." "Of course, their full clout has not yet been felt in Washington—or in their paychecks. But with the ides of March approaching, the polls certainly suggest the President has reason to beware," she warned.[56]

In *Gender Gap*, Abzug and Kelber more fully delineated the connections between economic and political power. The fact that women did not "occupy the seats of power" was "more than a gap"; it was "a wide and deep chasm," they argued. And "yet another entrenched gender gap" faced women—"the one that keeps women locked up in an economic ghetto and enriches American industry and business by billions of dollars."[57] Thus, because women's lack of political representation exacerbated their economic precarity as a whole group, it was essential for them to take collective action as voters to demand greater rights and protections. In other words, increasing their political clout would make leaders more accountable. With greater women in office to follow, they assumed, more progressive outcomes could be achieved.

In making this case, Kelber and Abzug revealed their difference in approach from other feminist leaders. As in Eleanor Smeal's 1984 book, *Why and How Women Will Elect the Next President*, Abzug and Kelber used the popularizing language of choice and nodded to White middle-class interests.[58] Yet, what set their work apart from Smeal's was its greater attention to the concerns of women of color, working-class women, and women living in poverty. After the ERA failed, Abzug and Kelber sought to move the conversation forward. Legal personhood, they reminded, was about more than equalizing the law in the area of sex discrimination. They incorporated the language of antipoverty activists and unionists working for labor and welfare rights, liberally using the term economic justice. Their insight that "the feminization of poverty leads directly to the feminization of politics" reflected this orientation.[59]

In *Gender Gap*, Kelber and Abzug drew on their ideological grounding in the US Popular Front, where they first gained an intersectional understanding of how the "labor question" interacted with race and gender. Equally, they called upon recent conversations they had with women's rights activists working around the globe, many of whom critiqued US human rights discourse as not doing enough to address economic parity. These influences, new and old, shaped their view that a racialized and gendered class critique was necessary to combat women's precarious status during the Reagan presidency, which they correctly saw as a reactive effort to constrict gains of 1960s and 1970s rights movements. World War II, they argued, created an economic disruption that brought more women into the workforce and brought them "smack up against the sexist barriers of occupational segregation, pervasive discrimination, and the continuing wage gap."[60] Seeing this long pattern of neglect and discrimination led first to a mass feminist movement and ultimately a growing partisan gender gap.

While Abzug and Kelber were attentive to race, *Gender Gap* could have delivered a more thorough treatment of the mutual struggles against White and male supremacy alongside their class critique. They did this work better in an editorial timed with their book's release that critiqued Reagan's State of the Union address. Reagan's "cosmetic, callous and unconvincing" response to the gender gap was clear in the example he made of Black business owner Barbara Proctor. Reagan suggested Proctor "rose from a ghetto to build a multimillion dollar advertising agency," a fictitious Horatio Alger narrative that Proctor herself punctured, revealing that she achieved economic success with the help of federal loans and affirmative action laws. Kelber and Abzug highlighted this "atypical case" to stress that the reality for many American women was quite different. "Only one percent of American women earn more than $25,000; three out of five working women earn less than $10,000; and the wage gap for black women is 54 cents on the dollar and 49 cents for Hispanic women—if they are fortunate enough to have jobs," they reported. For the gender gap to swing Reagan's way, they predicted, he would have to "stop picking their pockets."[61]

Abzug and Kelber considered a confluence of domestic and global concerns, arguing that more women in power would help alleviate a male-made mess of "international economic problems" and quite possibly stave off "nuclear holocaust." Two chapters—"The Possible Dream," imagining a woman as president, and "The Bella Abzug Agenda," outlining a progressive future—dealt with the ongoing Cold War, linking this lengthy conflict to the expansion of US-led global capitalism. At their most prescient, they cautioned that the United States was "caught in an international economic crisis that its own policies have helped to create" that would only get worse. In this unfair system, women had the most to lose. Around the globe, they "make up one third of the world's official labor forces but work twice as many hours as men—for much less pay" and "receive only 10 percent of its income, and own less than 1 percent of private property." At home, "American women, too, are the majority of the poor."[62]

The Bella Abzug Agenda

Abzug and Kelber delivered their strongest anticapitalist, justice-centered argument in their book's final chapter. They talked openly of an ongoing "conflict between classes" linked to "male rule and female subordination." They also challenged what they saw as a daily assault on basic human rights by the Reagan administration. "Eating every day, having work, shelter, clothing, education, and health care are ideas that will never go out of style, no matter how much heads of corporations hope that robots will replace human beings and that women will meekly continue to accept lower wages and inferior status," they asserted.[63] Here, they directly responded to White House officials' criticism of feminists' gender gap campaign, which one aide characterized as "the Bella Abzug agenda." This "liberal agenda" is "contrary to the Reagan philosophy," a Reagan advisor encouraged in the press; it would put the nation "back 40 years to the bankrupt ideas that have failed before."[64]

Kelber and Abzug's most biting economic critique did not spare Democrats. "The Democratic Party, too, must take responsibility for the state of our nation," they emphasized. Party leadership have "allowed the boundaries of national debate to move to the right, while millions of Americans who provide the base of support for the Democrats are moving in the other direction." They saw the shift underway from being a party of social welfare and collective security to one that advocated a tradition of rights and multiculturalism tied to individualism. While correct in this view, they nonetheless believed that "millions of Americans" could and would still move toward their progressive vision of democracy. They presented this program in their book's final pages, outlining an agenda that closely resembles progressive Democrats in the twenty-first century: a nationalized health care system, federally funded childcare, expanded welfare, environmental safety, improved public transportation, retooling the economy in the service of labor, equal access to abortion, full employment, and equal rights and opportunity for all. Their simple funding solution is also one that progressive Democrats still imagine could work: Capital "will come from the benefits of full employment, reforming the tax structure, and cutting the Pentagon budget."[65]

It is striking that Abzug and Kelber decided to end their book on this overtly leftist note "without shame or apology."[66] Even so, Kelber, more than Abzug, understood their outlined agenda to be greatly aspirational. As she admitted in a 1983 oral interview, "There is a left, but it's a fairly small left, in this country, we specialize in fireworks politics."[67] More pragmatic than many leftists, Abzug focused primarily in 1984 on the singular purpose of pressuring Democratic presidential nominee Walter Mondale to select a woman as his running mate. This goal—the narrowest path to victory outlined in *Gender Gap*—became the primary focus of feminists who had gathered at Frances Lear's think sessions, ultimately spurring the Women's Presidential Project. Joining a growing chorus, Abzug asked, "Why not a woman vice president?" in a *New York Times* editorial.[68] Addressing a different crowd in *The Nation*, Kelber worried out loud, "The GOP just might one-up the Democrats in 1988 by selecting Jeane Kirkpatrick or some other American version of Margaret Thatcher to balance the ticket and restore its eroding base among women voters."[69]

Abzug and Kelber understood it was a long shot, but a risk they believed worth taking because the political glass ceiling would not break without cracks. Still influencers, they encouraged women to boycott the election if Mondale did not make good on this ask. Responding to this pressure campaign, he picked Queens Representative Geraldine A. Ferraro, who had publicly noted, "I am committed to having a Democrat defeat Ronald Reagan. I don't think we should be talking about a possibility of women staying home."[70] Ferraro, in Kelber's view, was a "more malleable" establishment favorite than her pick, Representative Patricia Schroeder of Colorado.[71]

Mondale's historic selection of Ferraro did little to move the needle forward for feminists or Democrats. Instead, this vice presidential pick revealed an underlying voter perception that identity politics were divorced from economics and the primary reason that a woman would be added to a presidential ticket was to benefit the former at the expense of the latter. In an exit poll conducted by ABC, only 11 percent of voters deemed Ferraro on the ticket as important. This same poll found that among men, 29 percent noted that they were less likely to vote Democratic because of Ferraro, while 12 percent said they were more likely. Among women, 19 percent noted Ferraro motivated them to vote Democratic, whereas 24 percent found Ferraro's nomination prompted them to vote Republican. Assessing these results, Mary Thornton of the *Washington Post* concluded, the "so-called 'gender gap' . . . has narrowed somewhat."[72]

Some journalists had already indicated, "The Gender Gap: It May Cut Both Ways," before the outcome of the 1984 election had been determined.[73] Abzug and Kelber paid close attention to this coverage when working on *Gender Gap*, concerned this assessment might be true. Most troubling to them, Reagan aides openly discussed cultivating a "male vote" to be a counterweight to feminist-oriented women voters. "It's the fact that Ronald Reagan is very popular among men and he is taking the male vote away from the Democrats," commented Michael K. Deaver, his deputy chief of staff.[74] Abzug and Kelber found Republican women's response to the gender gap less concerning. Elizabeth Dole led the charge with a much discussed 1982 editorial, "The Real Gender Gap," in which she argued that the gender gap was "not political but financial and legal."[75] Thereafter, President Reagan tapped her to lead a White House Coordinating Council on Women to help "demonstrate our compassion, gentleness and caring."[76] Dole believed the disconnect between women and Reagan was temporary. Republicans needed to convince women that they were the party that would underwrite their career advancement. Indeed, Dole paved the way for Republicans to claim women's empowerment as a tenet of free-market individualism.

Kelber and Abzug did not anticipate this dialogic shift. After the 1984 election, they penned editorials trying to make sense of what went wrong that largely pointed the finger at moderate Democrats. "It would be disastrous to think that the party should abandon its base among women, minorities and working people," they warned in the *New York Times*. They believed that new voters would be attracted to "the gender gap issues of peace and economic justice" and called on fellow Democrats to adjust the party's traditional bread-and-butter issues to be more relevant to a diversifying populace.[77] The new constraints of a globalizing economy with a feminized service sector, outsourced industrial jobs, new immigration, and stagnating wages had to be addressed. Likewise, the campaign for greater inclusion must be tied to workers' economic concerns.

It is instructive to return to *Gender Gap* in the twenty-first century, particularly after President Donald Trump's 2016 and 2024 elections made the "Reagan Revolution" seem tame. In both instances, Trump overcame Democratic Party nominees who were women: first former Secretary of State Hillary Clinton and next Vice President Kamala Harris. In both campaigns, journalists predicted a widespread gender gap that ultimately did not lead to the first woman president. A few months out, pollsters expected a gender gap of 18 points on Election Day in 2024. In the end, it was a 10 percent divide with 45 percent of women and 55 of men voting for Trump. This difference fell lower than the 12 percent gender gap that helped boost President Joe Biden in 2020 and is close to the spread that convinced Abzug and Kelber in 1980 to study how the gender gap could be harnessed for progressive purposes.[78]

Revisiting *Gender Gap* can help us understand what did not unfold as much as what could be. After the 1984 election, Abzug and Kelber were forced to face the reality that a growing gender gap did not preclude a Republican presidential victory. Their work would continue, shifting increasingly toward global feminist organizing as they became further disillusioned with the prospects of progressive change in the United States. While *Gender Gap* did not predict an election outcome, it did leave behind a record of activism and a blueprint for political organizing worth a second look. It traced a recent past where feminists called out Democrats for lukewarm support of women candidates and superficial lip service to the diverse needs of diverse American women. And it mapped out how these women of diverse backgrounds might help forge a progressive coalition to offset a growing conservative opposition buoyed by neoliberal acquiescence. This counterforce in the Democratic Party, reasserting its might since Trump first took office, has been important in a period where economic disparities are obfuscated using the language of empowerment to mask entitlement.[79] What *Gender Gap* reminds us most is that it is essential to clearly and creatively address this economic heart of identity politics.

Notes

1. Bella Abzug with Mim Kelber, *Gender Gap: Bella Abzug's Guide to Political Power for American Women* (Boston: Houghton Mifflin, 1984), 240. I refer to Abzug and Kelber as co-authors to acknowledge their full collaboration. For drafts and reviews, Boxes 954, 955, and 956, Bella Abzug Papers, Rare Book and Manuscript Library, Columbia University, New York [hereafter: BSA]; Folder 8, Box 27, Mim Kelber Papers, Archives and Special Collections, Hunter College, New York [hereafter: MK].

2. Abzug and Kelber, *Gender Gap*, 8, 17.

3. Gary Gerstle, *The Rise and Fall of the Neoliberal Order: America and the World in the Free Market Era* (Oxford, UK: Oxford University Press, 2022); Kim Phillips-Fein, "The History of Neoliberalism," in *Shaped by the State: Toward a New Political History of the Twentieth Century*, ed. Brent Cebul, Lily Geismer, and Mason B. Williams (Chicago: University of Chicago Press, 2019), 347–362.

4. See also Bruce Miroff, *The Liberal's Moment: The McGovern Insurgency and the Identity Crisis of the Democratic Party* (Lawrence: University Press of Kansas, 2007); and Leandra Zarnow, *Battling Bella: The Protest Politics of Bella Abzug* (Cambridge, MA: Harvard University Press, 2019).

5. For the best early collection, *The Politics of Gender Gap: The Social Construction of Political Influence* (Newbury Park, CA: Sage Press, 1988). See also *Voting the Gender Gap*, ed. Lois Duke Whitaker (Urbana: University of Illinois Press, 2008); *Political Women and American Democracy*, ed. Christina Wolbrecht, Karn Beckwith, and Lisa Baldez (Cambridge, UK: Cambridge University Press, 2008); *Gender and Elections: Shaping the Future of American Politics*, ed. Susan J. Carroll and Richard L. Fox (Cambridge, UK: Cambridge University Press, 2018, 4th ed.).

6. Studies attentive to labor feminism include Katherine Turk, *Equality on Trial: Gender and Rights in the Modern American Workplace* (Philadelphia: University of Pennsylvania Press, 2016); and Dorothy Sue Cobble, *The Other Women's Movement: Workplace Justice and Social Rights in Modern America* (Princeton, NJ: Princeton University Press, 2004).

7. Works include Daniel T. Rogers, *Age of Fracture* (Cambridge, MA: Harvard University Press, 2012); Marjorie Spruill, *Divided We Stand: The Battle over Women's Rights and Family Values That Polarized American Politics* (New York: Bloomsbury, 2017); Lily Geismer, *Left Behind: The Democrats' Failed Attempt to Solve Inequality* (New York: Public Affairs, 2022).

8. Zarnow, *Battling Bella*, 288–295; February–April 1979, "Calendars—1978–80, 1982, 1983," Box 920, BSA.

9. March 1982 Calendar, ibid.

10. Kelber, "What Bella Knew: NO, it was a little thing—like her personality, it was a big thing—like his power," *Ms.*, April 1979, in *The Bella Abzug Reader*, ed. Kelber and Libby Bassett (New York: Self-published by Mim and Harry Kelber, 2003), 153–155, 153.

11. Kelber, "How Women Are Changing Our Political Landscape," *Redbook*, November 1979, *The Bella Abzug Reader*, 156–161, 156.

12. "Reminisces of Miriam Kelber," Interview by Ken Miller, February 14, 1983, 20, Columbia Center for Oral History Archives, Columbia University [hereafter: Kelber OHRO].

13. Kelber OHRO, 19, 22–23; Zarnow, *Battling Bella*, 12–39.

14. Kelber quoted in Suzanne Braun Levine and Mary Thom, *Bella Abzug: How One Tough Broad from the Bronx Fought Jim Crow and, Joe McCarthy, Pissed Off Jimmy Carter, Battled for the Rights of Women and Workers, Rallied Against War and for the Planet, Shook Up Politics Along the Way* (New York: Farrar, Straus and Giroux, 2007), 16.

15. Kelber OHRO, 4; Miriam Kolkin (Kelber), "Hopes of Common People Hang on San Francisco Outcome," *Federated Press*, April 19, 1945, Folder 328, Box 22, Betty Friedan Papers, Schlesinger Library, Harvard University; Kolkin, "Union Lawyer Disturbs Western Union Agenda," *Federated Press*, April 11, 1946, Folder 329, ibid.; Daniel Horowitz, *Betty Friedan and the Making of the Feminine Mystique: The American Left, the Cold War, and Modern Feminism* (Amherst, Mass.: University of Massachusetts Press, 1998), 102–120.

16. Reminisces of Bella Abzug, 1995 and 1996, 88, Columbia Center for Oral History Archives, Columbia University [hereafter: Abzug OHRO].

17. Kelber OHRO, 6–17; Abzug OHRO, 287.

18. Amy Swerdlow, *Women Strike for Peace: Traditional Motherhood and Radical Politics in the 1960s* (Chicago: University of Chicago Press, 1993); Zarnow, *Battling Bella*, 39–63.

19. Karli and Laura Kelber, Interviewed by Leandra Zarnow, June 6, 2011, Brooklyn, New York.

20. Abzug quoted in Randi Henderson, "Bella Abzug: It's Not If She Runs but When," *The Sun*, February 19, 1980, B1.

21. Abzug, "Dear Friend," October 1, 1979, "Women USA Inflation Mailing (Send Your Bills to Congress) Oct. 79," Box 1006, BSA; Margaret Mason to Abzug, September 11, 1980, "Women USA—Margaret Mason, Memos," Box 1008, ibid.

22. Judy Flander, "Commentators Clamor for Attention at CNN," *On Cable*, November 1981, 17–20; and Author unknown, "Cable Courts Women," *On Cable*, January 1981, 19–22, "Cable News Network Agreement," Box 1020.

23. Abzug, "CNN Spot," June 5, 1980, "CNN, June 1980–Sept. 1980," Box 1019, BSA

24. Abzug, "A Proposed Strategy for Women in the 1980 Election Campaign," Confidential Memo, December 21, 1979, "Democratic Convention, 1980," Box 968, BSA.

25. *The Spirit of Houston: An Official Report to the President, the Congress and the People of the United States* (Washington, DC: US Government Printing Office, 1978).

26. "Women Leaders Endorse Kennedy," *Washington Post*, March 10, 1980, A3; Abzug and Kelber, *Gender Gap*, 81.

27. Abzug and Kelber, *Gender Gap*, 85, 86.

28. Abzug, Handwritten Notes, n.d., "Democratic Convention 1980," Box 969, BSA.

29. Spruill, *Divided We Stand*; Zarnow, *Battling Bella*; Donald Critchlow, *Phyllis Schlafly and Grassroots Conservatism: A Woman's Crusade* (Princeton, NJ: Princeton University Press, 2005).

30. Kelber, "Speech to the Mid-Atlantic Association of Radical Historians," November 14, 1980, *The Bella Abzug Reader*, 185–195, 188.

31. Kelber, "Speech to the Mid-Atlantic Association of Radical Historians," 193, 194.

32. Adam Clymer, "Displeasure with Carter Turned Many to Reagan," *New York Times*, November 9, 1980, 28; quoted in Kelber, "Speech to the Mid-Atlantic Association of Radical Historians," 188; Abzug and Kelber, *Gender Gap*, 215.

33. Abzug notation on "Vote by Sex in Presidential Elections, 1952–1980," n.d., "Gender Gap: Bella Abzug with Mim Kelber—Research Materials—Voting Records, Polls, Statistics," Box 954, BSA.

34. Margaret Heckler quoted in Leslie Bennetts, "A Day of Lobbying for Women's Rights," *New York Times*, February 6, 1981, B6; Abzug and Kelber, *Gender Gap*, 214.

35. Eleanor Smeal, *Why and How Women Will Elect the Next President* (New York: Harper & Row, 1984), 10; Carol M. Mueller, "The Empowerment of Women: Polling and the Women's Voting Bloc," in *The Politics of Gender Gap: The Social Construction of Political Influence* (Newbury Park, CA: Sage Press, 1988), 16–36; Kathy Bonk, "The Selling of the 'Gender Gap': The Role of Organized Feminism," ibid., 82–101.

36. Judy Mann, "Women," *Washington Post*, October 16, 198, C1.

37. Abzug and Kelber, *Gender Gap*, 218.

38. Lois Duke Whitaker, "Introduction," in *Voting the Gender Gap*, ed. Loise Duke Whitaker (Urbana, IL: University of Illinois Press, 2008), 1–8, 3; Barbara Norrander, "The Gender Gaps," in ibid., 9–32.

39. Abzug and Kelber, *Gender Gap*, 222, 227; "Frances Lear, a Mercurial Figure of the Media and a Magazine Founder, Dead at 73," *New York Times*, October 1, 1996, B10.

40. Abzug and Kelber, *Gender Gap*, 53, 95; Jimmy Carter, *Keeping Faith: Memoirs of a President* (Westminster, MD: Bantam Books, 1982).

41. Research material with Abzug's notations, "Manuscript, Gender Gap (1st draft), Bella Abzug with Mim Kelber—Misc. Related Articles, Research Materials," Box 954, BSA; "Polls (CBS News, Wash Post) 1983," ibid.; "Voting Records, Polls, Statistics," ibid.; "Untitled," Box 956, BSA.

42. Carol F. Casey, "Election Campaigns: Organizational Strategies and Techniques: A Select Annotated Bibliography," Congressional Research Service Reports, Library of Congress, November 1, 1975.

43. Abzug and Kelber, *Gender Gap*, 203.

44. Ruth B. Mandel quoted in Kathleen Hendrix, "Women in Politics: See How They Run," *Los Angeles Times*, November 24, 1982, F1.

45. Abzug and Kelber, *Gender Gap*, 152, 168; Mandel, *In the Running: The New Woman Candidate* (New Haven, CT: Ticknor & Fields, 1981); "Ruth B. Mandel, a Voice for Women in Politics, Dies at 81," *New York Times*, April 11, 2020. Abzug and Kelber also credited Mandel's colleague at CAWP, Kathy Stanwick.

46. Those surveyed were Barbara Boxer, Dianne Feinstein, Katie Hall, Barbara Kennelly, Madeline Kanin, Barbara Mikulski, Patsy Mink, Ann Richards, Claudine Schneider, Pat Schroeder, Olympia Snowe, Kathy Whitmire, and Harriett Woods. "Untitled," Box 956, BSA.

47. Feinstein, "Survey of Elected Women Officials," Response, 1, ibid.

48. Schroeder, "Survey of Elected Women Officials," Response, 1, ibid.

49. Mikulski, "Survey of Elected Women Officials," Response, 9, ibid.

50. The Social and Demographic Research Institute records have not been saved and Alice S. Rossi's papers at the Schlesinger Library do not pertain to this research. Rossi, *Feminists in Politics: A Panel Analysis of the First National Women's Conference* (New York: Academic Press, 1982), xxiii; "Alice S. Rossi, Feminist Icon": https://www.veteranfeministsofamerica.org/legacy/ALICE%20ROSSI.htm; *Gender Gap*, 60, 113.

51. Marjorie Lansing and Sandra Baxter, *Women and Politics: The Invisible Majority* (Ann Arbor, MI: University of Michigan Press, 1980); Abzug and Kelber, *Gender Gap*, 109; Robert C. Grady and David W. Hortin, "In Memoriam: Marjorie Lansing," *PSOnline*, September 1998, 647: https://www.cambridge.org/core/services/aop-cambridge-core/content/view/0DB8D4C1CCFD8BDB9662164D780D099A/S1049096500055025a.pdf/marjorie_lansing.pdf.

52. Ethel Klein, *Gender Politics: From Consciousness to Mass Politics* (Cambridge, MA: Harvard University Press, 1984); Abzug and Kelber, *Gender Gap*, 220–222; Ethel Klein: https://cawp.rutgers.edu/ethel-klein-legacy-fund; Denise L. Baer, "Political Parties; The Missing Variable in Women and Politics Research," *Political Research Quarterly* 46, no. 3 (September 1993): 547–576.

53. Barbara Farah and Klein quoted in Abzug and Kelber, *Gender Gap*, 221; "The Women's Vote," n.d., "Manuscript: Gender Gap—Chapter 3 and 9," Box 954, BSA.

54. Lynch, "Women, Reagan and Economic Justice," n.d., 1–3, 1, 2, "Gender Gap: Bella Abzug with Mim Kelber—Research Materials—Voting Records, Polls, Statistics," Box 954, BSA; Paul Vitello, "Dotty Lynch, Pollster Who Saw the Gender Gap, Is Dead at 69," *New York Times*, August 11, 2014. Abzug and Kelber also drew on work by Kathleen Frankovic, Martin Plissner, Elda Vale, and Laurily Epstein of CBS, Jeffrey Alderman and Peter Begans at ABC, and Democratic strategist Curtis Gans, *Gender Gap*, viii.

55. Coalition of Women on the Budget, "Inequality of Sacrifice: The Impact of the Reagan Budget on Women," March 1983, quoted in Abzug and Kelber, *Gender Gap*, 146, see generally, 145–147, 214–215.

56. "Women and Reagan," March 7, 1983, "CNN Spot, Jan. 3, 1983 through June 14, 1983," Box 1020, BSA.

57. Abzug and Kelber, *Gender Gap*, 4.

58. *Why and How Women Will Elect the Next President* and *Gender Gap* were reviewed together. Barry Sussman, "The Sexual Balance of Power," *Book World*, March 4, 1984; Nancy J. Walker, "Making Women's Votes Count," *New York Times*, March 11, 1984, 10.

59. Abzug and Kelber, *Gender Gap*, 115.

60. Abzug and Kelber, *Gender Gap*, 17.

61. Abzug and Kelber, "Women vs. Reagan," *New York Times*, February 12, 1984, E19.

62. Abzug and Kelber, *Gender Gap*, 14, 240.

63. Ibid., 240.

64. Unnamed White House official quoted in Juan Williams, "Reagan's Aides Say Gender Gap Is GOP Problem," *Washington Post*, September 9, 1983, A1.

65. Abzug and Kelber, *Gender Gap*, 238, 240.

66. Ibid., 240.

67. Kelber OHRO, 35.

68. Abzug, "Why Not a Woman Vice President?" *New York Times*, November 10, 1983, G7; Alison Muscatine, "Women to Meet with Mondale on Choice of Running Mate," *Washington Post*, June 28, 1984, A12; Robert Shogan, "Women's Group Asks Democrats to Take Stands," *Los Angeles Times*, April 20, 1983, B16; Abzug and Kelber, *Gender Gap*, 227–228.

69. Kelber, "The De-feminization of the Democratic Party," *The Nation*, May 1, 1984, *The Bella Abzug Reader*, 243–249, 249.

70. Abzug and Geraldine Ferraro quoted in Jane Perlez, "Democratic Women Split on Best Strategy for '84," *New York Times*, May 10, 1983, A20.

71. Kelber, "The De-feminization of the Democratic Party," 244.

72. Mary Thornton, "Ferraro Loss Shadows Gains by Women: Exit Polls Suggest 'Gender Gap' Narrowed," *Washington Post*, November 8, 1984, A46.

73. Ellen Goodman, "The Gender Gap: It May Cut Both Ways," *The Sun*, July 29, 1983, A15.

74. Michael K. Deaver quoted in Juan Williams, "White House Sees Two Sides to Gender Gap," *Washington Post*, July 25, 1983, A1. For Abzug's analysis of Republican strategy, "Repubs. and Gender Gap," Box 956, BSA.

75. Elizabeth Dole, "The Real Gender Gap," *Christian Science Monitor*, October 29, 1982, 23.

76. White House Coordinating Council Report quoted in Marissa Chappell, "Reagan's 'Gender Gap' Strategy and the Limitations of Free-Market Feminism," *Journal of Policy History* 24, no. 1 (2012): 115–134, 118.

77. Abzug and Kelber, "Despite the Reagan Sweep, a Gender Gap Remains," *New York Times*, November 23, 1984, A35.

78. Mike Allen, "Gender Gap Widens Support for Harris vs. Trump: Poll," *Axios*, September 2, 2024; Amanda Becker, "Harris Lost Support from Women Overall—but Not Women over 65," *The 19th*, November 20, 2024. Breaking down the gender gap by race, age, religion, and education, "Gender Differences in 2024 Vote Choice Are Similar to Most Recent Presidential Elections," Center for American Women in Politics, https://cawp.rutgers.edu/blog/gender-differences-2024-presidential-vote

79. Zarnow, "'Send Her Back': Trump's Feud with Feminists and Conservative Women's Triumph" and Michael Kazin, "The Path of Most Resistance: How Democrats Battled Trump and Moved Left," in *The Presidency of Donald J. Trump: A First Historical Assessment*, ed. Julian Zelizer (Princeton, NJ: Princeton University Press, 2022), 121–143, 335–350.

PART III

Adrift in a New World Order

CHAPTER 7

"We're Taking All the Risks and They're Getting All the Profits": Capitalism, Labor, and Democracy in the Wastelands of Southeastern Louisiana

Jennifer Klein

The landscape of St. Gabriel Prison Camp for women festered with stagnant pools of water, impassible mud, raw sewage flowing through open ditches, torn screens, and rotting wood. The decaying camp, fifteen miles south of Baton Rouge, Louisiana, lay between the East Bank of the Mississippi River and the vast Spanish Lake Basin wetland. Rain always meant flooding and extensive mud. Thunderstorms, hurricanes, tornadoes brought worse: collapsed buildings, blown-away roofs, downed electrical poles, ruined foodstuffs. These environmental nuisances were not new to the incarcerated women; the Women's Division of the Louisiana State Penitentiary had only relocated from Angola to St. Gabriel in 1961. In both locales, the conditions of incarcerated existence—smells, sights, sounds, eating, sleeping, waking, laboring—were defined by a constant battle with and through the torrential riverine ecology and, in prisoners' own words, "violent climatic conditions."[1]

Climate, weather, and topography are not solely responsible for this area's historic significance. Since the 1890s, southeast Louisiana from Baton Rouge to New Orleans, approximately 100 miles along the west and east banks of the Mississippi River, has been the site of a leper colony, psychiatric hospital, various prisons, chemical and oil plants, waste storage facilities, and hazardous waste sites. The area both literally and figuratively has been a prison, a repository of expulsion and waste—chemical, medical, social. Powerful institutions classified, circumscribed, and used people in particular ways. Eighteenth-century French colonialists laid waste to Indigenous riverside villages and mounds, enslaved Native peoples, and destroyed natural levees to turn land into divisible property. Nineteenth-century slave-plantation sugar cultivation bundled human and extrahuman nature in particular ways with severe deleterious effects. During the US Civil War, Union troops deliberately burned or sabotaged sugar plantations; new forms of confinement institutions for expelled individuals subsequently took root on those cast-off sugar plantations. Beginning in the mid-twentieth century, a state-subsidized chemical industry disgorged and emitted massive amounts of waste as a part of its daily functions.

The dominant modes of capitalist production here reveal how capitalism is a mode of organizing nature—the web of life that, as Jason W. Moore explains, includes human organization and "extra-human flows, relations, and substances." Capitalism survives by compelling the web of life to work harder and harder—for free or at very low cost. Looking at the geographical layers of human experience, we can see how energy (the capacity to do work)—by humans and nonhuman actors—is transformed into value, wealth, and hierarchies of power.[2] The degradation of human and nonhuman in this area makes it *useful* for capitalists and the state as opportunities to offload waste. A sacrifice zone,[3] though, is never a static place of dumping. It always sets up a new phase of appropriation and exploitation and thus capital accumulation. Once people have been turned into wasted humans they become part of a calculation or supply of unpaid energy (labor power) and nature. They get reintegrated back into the process of capital accumulation because they can be exploited and appropriated on the cheap.

Those processes made southeast Louisiana into the Chemical Corridor and "Cancer Alley." Yet Louisiana, by the end of the twentieth century, held another notorious distinction: the highest rate of incarceration in the United States, far exceeding the national rate. This was true not only for adults but also for children; both populations faced persistent physical abuse and extended periods of solitary isolation.[4] Louisiana developed an entire political economy of incarceration over a century and a half that involved expulsion, marginalization, compulsory labor, and commodity production and sale. The landscape of incarceration both predated the chemical industry and eventually overlapped with it geographically and functionally. It linked expendable nature and expendable bodies.

Louisiana's Chemical Corridor has also been a site of conflict and struggle. State officials labored to attract petrochemical industries after World War II.

Along with prewar oil companies, those businesses quickly dominated Louisiana's politics and environment. That power did not go unchallenged. In the 1970s and 1980s, Louisianans became aware of how dangerous chemicals and waste were. They fought to clean up and protect the area's free and unfree residents. Black and White communities, rural and urban, actively demanded aggressive state intervention. They wanted the regulation and oversight that the liberal and countercultural thinkers in Reuel Schiller's chapter had spent the 1960s and 1970s attacking. But the US Environmental Protection Agency (EPA) and Louisiana's new Department of Environmental Quality (DEQ) showed, for a time, how such agencies could enhance the democratic process; EPA and DEQ became a partner to people, communities, and groups in the way that the activists in Daniel Geary's and Leandra Zarnow's chapters would have applauded. Chemical and waste removal enterprises had too much power in Louisiana, pressuring the legislature and other government officials to underfund and understaff DEQ and subvert the environmental movement with which it was allied.

Making a Petrochemical Gold Coast

The chemical industry took firm root in southeastern Louisiana and the state government during World War II. Wartime contracts paid firms to make essential materials such as synthetic rubber and nylon. Legislators and voters wanted industrial development to continue. They amended the state constitution in 1946 to make a ten-year tax exemption on all property taxes and ad valorem taxes (state, parish, and municipal) permanent. Any corporation that moved into Louisiana from elsewhere or even relocated within the state was eligible. Companies could also reapply for an extension of that exemption for another five to ten years if they made capital improvements. The State Board of Commerce and Industry (BCI) then consolidated control over all elements of what state boosters called the "Right to Profit" law. No public employees or elected officials sat on this board, just business executives whom the governor appointed. BCI did a lot of work for a state eager for industry. They sent recruiters around the country to lure companies to Louisiana, reviewed applications for tax exemption, granted the tax breaks, and ensured companies had unrestrained prerogatives once they arrived.[5]

Postwar recruitment had deep connections to the state's antebellum past. One pamphlet promised a "Petrochemical Gold Coast," where "steel towers and tanks" existed alongside "the familiar moss-draped cypresses, the antebellum plantations, the fields of sugar cane, and lovely bayous."[6] That unapologetic nod to the slave South befitted the powerful board, whose members continued to serve regardless of electoral turnover. It operated unchecked, unregulated, and unaccountable to the state legislature, to the parishes wherein companies settled, or to voters and residents in those localities.[7]

Southeast Louisiana appealed to chemical companies. Raw materials, like salt and sulfur, as well as plentiful, cheap gas supplies were important to those businesses. But the three reasons most companies gave for moving were promised tax exemptions or a "favorable tax picture" (sometimes both were given); access to raw materials; an abundant water supply; and use of the river. "Available labor supply" and "friendly labor supply" frequently appeared in the 5,000 tax-exemption applications that the BCI approved by the early 1970s, polite answers that other firms moving into other parts of the then-emergent Sunbelt also gave.[8]

Chemical firms benefited from how sugar had transformed an area where sugar (not cotton) had once been king. After the Civil War, a new sugar oligarchy arose among White creoles, "Anglo" Southerners, and Northern transplants. These same parishes would become the strongholds of the powerful chemical and oil industry. Chemical and oil companies bought out the plantations with the best features, including access to the river and a "Big House" serving as corporate offices molded into the nostalgic grandeur of old plantation society. DuPont Chemicals located on the site of Belle Pointe and Sunnyside Plantations. Beker Industries Corp. (which processed sulfuric acid, phosphoric acid, and diamonium phosphate) moved into Hahnville (once the Native village of Quinipissa) and then the Hahn Sugar Plantation and Flagg Home Place Plantation. After Union Carbide bought the Star Plantation, management used the old plantation house as its offices. Freeport Chemicals and Mosaic Agrico split the former Uncle Sam Plantation, and Hercules Chemical built in Plaquemine, once Chitimacha lands.[9] Marathon Petroleum constructed its refinery in the 1970s on the former San Francisco Plantation, which is, as the company still avows, "a designated National Historic Landmark."[10]

Nearby African American landholders and communities had little say in who or what would be neighboring them. Southeast Louisiana had a checkerboard pattern of large, White-owned plantations, interspersed with small African American land holdings and freetowns or freedmen's towns. Those farms and hamlets could be traced back to the US Freedmen's Bureau, which had actually given former slaves some acres during Louisiana's comparatively radical Reconstruction. Among the African American freetowns, many of which were unincorporated, that got sucked into the orbit of the chemical economy were Geismar, Diamond, Sunshine, Morrisonville, Alsen, and Scotlandville. African American residents lacked the ability or power to influence zoning and land use matters as the chemical industry moved in, especially before passage of the 1965 Voting Rights Act.[11] Chemical plant clusters quickly formed in East Baton Rouge Parish around Alsen and Baker; Iberville Parish, especially in and around St. Gabriel, Sunshine, Reveilletown, Morrisonville, and Carville; Ascension Parish in Geismar; and St. Charles in Good Hope and Norco.

Those freetowns were not the only reminders of chattel slavery; the many African Americans imprisoned reflected how the lower Mississippi plantation landscape had been reformulated as a territory of expulsion, confinement, and coercion. Northeast of Baton Rouge lay the notorious Angola State Penitentiary; separately, it maintained 2,200 acres of sugar land at St. Gabriel in Iberville Parish as a prison camp extension for African American male inmates since 1906. Prisoners at Angola and St. Gabriel spent their days cultivating cotton, cutting cane, and pressing sugar—the two slave crops of Louisiana—until the 1970s.[12] Overcrowding and violence at Angola pushed the Board of Institutions to relocate female prisoners and the Women's Division to the decaying prison farm at St. Gabriel in 1961. The dilapidated prison farm expanded alongside the area's growing petrochemical sector. Even state officials described the repurposed, segregated St. Gabriel as a "miserable facility," so "deplorable" it posed "a definite health hazard."[13]

Women did not do the field work that men had done at St. Gabriel. St. Gabriel's inmates made clothing and textile products for reform and correctional schools, state penal institutions, parish jails, state hospitals, and rehabilitation centers in the prison's garment factory. There were no medical facilities or medical personnel on site for the prisoners, whom reformers, journalists, and state officials called "forgotten women."[14]

The minors upriver from St. Gabriel in the State Industrial School for Colored Youth (SISCY) were also overlooked. SISCY opened as a youth detention center for both boys and girls on the former Loveland Plantation in 1946.[15] Numbers perpetually rose. By the end of the 1960s, at least 60 percent of the juveniles held there came from Orleans Parish about ninety miles away. As multiple observers at the time noted, "the juvenile correctional institutions are not used solely for commitment of delinquents"; many "mentally retarded," "emotionally disturbed," "neglected, or dependent juveniles" were held in "primitive dormitories" with "abuse meted out wantonly." Youth inmates, like adults at St. Gabriel, also had to work but minors toiled in fields and in a canning plant.[16]

The penitentiary, prison farm, and SISCY, as well as the former freetowns, were a part of the rapidly developing Chemical Corridor that produced one-fifth of US petrochemicals by the late 1970s. Over 130 chemical plants and oil refineries came to occupy both sides of the Mississippi River across parts of a dozen parishes. The sector burgeoned, until all the basic building blocks of the industry (nearly 200 different chemicals) were produced in southeast Louisiana, including petrochemicals, inorganic chemicals, fertilizers, plastic feedstocks, resins, rubber, and elastomers.[17] Besides the river, 26,000 miles of pipeline and "a web of canals [that] cut through pastures and marshlands" facilitated transport.[18]

From Waste Problem to Economic Opportunity

Politics protected petrochemical plants' power, but the millions of tons of hazardous waste they produced could not be contained; expulsion and waste were central to the operation of these companies. By the early 1980s, firms in East Baton Rouge, Iberville, and Geismar/Ascension were among the top generators of hazardous waste in Louisiana. Sometimes a firm had plants in two of those locales. These include Allied Chemical in Baton Rouge and Geismar, American Hoechst, BASF, Ciba-Giegy, Cos-Mar, Dow, Ethyl Corp., Exxon Chemical, Kaiser, Marathon, Monsanto, Ohmatede, Regency Chemical, Rubicon, Rollins Environmental, and Stauffer.[19]

Initially, firms disposed of almost all of their waste in land-based forms, typically untreated and unregulated. Firms used landfills, waste pits, holding ponds, storage lagoons, injection wells, salt domes, and other underground caves. Iberville Parish contained each of these forms. Whether above ground or underground, they tended to be unlined or improperly lined. The sites never underwent any initial review for impacts to human health, drinking water, or the environment more generally. This waste, primarily in liquid form, was discharged into streams, swamps, and marshes, with the assumption that these natural bodies of water would absorb it or flush it out to the sea via the river.[20]

Waste seriously impacted rural parishes' unincorporated townships, hamlets, villages, small farms, sugar plantations, and prisons. Chemical production processes involved continuous, high-volume usage of water; they also expunged massive amounts of wastewater and other waste liquids. Louisiana eventually ranked first among all states for industrial water usage: 2,680 million gallons per day.[21] The infrastructure to handle this exponentially different use and circulation of water simply did not exist. Surrounding communities still relied on septic tanks. St. Gabriel prison likewise had no sewage treatment system, yet a pipeline ran across the grounds. Nor could parishes tax their new corporate neighbors in order to develop modern water systems, thanks to ongoing state exemptions.[22]

The area's climate and topography did not help. Heavy rains swelled the Mississippi River regularly, which sent untreated sewage and wastewater into surrounding floodplains, bayous, or swamps. Low-lying communities, like St. Gabriel and Geismar, were particularly vulnerable to the hurricanes and tropical storms that also caused flooding, which made life at St. Gabriel Prison Camp even worse for incarcerated women. [23] Those living outside the prison camp also suffered. Solid waste, sludge, and liquid waste floated and settled around these communities. Septic tanks overflowed or backed up into people's homes. That threat was more visible than the chemicals that had seeped into the groundwater and drinking-water aquifers by the 1970s. Industry had also pumped 94,000 tons of pollutants, including sulfuric acid and ammonia, into the air. Unaccounted for were the contents of abandoned waste sites connected to petrochemical plants. A decade later, Geismar–St. Gabriel communities allegedly faced 198 million pounds of pollutants in air, water, and land.[24] St. Gabriel's prison, the Louisiana Correctional Institution for Women, and Elayn Hunt Correctional Facility lay between these sites.

By 1970, there was clearly a toxic waste crisis in Louisiana. Yet the state did not just have a waste problem. For alert, shrewd entrepreneurs, Louisiana also offered a waste opportunity, especially once the federal government ushered in a new regulatory regime with the 1970 Clean Air Act, the 1970 establishment of the Environmental Protection Agency (EPA), and the 1972 Clean Water Act. Rollins-Purle Inc., for example, arrived in Louisiana in 1969 seeking to position itself as a new kind of firm: a company that would solely handle and dispose of the industrial wastes produced by heavy manufacturing. Hailing from New Jersey, Rollins-Purle spent several months introducing itself to relevant Louisiana pols and executives, holding press conferences, and courting shareholders to introduce its services. The company acquired 132 acres along Scenic Highway, five miles north of Baton Rouge and extending into the African American area of Alsen. It was three miles from Southern University of Louisiana, a historically Black college. Not only did Rollins-Purle apply for a permit to operate a regional waste treatment facility, including landfills, holding pools for liquid wastes, and an incinerator for semisolid and solid wastes, the firm also immediately submitted an application for tax exemption in November 1969.[25]

Rollins received state approval even though it had no experience in waste treatment. The company was actually Rollins International, Inc.—a truck leasing and hauling company. The firm was in the business of transporting, distributing, and warehousing bulk commodities for other companies. It leased trucks and autos and then expanded into financial services. Rollins nonetheless boasted of its ability to "apply chemical, biological, and physical methods of waste treatment and disposal of 250,000 gallons of concentrated residues per day."[26]

Rollins was ambitious. Executives projected $50 million in revenue in this new market and promised "fantastic growth in pollution control" when they signed a leasing agreement with Purle Brothers Holding Company of England, an industrial collection and treatment company. Instead of the typically fragmented and local waste handling, what Rollins was offering was regional treatment of industrial waste: Its large fleet of trucks would haul the wastes of numerous industrial plants, no matter what they produced, transport them to a central treatment facility, and "make industrial pollutants harmless before disposing of them." Over the next decade, Rollins went on a merger and acquisition spree, buying up smaller waste hauling companies or trucking firms. A decade later it was one of the largest national waste hauling/waste disposal companies. Similarly, Texas-based Browning Ferris Machinery Co. merged with American Refuse Systems in 1969 to become Browning-Ferris Industries. It too began buying and consolidating a specialty in hazardous waste land disposal and became one of the first waste disposal companies listed on the New York Stock Exchange.[27]

Rollins International executives boasted that the rapidly expanding number of chemical producers needed their company. At the groundbreaking ceremony for the waste treatment plant, Louisiana's executive director of the state Department of Commerce acknowledged that this new stage of capital development—regional waste treatment—would in itself "make this area even more attractive to industry." Rollins's East Baton Rouge waste disposal site would "become the nucleus of a new industrial park to serve Greater Baton Rouge."[28] Indeed, in 1974, the company euphemistically renamed itself Rollins Environmental Services Inc. It then used the cheeky slogan, "Call Us By Our Middle Name."[29] By the 1980s, even the state's Hazardous Waste

Advisory Board pointed to "the future opportunity for Louisiana to share in the growth industries related to hazardous waste control and destruction, other than land disposal."[30]

Rollins benefited from the lack of state regulation. With East Baton Rouge Parish as its domain, the company eventually expanded to 340 acres, bordering a vast wetland area known as Devil's Swamp and just 2.5 miles from the Jetson juvenile prison. Rollins also began operating a waste "landfarm" in historically Black Baker-Scotlandville, the location of Jetson, and used the Baker Canal, which runs alongside the prison, for discharging waste. Landfarming was a process by which sludge wastes were degraded by injection in the ground and covered in dirt—again, transforming nature into value. Rollins additionally maintained open waste pits and an injection well in Iberville Parish. In 1980, the Department of Natural Resources (DNR) reported that most of the petrochemical enterprises in Louisiana (ninety-three firms) were Rollins's clients. In the mid-1980s, Rollins stock became one of the biggest winners on Wall Street.[31]

Rollins did not mitigate Louisiana's hazard waste problems; the firm instead intensified and spread the toxic soup already harming the river parishes. Rollins's inexperience, poor knowledge, general carelessness, and, in some cases, fraudulent secrecy created more hazards for people, animals, and the environment in the 1970s and 1980s. The Rollins incinerator, for example, mixed together chemicals from dozens of plants, which caused dangerous emissions that regularly sickened residents of the Alsen, Scotlandville, and Baker sections of East Baton Rouge. Odors were apparently so bad that workers from neighboring chemical plants, such as Allied Chemical, filed written complaints. Rollins accidentally spilled or deliberately dumped waste oil, sludges, and effluents into drainage ditches, canals, Baton Rouge Bayou, Bayou Sorrel, and Devil's Swamp. The use of sand pits contributed to seepages. Its South Landfill, operating from 1971 to 1982, had twenty-four insufficiently lined waste cells, storage drums, and free liquids. Storage barrels burst and overflowed. These liquids traveled a mile underground through a channel of sand, contaminating the groundwater of its neighbors, including Allied Chemical Corp.[32]

Rollins found a new profitable market through importing hazardous wastes from out of state and laying them to rest in the wetlands and former sugar lands of Louisiana. At first, it did so secretly and illicitly. One of its earliest such arrangements involved dangerously and illicitly bringing Dioxin, TCCD, from a hazardous contaminated site in Missouri. But Rollins struggled to deal with this herbicide, a critical component of "Agent Orange" used during the Vietnam War and once described as "the most toxic manmade chemical." Rollins still struck deals throughout the 1970s to bring more waste, including PCBs, from 17 states to its landfarm. Soon other companies, including Dow Chemical, found it profitable to dispose of hazardous waste compounds in the region.[33] These companies were, in effect, putting southeastern Louisiana into a rapidly developing and consolidating national political economy of waste to profit from other states' eagerness to expunge highly toxic and nondegradable compounds.

Resistance and the Struggle for Democracy

Both free and imprisoned Louisianans challenged the chemical and waste removal companies, as well as the politicians and policies that enabled them. Southeastern communities and the state of Louisiana were initially ill-equipped to confront or even understand the waste problem. Unincorporated communities had no power to levy taxes on these companies, and the state had granted open-ended tax relief to many corporations. Hence, there was no money for infrastructure modernization. The state had almost no information regarding transport routes of particular chemical wastes, disposal sites, or what was contained in particular sites, nor a pertinent regulatory code. Louisiana agencies also lacked any systematic record of abandoned industrial waste sites.

Neither the DNR nor the Board of Commerce and Industry challenged chemical or waste removal companies. Up until the early 1980s, both agencies enabled and allowed corporations to claim siting decisions, production processes, emissions, and waste disposal as private matters of "proprietary knowledge" and managerial prerogative. DNR also maintained a decidedly deferential relationship toward corporations, generally allowing egregious practices of waste disposal to quite literally spread. DNR only implemented a tepid Hazardous Waste Management Program in 1979, with reassurances of "meeting the needs of industry."[34] DNR citations for negligence or hazard would be quietly settled on terms favorable to the company and often included release from future liability.[35]

Organized labor had some power to challenge the petrochemical industry. Prior to 1976, Louisiana did not have the kind of comprehensive right-to-work law discussed in Jean-Christian Vinel's chapter.[36] The Oil, Chemical and Atomic Workers Union (OCAW) had therefore been able to make slow but steady gains organizing refineries and chemical plants in Louisiana during the 1950s and 1960s. In its early years, OCAW was deferential to the industries bolstering the national security state because a significant percentage of its workers produced weaponry, uranium, nuclear bombs, and energy. But multiplying safety and health lapses amid ratcheted up production and environmental hazards led OCAW to shift its political orientation in the late 1960s.

OCAW assertively sought greater state intervention regarding workplace hazards, safety, and health. OCAW legislative director Tony Mazzocchi forged the coalition to enact the 1970 Occupational Safety and Health Act, after which the union became an active partner with the Occupational Safety and Health Administration (OSHA). In the 1970s, the union's approach to chemical and environmental hazards was threefold: prodding OSHA to issue comprehensive regulations and standards (rather than piecemeal actions); leveraging the state authority of OSHA and the EPA to pry open managerial secrecy about chemicals; and using collective bargaining to include union Hazardous Waste Training programs in contracts. The latter were meant to include workers in workplace safety programs. The union also presented its locals as enforcers of the 1976 Resource Conservation and Recovery Act, enacted to monitor treatment, storage, and disposal of hazardous wastes.[37] After continuous pressure in the late 1970s and early 1980s, OCAW managed to get the EPA to engage in direct review of the disposal permits for BASF, one of the major firms in Geismar. BASF's decision to lock out its employees likely emerged from that victory, turning the dispute into a five-year fight between OCAW and the corporation.[38]

OCAW leaders' bold "Right to Know" campaign also reflected how intertwined were labor rights and democratic accountability. OCAW insisted that workers should share in all pertinent information about environmental conditions. In this case, it specifically included lists of generic names of substances used and produced as well as any medical or environmental test data. But there were limits to labor's campaign to turn collective bargaining into broader political power. While the union was in sync with the political claims of the emerging community grassroots groups along the Chemical Corridor, racial segregation in both arenas obstructed labor's ability to fight beyond its base in the plants. In East Baton Rouge, Iberville, and Ascension parishes, OCAWs members were primarily White and the surrounding communities were primarily Black.

Southeastern Louisiana's racial inequity was also visible in its prisons where inmates also pushed for basic rights. Like the larger prison rights movement of the 1960s and 1970s, they looked to litigation. In 1971, for example, nine female inmates at St. Gabriel's, who were repeatedly beaten and gassed in solitary confinement, filed a class-action lawsuit "to halt cruel and unusual punishment" and guarantee due process. Male and female inmates protested the fact that they suffered work injuries or disability doing prison labor and yet did not qualify as "workers" under state workers' compensation laws.[39] Nor did the then developing law around prisoners' rights extend to prison environs. Inmates, who were neither workers nor full "citizens," could not look to the EPA or OSHA to challenge the toxic waste surrounding them.

Those outside the prisons could take advantage of the federal government's new environmental programs and policies. Parishes applied to the EPA in the late 1970s and early 1980s for federal grant money to underwrite sewage construction. Hundreds of people, rural Whites and Blacks, also wrote to their congressional representatives urging them to intervene and block new permits for waste discharge into smaller bodies of water, where residents had long fished and hunted, and into the Gulf. They wrote to state representatives, the governor, and the attorney general to report illegal dumping, conditions around waste pits and incinerators, and their own health problems, including the seeming increase in the number of cancers and miscarriages. Mayors and clerks from small rural towns also wanted higher-level officials to take aggressive action on these problems. Police juries, a form of parish government, even passed official resolutions to block waste sites.[40]

Yet Louisianans could not get state officials to respond. Bureaucrats simply did not show up to public hearings. Inaction frustrated concerned Louisianans. "They're a joke. All we get from them," Bayou Sorrel resident Columbus Millet Jr. fumed, "is the round-around and it smacks of cover up." Companies seemed to contribute little to their communities, Millet insisted: "As it stands now, we're taking all the risks" and "they're getting all the profits."[41]

The death of nineteen-year-old Kirtley Jackson in July 1978 proved a breaking point and a political rallying moment for grassroots organizing and action. The young truck driver became fatally overwhelmed while unloading hazardous waste into an open pit in Bayou Sorrel, located in southeast Louisiana's Iberville Parish. The EPA and coroner's report blamed "toxic fumes" from "a reaction of mixing liquids in an open pit." The enormous pit operated twenty-four hours a day, receiving waste from Texas, Arkansas, and Illinois as well as Louisiana; it had also overflowed. The permit, however, was for an injection well, not an open pit. Moreover, since no one from Louisiana's state government ever went out there to check, they seemed unaware that the site had developed into *four* open pits surrounded by a river, bayou, canal, and fishing lake in a floodplain area.[42]

Jackson's death provoked outrage and substantial media attention. Irate citizens were able to force state officials to come to town for a public hearing. State officials were either intransigent or feckless: They said there was nothing they could do. Local citizens refused to believe them and rose up to take matters into their own hands. They marched over to the bridge leading to the pits and burned down the only entrance to the facility. The EPA regional director, while acknowledging the illegality of this act, also observed that it was effective! The deputy sheriff still feared citizens would engage in further violence. Yet instead of turning to state officials, he actually called in the federal EPA from the regional headquarters in Houston. EPA representatives came in with a local OSHA official to quell the community and conduct an inspection of Jackson's death. Not only were they denied entrance to the facility; a state judge refused to give them a search warrant. EPA and OSHA officials therefore had to go to a federal judge for the warrant, after which US Marshals accompanied them into the facility. Company staff still withheld the actual logbooks from them.

It took weeks of federal and state wrangling, but investigators finally got what they needed. They determined Jackson died of asphyxiation from hydrogen sulfide at six times the lethal level. A federal district court judge ordered an immediate cleanup of the area and removal of "existing health hazards." The DNR tried to stymie these efforts, but the federal judge and EPA officials remained vigorous in their enforcement.[43]

Having backed the inquiry, angry residents began challenging the DNR and BCI's business-first policies. After the BCI issued a permit to Rollins to reopen a troubled deep waste injection well in Bayou Sorrel, near the pit where Jackson died, outraged Louisianans demanded greater democratic control over the industry. Attendees at an August 14, 1978, Iberville Parish Police Jury meeting went beyond criticizing the state's approval of the permit; they demanded the state create a process for public hearings in which residents could participate and voice opinions prior to permitting. The poor and working-class White residents of the community made clear they understood class politics and waste regulation as tightly linked. "It seems like, again," Columbus Millet Jr. argued, "the Big Boy gets to stick you with the junk, whether you like it or not."[44]

Residents soon became much more organized in their fight. They formed numerous grassroots groups all along the Mississippi River parishes, including Ascension Parish Residents Against Toxic Waste (Geismar), Save Ourselves (Burnside), and AWARE in Plaquemine (Iberville Parish); Citizens for a Clean Environment (Baton Rouge); Ecology Center's Toxics Task Force; Louisiana Environmental Action Network; several Sierra Club chapters; Gulf Coast Tenant Organization; and Association of Community Organizations for Reform Now (ACORN). Well aware that state officials sought to protect industry, the grassroots groups reached out to the EPA and formed an alliance with that federal agency and the departments of Health, Education, and Welfare and Health and Human Services. Local groups used the technical assistance and information from the EPA to embark on a self-education and popular education process. They held local workshops, symposia, and conferences from 1979 onward.[45]

Federal EPA officials shrewdly helped form a citizen movement called Waste Alert!, which emphasized citizen involvement in decision-making for municipal and commercial hazardous waste management. It brought together activist groups for workshops and training that built up the skills, knowledge, and understanding of citizens so that they could be an active part of efforts in their area. That organizing empowered local residents to enforce federal laws, including the new federal Resource Conservation and Recovery Act, which sought to monitor chemical wastes, classify particular substances as hazardous, and phase out all land disposal forms of hazardous waste (like the landfarm Rollins used).[46]

Activist citizens also began to use the courts. Ascension Parish residents, for example, filed for an injunction against any permits for discharge of hazardous waste chemicals into streams, land disposal, and injection wells. Alsen residents filed a class action lawsuit to block Rollins's application to burn PCBs in their neighborhood; the court action and a militant public hearing did force Rollins to withdraw the application in December 1984—at least for the time being. A Baton Rouge environmental group, RESTORE, appealed to the Circuit Court in October 1986, charging a pattern of racism inherent in company decisions and activities that created toxic zones. Amanda Lee, an African American resident of Alsen, sharply explained why her community had unfairly borne the costs of pollution. "They gave us the plants, Devil's Swamp [landfill], the airport, the parish prison, Rollins. They wouldn't put Rollins in Sherwood Forest or Villa Del Rey. . . . We're just a bunch of black people out here." As her lawyer put it, elites figured "people aren't likely to complain." Other communities filed suit to close Browning-Ferris facilities, and even Rollins reached a settlement agreement to shut down a landfarm northeast of Baton Rouge and pay for cleanup.[47]

What Louisiana residents also needed was institutionalization of regulatory standards and enforcement power. That could not happen at the local level. Iberville Parish had tried to take action on its own by passing a parish prohibition of hazardous waste disposal. When Rollins acquired a facility "to dispose of liquid industrial residue by injecting it into the earth," the police jury passed an ordinance specifically restricting injection wells. Rollins Environmental Services, however, sued the parish and kicked the case up to a higher state court. Eventually, at the level of the state supreme court, Rollins won the case and abrogated the parish prohibition.[48]

Louisianans did not get the kind of state agency that could further empower them to clean up and protect their communities until the mid-1980s. The legislature passed the Louisiana Environmental Quality Act in 1983, which Republican Governor David Treen, a former US congressman, signed in the spirit of his 1980 campaign promise for government reform. That law reflected the two strong currents pushing action at the state level: local activism and federal laws that states had to follow. The 1983 legislation promised that the state would comply with RCRA's federal mandate to phase out land disposal and would create a new Department of Environmental Quality. DEQ, unlike the Board of Commerce and Industry and DNR, was independent of the petrochemical, oil, and gas industries. The law mandated that DEQ work with the existing Hazardous Waste Advisory Board in order to counter corporate power over waste disposal and fight for adequate funding for DEQ.

DEQ Secretary Patricia Norton was an active, committed enforcer. She faced a formidable task: Louisiana generated sixteen million tons of hazardous waste when she assumed office in 1984. DEQ took on the responsibility of aligning state classifications of hazardous substances, rulings on substances, and regulatory codes with those of the EPA, especially as these continued to develop over time.[49] DEQ also did the actual job of discharge testing—particularly through surprise visits. Thereafter, Rollins Environmental Services Inc., Petro Processors, and Browning-Ferris/CECOS were continually put on the defensive. Those firms faced fines, injunctions, and suits. In 1985, following a particular egregious episode at Rollins, DEQ actually ordered the entire facility shut down.[50]

DEQ, along with EPA, finally confronted Rollins over the area known as Devil's Swamp. Locals swam, fished, and boated in that thirty-one-square-kilometer freshwater wetland and thriving wildlife refuge. Yet Petro Processors and Rollins surrounded Devil's Swamp with enormous waste pits that leached into it. Rollins also used it as a dump. Because of Devil's Swamp location, a lot of that waste ended up in the Mississippi.[51] DEQ and EPA testing in the 1980s showed the site contaminated with chemicals ranked highest on the Hazardous Ranking System scale for toxicity, persistence, quantity, and lack of natural or artificial containment. Living creatures were already gone. The vegetation was desiccated; dead cypress trees floated in the swamp. "Devil's Swamp was so bad," longtime activist and founder of the Louisiana Environmental Network remembered, "even the devil left."[52] Norton issued the emergency order to close off public access to the waters.[53] DEQ then got it listed as a Superfund site, which has taken more than twenty-five years to clean up.

DEQ also became a partner to people, communities, and groups, connecting them to the state government and federal EPA. Norton actively invited citizens to participate in DEQ's work and labored to open up the once secret and private decisions about waste disposal. She wanted these to become public decisions. So DEQ started requiring public hearings to review the waste and water discharge permits that corporations sought. DEQ started with public "fact finding" hearings for companies seeking hazardous waste disposal permits. Norton established a policy that EPA and DEQ would receive and jointly consider written comments related to waste siting proposals. Open, public adjudicatory hearings were next. DEQ also provided grassroots groups with data about companies that they could use in testimonies before legislative committees. Transparency was also a part of DEQ's 1986 initiative to assess a monitoring and maintenance fee for waste management, which required registration of all underground storage tanks.[54]

Pat Norton herself responded to calls about noxious odors, spills, or illegal dumping. In one of her most celebrated actions, Norton took an evening call in August 1985 from E. W. Pate, who lived near Rollins's Baton Rouge incinerator and landfill. While hosting a birthday crawfish boil in his yard, a plume of black smoke came up from the incinerator. The stench was so noxious that people got headaches, nausea, and burning eyes. Pate called Norton and she arrived within thirty minutes, experienced the smell, and also got a terrible headache. When Norton and two staff members inspected the incinerator, they found leakage as well as instruments that were malfunctioning and in code violation. She ordered the incinerator shut down immediately and the next day issued a DEQ order to shut down the entire Rollins site in North Baton Rouge. As one journalist noted, "Rarely has a Louisiana public official rocked boats and ruffled feathers in the Norton manner. Certainly, no public official has challenged the state's most sacred cow—the oil, gas, and chemical industry—as she has."[55]

A bitter fight between DEQ and Rollins followed. Norton instructed the company to plan for permanently closing the incinerator, landfill, and waste treatment plant at the site by March 1986. Rollins executives balked and claimed that Norton could not issue such an order, since it would in essence revoke the company's permit. Instead, they demanded a hearing in order to challenge DEQ's authority to close its site.

A permanent shutdown would have been costly because Rollins was believed to reap almost 20 percent of its profits from the Baton Rouge site. The previous year, Rollins had earned $6.5 million there. It was reported to be the second largest such site in terms of capacity in the nation. Apparently, the company had also tampered with equipment and instruments so as to accept a greater, illegal volume of waste.

That chicanery was the final straw for DEQ. "Our position is that the facility is going to be closed," Norton publicly insisted. "We're going to use every legal means we have to close it." DEQ rejected Rollins's proposal to make improvements to the site and thereby keep it open and running. Standing with African American residents who had joined the lawsuit against Rollins, Norton declared, "Alsen residents should not be subjected to further experimentation."[56]

Rollins, however, had friends at the highest levels. Executives turned to Governor Edwin Edwards, who had lost the governor's mansion to Treen in 1979 but won it back in 1983. This Democrat, like a lot of Louisiana politicians, had always been a petrochemical ally. When asked about hazardous waste in the late 1970s, Edwards responded in a way the DNR and Board of Commerce and Industry would have applauded: "This is the price we pay [for economic growth] and we have no apologies for it."[57] He had not changed his mind while out of office or after his return. Edwards therefore urged Norton to "reconsider" her ruling.[58] She did not. So he granted the company's request and personally appointed the hearing officer for the case in administrative court, where the company was represented by Governor Edwards's former law partner. Ultimately, the judge found Rollins guilty of only two minor air pollution infractions out of the forty-four pollution violations charged.

Rollins's permits were safe because they had not been found guilty of any hazardous waste violations.[59] Both Rollins and Browning-Ferris filed motions in state court arguing the "Secretary" (i.e., Norton) was biased and therefore should not be permitted to adjudicate such hearings.[60]

Pat Norton's grassroots base of support and alliance with the EPA was not enough political capital in Louisiana. Edwards forced her out of office a year later, and the state legislature underfunded and understaffed DEQ from then on. Industry went on a new offensive against regulatory requirements, disclosing less information about their internal processes and products.

Louisianans for a time had fought for something better than the Chemical Corridor and Cancer Alley that had become enmeshed with the much older and profitable systems of sugar and incarceration. Inmates had dared to sue for better treatment in the prisons and ask for the kind of labor rights they would have had as free men, women, and children. There were limits to what they could achieve in prison fields, St. Gabriel's garment factory, SISCY's canning plant, and Hunt Correctional's chemical plant because they did not have the same rights and protections enjoyed by OCAW's largely White membership. The largely Black inmate population in those correctional facilities could not look to OSHA or the EPA to clean up and fix the deplorable conditions in which they lived and worked.

But free Black and White Louisianans could. Many had been angry before Kirtley Jackson's shocking death. Their outrage and activism made a real difference after. The investigation that residents demanded laid the groundwork for the kind of work the EPA and, eventually, the DEQ would partner with them to do. Communities, OCAW, the EPA, OSHA, and the DEQ became a tangible threat not only to the bottom line at Rollins and other companies, but also to the power they wielded over southeastern Louisiana. The struggle to shut down Rollins in the mid-1980s shows that the work necessary to make American capitalism more democratic has been and will continue to be a bitter and prolonged struggle at the local, state, and federal levels.

Notes

1. *Angolite*, Feb. 20, 1954; May 8, 1954; Jan. 1, 1955; Feb. 12, 1955; Feb. 18, 1956; Mar. 10, 1956; Nov. 9, 1957; Nov. 23, 1957; Mar. 15, 1958; Oct. 1958; April 25, 1959; April 15, 1961, Louisiana State University Special Collections, Baton Rouge, LA.

2. Jason W. Moore, *Capitalism in the Web of Life: Ecology and the Accumulation of Capital* (Verso, 2015), 2, 12–13.

3. Sacrifice zones refers to communities, particularly with low-income residents, "exposed to disproportionately elevated levels of hazardous chemicals." Writes Steve Lerner, "Environmental justice activists . . . tend to call these areas 'sacrifice zones,' 'fence-line communities,' or 'hot spot of pollution.'" Lerner argues for the first term since it emphasizes that these residents "are required to make health and economic sacrifices that more affluent people can avoid." Steve Lerner, *Sacrifice Zones: The Front Lines of Toxic Chemical Exposure in the United States* (Cambridge: MIT Press, 2010), 3.

4. "Louisiana Profile," Prison Policy Initiative, https://www.prisonpolicy.org/profiles/LA.html, accessed Nov. 22, 2019; Human Rights Watch Children's Rights Watch, *Children in Confinement in Louisiana* (US: Human Rights Watch, 1995), https://www.hrw.org/legacy/reports/1995/Us3.htm, accessed Nov. 22, 2019; Adam Gelb and Elizabeth Compa, "Louisiana No Longer Leads Nation in Imprisonment Rate: Louisiana Drops to No. 2 [in 2018]," Pew Charitable Trusts, https://www.pewtrusts.org/en/research-and-analysis/articles/2018/07/10/louisiana-no-longer-leads-nation-in-imprisonment-rate, accessed Nov. 22, 2019.

5. "What Has Louisiana Done for Business and Industry Lately? Voted into Its Constitution Industry's Right to Profit Law!," State Board of Commerce and Industry, P79–297, 8869, A-P-1, Box 1; BCI, "Why Industry Moves to Louisiana," n.d. In general, all these materials can be found in Boxes 1–5, Louisiana State Archives (hereafter LSA), Baton Rouge, LA.

6. Source: "Petro-Chemical Gold Coast," Fall 1970, P79–279, 8873, A-P-5, Box 5, Folder: Board Meeting Executive Minutes, Dec. 9, 1970, LSA.

7. "What Has Louisiana Done for Business and Industry Lately? Voted into Its Constitution Industry's Right to Profit Law!"; BCI, "Why Industry Moves to Louisiana."

8. For Tax Exemption Applications to the Board of Commerce and Industry, See Applications in State Board of Commerce and Industry Records (hereafter BCI), P79–297, 8869, A-P-1, Box 1, and 8873, A-P-5, Box 5, LSA. Elizabeth Tandy Shermer, *Sunbelt Capitalism: Phoenix and the Transformation of American Politics* (Philadelphia: University of Pennsylvania Press, 2013); Tami Friedman, "Exploiting the North-South Differential: Corporate Power, Southern Politics, and the Decline of Organized Labor After World War II," *Journal of American History* (Sept. 2008).

9. St. Charles Parish Virtual Museum, www.stcharlesgov.ne/departments/economic-development-and-tourism/parish-history.

10. Marathon Petroleum, "Grayville Refinery Fact Sheet," https://www.marathonpetroleum.com/content/document/fact_sheets/MPC-Garyville_FactSheet-1218.pdf, accessed Dec. 28, 2018.

11. Richard Misrach and Kate Orff, *Petrochemical America* (Aperture, 2014), 115; Barbara Allen, *Uneasy Alchemy: Citizens and Experts in Louisiana's Chemical Corridor Disputes* (Cambridge: MIT Press, 2003); Robert D. Bullard, *Dumping in Dixie: Race, Class, and Environmental Quality*, 3rd ed. (Westview Press, 2000).

12. Report to the Director of the Board of Institutions, May 18, 1954, Corrections/Board of Institutions Records, P88–177, Box 1, Folder: 13176; Report of the Director of the Board of Institutions, Oct. 21, 1960, Box 1, Folder: 13176, State Archives of Louisiana, Baton Rouge, LA; *State of Louisiana Department of Institutions Annual Report 1961–1962*, 26, State Library of Louisiana, Baton Rouge, LA. On prisons and plantation work, see Robert Perkinson, *Texas Tough: The Rise of America's Prison Empire* (New York: Metropolitan Books, 2010).

13. Annual Report of the Board of Institutions, 1965–1966; Louis Sowers to Dr. Bernard Sliger, May 23, 1969, Acc. P83–580, Box 7652, Folder: Divisions of Administration, 1969, State Archives; David Wade to Mrs. Mary Evelyn Parker, Commissioner of Administration, June 1967, Box 7652, Folder: Divisions of Administration, 1969, State Archives; A Report to the

Governor by the Department of Institutions, Oct. 15, 1968, Acc. P83–580, Box 7652, Folder: Governor McKeithen, State Archives; Clarence Doucet, "Suit by Women Inmates Upheld," *Times-Picayune*, Oct. 2, 1971.

14. "Prison Study Lists Women as Forgotten," April 27, 1972; Kathleen Mulvhill, "It's Home for Women Prisoners," *Times-Picayune*, Nov. 29, 1981.

15. *East Baton Rouge Police Digest*, June 1945, East Baton Rouge Parish Library On-line Archive; *State of Louisiana Department of Institutions Annual Report 1960–61*, 43, State Library of Louisiana.

16. *State of Louisiana, Department of Institutions Annual Report 1961–1962*, 68–69; A Report to the Governor by the Department of Institutions, Oct. 15, 1968, Acc. P83–580, Box 7652, Folder: Governor McKeithen, Louisiana State Archives; Betsy Halstead, " 'School' Prepares Youths for Bigger Things—Angola," *New Orleans Times Picayune*, June 23, 1970; Warren Gadpaille, "Psychiatric Problems of Delinquency in Louisiana," Research Division, Louisiana State Department of Institutions, 1957, 5.

17. Donald E. Kirsopp, "Product Line Expansion in the Chemical Industry Along the Mississippi River in Louisiana," Chemical Industry Study, Resource Development Project, Louisiana Department of Commerce and Industry (Sept. 1969), State Library of Louisiana; Petrochemical Targets Study for Louisiana, 1983, State of Louisiana; Louisiana Directory of Petrochemical Industries, Homesite Company; Raymond Edgar Shanefelt, "The Baton Rouge–New Orleans Petrochemical Industrial Region: A Functional Regional Study," Vol. 1 (PhD Dissertation, Louisiana State University, 1977), 20.

18. Misrach and Orff, *Petrochemical America*, 6.

19. John Jacobus, A. J. Englade Jr., and G. D'Amour, "Louisiana Industry-Resource Recovery and By-Product Conversion and Disposal Technologies," Report Prepared for State of Louisiana, Board of Regents, Feb. 1985, LA Department of Environmental Quality Records, Acc P1994–93, 20870–10, Box 10, LSA.

20. Environmental Action Foundation, "Hazardous Wastes: Hidden Danger," *Garbage Guide*, RCRA Resource Guide No. 2, 1978, Ecology Center of Louisiana Records (hereafter EC), Coll. 32, Box 69, Folder: 11, Loyola University Special Collections, New Orleans, LA. On the history of landfills, see Heather Rogers, *Gone Tomorrow: The Hidden Life of Garbage* (New York: The New Press, 2005).

21. U.S. Department of the Interior, U.S. Geological Survey, "Industrial Water Withdrawals by State, 2000," Survey (Dec 2010), http://ga.water.usgs.gov/edu/wuin.html, accessed Nov. 20, 2019.

22. Louis Sowers, "A Report to the Governor by Department of Institutions," Oct. 15, 1968, BCI, Box 7652; David Wade to Mary Evelyn Parker, June 7, 1967, Box 7652, Folder: Division of Administration 1969, LSA; "Advisory Board Visits Angola," *State-Times*, Jan. 29, 1966; "Nat'l Business Women's Week Celebrated Here, Col. White Is Speaker," *State-Times*, Oct. 20, 1967; "Prison on the Move," *Morning Advocate*, Oct. 21, 1973.

23. *Angolite*, Feb. 20, 1954; May 8, 1954; Jan. 1, 1955; Feb. 12, 1955; Feb. 18, 1956; Mar. 10, 1956; Nov. 9, 1957; Nov. 23, 1957; Mar. 15, 1958; Oct. 1958; April 25, 1959; April 15, 1961, Louisiana State University Special Collections, Baton Rouge, LA.

24. David Snyder, "Wastes Chokes Scenic Bayou," *The Times-Picayune*, Sept. 10, 1985, p. 1.

25. Rollins-Purle Inc., Application No. 4747, Nov. 19, 1969, BCI Records.

26. Rollins Press Kit, "Introducing Sludge Gulper: Sludge, Oil, Chemicals, Rollins-Purle Inc. A Complete Pollution Abatement Service," 1970, BCI Records, P79–279, A-P-5, Box 5, LSA.

27. See Rollins Purle and Rollins Environmental Materials in BCI Records, Box 5; "Rollins Leasing Forms Firm for Waste Disposal," *The Philadelphia Inquirer*, Dec. 20, 1968, p. 34; "Company Profiles: Rollins Leasing," *The Philadelphia Inquirer*, Oct. 15, 1969, p. 25; Andrew Wallace, "Firm Building Plant to Control Pollution," *The Philadelphia Inquirer*, Oct. 23, 1969, p. 22. More generally, see Craig Colten and Peter Skinner, *The Road to Love Canal: Managing Industrial Waste Before EPA* (Austin: University of Texas Press, 1996).

28. Gray and Rogers Inc. Press Release, "New Pollution Control Could Figure in Economic Growth," Nov. 12, 1969, BCI Records, Box 5, LSA.

29. Rollins Environmental Services Inc, "Call Us by Our Middle Name," Larry Lynch Papers, P93–174, 9989-2-P, Box 2.

30. Velma Campbell, MD, to Brenda Kelly, Memorandum: Draft Policy Statement for Land Disposal, Jan. 4, 1986, EC Records, Coll. 32, Box 69, Folder 8, Loyola, NOLA.

31. "Rollins Dump Receives Waste from Across the U.S.," *Baton Rouge State-Times*, April 22, 1980.

32. "Rollins Order to Fix Ground Water Problem," *States-Times*, May 4, 1989.

33. Department of Environmental Quality, "Notice: Fact Finding Hearing," 1986, Larry Lynch Papers (hereafter LL), P93–174, 9989, Box 1-P, Folder: Fact Finding, LSA.

34. Department of Natural Resources, *Hazardous Waste Bulletin*, vol. 1, no. 1 (Dec. 1979), EC Records, Coll. 32, Box 69, Loyola; "Early Action Was Met with Disbelief," *The Times-Picayune*, Sept. 8, 1985, p. 18.

35. "Penalty Hike Refused for Stream Pollution," *State-Times*, April 19, 1974.

36. Berkeley Miller and William Canak, "Gumbo Politics: Unions, Business, and Louisiana Right-to-Work Legislation," *Industrial and Labor Relations Review* 43, no. 2 (January 1990), 258–271; Thomas Becnel, *Labor, Church, and the Sugar Establishment: Louisiana, 1887–1976* (Baton Rouge: Louisiana State University Press, 1980), 21–22, 180–186; Elizabeth Tandy Shermer, "Counter-Organizing the Sunbelt: Right to Work Campaigns and Anti-Union Conservatism, 1943–1958," *Pacific Historical Review* 78 (February 2009): 81–118.

37. "Draft of Grospiron Speech to AFL-CIO Health & Safety Conf," 9/10/1978, OCAW Records, Acc. 1193, Health & Safety Series, Box 9, University of Colorado Special Collections, Boulder, CO; Steve Wodka, OCAW International Rep, to Joe Velazquez, OSHA, Oct. 31, 1978, OCAW Records, Box 9; Report of Christine Oliver, MD, and OCAW to Fulfill Labor Dept. Services Contract B-9-F-8–3424 for Six Health Hazard Evaluations, Oct. 31, 1978, Box, 9; Sylvia Krekel to Robert E. Wages, 12/5, 1988, Re: Hazmat Training for Witco, Gretna, Louisiana, Local 4–447, Nov. 12, 1988, Box 7, Folder: OSHEC; Robert Wages to District Directors, RE: Bargaining for Haz. Waste Training, 12/7/1988, Box 7, Folder: Grant Correspondence; Krekel to All HAZMAT OSHECS, 12/9/88, RE: RCRA Site List, Box 7; Krekel to All HAZMAT OSHECS, 6/6/1989, RE: Agency for Toxic Substances & Diseases Registry, Box 7; Sylvia Krekel to John Knauff, 3/29/1989, Box 7, Folder: Grant Corresp; Kerkel to Dick Sheldon, Refinery Manager, AMOCO, 4/26/1989, Box 7; Hess Oil to Kerkel, 4/17/89, Box 7, Folder: Grant Corresp, all in OCAW Records, Health & Safety, Boulder, CO. See also, Les Leopold, *The Man Who Hated Work and Loved Labor: The Life and Times of Tony Mazzocchi* (Chelsea Greene Publishing, 2007).

38. OCAW correspondence, memos, reports are in EC Records, Coll. 32, Box 34, Folders 2–7, Loyola, NOLA.

39. Clarence Doucet, "Suit by Women Inmates Upheld," *Times-Picayune*, Oct. 2, 1971. On workers' comp., see *The Angolite*, Oct. 3, 1953.

40. See letters for example to US Representative David Treen, starting as early as 1973–1974. Hundreds of angry letters over DuPont application for waste discharges. See also David Treen papers as governor in early 1980s. David Treen Papers, Coll. 651, Box 341, Folders: EPA; also in Ecology Center of Louisiana Records, Coll. 32, Loyola University Special Collections, NOLA.

41. "Tragic Death May Be Disguised Blessing," *The Times-Picayune*, June 13, 1979.

42. Peyton Davis, "A Death in Louisiana," *EPA Journal* 5, no. 2 (February 1979), 14–16.

43. Davis, "A Death in Louisiana," 14–16.

44. "Louisiana: The State We're In," Louisiana Public Broadcasting, Episode 249, Aug. 25, 1978, American Archive, https://americanarchive.org/catalog/cpb-aacip_17-87pnwx6j, accessed 4/19/23.

45. Activist groups' newsletters, pamphlets, and announcements in the Larry Lynch Papers, P93–174, 9989, Boxes 1 and 2, LSA.

46. LL Collection, P93–174, 9989, Box 1; EC Records, Coll. 32, Box 40, Folder 10; Box 41, Folders 5, 12, and 14; Box 70, Folder 1. On Waste Alert! see "Memo: Waste Project, National Wildlife Federation to Subscribers to the Rural Solid Waste Newsletter," Dec. 1979, EC Records, Coll. 32, Loyola; also Carol S. Lawson, "Waste Alert!," *EPA Journal* 5, no. 2 (Feb. 1979). Sierra Club Delta Chapter, "A Preliminary Report to the Louisiana House Natural Resources Subcommittee on Oversight Concerning Annual Dumping of Almost 200 Million Pounds of Toxic Chemicals into the Air in Geismar and Saint Gabriel Communities," Oct. 21, 1981 and accompanying press releases, LL Papers, 9989, Box 1-P.

47. Ascension Parish Residents Against Toxic Pollution v. Martha Nadden, DEQ, "Motion for Preliminary and Permanent Injunction," EC Records, Coll. 32, Box 96.5, Folder 4; State v. Rollins Environmental Services, Inc., Supreme Court of Louisiana, May 18, 1981, No. 80-K-2968; Environmental Control Com v. Browning-Ferris Industries, Court of Appeal of Louisiana, First Circuit, Dec. 28, 1983, No. 83 CA 0855; "Environmental Group Appeals Rollins Findings," *Baton Rouge Morning Advocate*, Oct. 29, 1986, LL Papers, Box 2; Coalition for Community Action, "The Alsen Story: People v. PCBs," 1984, LL Papers, P93–174,9989, Box 1-P, Folder: Misc. Pollution/Chemical Propaganda, LSA. Steve Culpeper, "Alsen Residents Suing Rollins Complain Noxious Fumes Back," *Baton Rouge State-Times*, July 30, 1985. On race and waste sites, see Robert Bullard, *Dumping in Dixie*.

48. *Rollins Environmental Services Inc. v. Iberville Police Jury*, Supreme Court of Louisiana, May 21, 1979, No. 63502. (371 So. 2nd 1127).

49. "Hazardous Waste Advisory Board Recommendations," EC Records, Coll. 32, Box 69, Folder 8, Loyola, NOLA; Dr. Velma Campbell, MD, to Brenda Kelly, "Memorandum: Draft Policy Statement for Land Disposal," Jan. 4, 1986, EC Records Coll. 32, Box 69, Folder 8, Loyola, NOLA.

50. "Rebel: DEQ Captain Rocks the Boat," *The Times-Picayune*, Sept. 13, 1985; "Prosperity in Paradise: What Was Once Pate's Paradise Now His Hell," *Baton Rouge Morning Advocate*, April 25, 1985; "Rollins Seeks Hearing Over Its Waste Site in Baton Rouge, LA," *Wall Street Journal*, Aug. 26, 1985, LL Papers, Box 2, LSA; Mike Dunne, "Norton Rejects Rollins' Plan," *Baton Rouge Morning Advocate*, Aug. 20, 1985, LL Papers Box 2; David Snyder, "Stench: Friendships and Dreams Killed by Fumes," *The Times-Picayune*, Sept. 8, 1985, p. 17.

51. Jerry Spier, Chair, Hazardous Waste Committee, Delta Chapter Sierra Club, to Martha McKee, Chief, Superfund Site Assessment Section, EPA Region VI, Aug. 19, 1986, LL Papers, 9990–2-P, Box 2, Folder: Devil's Swamp, Rollins/Petro Processors, State Archives; *Baton Rouge Morning Advocate*, April 25, 1985; Bob Anderson, "DEQ to Close Section of Devil's Swamp,"

Baton Rouge Morning Advocate, July 31, 1986. See also EPA Superfund Site, "Devil's Swamp Lake, Scotlandville, LA," Superfund Site Profile, https://cumulis.epa.gov/supercpad/SiteProfiles/index.cfm?fuseaction=second.Cleanup&id=0600652#bkground, accessed Dec. 24, 2018.

52. J. Klein Interview with Darryl Malek-Wiley, New Orleans Sierra Club Office, Nov. 30, 2018, notes in author's possession.

53. Ibid.

54. See Notices of Fact Finding Hearings and Notice of Adjudicatory Hearings in LL Papers, P93–174, 9989, Box 1-P, Folder: d base,III; Folder: Fact Finding, LSA; Testimony of Peggy Hoffman, resident of St. Gabriel, and Les Ann Kirkland, Iberville, AWARE, Oct. 21, P93–174, 9989, Box 1-P, LSA.

55. "Rebel: DEQ Captain Rocks the Boat," *The Times-Picayune*, Sept. 13, 1985; "Prosperity in Paradise: What Was Once Pate's Paradise Now His Hell," *Baton Rouge Morning Advocate*, April 25, 1985.

56. "Rollins Seeks Hearing over Its Waste Site in Baton Rouge, LA," *Wall Street Journal*, Aug. 26, 1985, LL Papers, Box 2, LSA; Mike Dunne, "Norton Rejects Rollins' Plan," *Baton Rouge Morning Advocate*, Aug. 20, 1985, LL Papers Box 2; David Snyder, "Stench: Friendships and Dreams Killed by Fumes," *Times-Picayune*, Sept. 8, 1985, p. 17; David Snyder, "Burning Fumes Sear Workers' Memory," *Times-Picayune*, Sept. 8, 1985, p. 17.

57. Stella Pitts, "Waste Sites: Who's at Fault?" *The Times-Picayune*, June 17, 1979, 1, 12.

58. "Lawmakers Get Behind Fight to Shut Down Toxic Waste Site," *Times-Picayune*, Aug. 29, 1985.

59. Mike Dunne, "Guste to Plead Rollins Case as an Intervenor," *Baton Rouge Morning Advocate*, Dec. 4, 1986, LL Papers, 9990–2-P, Box 2, Folder: Devil's Swamp, Rollins/Petro Processors; John Eberhart, "Attorney Challenges Rollins' Witness," *State Times*, Aug. 6, 1986, LL Papers, Box 2, LSA; H. David Vaughn II, "In Re Rollins Environmental Services: The Disqualification of an Administrative Agency Decision Maker," *Louisiana Law Review*, vol. 47 (1987).

60. Charles Hargroder, "Norton Replaced for Rollins Case," *Times-Picayune*, Jan. 16, 1986, A 31; H. David Vaughn II, "In Re Rollins Environmental Services: The Disqualification of an Administrative Agency Decision Maker," *Louisiana Law Review*, vol. 47 (1987).

CHAPTER 8

From the "Labor Question" to the "Immigration Question": Newcomers, Politics, and Democracy in the Contemporary United States

Carl Bon Tempo

In the early and middle decades of the twentieth century, few questions were more important to politics and society in the United States than the "labor question." That query addressed how the demands of capital and labor might find a peaceful and beneficial equilibrium. Historians, like Nelson Lichtenstein, have shown how labor unions, workers, the New Deal state, and businesses and management crafted a contentious and incomplete answer to that question beginning in the 1930s.[1] After the 1960s, the labor question receded from the center of politics. Political conservatives, empowered as the country turned to the right, had their own answers to the labor question and increasingly the ability to enforce them. At the same time, and related to conservatism's rise, labor union membership plummeted, especially in the private sector, further sidelining the labor question.

In the early twenty-first century, though, a new question emerged as a vital issue in American politics and society: the "immigration question." The retreat of the labor question surely aided in the rise of the immigration question, but it was not a simple substitution. For one thing, elements of the labor question folded into the immigration question. Moreover, the immigration question's salience arose not only from labor and work issues, but also from concerns around culture, nationality, and race.

What was the immigration question? It took a few forms, as this chapter suggests, but, broadly, the immigration question asked how, and whether, newcomers might find a place in contemporary American society. This chapter seeks to explain the immigration question's central role in modern America and how its rise revealed a reshaped American politics that many consider to reflect a profound democratic crisis.

To be sure, the immigration question confounded Americans at other points in their history. In the 1850s, a surge in German and Irish immigration against the backdrop of a splintering political system produced a powerful nativist movement. In the late nineteenth and early twentieth centuries, the millions of Europeans entering the United States recast the country's economic, social, and cultural structures and fueled vigorous defenses of, and attacks upon, the newcomers. In these instances, as in the current era, immigration unleashed debates that focused on the country's future and how it defined itself. The conversations in the current era, then, have more than a few echoes with the past.

Any account of how the United States arrived at this moment, and this iteration of the immigration question, must grapple with Donald Trump. From his 2015 speech officially announcing his candidacy, when he derided Mexican immigrants as "people that have lots of problems . . . bringing drugs . . . bringing crime. . . . They're rapists," through the end of his first term in 2021, Trump did more than any individual to keep immigration on the front pages.[2] Yet concentrating on Trump's role in the rise of the immigration question oversimplifies immigration politics. Such a focus misses longer and larger changes in immigration to the United States, in immigration policy, and, most importantly, in the politics surrounding immigration that have all unfurled over the preceding decades. As such, it makes more sense to see Trump as the crystallization of ascendancy of the immigration question rather than his being generative of it.

What propelled the immigration question to prominence? From a longer historical perspective, there were the enormous changes in the sources, numbers, and types of immigration to the United States in the twentieth century's last decades. These developments contributed to a demographic revolution in the country's population and racial and national makeup during the same decades that there were, as previous chapters in this volume have shown, profound battles over and changes to American democracy and capitalism on the job, within the two major parties, and in governance.

More immediate than these slow and seismic shifts were a few political and immigration policy and politics controversies that erupted on both sides of the political and ideological divide, fueling the immigration question's relevance. On the right, elements of the Republican Party embraced strongly restrictionist and anti-newcomer policies, rhetoric, and politics that rather quickly marginalized pro-immigration members of the GOP. This development started with the internecine warfare that broke out in the GOP as it battled over comprehensive immigration reform in the Bush years, continued with the rise of the Tea Party, and found its way into former Massachusetts Governor Mitt Romney's immigration proposals in the 2012 presidential campaign. Immigration supporters among liberals and the left played a role too in elevating the immigration question, protesting border policies (authored and supported by both Republicans and Democrats) and attacking the Right's anti-immigrant rhetoric. But it was the restrictionist GOP that emerged as the most vital player in raising the immigration question, as many Democrats and liberals to a striking degree still subscribed to political and policy formulations that originated in the late twentieth century before the contemporary uproar over immigration.

The immigration question's centrality to contemporary politics also reveals some of the processes by which democratic governance has broken down in recent years. Immigration politics has moved from an era of dealmaking and compromise (which should not be lionized in any event as plenty of harmful policies arose out of those compromises) to one of unbridgeable divides and stasis on the policy front. More important, the immigration question, with the politics it has produced, portends the deterioration of the promise of democracy itself if one considers the fate of the "Dreamers" and their second-class status in American life, as well as the normalization of violence at the border that dehumanizes so many newcomers.

Formulating the Immigration Question

Public polling was one blunt measure of the importance of the immigration issue. Polling showed that immigration surged as "the most important problem" in the view of the public at points between 2001 and 2014, and it remained near the top of the agenda from 2014 through 2019. By 2019, 23 percent of Americans named it the top problem.[3] By the end of 2021, only about 10 percent of Americans cited it as the "top problem," but that figure uncovered a strong partisan split in which Republicans were much more likely to identify it as a top problem than Democrats.[4] When the pollsters asked the public about "illegal immigration," even larger percentages of respondents saw it as a "big problem," with Republicans again particularly sounding the alarm.[5]

But the immigration question was not as straightforward as the pollsters laid it out to the public. As it emerged in the late twentieth and early twenty-first centuries, the immigration question took a few forms. Each of these iterations points to the complex ways that newcomers shaped American life and the equally complex forms that the politics surrounding newcomers took.

At times, the immigration question really was a border question, focused especially on the US–Mexican border. With a growing population of unauthorized newcomers (the majority from Mexico) in the United States in the late twentieth century, the border became a more central facet of how Americans conceived of immigration. This phenomenon was not entirely new. In the late nineteenth century, the border figured prominently in the origins of Chinese exclusion and in the framing of Ellis Island and the Statue of Liberty as exemplars of the so-called "open door" to the United States. Nor was "unauthorized entry" a new idea in late twentieth-century America.

But the sanctification of the border as a securitized, tangible place that contained—and gave physical presence to—the nation's sovereignty achieved an almost talisman-like position in US politics, especially on the political right.[6] It led many Americans to formulate the immigration question as "How should the United States maintain a border to regulate the arrival of immigrants, and what does the state of the border indicate about American sovereignty?" The thrust of the question—no matter the answer—presupposed that the border and its (un)permeability revealed something deeply resonant about the United States.

Another formulation of the immigration question had an even longer history. Since the colonial era, individuals living in the British North America/the United States have wondered about how newcomers changed their society and whether (and how) they fit into that future. Simply, immigration opened questions of identity and the shape of the imagined nation. On this front, the immigration question boiled down to "Who are we if all these newcomers live among us?"[7]

The answers multiplied and scattered in all directions at the dawn of the twenty-first century (as they had throughout American history). The renowned historian Arthur Schlesinger's 1991 book *The Disuniting of America* worried that an increasingly diverse United States lacked "the language, the institutions, and the political ideals" to unify the nation.[8] More than a decade later, eminent political scientist Samuel Huntington warned ominously of a "Hispanic challenge" that threatened "the American dream created by an Anglo-Protestant society."[9] Republican Patrick Buchanan powered his 1990s quests for the presidency on many of these ideas, stoking White fears of being outnumbered and left behind in an immigrant-driven society, an approach later mirrored by Donald Trump. Meanwhile, Presidents Barack Obama, a Democrat, and George W. Bush, a Republican, emerged as exemplars of various forms of pluralism. The nation's first Black president, for instance, presented his multicultural family history that stretched across continents, oceans, and cultures as prototypically American.[10] You could hardly find more different personalities and approaches to immigration than these individuals, yet they all asked the same version of the immigration question.

A final rendering of the immigration question folded in issues of labor and work. Many of these newcomers in the late twentieth century came for work, and they contributed vitally to the American economy. But with the number of newcomers increasing after 1965 and amounting to a proportion of the population not seen since the 1880–1914 period, the work–immigration nexus's importance grew.[11] The immigration question from this perspective was "How do immigrants fit into the modern economy and country's work life?"

This version of the immigration question emerged largely because of the neoliberal economic regime that unleashed wrenching changes on modern America. As income inequality grew and economic and social mobility stagnated, some blamed newcomers. Immigrants seemed an easy and cheap source of labor that fed the capitalist engine while eroding economic and living standards for working-class Americans who had enjoyed relative economic prosperity in the century's middle decades.[12] Newcomers, in this line of thinking, might help generate national wealth, but to what ends and for whom? From a different direction, others recognized that immigrants too often worked in intolerable conditions, leading to demands from some Americans, and newcomers themselves, that the state, and management, step in to offer protections.[13] Finally, unions were one of the main vehicles for immigrant political mobilization—and newcomers an important wellspring of labor organizing—and thus politics and the economy potently mixed in immigrant and laboring communities.[14]

This thicket of newcomers, economics, and capitalism suggests that the immigration question of the twenty-first century bore some deep connections to the twentieth century's labor question. In the 2000s, the fate of laboring people was, per se, the fate of newcomers, given the vital role that the latter played in the modern US economy and labor market.

A Revolution in Immigration

The starting point for each of these versions of the immigration question was the massive changes in immigration to the United States over the last decades of the twentieth century. The 1965 landmark reform of immigration law jumpstarted these transformations, most of which were unintended.[15]

The numbers alone tell one startling story. In the 1960s, 3.3 million authorized immigrants entered the United States, a figure that grew to almost 4.5 million in the 1970s, and then to 7.3 million and 9.0 million in the 1980s and 1990s respectively.[16] These leaps occurred even though the 1965 reforms capped annual immigration to the United States at levels roughly equal to the preceding decades under the national origins quota immigration laws. But the 1965 law contained a provision that allowed close family members of US citizens to enter with authorization but not count against the caps.[17] The results were clear: The number of immigrants entering the United States by the end of the twentieth century was the most since the first fifteen years of the twentieth century.

The origins of the newcomers changed too. North Americans, individuals from the Caribbean, and Europeans entered in the largest numbers in the 1960s. In the decades that followed, the number of Europeans diminished while those entering from the Americas grew and those from Asia surged. After 1980, Mexico, the Philippines, Vietnam, China, and India (in that order) sent the most newcomers—evidence of the new centrality of Asia in US immigration, a stunning reversal considering the decades of efforts to slow Asian migration to the United States.[18] This change in the origins of newcomers helped change the composition of the United States at the twenty-first century's dawn. The foreign-born made up 10 percent of the US population in 2000 (up from 5 percent in 1970), and the percentage of individuals of Hispanic and Asian descent in the United States rose sharply to 12.5% and 3.6% respectively.[19]

Refugee and asylee admissions patterns during these years followed similar trends as immigrants. Under the Refugee Act of 1980, the number of refugees entering the United States grew substantially (anywhere between

50,000 and 100,000 most years), and they came from different parts of the world—Asia, Africa, and the Middle East—than their largely European predecessors. The number of applications for asylum also exploded in the late twentieth century, the product of instability in the Americas, but the number of grants of asylum lagged far behind. Advocates for asylum-seekers lamented this backlog and saw it as needlessly cruel. Immigration opponents, meanwhile, erupted in anger over the large number of asylum claimants waiting in the United States for immigration authorities to adjudicate their cases. Those awaiting an asylum hearing could, until late in the Trump administration's first term, basically remain in the United States until their hearing. For this reason, immigration opponents saw asylum as a backdoor and illegitimate path to entry—even though asylum seekers were entitled to wait in the United States for their cases' resolution.[20]

The final big change of the late twentieth century was the arrival of large numbers of unauthorized individuals in the United States. In 1980, an estimated 2 million unauthorized persons lived in the United States, a number that increased to an estimated 8.0 million by 2000. In the twenty-first century, the unauthorized population peaked in 2007 (just before the Great Recession) at 12.2 million and then receded slightly to around 11 million for the next decade. Mirroring trends in authorized entrants, unauthorized individuals from Mexico were the single largest group in these decades, but the equally important story was the growth of unauthorized entry from Central America and Asia, especially India and China.[21]

These slowly emerging trends in immigration to the United States were punctured at times by singular events. In the early 1990s, an increase in Cuban refugees arriving in Florida put Democrat Bill Clinton's administration on the defensive, leading to the implementation of the "wet foot, dry foot" policy that satisfied almost no one. If American authorities interdicted Cubans at sea—the so-called wet foot—then the Cubans were returned to the island, but if the Cubans made it to US soil—the dry foot—then they could apply for, and very likely receive, asylum.[22] Likewise, the wars and violence that roiled Central America and Mexico in the first decades of the twenty-first century caused hundreds of thousands to flee to the United States.[23] A full accounting of the various unexpected and sudden shocks in migration to the United States involves many more episodes, but these two examples illustrate the futility of boiling down immigration to annual admissions statistics.

No matter how, from where, or when they arrived, these immigrants proved essential to the functioning of the US economy. Immigrants harvested and produced the nation's food, built and maintained its homes and infrastructure, cared for the young and old, the sick and the well, and helped make the tech sector the envy of the world. The modern American economy absolutely depended upon the skills, energy, and labor of these newcomers, which helps explain the labor component of the immigration question.

As the numbers, origins, and circumstances of those arriving in the United States evolved, so did the policy and legal apparatus that governed their arrival, which reflected the challenges to democratic governance examined in Reuel Schiller's and Joseph Thorndike's chapters in this volume. Most of the changes to immigration policy and law in the first two decades after 1965 merely consolidated the original reforms. In a sign of things to come, though, Congress's annual appropriations for border control and border control personnel began to shoot up after 1980.[24] The first significant policy departure came in 1986 with the Immigration Reform and Control Act (IRCA), a bipartisan measure many years in the making. Immigration advocates won a path to permanent residency and citizenship for many of the over 3 million unauthorized individuals in the United States, what almost all involved described as IRCA's "amnesty" provisions. Those legislators who decried what they called "illegal immigration" were heartened by IRCA's proposed sanctions against employers who hired the unauthorized and by even more funding for border control.[25]

In the decades after IRCA, law and policy turned even harder toward restricting immigration and limiting the rights of immigrants in the United States. The federal government set up several border security operations—with almost laughably macho code names like "Operation Gatekeeper" and "Operation Hold the Line"—in the early 1990s that surged resources to the border in a show of deterrent force that aimed to slow unauthorized entry. Their effects were hardly funny, though. Individuals crossed the border in more inhospitable and dangerous spots, leading to more than a thousand deaths by the end of the 1990s, though some estimates push the body count higher.[26]

Change came in the legislative arena too, and along the same lines. The 1996 Illegal Immigration Reform and Immigrant Responsibility Act (IIRIRA) gave the government greater deportation powers, provided for five thousand more border patrol agents over the next five years, and made it harder for individuals to adjust their immigration status. Likewise, the landmark welfare reform law (the Personal Responsibility and Work Opportunity Act) of that same year found many of its fiscal savings in cutting newcomers of all types out of the social safety net, just as the feminist thinkers in Leandra Zarnow's chapter feared a decade before. Immigration opponents triumphed at the state level, too. In California, virulent anti-immigrant politics boiled over with that state's passage of Proposition 187, which denied newcomers access to social services. While the courts quickly neutered much of Prop. 187, its passage confirmed the general direction of immigration politics and policy.[27]

These trends intensified in the early twenty-first century. In the wake of the 9/11 attacks, the Republican Bush administration toughened policies toward all sorts of newcomers with the 2001 Patriot Act and the development of the Department of Homeland Security (DHS). Bush sliced admissions to the United States of refugees via the Refugee Act, numbers that only recovered by about 2007. Asylees faced huge backlogs in trying to push their cases through an overburdened system that added the prevention of the entry of suspected terrorists to its generally skeptical attitude toward asylum claims.[28] Nonimmigrants—tourists, students, and temporary workers, for instance—also saw their avenues of entry into the United States narrowed.

Away from the border, the Bush administration began a surveillance and monitoring program called National Security Entry-Exit Registration System (NSEERS) that required male, aged 16 and older, newcomers from over twenty countries with large Muslim populations (and North Korea) to register with the DHS. NSEERS, which lasted until 2011, did not identify any terrorists but it did prove effective at identifying unauthorized individuals in the United States. Finally, if California led the anti-immigrant surge in the 1990s at the state level, then two other states took over in the 2000s. Arizona made national headlines for Sheriff Joe Arpaio's stridently anti-immigrant policies and the anti-newcomer legislation SB. 1070, which Republican governor Jan Brewer supported. On the other side of the country, Georgia drew attention for trying to cut off some newcomers from the state's institutions of higher education.[29]

As scholars like Daniel Tichenor have demonstrated, the political configurations and alliances at the foundation of immigration lawmaking and policymaking stayed relatively stable across most of the twentieth century.[30] The restrictionist (immigration opponents and skeptics) and liberalizer (immigration supporters) blocs were relatively evenly matched. Each contained regional diversity, each were bipartisan, and each mixed different political ideologies. They were stable too, though some movement occurred: Labor unions moved from the restrictionist to the liberalizer camp in the last half of the twentieth century. After 1945, immigration legislation almost always arose out of horse-trading between the two blocs. That bargaining could take years—the discussions that resulted in the 1986 IRCA began in 1981—and brought together strange bedfellows, but the pattern was fairly clear. Each side retreated somewhat from its beginning positions to craft compromise laws, even if a particular law sometimes saw one bloc gaining more than the other.

The late twentieth-century makeup of the liberalizer and restrictionist camps highlights how the immigration question's evolution illuminates the political fault lines deeply interwoven into the health of the American labor market and democratic capitalism. Among those happy to see the admissions of newcomers expanded, for example, were conservative free marketers, large industrial or farming interests, ethnic interest groups, human rights and immigrant rights organizations, and pluralist, cosmopolitan liberals. On the restrictionist side stood some liberals and environmental groups (who worried about newcomers overcrowding the job market and degrading the environment, respectively), joined by conservative nationalists, like Patrick Buchanan, and anti-newcomer interest groups like the Federation for American Immigration Reform (FAIR). These partnerships on the issue of newcomers entering the country did scramble a bit when it came to the rights of immigrants in the United States. Free-marketers, for instance, wanted immigrants to enter the United States, but had little interest in ensuring their rights once in the country, while liberals wary of too many immigrant admissions did switch to the immigrant side on rights issues.[31]

These basic dynamics held in immigration politics into the 1990s and even as the policies writ large turned more restrictionist. The 1996 IIRIRA saw these heterogenous restrictionist and liberalizer blocs hold together much as they had in previous decades. And the parties continued to be divided internally by immigration. Welfare reform in 1996, for instance, demonstrated the typical splits among Democrats. Some restrictionist Democrats joined with restrictionist Republicans to support reforms that further cut all sorts of newcomers from the social safety net (and generated massive savings in welfare expenditures), while a good number of liberal Democrats saw those cuts as harshly punitive. The Clinton administration proposed a middle path, but when much of the final legislation's welfare savings targeted newcomers, the Clinton White House vowed to try to reverse them in the coming years. Welfare reform enacted via immigration policy showed deep fissures among Democrats.[32]

The cracks in these political configurations did begin to appear, slightly, in the 1990s, especially in California's battle over Prop. 187. California voters,

Democrats and Republicans, supported the measure by large margins. But Republicans in California, especially GOP Governor Pete Wilson, led the charge for 187 while Democrats and liberals led the pushback. As historian Sarah Coleman points out, 187 taught many in the California GOP the value of immigration restriction, and thus led them to marginalize more moderate voices on immigration, especially business interests. Democrats, meanwhile, saw an opportunity to shore up their support among Latinos by advocating for immigrants.[33]

But the possibility of partisan polarization revealed by the battle over 187 should not be overstated. A large contingent of Democrats, including Clinton, supported a variety of border control measures and some were open to cutting newcomers from the social safety net, just perhaps not the way that 187 did. In the GOP, the free-marketers and business community still offered an agenda that welcomed newcomers while figures like the Bush family rejected outright cultural nationalism. Immigration politics after 9/11 frankly did little to clarify the state of play when momentous reforms like the Patriot Act passed the Senate with only one dissenting vote and the House with only sixty-six "nay" votes. These outcomes were largely the result of rally-round-the-flag patriotism that surged through the United States, with no real antecedent in immigration politics.

The Immigration Question, Front and Center in the New Millennium

And yet, it was at that moment, as the twenty-first century began, that the familiar patterns of immigration politics really began breaking down and the immigration question catapulted to the fore. A few episodes brought on this new era.

A key early moment came in 2005 as immigration reform proposals bubbled out of a Republican-controlled Congress. A group of Republican immigration hardliners in Congress, led by Rep. James Sensenbrenner of Wisconsin, rushed a stunningly restrictionist reform bill through Congress right before Christmas almost exclusively on the strength of GOP votes. The aptly named "Border Protection, Antiterrorism, and Illegal Immigration Control Act" included greater funding for border control and aimed to jail those who entered the United States without authorization. The former was unsurprising, but the latter proposed a significant alteration of existing policy, which, in most cases, returned to their country of origin those apprehended after entering without authorization. The Sensenbrenner proposal was strikingly escalatory.[34]

Key GOP Senate leaders, though, had little interest in passing such an anti-immigrant measure. Taking their cues from President Bush and working with Democrats like Senator Ted Kennedy, they responded with proposals that would increase border security but also start a guest worker program and create a path for the unauthorized living in the United States to win permanent residency.[35]

This Senate approach was not new. President Bush had nearly crafted just such a deal with Mexican President Vincente Fox in the late summer of 2001 before the 9/11 attacks scuttled that opportunity. Moreover, the sort of trade-offs inherent in the Senate proposal—more border security in return for a path for permanent residency for the unauthorized—fell in line with other legislative maneuvering over the previous decades, for instance the 1986 IRCA. And yet, in this case, the House Republicans refused to bend or compromise, setting up a standoff and a grand debate over immigration and immigration policy as 2005 came to an end.

The House Republicans' punitive approach stirred up a hornets' nest of opposition. Republicans' aggressive legislative approach energized advocates and supporters of immigration. The most stunning moment came with the "Day Without an Immigrant" protests that reached a crescendo on May 1, 2006. Organizers managed to convince hundreds of thousands of immigrants and their political allies to walk out of work and school to protest. Four hundred thousand hit the streets in Los Angeles, 300,000 protested in Chicago, and another 12,000 locked arms as human chains in New York City. Some industries, like meat processing plants, had to close for the day because their workers were protesting.[36]

Those protests highlighted, as this volume does, the intertwining of democracy, capitalism, and work with the immigration question. Indeed, from this perspective, the labor question was not dead; it had morphed into an immigration question. Some "Day Without an Immigrant" protesters carried signs attacking the House Republican December 2005 bill, declaring: "This is not democracy; it's hypocrisy." Others told their personal stories. One man from Guatemala, who arrived in the early 1990s, revealed: "I crossed a river and came here as an illegal and now I have a green card and a profession. I want others to have the same opportunity. The way we treat immigrants at the moment isn't just."[37] The overall attitude of the "Day Without an Immigrant" demonstrations was best reflected by one of the protests' supporters, who declared: "I think people have to realize that enough is enough in the bashing of immigrants. . . . We can't be the scapegoats for everything that happens in this country. We're just as American as everyone else."[38]

Unsurprisingly, the "Day Without" movement heightened the ire of some of the most virulent anti-immigrant activists. One member of the Washington, D.C.–area chapter of the Minutemen, a national group that opposed what it called "illegal" immigration, was upset that the protests were even occurring. In advance of the May 1 event, and not knowing how large they would be, he declared: "Unfortunately, American laws do not ban foreigners from protesting on our soil." He comforted himself, though, by concluding, "Who are they influencing? They're not influencing Congress."[39] It was another piece of evidence suggesting the links that participants in immigration politics made to democracy.

The actions of Republican politicians and interest groups were equally telling. Moderates pressed ahead with their approach, which only accelerated the political war between the immigration hardliners and the moderates in the GOP. Conservative media, especially talk radio and Fox News, buzzed with blistering attacks on the GOP senators who supported the more moderate approach. One policy expert who worked with the Democrats remembered the moment as a turning point because leading restrictionist organizations like the Federation for American Immigration Reform (FAIR) "managed to convince Fox News back then to be their twenty-four hour news channel of the anti-immigrants point of view."[40]

No one took more flak than longtime allies and immigration moderates Senators John McCain and Lindsey Graham. Those Republicans earned the nicknames "Amnesty John" and "Lindsey Gomez." As McCain recalled later, "I remember being on talk shows and the host wouldn't let me get a word in. . . . Then listening to the talk shows in the car: 'Amnesty John' and 'Lindsey Gomez.' It became pretty apparent that the depth of emotion on the issue was quite significant."[41]

The quest by immigration deal-makers like McCain and Kennedy for some sort of compromise law continued into 2007, when the effort finally died. Immigrant advocates, many of whom had rallied in the streets in the "Day Without" protests, largely backed the compromise approach, though support was not unanimous. While the Service Employees International Union (SEIU) and its sizeable immigrant rank and file signed on, the AFL-CIO rejected the Kennedy-McCain framework because of its inclusion of a guest worker program.[42] All in all, Democrats and liberals probably pulled their weight in bringing enough of their supporters to the compromise bill. The changed dynamic lay on the Republican side where those hardliners would not cave and the fight actually made clear their—and their media allies'—power. McCain even pointed to the immigration fight later as a drag on his fundraising abilities in the 2008 presidential contest, indicative of the split in the party, the harm and dangers it created for titular leaders like Bush and McCain, and the salience of the hardline position.

The immigration debates of 2005–2007 ended without resolution, only seeding the ground for the next confrontations. But it was clear that there was little room for the compromise and cross-party legislative bargains that had emerged in decades of prior policy discussions. The Bush, McCain, Graham, and Kennedy set just did not have the votes to make a deal. And while both immigrant advocates and immigrant opponents rallied to their respective causes with an energy not seen in previous years, the latter, largely in the hothouse of conservative politics and media, were especially fervent. Bush, McCain, and Graham, representative of the mildly liberalizer approach so important to the party for years, were the ones crowded out.

By 2009, a new group—the Tea Party—kept the immigration question front and center. Most observers trace the birth of the Tea Party to early 2009, when a TV reporter on CNBC blasted financial aid for those with underwater mortgages and called for a return to his definition of the country's first principles.[43] That call to arms struck a chord with conservatives and Republicans who were rudderless in the wake of Democrat Barack Obama's election to the presidency. GOP leaders happily co-opted the energy and anger that many grassroots Republicans felt in claiming the Tea Party moniker. Of course, it was not all a grassroots movement. Big money donors, like the Koch family, sat behind at least parts of the Tea Party movement.[44]

Demographically, Tea Party members tended to be middle-aged or elderly middle-class and upper-class Whites. Tea Partiers expressed intertwined elements of economic and cultural conservatism, though too many contemporary observers stressed the former, neglected the latter, and failed to see their connections. Tea Partiers lambasted government spending, lamented high taxes, and questioned the welfare state—with a large caveat. In the mental world of the Tea Party, Americans like themselves had worked and paid those taxes and thus deserved, in the logic of fiscal citizenship laid out in Joseph Thorndike's chapter, government aid via the welfare state. They had, after all, earned it. Tea Partiers contrasted themselves sharply to younger Americans, to people of color, and to those individuals they viewed as just plain lazy, none of whom had earned the help that government programs provided.[45]

There is some debate about the breadth of anti-immigrant sentiment in the Tea Party. Some evidence suggests decent support among the Tea Party for newcomers of all types, and a number of Tea Partiers wholeheartedly backed what they called "legal immigration."[46] Moreover, a majority of Tea Party members, according to one reputable survey, supported a path to permanent residence for unauthorized individuals. Even larger majorities in that survey rejected the idea of mass deportations of unauthorized immigrants.[47] Other observers, including the two leading scholars (Theda Skocpol and Vanessa Williamson) of the Tea Party, who studied its grassroots organizations and members, dismissed this interpretation. They believed that immigration "more than anything else" motivated the group's rank and file, noting that "the fear and hatred of particularly Hispanic immigrants is very, very strong."[48] As Skocpol and Williamson concluded of the Tea Party members: "Virtually all want government to police immigrants."[49]

Indeed, a good number of Tea Partiers were suspicious of, or outright opposed to, immigration and immigrants. What did those Tea Partiers believe? For many, that immigrants of all types put stresses on local communities, especially schools, the implication being that the immigrant presence destroyed the school system for long-standing community members. Relatedly, others feared that so-called "illegal immigrants" came to the United States and siphoned the country's hard-earned wealth by taking advantage of, and abusing, the modern welfare state. In this zero-sum game scheme, those newcomers took directly from older American citizens who had contributed to the United States for decades. But such claims did not reflect reality; both authorized and unauthorized immigrants—less so refugees—were excluded from much of the social safety net. Nonetheless, this story about newcomers, and especially the unauthorized, mapped on to the larger concerns that many Tea Partiers had about how aid and resources found their way to supposedly unworthy populations.[50]

Some Tea Party members expressed disgust with how the unauthorized broke American laws to either enter or remain in the United States. Tea Partiers saw unauthorized individuals as both lawbreakers and as a stain on American sovereignty. The US–Mexican border emerged as a key concern of some Tea Party members, who wanted a stronger presence at the border to deter so-called "illegal immigration." More than 4 in 5 Tea Partiers in a 2010 poll called "illegal immigration" a "very serious" current issue. No wonder a popular Tea Party bumper sticker declared "Law and Border."[51] This call for a tougher border regime of course involved not just deterring the unauthorized, but naturally scrutinizing everyone arriving at the country's gates.

Finally, many Tea Partiers felt a cultural disconnect with newcomers. One Tea Party member stated that in modern America, "you have to select English for daily transactions,"[52] tracking with long-standing anti-newcomer complaints that English had become a second language in the United States (and echoing Patrick Buchanan's infamous "Meatball" presidential ad from 2000).[53] Mississippian Chris McDaniel, a Tea Party candidate who tried to unseat Senator Thad Cochrane in the Republican primary, described his displeasure with a more diverse America this way: "Millions in this country feel like strangers in this land. You recognize that, don't you? An older America is passing away. A newer America is rising to take its place. We recoil from that culture. It's foreign to us. It's offensive to us."[54]

The Tea Party's rise helped cement the immigration question at the center of American politics. The Tea Party's general prominence in American politics, via its role in attacking the Obama health care proposal[55] and its efforts that propelled the GOP to victory in the 2010 midterm elections, brought attention to other aspects of its agenda, like immigration. Tea Party activists used the immigration issue to blast away at fellow Republicans whom they considered insufficiently dedicated to Tea Party concerns. Nowhere was this clearer than in the Tea Party's signature triumph over a GOP standard bearer: underdog Tea Party candidate Dave Brat's victory over House Majority Leader Eric Cantor in the GOP primary in the summer of 2014. Brat harangued Cantor on immigration, claiming that Cantor supported a path to permanent residence for unauthorized individuals, something Brat and others derisively labeled "amnesty."[56] Brat's win indicated the appeal of tougher and less accommodationist immigration policies and rhetoric to the GOP. As such, the Tea Party pushed ever larger numbers of Republicans toward a harder line on immigration.

One indication of how comfortable the Right was with this anti-newcomer thinking—and a charge that further fueled anti-newcomer animus—came in 2011 when Republicans began questioning the legitimacy of President Obama's birth certificate and therefore his eligibility for holding the White House. Donald Trump and Fox News trumpeted this fantastical, and easily disproven, charge. But the idea that Obama was not a citizen and had essentially invaded the White House mirrored ideas on the Right about immigrants and the United States. This "birther" charge also meant that there was little Obama could do to assuage anti-immigrant forces on the right; there was no way he could be tough enough on immigration to satisfy them.[57]

Elements of this Tea Party thinking, as well as the GOP's birtherism, found its way into Republican presidential nominee Mitt Romney's 2012 campaign. Romney adopted some of the Tea Party rhetoric about the deserving and undeserving of government aid in his remarkable "47 percent" comments, recorded at an event with GOP donors: "There are 47 percent of the people who will vote for the president no matter what. All right, there are 47 percent who are with him, who are dependent upon government, who believe that they are victims, who believe the government has a responsibility to care for them, who believe that they are entitled to health care, to food, to housing, to you-name-it. . . . These are people who pay no income tax."[58]

Romney went further down the Tea Party route with his comments about unauthorized immigration, especially as he sought the GOP nomination. He explained that his policy to reduce the number of unauthorized immigrants in the United States amounted to "self-deportation," by which he meant "people decide they can do better by going home because they can't find work here because they don't have legal documentation to allow them to work here." While he added a caveat—"We're not going to round people up"—the theory behind self-deportation was brutalizing.[59] Borrowed from immigration activist and Tea Party darling Kris Kobach, who advised the campaign—and later advised Donald Trump on immigration—the self-deportation approach demanded that communities make life so uncomfortable and unwelcoming to unauthorized immigrants that they would decide to give up on living in the United States and leave. While Romney did offer support to "legal" immigrants and did retreat from criticizing some unauthorized individuals living in the United States, mainly the so-called Dreamers, as the general election campaign heated up, he still repeatedly trumpeted his opposition to unauthorized entry.[60]

Immigration was not a top-line issue in Romney's campaign, but it was revealing on a few fronts. Romney chose a much more aggressive approach to immigration than McCain had only four years before, a sign that the candidate surely knew which way the winds were blowing in his party. Moreover, his use of Tea Party rhetoric on immigrants and the related dichotomy of the deserving/undeserving demonstrated that group's power. Romney, then, did not do as much as others to turn up the heat on the immigration issue, but he surely kept it on the stove, simmering away.

Republicans and a subset of hardline immigration opponents within the party did the most to elevate the immigration question in American politics in the early twenty-first century. But immigration liberalizers and key Democrats also played an important role. As already noted, activists pushed back against the punitive legislative proposals authored by House Republicans in 2005 and 2006 with the "Day Without an Immigrant" demonstrations. Those large national protests should not obscure smaller, community-based campaigns. In Charlotte, North Carolina, recent newcomers from Mexico fought back after experiencing a backlash as they moved to that region's exurbs in the early twenty-first century.[61] Similar drives popped up among Hispanics, especially younger individuals, in Georgia and Arizona when state governments initiated a slate of anti-immigrant policies at the end of the twenty-first century's first decade.[62]

The work of those advocating for immigrants and immigration helped elevate the immigration question in politics, but they did not only rail against GOP hardliners. Instead, the Obama administration also came in for criticism from these activists.[63] Obama's approach on immigration through most of his first term was to seek a grand bargain on immigration policy. Obama kept in place the stringent border and deportation policies of the preceding years, even showing a willingness to accelerate them in the hope that demonstrating a commitment to border security would convince skeptical Republicans to join Democrats in supporting a path to permanent residence in the United States for the unauthorized and other smaller liberal reforms to immigration law. In this approach, Obama had the support of many congressional Democrats. He also was walking in the footsteps of previous reformers like Kennedy and McCain.

The strategy failed on two fronts. First, immigration skeptics were not swayed by the Obama administration's border security policies, and no compromise legislation made it through Congress. Obama ran into problems trying to bring around the shrinking number of Republicans who supported the grand bargain approach but just could not stand the political heat immigration generated in their party. Again, conservative media and activists like Rush Limbaugh played a key role as they blasted the bipartisan approach for offering an easy path to citizenship for unauthorized individuals.[64]

Second, members of the immigration advocacy community lambasted the Obama administration for employing stricter border enforcement and deportation regimes—and the attendant costs in lives ruined trying to cross the border—to win immigration reform. Most famously, the National Council of La Raza's (NCLR) president in 2014 labeled Obama "the deporter in chief."[65] A number of Latinos and immigration advocates displayed a real sense of betrayal. One woman, whose husband immigration authorities detained in early 2014, remarked: "President Obama has the right to stop deportations; he just don't want to do it. When I first saw President Obama, tears came to my eyes because I said 'He's the one who is going to bring us out of the shadows.' Now when I see him, I see a future that is uncertain for myself and everyone else."[66]

Even before the noteworthy confrontation with the NCLR in 2014, Obama began to switch his approach in 2012 as his reelection efforts picked up steam. Most famously, he promulgated the Deferred Action for Childhood Arrivals (DACA) program in 2012, which protected individuals brought to the United States as minors from deportation. As his second term went on, Obama seemed to give up hope of bringing Republicans around and instead ratcheted down the border security effort and began issuing other executive orders and executive actions that allowed more unauthorized newcomers to remain in the United States.[67] But the critiques of his actions from his putative allies like the NCLR had purposefully kept the immigration question front and center in politics in the hope of spurring just such a change. In this sense, immigration advocates, by utilizing such jarring language and stories, did their part to catapult immigration to the top of the agenda.

Even then, there is an important difference to consider as the immigration question found its way to prominence through the work of supporters of newcomers. Obama took loud criticism for his border control policies that stressed enforcement and deportation, but his critics never booted him (or less prominent politicians than the president who shared his policy predilections) from the coalition that sought to remake immigration law. The contrast with the GOP was clear. Immigration restrictionists had always been in the modern Republican party, but many of the most prominent restrictionists of the twentieth century were willing to deal. Those types of dealmakers just could not find the political space to operate in the twenty-first century. Put another way, the great Republican immigration lawmaker of the late twentieth century was Senator Alan Simpson—a man of restrictionist leanings who played a key role in birthing the legislation of the 1980s and 1990s—but his heirs like McCain and Florida Senator Marco Rubio worked in a drastically different environment. And Simpson, McCain, and Rubio as restrictionists were miles away from someone like Senator Jeff Sessions, the face of recalcitrant immigration restriction in the new century.

A Twenty-First-Century Stalemate

The prominence of the "immigration question" in American politics is important in its own right, but also for what it reveals about the health of democratic governance in modern America. Two points stand out in particular.

It is not a stretch to conclude that legislating on immigration issues has become nearly impossible in the twenty-first century. Even relatively small-bore proposals, like the Afghan Adjustment Act, which would offer a pathway to permanent resident status for thousands of Afghan refugees paroled into the United States in the aftermath of the US withdrawal from that country, cannot find their way through Congress.[68] Bigger immigration reforms, like a pathway to permanent residence for unauthorized individuals, a rethinking of American asylum policy, a reform of the preference system that guides the allocation of immigrant visas, have no hope of passage. The proposals, when they even appear, are dead on arrival, and the largest impediment is conservatives within the restrictionist camp. This is a relatively recent development. Adjustment acts for Hungarian, Cuban, and Indochinese refugees in similar situations passed easily and with support from restrictionists and liberalizers, Democrats and Republicans.[69] Major immigration legislation in the 1980s and 1990s had equally broad origins.

Nowhere was this new state of play more apparent than in the border security/immigration proposal agreed upon by the Biden administration and Senate Republicans in 2024. The legislation would have poured more resources into border control and would have severely limited access to asylum, all in the hopes of considerably slowing the number of individuals crossing the country's borders. Immigration and refugee advocates were aghast at the specifics and hardly pleased with Democrats, including the president, who adopted increasingly restrictionist approaches. Eyeing his campaign for the White House, though, Donald Trump rallied immigration hardliners and they submarined the proposal. The hardliners in the GOP triumphed again.[70]

The point here is not to blindly praise bipartisan legislation generally, or, in particular, immigration policy that emerged out of compromise between the heterogenous liberalizer and restrictionist camps. Any political historian can rattle off a number of awful laws and policies produced via these compromises; an immigration historian quickly notes the bipartisan support for the 1920s national origins quota system. But it is to recognize that this new era of immigration politics has stalled out any policy or legislative solutions, even imperfect ones that might be improved upon or revised at later dates. In this sense, immigration policy, and the political configurations underlying it, is no different than climate, energy, or health care policy, to name a few, and all part of the larger stalemate in politics and policymaking that too often makes the country seem nearly ungovernable.

The rise of the immigration question has also been accompanied by the marginalization and debasement of newcomers, especially by restrictionists and immigration skeptics, but also by some liberalizers. The utmost promise of democratic governance is the development and extension of certain values, especially those relating to individual political and civil rights, social and economic equality and opportunity, and bodily autonomy and integrity. Yet, in modern immigration affairs, the Dreamers remain in limbo, unauthorized individuals must live in society's shadows, and immigrant bodies are inspected, and too often brutalized, at the border. And there seems no end to the cruelty. The Biden administration not only announced in late February 2023 new rules for asylum-seekers that meant those arriving at the border seeking protection will find those avenues increasingly closed shut, but tried in 2024 to win further restrictions.[71]

Time and again, the politics and policies produced in the era of the "immigration question" reveal that newcomers fail to enjoy the promises of democratic governance. Instead, immigrants are both the victims of its deterioration and their treatment is one of the vehicles by which democratic governance deteriorates. Changing the shape of the "immigration question"—the ways we talk about and create policy around newcomers—is one path toward a revival of democracy's promise. It is hard to envision a more vital task.

Notes

1. Nelson Lichtenstein's works stand at the center of this scholarship. Nelson Lichtenstein, *State of the Union: A Century of American Labor* (Princeton: Princeton University Press, 2013, revised edition); *Walter Reuther: The Most Dangerous Man in Detroit* (New York: Basic Books, 1995).

2. "Here's Donald Trump's Presidential Announcement Speech," *Time*, June 16, 2015, available at https://time.com/3923128/donald-trump-announcement-speech/.

3. Gallup, "Immigration Surges to Top of Most Important Problem List," July 18, 2018, https://news.gallup.com/poll/237389/immigration-surges-top-important-problem-list.aspx; Gallup, "New High in U.S. Say Immigration Most Important Problem," June 21, 2019, https://news.gallup.com/poll/259103/new-high-say-immigration-important-problem.aspx.

4. Gallup, "Most Important Problem," November 2021, https://news.gallup.com/poll/1675/most-important-problem.aspx; Gallup, "Fewer in U.S. Cite Coronavirus as Major Problem,"

April 28, 2021, https://news.gallup.com/poll/349205/fewer-cite-coronavirus-important-problem.aspx.

5. Pew, “Americans Views of the Problems Facing the Nation,” April 15, 2021, https://www.pewresearch.org/politics/2021/04/15/americans-views-of-the-problems-facing-the-nation/pp_2021-04-15_biden-100-days_03-01/.

6. Greg Grandin’s *The End of the Myth* is a thoughtful rumination on this phenomenon. Greg Grandin, *The End of the Myth: From the Frontier to the Border Wall in the Mind of America* (New York: Henry Holt, 2019), especially pages 267–269.

7. Gary Gerstle, *American Crucible: Race and Nation in the Twentieth Century* (Princeton: Princeton University Press, 2001.)

8. Arthur Schlesinger, *The Disuniting of America: Reflections on a Multicultural Society* (New York: W. W. Norton, 1991), 147.

9. Samuel Huntington, “The Hispanic Challenge,” *Foreign Policy*, March/April 2004.

10. Gary Gerstle, “Minorities, Multiculturalism, and the Presidency of George W. Bush,” Julian Zelizer, ed., *The Presidency of George W. Bush* (Princeton: Princeton University Press, 2010), 252–281; Sarah Coleman, “A Promise Unfulfilled, an Imperfect Legacy: Obama and Immigration Policy,” Julian Zelizer, ed., *The Presidency of Barack Obama* (Princeton: Princeton University Press, 2018), 179–194.

11. Abby Budiman, Pew Research Center, “How Many People in the U.S. Are Immigrants?,” August 20, 2022, available at https://www.pewresearch.org/fact-tank/2020/08/20/key-findings-about-u-s-immigrants/.

12. For a starting point on this line of thinking, see George Borjas, “Yes, Immigration Hurts American Workers,” *Politico*, September/October 2016, available at https://www.politico.com/magazine/story/2016/09/trump-clinton-immigration-economy-unemployment-jobs-214216/.

13. See, for example, Eric Schlosser, “Why It’s Immigrants Who Pack Your Meat,” *The Atlantic*, August 16, 2019, available at https://www.theatlantic.com/ideas/archive/2019/08/trumps-invasion-was-a-corporate-recruitment-drive/596230/. For insights into the laboring experiences of Chinese immigrants, see Xiaojian Zhao, *The New Chinese America: Class, Economy, and Social Hierarchy* (New Brunswick: Rutgers University Press, 2010).

14. See, as a starting point, Ruth Milkman, “Immigrants Didn’t Kill Your Union,” *Dissent*, Spring 2019, 57–64.

15. Carl J. Bon Tempo and Hasia Diner, *Immigration: An American History* (New Haven, CT: Yale University Press, 2022), 261.

16. Bon Tempo and Diner, *Immigration: An American History*, 273.

17. Aristide Zolberg, *A Nation by Design: Immigration Policy in the Fashioning of America* (Cambridge, MA: Harvard University Press, 2009), 333–338.

18. Bon Tempo and Diner, *Immigration: An American History*, 273–274.

19. Bon Tempo and Diner, *Immigration: An American History*, 276.

20. Carl Bon Tempo, *Americans at the Gate: The United States and Refugees During the Cold War* (Princeton: Princeton University Press, 2008); Maria Cristina Garciá, *The Refugee Challenge in Post–Cold War America* (New York: Oxford University Press, 2017).

21. Randy Capps et al., “Unauthorized Immigrants in the United States: Stable Numbers, Changing Origins,” Migration Policy Institute, December 2020, available at https://www.migrationpolicy.org/research/unauthorized-immigrants-united-states-stable-numbers-changing-origins; Bon Tempo and Diner, *Immigration: An American History*, 275, 333.

22. García, *The Refugee Challenge in Post–Cold War America*, 58–59, 63–64.

23. Liliana M. González and Michael Feil, "Public Insecurity and International Emigration in Northern Mexico," in *Mexican Migration to the United States: Perspectives from Both Sides of the Border*, ed. Harriet Romo and Olivia Mogollon-Lopez (Austin: University of Texas Press, 2016).

24. Joseph Nevins, *Operation Gatekeeper and Beyond: The War on "Illegals" and the Remaking of the U.S.-Mexico Boundary*, 2nd ed. (New York: Routledge, 2010), 5, 44, 84, Appendix F.

25. Bon Tempo and Diner, *Immigration: An American History*, 302–305.

26. Nevins, *Operation Gatekeeper and Beyond*, is the best overview of these operations. On the fatalities, see Mike Davis, *Magical Urbanisms: Latinos Reinvent the U.S. Big City* (New York: Verso, 2000), 41–42.

27. All of these events are covered in Bon Tempo and Diner, *Immigration: An American History*, 302–309, 313.

28. The best overview of these changes is available in Garciá, *The Refugee Challenge in Post-Cold War America*, pages 130–135. See Center for American Progress, "Rebuilding the U.S. Refugee System for the 21st Century," October 26, 2020, available at https://www.americanprogress.org/article/rebuilding-u-s-refugee-program-21st-century/.

29. For an overview of the post-9/11 immigration policies, see Gary Gerstle, "Minorities, Multiculturalism, and the Presidency of George W. Bush"; Bon Tempo and Diner, *Immigration*, 324–328, 343–345, 348–350.

30. Daniel Tichenor, *Dividing Lines: The Politics of Immigration Control in America* (Princeton: Princeton University Press, 2001).

31. Tichenor, *Dividing Lines*, 276.

32. Sarah Coleman, *The Walls Within: The Politics of Immigration in Modern America* (Princeton: Princeton University Press, 2021), 108–141; John F. Harris and John E. Yang, "Clinton to Sign Bill Overhauling Welfare," *Washington Post*, August 1, 1996, page A1; Peter Edelman, "The Worst Thing Bill Clinton Has Done," *The Atlantic*, March 1997, 43–58.

33. Coleman, *The Walls Within*, 127–130.

34. Rachel Weiner, "How Immigration Reform Failed, Over and Over," *Washington Post*, January 20, 2013, available at https://www.washingtonpost.com/news/the-fix/wp/2013/01/30/how-immigration-reform-failed-over-and-over/; Jonathan Weisman, "Immigrant Bill Fallout May Hurt House GOP," *Washington Post*, April 12, 2006, available at https://www.washingtonpost.com/wp-dyn/content/article/2006/04/11/AR2006041101643.html?itid=lk_inline_manual_19. For the vote tally, see "H.R. 4437 (109th): Border Protection, Antiterrorism, and Illegal Immigration Control Act of 2005," https://www.govtrack.us/congress/votes/109-2005/h661.

35. On Bush and immigration, I draw on Gary Gerstle, "Minorities, Multiculturalism, and the Presidency of George W. Bush," in Zelizer, ed., *The Presidency of George W. Bush*.

36. Ines Ferre et al.,"Hundreds of Thousands March for Immigrant Rights," CNN.com, May 3, 2006, available at http://www.cnn.com/2006/US/05/02/immigrant.day/.

37. Dan Glaister and Ewen MacAskill, "US Counts Cost of Day Without Immigrants," *The Guardian*, May 1, 2006, available at https://www.theguardian.com/world/2006/may/02/usa.topstories3.

38. Nancy Trejos and Aruna Jain, "Organizers Expect Crush for Immigrants Rights Rally," *Washington Post*, April 10, 2006.

39. Trejos and Jain, "Organizers Expect Crush for Immigrants Rights Rally."

40. Ryan Lizza, "Getting to Maybe: Inside the Gang of Eight's Immigration Deal," *The New Yorker*, June 24, 2013.

41. Dan Balz and Haynes Johnson, *The Battle for America: The Story of an Extraordinary Election* (New York: Penguin Press, 2010), 254.

42. Krissah Williams, "Unions Split on Immigrant Workers," *Washington Post*, January 27, 2007, available at https://www.washingtonpost.com/wp-dyn/content/article/2007/01/26/AR2007012601635.html?itid=lk_inline_manual_24.

43. Andrew Kirell, "When CNBC Created the Tea Party," *The Daily Beast*, October 30, 2015, available at https://www.thedailybeast.com/when-cnbc-created-the-tea-party.

44. Jane Mayer, "Covert Operations," *New Yorker*, August 30, 2010.

45. The best overview of the Tea Party is Theda Skocpol and Vanessa Williamson, *The Tea Party and the Remaking of Republican Conservatism* (New York: Oxford University Press, 2012).

46. Charles Clark, "These Tea Partiers Aren't Anti-Immigration. They Just Want to Close the Border," *National Journal*, July 24, 2014, available at https://www.nationaljournal.com/s/52086/ and at https://www.theatlantic.com/politics/archive/2014/07/these-tea-partiers-arent-anti-immigration-they-just-want-to-close-the-border/431157/.

47. Michael Dimock, "Tea Partiers Are Not All Immigration Hawks," Pew Research, June 11, 2014, available at https://www.pewresearch.org/fact-tank/2014/06/11/tea-partiers-are-not-all-immigration-hawks/.

48. Indeed, even the surveys that highlight the pro-immigration bent among some Tea Partiers admit that sizable minorities of Tea Partiers wanted a national deportation campaign and to deny the unauthorized any path toward citizenship or permanent residence—two positions that were more popular among the Tea Party than in either the GOP or the public at large. For the quotes, see Bryan Schatz, "The Tea Party Got What It Wanted," *Mother Jones*, September 10, 2019, available at https://www.motherjones.com/politics/2019/09/the-tea-party-got-what-it-wanted/.

49. Skocpol and Williamson, *The Tea Party* (2012 edition), 56.

50. Skocpol and Williamson, *The Tea Party*, 71–72; Clark, "These Tea Partiers Aren't Anti-Immigration"; Jay Root, "Updated: Tea Party Presses Perry on Immigration," *Texas Tribune*, September 19, 2011, available at https://www.texastribune.org/2011/09/19/tea-parties-press-rick-perry-immigration/.

51. Skocpol and Williamson, *The Tea Party*, 57.

52. Skocpol and Williamson, *The Tea Party*, 46.

53. For Buchanan's "Meatball" ad, see https://youtu.be/4-KkiYcK7IA.

54. William Galston, "Strangers in This Land—The Tea Party's Lament," March 28, 2014, available at https://www.brookings.edu/blog/fixgov/2014/03/28/strangers-in-this-land-the-tea-partys-lament/.

55. Jonathon Cohn, *The Ten Year War: Obamacare and the Unfinished Crusade for Universal Coverage* (New York: St. Martin's Press, 2021), 161–163.

56. "5 Takeaways from Cantor Shocker," *Politico*, June 10, 2014, available at https://www.politico.com/story/2014/06/2014-virginia-primary-eric-cantor-five-takeaways-107694?hp=t3_3.

57. Adam Serwer, "Birtherism of a Nation," *The Atlantic*, May 13, 2020, https://www.theatlantic.com/ideas/archive/2020/05/birtherism-and-trump/610978/; Anthony Zurcher, "The Birth of the Obama 'Birther' Conspiracy," *BBC*, September 16, 2016, https://www.bbc.com/news/election-us-2016–37391652.

58. Romney quoted in David Corn, "Romney Tells Millionaire Donors What He REALLY Thinks of Obama Voters," *Mother Jones*, September 17, 2012, https://www.motherjones.com/politics/2012/09/secret-video-romney-private-fundraiser/.

59. Lucy Madison, "Romney on Immigration," CBS News, January 24, 2012, https://www.cbsnews.com/news/romney-on-immigration-im-for-self-deportation/.

60. Jefferson Morley, "The Man Behind Romney's 'Self-Deportation' Plan," Salon.com, February 22, 2012, https://www.salon.com/2012/02/22/the_man_behind_romneys_self_deportation_dreams/; Maggie Haberman and Annie Karnie, "A Would-Be Trump Aide's Demands," *New York Times*, May 20, 2019, available at https://www.nytimes.com/2019/05/20/us/politics/kris-kobach-trump.html; Ed Pilkington, "Romney Softens Immigration Stance on Self-Deportation at Debate," *The Guardian*, October 17, 2012, available at https://www.theguardian.com/world/2012/oct/17/romney-immigration-presidential-debate.

61. Julie Weise, *Corazón de Dixie: Mexicanos in the U.S. South Since 1910* (Chapel Hill: University of North Carolina Press, 2015), 179–216.

62. Bon Tempo and Diner, *Immigration: An American History*, 349–350.

63. Sarah Coleman, "A Promise Unfulfilled, An Imperfect Legacy," in Julian Zelizer, ed., *The Presidency of Barack Obama* (Princeton: Princeton University Press, 2018).

64. Kevin Cirilli, "Limbaugh: Up to Me and Fox News," *Politico*, January 28, 2013, https://www.politico.com/story/2013/01/rush-limbaugh-immigration-fox-amnesty-086823.

65. Seung Min Kim and Carrie B. Brown, "The Death of Immigration Reform," *Politico*, June 27, 2014.

66. Kathleen Hennessy, "Immigration Advocates Step Up Pressure on Obama to Ease Deportations," *Los Angeles Times*, March 7, 2014, available at https://www.latimes.com/nation/politics/politicsnow/la-pn-obama-immigration-deportations-20140306-story.html#ixzz2vHbJfy00.

67. Sarah Coleman's "A Promise Unfulfilled, An Imperfect Legacy" is the best overview of these changes.

68. Luke Broadwater, "Bill to Grant Afghan Evacuees a Path to Residency Hits Snag," *New York Times*, September 23, 2022, p. A15; Farah Stockman, "Do Right by Our Afghan Allies. Pass the Afghan Adjustment Act," *New York Times*, December 17, 2022, p. A22.

69. See Bon Tempo, *Americans at the Gate*.

70. Luke Broadwater, "Senate to Vote Again on Border Bill as Democrats Seek Political Edge," *New York Times*, May 20, 2024, https://www.nytimes.com/2024/05/20/us/politics/senate-schumer-border-immigration.html.

71. Pedro Gerson, "Joe Biden Is Now Taking Immigration Policy Directly from Stephen Miller," Slate.com, February 27, 2023, available at https://slate.com/news-and-politics/2023/02/joe-biden-immigration-policy-stephen-miller-asylum-rules.html; Miriam Jordan, "Biden Administration Announces New Border Crackdown," *New York Times*, February 22, 2023, p. A16.

CHAPTER 9

Management and Power in Global Supply Chains: The Need for History in an Ahistorical Field

Shane Hamilton

Supply chain management is taught in business schools around the world, training the managers of the future to seek and capture value in global supply chains. Perhaps 130,000 Americans are employed as "supply chain managers," despite that being an occupational category so new that it is not directly counted in US Bureau of Labor Statistics employment figures.[1] They are very well-paid (average US salary is $108,311), they are overwhelmingly male (75%), and employment demand for them exceeds supply by a ratio of six to one.[2] Their work is routinely lauded as essential to the modern global economy, embodying and enabling capitalism's future.[3]

Supply chain management may in fact be the most future-oriented field in the contemporary business world. A veritable "historic turn" has taken root in other business and management fields in recent years, revivifying critical historical contextualization in areas ranging from entrepreneurship to organization studies to strategic management and international business.[4] The historical turn, however, seems completely off the map for the field of supply chain management. The vast bulk of research in the field is ahistorical, and as I demonstrate in this chapter, when history is invoked it is done in epistemologically and ethically problematic ways, which I call "disowning history" and "selectively interpreting history." Rather than critically considering the historical development of the political and economic contexts that have made supply chain management into the world's newest profession, supply chain managers are trained to think of their work as necessary and predetermined, driven by technological and economic "forces."

In the following pages I consider a range of (a)historical narratives produced by supply chain theorists and practitioners since the 1980s, when the term "supply chain management" first came into widespread use. These histories will seem jarring to labor and business historians and historians of capitalism. The pioneering 1970s publications of new labor historians (discussed in this volume's final section) swept aside abstract notions of determinist "forces," insisting instead that capitalist conflicts were always cultural as much as economic. Whether practicing labor history, sociocultural business history, or history of capitalism, most historians now consider it uncontestably true that the dynamics of power between workers and managers—whether on a factory floor or in a movie theater—are embedded in sociopolitical relationships, not abstract timeless institutions.[5] Even Peter Drucker understood this. The famed mid-century management theorist pioneered the analysis of distribution in the industrial economy in the 1960s, chiding CEOs for failing to think of workers in distribution fields as actual people: people with ideas, experiences, and interests, rather than as abstract "allocations," "administrative expense," or worst of all, mere "donkey[s]."[6] Two decades after Drucker rebuked managers for ignoring the labor processes of distribution, I argue, theorists of the "new" field of supply chain management developed formal models for doing precisely that, imagining a past burdened by administrative expenses, antithetical to a future of seamless transactions across the boundaries of firms and nation-states.

Today, by imagining linear deterministic pasts, supply chain management researchers and practitioners are engaged in erasing alternative paths for the supply chains of the future. Recent events have highlighted the uncertainty embedded in global supply chains, however. Breakdowns in global supply chains—container ships stuck in canals, shortages and rationing at major multinational retail chains, skyrocketing commodity costs, renationalization of manufacturing sites—suggest the possibility that the loci of power may be shifting. The Wal-Mart-style, buyer-driven, tightly coordinated supply chains of the late twentieth century may be in the process of giving way to more fragmentary networks, characterized by increasingly dispersed contestations of power by multiple stakeholders. In our contemporary moment, then, the work of historians and historically sensitive social scientists who have studied the broader contexts of supply chains is increasingly important. How historians can—and why they must—reshape the public understanding of supply chain management is the subject of the pages that follow.

A Historiography of "Supply Chain Management"

As a concept, field of practice, and area of academic research, "supply chain management" is routinely understood to be a very new phenomenon, generally dated to the early 1980s, after the embrace of deregulation explored by Reuel Schiller in his chapter. On this matter, historians, management theorists, and business practitioners largely agree.[7] Yet whereas historians and social scientists might see the rise of a new field of management as a product of broad political, social, and economic transformations (like those transforming the immigration question in Carl Bon Tempo's chapter), members of the field itself routinely insist that its central concepts emerged from finely honed business practice. Most often, the internal historiography of supply chain management points to a 1982 report highlighting the work of London-based strategy consultants at Booz Allen Hamilton who used the term "supply chain management" to describe their work in pushing US and European firms to integrate previously distinct operations of purchasing, manufacturing, sales, and distribution, following the lead of "lean" Japanese automotive manufacturers.[8] The *Financial Times* highlighted the Booz Allen Hamilton approach in June 1982, bringing the term "supply chain management" into wider public discourse for the first time.[9]

From the moment of the term's coinage, supply chain management was understood to be integrative of other related business functions, including purchasing, logistics, distribution, and marketing. Yet while Booz Allen Hamilton consultants emphasized that "the supply chain has to be managed as a single entity," implying that lead firms (manufacturers) would run the show, supply chain management has also been understood as a "wider, intercompany, boundary-spanning concept" requiring noncentralized coordination and information sharing among multiple firms of different types and sizes.[10] In this latter vein, some alternative histories of supply chain management see the field emerging not from one report by a strategy consulting firm advising multinational manufacturing firms, but instead from a more collaborative approach developed by manufacturers, retailers, and consultants in the US textile industry in the 1980s.[11] Although hardly a raging historiographical debate in the field, such contradictions reveal the lack of historically contextualized analyses of where the power lies in modern supply chains (a point to which I return below).

Within academic business and management research, the concept of supply chain management was not immediately adopted as significantly innovative.

When business journals first published work in the field, it was initially produced by practitioners rather than theorists.[12] Supply chain researchers seeking to put the field on firmer intellectual ground have occasionally emphasized in recent years that in many ways there is not so much that is new about the concept. One stream of reflection suggests that supply chain management is simply a reformulation of what used to be called purchasing and supply management, a field with theoretical foundations stretching back to the nineteenth-century British polymath Charles Babbage and more substantially to work done at Harvard Business School in the 1920s, primarily focused on systemic cost reduction for large firms. Supporting this view is the fact that the journal once known as the *International Journal of Purchasing and Materials Management* changed its title in 1999 to become the *Journal of Supply Chain Management.*[13]

Other theorists in the field instead see the intellectual roots of the field in demand-side logistics and distribution. Here the founding theoretician is generally acknowledged to be management scholar Peter Drucker, whose 1962 article in *Fortune* declared distribution to be the "dark continent" of the industrial economy, in great need of being more carefully and thoughtfully "managed."[14] Drucker overstated the case, however, as the study of "physical distribution" was already established in the late nineteenth century, as agricultural economists sought to understand the problems of moving surplus agricultural goods across regional and national boundaries.[15] Nonetheless, it is certainly the case that beginning in the 1960s, "physical distribution" increasingly came to be understood as one component of a wider field of "logistics." Previously associated with military procurement and transportation, logistics was promoted in the 1960s by academic researchers as a "total cost approach" for firms, integrating previously siloed operations in transportation, inventory control, warehousing, and facility location. Logistics textbooks and university courses emerged in the 1960s, leading some scholars to suggest that supply chain management's roots are fully embedded in the "logistics revolution" that flourished in business practice in the 1970s, as retailers including Wal-Mart drew on transportation and information technologies to slash costs.[16] Crucial to this transformation was the uniting of distribution—traditionally a subset of marketing and thus inherently consumer-oriented—with logistics and procurement via new information technologies that enabled some firms (particularly Wal-Mart) to pit suppliers against each other to drive costs down.[17] By the late 1970s, this antagonistic conceptualization of logistics as a tool for suppressing the economic power of suppliers was formalized by Harvard Business School professor Michael

Porter. With his influential "Five Forces" framework, Porter declared that the bargaining power of suppliers was one of the most significant factors preventing anchor firms from attaining "supranormal profits" in an industry.[18]

Tying supply chain management to the history of distribution and logistics emphasizes the interests of retailers over manufacturers, consumers over workers. Some supply chain management scholars thus advocate different terminology, referring to "value chains" (or "networks") to suggest that it is possible to "manage" them in such a way as to collectively meet the needs of everyone involved from the point of production to the point of final consumption.[19] References to "value chains," however, rarely consider that there are two quite distinct historiographical traditions behind the concept. On the one hand, most business and management scholars drawing on the term are likely influenced by Michael Porter's mid-1980s work on the "value chain," which he conceived as a model for "systematically examining all the activities a firm performs and how they interact." Porter's value chain was inward-looking, focused on the structure of a large, vertically integrated firm, and he declared that such firms could sustain competitive advantage by coordinating "all of the activities of a firm acting in harmony."[20]

A distinct intellectual lineage that focused on inequality rather than harmony, however, also contributes to the contemporary concept of "value chains." Rooted in the world-systems theory associated with Immanuel Wallerstein, scholarly interest in "commodity chains" emerged as sociologists and historians sought to understand global inequality in structural terms in the 1970s. In stark contrast to the theories generally cited by supply chain management researchers as foundational to their field, the commodity chains approach incorporated the value of human labor into its theorizing and explicitly sought to explain why power was distributed unequally across organizational, social, and geographical boundaries. Firms' competitive strategies figured into the analyses, but not with the goal of advocating paths to "supranormal profits." In further contrast with business school theories, the world-systems approach to commodity chains rooted much of its theory in sweeping but empirically grounded historical analyses, generally tying the rise of global commodity chains to the capitalist transformations of the world economy in the long sixteenth century.[21] Global commodity chains (GCC) research morphed in the 1990s and early 2000s into global value chains (GVC), a theoretical paradigm touted most visibly by Gary Gereffi at Duke University and widely recognized for its valuable incorporation of governance into the field's theoretical approaches. As Jennifer Bair has noted, bringing governance to the forefront makes GCC and GVC theory attractive and relevant for policymakers, but often at the cost of losing the long-range historical and broadly contextualized approaches originally undertaken by world-systems theorists.[22]

There are, then, multiple ways to interpret the historical etymology of "supply chain management." Historicizing the concept as "new" in the 1980s (as mainstream supply chain management scholars do) stakes out the boundaries of the field as inherently future-oriented, focused on enabling asset-lean downstream firms to tightly integrate multiple business processes and deliver goods at low cost to consumers. By contrast, critical perspectives see supply chain management as one variation on a constantly shifting dynamic in global capitalism, revealing the possibility that other stakeholders—smaller firms, political institutions, and workers in production and processing industries—can shape the future of supply chain industries. How the history of supply chains is interpreted thus strongly determines the extent to which critical thinking about their futures is either enabled or restricted.

Disowning and Selectively Interpreting the Past in Supply Chain Theory

History is remarkably absent in supply chain management research and teaching. Between 1994 and 2022, the top fifteen journals in the field published 38,510 research articles. Of those, only 139 (0.36 percent) included any variation of the words "history" and "supply chain."[23] Most of the articles that include the keyword "history" or "historical" do not include any contextualized analysis of past events. For instance, references abound to "historical performance," for example, a time-series dataset of a firm's return on assets.[24] Some include the word "historically" in the abstract merely as a throwaway introductory term, with no historical content or analysis present in the article itself.[25] As two historically sensitive management scholars have argued, the field of supply chain management is "inherently future-oriented."[26] Promoting a linear and deterministic conceptualization of time, the field of supply chain management problematically distorts the lessons of the past in at least two ways: disowning the past and selectively interpreting history.

Disowning the past is an intentional process of erasure.[27] It is not a process of forgetting. Disowning acknowledges the existence of past events, yet refuses to recognize past actions, events, or knowledge as relevant to future decisions. The past becomes a problem that must be removed from present-day collective memory, similar to what Rolland Munro has called "rubbishing the past," to ensure that members of a community who might see value in previous modes of organizing work instead see those traditions as "outdated and outmoded."[28] Disowning the past is a strategic and intentional process, not a simple oversight.

The process of disowning supply chains history is perhaps most evident in the teaching of undergraduate and graduate students in supply chain management. Several systematic analyses of supply chain management courses in multiple countries reveal that in hundreds of syllabuses, there is no content explicitly labeled as historical. There is a tendency to "silo" the various topics taught—inventory management, supply chain design, information technology—with a fundamental lack of "integrative skill development" and little encouragement of "general knowledge skills."[29] Two influential supply chain theorists have suggested that existing approaches to educating supply chain managers involve "too much emphasis on the technical aspects of the role," with little effort to develop awareness of context or to develop the communications skills needed to work successfully with a wide range of stakeholders.[30] Many popular supply chain and logistics textbooks aimed at undergraduates have no historical content at all, with their authors and editors perhaps working on the assumption that business students do not care about history and only want to know "what works and what doesn't."[31] In a remarkably common trope, the only history in some textbooks is a line or two in the introduction declaring that supply chains have mattered since the construction of the Egyptian pyramids and the empire-building of Roman armies.[32] As Dana Orenstein has noted in her history of American warehouses, this "ancient history" trope is intended primarily to promote a universalized sense of historical authenticity without actually diving into the messy details and contingencies of change over time.[33]

Perhaps most problematic are texts that seek to mark out the boundaries of the field of supply chain management by explicitly disowning the past as a problem. This primarily takes the form of a declaration that prior to the 1980s, business managers simply could not conceive of integrated supply chains. Take one of the few textbooks in the field that has a substantive history section in its introductory chapter. Echoing Drucker's "dark continent" metaphor, *The Handbook of Logistics and Distribution Management* insists that in the 1950s and 1960s, "distribution systems were unplanned and unformulated" and only "some way or other" did goods reach consumers. It was not until the 1980s that "forward-looking companies" recognized the possibility of using information technologies as well as physical distribution technologies to develop "an effective logistics strategy."[34] Generally the failures of the past are attributed to managers compartmentalizing their focus on cost reduction in purchasing, production, and inventory, rather than viewing supply chains as integrated producers of value. As one historical review puts it: "Until the late 1990s, the possibility that revenue gains or returns on assets could come from supply chain activities hardly crossed their minds."[35] From such a perspective, history is more than useless, it is a burden, for in "today's hyper-dynamic environment" the only path to success is to "constantly seek to implement innovative but risky and unproven initiatives."[36]

Disowning the past thus poses an ethically disturbing epistemological claim: Perhaps supply chain managers *can* know the past, but they *should* not, for lurking in that "dark continent" are noninnovative ideas that could very well cannibalize global capitalism from within. Yet as such hyperbole suggests, disowning the past is a very difficult act to get away with. As a process of intentional rejection of past events that may have been formally documented, disowning might have the unintentional effect of making the past not forgotten but "remembered only too well."[37]

Selectively interpreting the past provides an alternative mode to disowning, though with a similar outcome for inculcating supply chain managers with a linear conceptualization of time. Selective interpretation is a concept generally familiar to historians as something we try hard to avoid lest we be deemed lacking in objectivity.[38] Yet as I and others have argued, selective interpretation of the past is often used intentionally in the business and management world as a means of strategically communicating with stakeholders.[39] In the intellectual world of supply chain management, selective interpretation often lays out the history of supply chains as a series of stages, each following the other in a predetermined fashion. In these selective readings of supply chain history, the key message is that the "evolution" of supply chains is teleological, always progressing to a higher plane of efficiency.

Much more common than the "old as the pyramids" trope in supply chain textbooks is the invocation of Wal-Mart as the organization that did more than any other to model the future of global supply chains. Wal-Mart's supply chain management techniques are routinely upheld as a model for other organizations—not just its initial successes, but its ongoing achievements in the early twenty-first century. Textbooks regularly offer Borders as the counterpoint to Wal-Mart, noting that the chain bookseller rose to prominence in the United States in the 1990s but then failed to successfully "adapt supply chains to a changing environment."[40] The success of Wal-Mart has led at least one supply chain management researcher to develop a historical analysis of the firm's buyer-supplier relationships, based on primary research including "field notes and industry interviews" and "company reports, Compustat queries, trade reports, and surveys."[41] At nine pages in length, the results of the historical analysis may seem thin to a professional historian, but the point here is that few firms other than Wal-Mart are likely to get a single page of historical treatment in a supply chain journal, let alone nine.

Selective interpretation of the past not only entails that just a handful of firms are upheld as models for the future, but also that the contextual factors to be considered as important in shaping the development of supply chains are quite constrained. For instance, regulatory policy, the subject of Reuel Schiller's chapter, is generally treated in supply chain research as a burdensome problem of the past, rather than the outcome of decades of electoral political battles, mass movements by farmers and workers and consumers, and ideological conflicts in democratic governance. Representative of this approach is one textbook's "good example" of the benefits of deregulation for FedEx, which was "constrained by burdensome government regulations in the United States in the 1970s" but after airline deregulation "was able to expand and grow."[42] Selective interpretation frames government regulation as a problem for supply chain managers, whereas more robust historical analyses might consider the possible benefits of regulation both for anchor firms and for other stakeholders, such as unionized employees or consumers unable to individually inspect the social or environmental harms embedded in supply chains. Supply chain theorists also routinely acknowledge that poor labor conditions in global supply chains have, in the past, posed reputational risks to lead firms, as with the impact of the child labor scandal on Nike in the 1990s and the similar results of the 2013 Rana Plaza disaster for major multinational fashion brands. Rather than being considered constitutive examples of the social harms embedded in contemporary supply chain practices, Nike's child labor episode and Rana Plaza are selectively upheld as examples of how organizations can learn to manage their supply chains (and reputational risks) even better: "Fashion brands' practices and organization, international standards and NGO campaigns have greatly evolved since the Nike scandal days."[43] (The International Labour Organization, meanwhile, notes that at least 109 accidents have occurred in Bangladeshi textile factories since Rana Plaza, leading to at least 27 deaths.[44])

Selectively interpreting the past furthermore enables radical compressions of time. Professional historians also compress and distort time, sometimes radically, when we periodize history for analytical purposes.[45] When supply chain theorists compress time, however, they do so in a strictly linear fashion. Complex events, technological systems, organizational relationships, and ideas are tersely summed up as "Supply Chain 2.0" or "3.0." A widely cited text in this stream of literature presents the "supply chain 4.0 strategy path" as an upward trending arrow. At the "initial stage," "disruptive technologies [are] not implemented," while at the "cutting-edge stage," disruptive technologies are not only in use but "evolving," with all "processes digitized."[46] This constrained presentation of historical development is explicitly intended as a user manual, to provide "frameworks to provide assistance in the formulation and deployment of Supply Chain 4.0 policies and strategies."[47]

The problem with teleological approaches to historical interpretation is that real-life events often throw a wrench in the works, disrupting the presumed path to progress. In supply chain theory, however, even setbacks are generally subject to selective interpretation, as with the apparent consensus that the 9/11 terrorist attacks and the 2008–2009 global financial crisis spurred the development of even better theories of supply chain resilience.[48] A less selective interpretation might have suggested that those disruptive events revealed systemic *fragility* in contemporary supply chains. What, then, might supply chain theorists learn from historical approaches that neither disown nor selectively interpret the past?

History, Context, and Alternative Futures for Supply Chains

While it is fair to castigate supply chain theorists for misrepresenting history, it is also fair to scold mainstream historians for ignoring supply chains and distribution until very recently. It might be enlightening, for example, to conduct an exercise like the one I recounted above, this time gathering not popular supply chain textbooks but instead survey texts in American history, to see how many of them include mention of the "logistics revolution" in terms even remotely equivalent to the attention afforded to Detroit assembly lines. The pioneering work of Nelson Lichtenstein on Wal-Mart, along with a handful of other scholars who have researched supply chains and distribution in broader sociopolitical and environmental contexts, may take time to work its way into the mainstream history textbooks.[49] While it does, I would suggest three specific modes by which historians of business, labor, and capitalism can critically intervene in public debates about the future of global supply chains.

First, whereas supply chain theorists begin with abstractions and assumptions, historians start with questions. The historian's inductive approach may not be as "logically rigorous" as the deductive methods prized by operations researchers and engineers, but as one pair of supply chain theorists has noted, the assumptions needed for deductive analysis "often fail to capture many features that are relevant in the real world."[50] Take for example Nelson Lichtenstein's history of the concept of "supply chain management" in a book chapter giving "two cheers" for a bygone era of vertically integrated firms: Rather than beginning with the consequences of the "logistics revolution" for the profitability of firms, Lichtenstein begins with the consequences for workers, consumers, and, above all, the structures of democratic governance in an economy driven by giant multinational retailers. Rather than assuming that what's good for Wal-Mart is good for America, Lichtenstein's work illustrates that Wal-Mart's rise to supply chain preeminence was driven not by technological forces but by political choices and contextually dependent business decisions. Ideas about how to efficiently structure a firm changed substantially over the course of the twentieth century, with important consequences for the ways in which workers employed by those firms could challenge the conditions of their work.[51]

The maintenance of epistemological doubt, rather than seeking prescriptive knowledge, is furthermore essential to the professional historian's toolkit. Rather than selectively interpret the past to present a linear path to the present/future, historians seek out surprising counterexamples and paths not taken that shed light on our current moment. Damon Yarnell, for instance, has convincingly demonstrated that Ford Motor Company, even during the supposed height of its vertical integration in the early twentieth century, in fact relied on thousands of suppliers. While contemporary supply chain theorists see anything before the 1960s as unplanned and unmanaged, Yarnell provides substantial documented evidence of the care and strategic foresight with which Ford purchasing agents maintained relationships with those suppliers. Acknowledging that the term "supply chain management" would be anachronistic in 1919, Yarnell nonetheless demonstrates how Ford purchasing agents did exactly that, managing systemic risks in the supply chain to ensure not just low costs but also long-term relationships to produce value for multiple stakeholders.[52] Likewise, Daniel Raff has convincingly argued that the bookseller Borders, far from being an example of failed supply chain management, was in its time a particularly sophisticated innovator. Unlike its one-size-fits-all competitor Barnes & Noble, Borders developed profitable supply chain management software, which enabled the firm to match a diverse array of books to diverse customers in far-flung locations.[53]

Finally, when considering context, historians cast their net widely. Rather than seeking monocausal explanations of change over time, in which "context" is treated as a control variable, historians embrace diversity, contingency, variation, and serendipity when exploring contexts.[54] Rather than assuming away context, historians elaborate it. In terms of supply chain history, one quite notable aspect of context is routinely overlooked by supply chain theorists: financialization. Whereas supply chain theorists tend to assume that the asset-lean corporation that outsources manufacturing and logistics functions is a product of rational managerial action, historians would suggest that the growing political, economic, and cultural power of financial institutions that characterized the 1970s and 1980s was a strong causal element driving the "leaning" of American corporations.[55] Even here, however, there is room for historians to situate the late twentieth-century transformations of capitalism in a broader context. Historians increasingly recognize, for instance, a long trajectory of financialization well before the 1970s. Additionally, historians of international business understand the long history of multinational corporations outsourcing nearly all their assets, well before the rise of the vertically integrated firms of the mid-twentieth century.[56] Furthermore, historical analysis can reveal surprising directionality in the causal relationship between financialization and supply chain management strategies: Ford Motor Company, as historian Stefan Link has argued, pivoted to vertical integration in the 1920s not primarily as a profit-maximizing strategy but largely due to a producer-populist rejection of financialized control of the firm's mission.[57]

Historians also tend to assume that context is not merely determinative (causal), but also a product (consequence) of changes. Take, for instance, Wouter Ronsijn's and Eric Vanhaute's history of Belgian food crises in the mid-nineteenth century, which traces the internationalization of Belgium's food supply chains. They argue that resultant food price shocks emerged not only from the economic restructuring of those supply chains but also from a decline of localized moral economies of food access. One consequence, then, was that market-dependent urban centers with proletarianized labor suffered most from the transformation of what, in retrospect, we can understand as global supply chains.[58] Indeed, such anachronistic uses of the concept of supply chains may be particularly useful for historians seeking not simply to explain the rise of contemporary supply chains, but instead to understand the wider context of the past—to neither disown nor selectively interpret that past, but to embrace its complexity and richness. Thomas Spain and David Turner, for instance, have recently argued for the usefulness of anachronism as a means of studying historical food supply chains, with concepts from supply chain theory and global value chain theory enabling new insights into regulatory policy, consumer culture, and the dynamic development of technological infrastructure.[59]

Applying these three aspects of historical methods—inductive reasoning, maintenance of epistemological doubt, and contextualization as a search for understanding and not just explanation—can shed light on two open questions that face contemporary supply chain management researchers and practitioners. First, exactly where is the power in contemporary global supply chains? And second, how tightly coordinated are these global supply chains?

Regarding the locus of power, it is difficult to ignore Wal-Mart and the historical context it emerged from and forcefully helped to shape. When Nelson Lichtenstein's *Retail Revolution* was published in 2009, evidence abounded to suggest that indeed the retailer had "created a brave new world of business."[60] In an earlier edited volume, Lichtenstein deemed Wal-Mart the "template for twenty-first-century capitalism," and a decade later doubled down on the argument that Wal-Mart's control over its supply chains was historically unprecedented, a power that "Ford would have envied."[61] As a not-inconsequential aside, it is interesting to note that the conference from which the 2006 edited volume emerged had a question mark rather than a period in regard to Wal-Mart's "template" status—punctuating the historian's epistemological doubt.[62] Perhaps a revival of that doubt is warranted. The M-Form vertically integrated industrial enterprise of the mid-twentieth century was once upheld by Harvard business historian Alfred Chandler Jr. as the epitome of capitalist efficiency, only to be dismissed as a form of egregious bloat by the end of the century. Perhaps the tightly integrated, retailer-driven global supply chains pioneered by Wal-Mart are likewise historically anomalous, with Wal-Mart serving not as a template but instead as an exception in the *longue durée* of supply chain history.

Some contemporary supply chain theorists, for instance, see digital platforms fundamentally disrupting existing chains. Companies such as Amazon and Alibaba are enabling the entry of small-scale niche producers into global markets while also doing much more than simply deliver goods to customers—selling, for instance, financial services and IT infrastructure to other firms, including competitors. Clearly Amazon is an incredibly powerful company, but its technologies may be in the process of redistributing power more diffusely through the multiple industries in which its servers and algorithms penetrate, opening up new possibilities for alternative economic activity and governance.[63] For a firm like Amazon, digitization coexists with the all-important physical assets of its logistics network. The firm's reliance on enormous, hyperefficient distribution centers has been seen by union organizers and labor scholars as a chokepoint at which workers can seize structural power to attain higher wages and improved working conditions. Limited successes to date in this realm, however, suggest that barriers to union organizing in logistics remain substantial.[64] Yet if digitization entails fundamental restructuring of supply chains, union organizers may benefit from rethinking the nature of "chokepoints." Strategy theorists are increasingly arguing that platform-based "ecosystems," in which firms maintain both independence and interdependence by joining platforms (e.g., Amazon's cloud-service AWS platform, or Android's user-centric software system), may be overtaking supply chains as a "distinct solution to the problem of inter-firm coordination." If the modularity and interdependence of such platforms means that individual firms, large and small, retain control over their own assets and make their own decisions about whether to participate in the platform or not, power is inherently more distributed in an ecosystem than in a supply or value chain.[65]

Historians might respond to such theories by noting that much depends on context. Ecosystems approaches dominate in certain industries—IT, telecommunications, finance, video games—where firms are staffed by highly educated, largely male workers and managers. Maintaining autonomy and choice is substantively different in such industries than it is in agrifood, textiles, or health care, where both workers and managers earn less and have far less autonomy.[66] Yet even here there is increasing evidence that the centrally coordinated, big buyer-driven supply chains of the late twentieth century are undergoing substantive change. In agrifood, for instance, the problem of reputational risk for national and multinational brands—from supermarkets to fast food chains to food processors—has in the past twenty years led to the rise of a coterie of "multi-stakeholder initiatives" (MSIs). Agrifood firms concerned about news or social media coverage of child labor or sexual violence in farm fields, outbreaks of *E. coli* and other pathogens in packaged foods, deforestation, animal cruelty, climate change, and so forth have turned to

MSIs as a collaborative, "pre-competitive space" in which such risks can be rooted out (e.g., via audits and inspections) before they damage a multinational firm's reputation.[67] Agricultural workers, socially conscious consumers, and small-scale entrepreneurs are generally not invited to the boardroom tables of these MSIs, but less empowered groups have nonetheless attempted to leverage the value of reputational risk to challenge the strategies of multinational agrifood firms. Organizations such as the Coalition of Immokalee Workers, Rainforest Alliance, and Fairtrade International have modeled collaborative approaches, seeking to redefine modes of governance in supply chains fraught with human and environmental exploitation. One such socially oriented MSI, the Ethical Tea Partnership, is for instance formulated on the assumption that big buyers of tea will increasingly be disempowered in global supply chains as atomized suppliers consolidate in response to price and reputational pressures.[68] Workers in agriculture rarely have recourse to unionization or sympathetic governments, but much like the women garment workers who shamed US textile jobbers into improving working conditions in their mid-twentieth-century supply chains, socially conscious MSIs uphold themselves as a vanguard of increasingly democratic modes of corporate governance.[69] Unlike their early twentieth-century predecessors who promoted "industrial democracy" and workers' control, however, twenty-first-century MSIs start with the premise that it is in corporate boardrooms where the key decisions for reform will be made, generally with little direct input from workers or consumers.[70]

Closely related to the question of where power has lain in the past and might lie in the future is the extent to which global supply chains have ever been or ever will be tightly integrated. Historical and theoretical work on Wal-Mart has generally emphasized the tightness of the firm's control and coordination over suppliers, and for good reason. The viability of a shower-curtain manufacturing firm was, at the time of publication of Lichtenstein's *Retail Revolution* as well as today, largely determined by the specifications for size, materials, and cost set by Wal-Mart managers in Bentonville, Arkansas, armed with reams of data on both the supplier's costs and on their customers' behaviors. Yet as historians as well as historically aware social scientists have always known, such centralized coordination is the product of substantial work, not magic. "Supply chains," as Anna Löwenhaupt Tsing argues, "are harder to control than corporations or state bureaucracies" because they are "unpredictable."[71] Even in the case of Wal-Mart, according to Löwenhaupt Tsing, Bentonville supply chain managers' aggressive demands for cost-cutting were expected to be fulfilled by entrepreneurs. Exactly how Global South entrepreneurs motivated or disciplined their employees to achieve the results was up to them, opening up potentially unanticipated consequences. Likewise, scholars of agrifood supply chains have argued that multinational buyer-driven chains expose small-scale entrepreneurs to greater oversight from state regulators and nongovernmental organizations than would be the case in atomized agrifood systems.[72] Geographer Susanne Freidberg has argued that not all players at the "bottom" of the supply chain are as powerless as we might assume; tightly organized Midwestern corn and wheat growers, for instance, exercise countervailing power by refusing to share valuable information and expertise with multinational agribusiness buyers.[73] Indeed, a common refrain in contemporary agrifood supply chains is how remarkably little giant multinational corporations—grain traders, supermarkets, food and beverage manufacturers—actually know about "their" supply chains.[74]

Waste is a concrete illustration of the lack of complete coordination. In electronics and agrifood, highly profitable, centrally coordinated buyer-driven supply chains must inherently coexist with shadow supply chains where waste products from the main channel are revalued and repurposed. Geographer Andrew Herod calls this a "Global Destruction Network," exemplified by aged merchant ships broken down in Asia for resale as scrap to Global North manufacturers, or electronics and automobiles stripped for parts in the Global North for resale to the Global South—routes of circulation so context-dependent, complicated, and often logic-defying as to suggest that Wal-Mart's supply chains are by comparison rather straightforward.[75] Food banks, likewise, exist in large part as a means of repurposing excess food inventories; the charitable enterprise America's Second Harvest, for instance, was initially formed by agrifood corporations in collaboration with a surplus foods broker to siphon off goods that could not be sold in mainstream supermarkets or restaurant chains.[76] One wonders whether Upton Sinclair would be in such awe of today's outsourced, disaggregated, "entrepreneurial" approaches to extracting value from undesirable commodities as he was when he witnessed Chicago meatpackers profiting from "everything but the squeal" in the early twentieth century.

By exploring context in greater richness, by maintaining epistemological doubt regarding the nature and permanence of global supply chains, and above all by digging up empirical evidence of contestations to "the one best way" of supply chain management, historians could potentially transform public understanding of the present and future of global supply chains.

In recent years, the business press has been abuzz with examples of supply chains breaking down or failing to deliver on promises. The visual imagery of the *Ever Given* mega-container ship, stuck for six days in the Suez Canal in 2021, will surely haunt supply chain managers for years to come. That same year, Swedish homeware multinational IKEA was compelled to announce that it could not predict its inventories, as soaring transportation costs and truck driver shortages during the COVID-19 pandemic resulted in shelves bare of flat-pack furniture across Europe.[77] A 2022 article in *Harvard Business Review*, surveying the ongoing disruptions, went so far as to query whether "the risks of global supply chains [are] starting to outweigh the rewards?"[78] One logistics expert has gone even further, suggesting that not only is there no such thing as "supply chain management" (because no supply system is as linear as the chain metaphor suggests, and the hubris of "management" is overhyped), but that the entire field should be "abandoned."[79] Epistemological doubt, it seems, may be creeping into the world of supply chain managers.

Conclusion

The past is not merely prologue to the present, and history is made, not given. The rise of Bentonville and Guangdong as important nodes in the global economy did not simply come about due to abstract "forces" of globalization. "Both were constructed by a set of political and policy choices," historian Nelson Lichtenstein has emphasized, choices that were inflected not only by the power of business leaders' ideas and actions, but also by structural assumptions about the unequal value of men's versus women's work.[80] The choices that powerful actors make have consequences, often at a grand scale, but not all consequences are intended. Some nation-states' efforts to restrict trade and slow the offshoring of high-wage manufacturing, for instance, have since the 1970s had the unintended effect of encouraging firms to restructure their supply chains to evade such restrictions. In some cases, this has led to "upgrading" of activities, enabling entrepreneurs and workers in countries previously on the economic periphery to increasingly shape their own economic futures.[81] Tragedies such as the 2013 Rana Plaza collapse, however, in which more than one thousand workers died due to exploitative working conditions driven by the demands of fast-fashion retailers, press upon us the importance of remembering the very real harms caused by the restructuring of the global economy in the late twentieth century. Among those for whom such remembrance is most important are the future generations of supply chain managers, who of course will continue to be powerful actors in the global economy. But one might also hope that through exposure to richer contexts, more diverse experiences, and the contingencies of the past as well as the present, such supply chain managers could approach their highly paid work with a sense that history might be something more than just an encumbrance to be disowned or selectively interpreted.

Notes

1. Bureau of Labor Statistics, United States Department of Labor, "Data for Occupations Not Covered in Detail," 2022, accessed May 4, 2022, https://www.bls.gov/ooh/about/data-for-occupations-not-covered-in-detail.htm#Management%20occupations.

2. Laura Birou, Heather Lutz, and Joseph L. Walden, "Undergraduate Supply Chain Management Courses: Content, Coverage, Assessment and Gaps," *Supply Chain Management* 27, no. 1 (2022): 1–11.

3. Mercedes Delgado and Karen Mills, "The Supply Chain Economy and the Future of Good Jobs in America," *Harvard Business Review* (March 2018).

4. R. Daniel Wadhwani and Christina Lubinski, "Reinventing Entrepreneurial History," *Business History Review* 91, no. 4 (2017): 767–799; Mairi Maclean, Charles Harvey, and Stewart Clegg, "Conceptualizing Historical Organization Studies," *Academy of Management Review* 41, no. 4 (2016): 609–632; Shane Hamilton and Beatrice D'Ippolito, "From Monsanto to 'Monsatan': Ownership and Control of History as a Strategic Resource," *Business History* 64, no. 6 (2022): 1040–1070; Stephanie Decker, "Introducing the Eventful Temporality of Historical Research into International Business," *Journal of World Business* 57, no. 6 (2022): 1–13.

5. Critical historiographies of "old" and "new" labor history, the cultural turn in business history, and the emergence of "history of capitalism" include: Leon Fink, *In Search of the Working Class: Essays in American Labor History and Political Culture* (Urbana: University of Illinois Press, 1994); David Brody, "Reconciling the Old Labor History and the New," *Pacific Historical Review* 62, no. 1 (1993): 1–18; Kenneth Lipartito, "Reassembling the Economic: New Departures in Historical Materialism," *American Historical Review* 121 (February 2016): 101–139; Seth Rockman, "What Makes the History of Capitalism Newsworthy?" *Journal of the Early Republic* 34, no. 3 (2014): 439–466; Sven Beckert et al., "Interchange: The History of Capitalism," *Journal of American History* 101, no. 2 (2014): 503–536.

6. Peter F. Drucker, "The Economy's Dark Continent," *Fortune*, April 1962, p. 266.

7. Nelson Lichtenstein, "Supply Chains, Workers' Chains, and the New World of Retail Supremacy," *Labor: Studies in Working-Class History of the Americas* 4 (Spring 2007): 17–31; Alison Ashby, Mike Leat, and Melanie Hudson-Smith, "Making Connections: A Review of Supply Chain Management and Sustainability Literature," *Supply Chain Management* 17, no. 5 (2012): 497–516.

8. Rafaela Alfalla-Luque and Carmen Medina-López, "Supply Chain Management: Unheard of in the 1970s, Core to Today's Company," *Business History* 51, no. 2 (2009): 204; C. M. Harland, "Supply Chain Management: Relationships, Chains and Networks," *British Journal*

of Management 7, no. 1 (1996): 63–80. The oft-cited document is R. Keith Oliver and Michael D. Webber, "Supply-Chain Management: Logistics Catches Up with Strategy," *Outlook* 5, no. 1 (1982): 42–47.

9. Arnold Kransdorff, "High Stock Levels Not the Answer for Volatile Demand," *Financial Times*, June 4, 1982, 18.

10. Kransdorff, "High Stock Levels Not the Answer," 18; John Mangan and Chandra Lalwani, *Global Logistics and Supply Chain Management*, 3rd ed. (Hoboken, NJ: John Wiley & Sons, 2016), 10.

11. Dennis W. Krumwiede, Rhonda R. Lummus, and Robert J. Vokurka, "The Relationship of Logistics to Supply Chain Management: Developing a Common Industry Definition," *Industrial Management and Data Systems* 101, no. 8 (2001): 426–432.

12. Alfalla-Luque and Medina-López, "Supply Chain Management," 204.

13. Michiel R. Leenders and Harold E. Fearon, "Developing Purchasing's Foundation," *Journal of Supply Chain Management* 44, no. 2 (2008): 17–27; Luis Araujo, Lars-Erik Gadde, and Anna Dubois, "Purchasing and Supply Management and the Role of Supplier Interfaces," *IMP Journal* 10, no. 1 (2016): 2–24.

14. Drucker, "Economy's Dark Continent."

15. Hanping Hou et al., "An Evolving Trajectory—from PD, Logistics, SCM to the Theory of Material Flow," *Journal of Management Analytics* 2, no. 2 (2015): 138–153.

16. Ronald H. Ballou, "The Evolution and Future of Logistics and Supply Chain Management," *European Business Review* 19, no. 4 (2007): 332–348; Edna Bonacich and Khaleelah Hardie, "Wal-Mart and the Logistics Revolution," in *Wal-Mart: The Face of Twenty-First-Century Capitalism*, ed. Nelson Lichtenstein (New York: New Press, 2006); Edna Bonacich and Jake Wilson, *Getting the Goods: Ports, Labor, and the Logistics Revolution* (Ithaca: Cornell University Press, 2008).

17. Lars-Erik Gadde, "The Rise and Fall of Channel Management," *IMP Journal* 10, no. 1 (2016): 129–153.

18. Michael Porter, "How Competitive Forces Shape Strategy," *Harvard Business Review* (March 1979): 21–38.

19. Susan A. Sherer, "From Supply-Chain Management to Value Network Advocacy: Implications for E-Supply Chains," *Supply Chain Management* 10, no. 2 (2005): 77–83.

20. Michael Porter, *Competitive Advantage: Creating and Sustaining Superior Performance* (New York: Free Press, 1985).

21. Jennifer Bair, "Global Capitalism and Commodity Chains: Looking Back, Going Forward," *Competition and Change* 9, no. 2 (2005): 153–180.

22. Bair, "Global Capitalism and Commodity Chains," 158.

23. The "top 15" journals in the field are those identified by Andreas Wieland, associate professor of supply chain management at Copenhagen Business School, on his blog "Supply Chain Management Research" (SCMresearch.org/tag/ranking). The rankings are determined by the Association of Business School's *Academic Journal Guide* ("the ABS list"). The literature search was performed on Web of Science, first searching across all 15 journal publications titles, filtered by items of type "Article" (e.g., excluding reviews, editorials, news items). That search was then refined to search within all fields for "hist*" and "supply chain."

24. Weihua Liu et al., "Effect of Buyer-Supplier Supply Chain Strategic Collaboration on Operating Performance: Evidence from Chinese Companies," *Supply Chain Management* 25, no. 6 (2020): 823–839.

25. Kirk Plangger et al., "Strategic Enablement Investments: Exploring Differences in Human and Technological Knowledge Transfers to Supply Chain Partners," *Industrial Marketing Management* 91 (2020): 187–195.

26. Olof Brunninge and Helgi-Valur Fridriksson, "'We Have Always Been Responsible': A Social Memory Approach to Responsibility in Supply Chains," *European Business Review* 29, no. 3 (2017): 375.

27. Hamilton and D'Ippolito, "From Monsanto to 'Monsatan.'"

28. Rolland Munro, "Belonging on the Move: Market Rhetoric and the Future as Obligatory Passage," *Sociological Review* 46, no. 2 (1998): 219.

29. Birou, Lutz, and Walden, "Undergraduate Supply Chain Management"; Heather Lutz, Laura Birou, and Joe Walden, "Survey of Graduate Supply Chain Courses: Content, Coverage and Gaps," *Journal of Business and Industrial Marketing* 27, no. 5 (2021): 625–636; Heather Lutz and Laura Birou, "Logistics Education: A Look at the Current State of the Art and Science," *Supply Chain Management* 18, no. 4 (2013): 463, 464.

30. John Mangan and Martin Christopher, "Management Development and the Supply Chain Manager of the Future," *International Journal of Logistics Management* 16, no. 2 (2005): 178–191.

31. Stephen Cummings and Todd Bridgman, "The Relevant Past: Why the History of Management Should Be Critical for Our Future," *Academy of Management Learning & Education* 10, no. 1 (2011): 77.

32. Sunil Chopra and Peter Meindl, *Supply Chain Management: Strategy, Planning, and Operation*, 5th global ed. (Harlow, England: Pearson, 2013); David Simchi-Levi, Philip Kaminsky, and Edith Simchi-Levi, *Designing and Managing the Supply Chain: Concepts, Strategies, and Case Studies* (Boston: McGraw-Hill, 2000); Christopher Martin, *Logistics & Supply Chain Management* (Harlow, England: FT Publishing, 2016).

33. Dara Orenstein, *Out of Stock: The Warehouse in the History of Capitalism* (Chicago: University of Chicago Press, 2019), 28–33.

34. Alan Rushton, Phil Croucher, and Peter Baker, *The Handbook of Logistics and Distribution Management*, 5th ed. (London: Kogan Page, 2014), 7, 8.

35. Chad W. Autry, "Supply Chain Research: Considering the Discipline's Evolving Relationship with Marketing, Current Issues, and Future Research Directions," *Journal of Marketing Theory and Practice* 29, no. 1 (2021): 101.

36. Autry, "Supply Chain Research."

37. Hamilton and D'Ippolito, "From Monsanto to 'Monsatan,'" 21.

38. Peter Novick, *That Noble Dream: The 'Objectivity Question' and the American Historical Profession* (Cambridge: Cambridge University Press, 1988); Peter Charles Hoffer, *The Historians' Paradox: The Study of History in Our Time* (New York: New York University Press, 2008).

39. Hamilton and D'Ippolito, "From Monsanto to 'Monsatan,'" 8–9; Olof Brunninge, "Using History in Organizations: How Managers Make Purposeful Reference to History in Strategy Processes," *Journal of Organizational Change Management* 22, no. 1 (2009): 8–26; Mike Zundel, Robin Holt, and Andrew Popp, "Using History in the Creation of Organizational Identity," *Management and Organizational History* 11, no. 2 (2016): 211–235.

40. Chopra and Meindl, *Supply Chain Management*, 17.

41. Jared M. Hansen, "The Evolution of Buyer-Supplier Relationships: An Historical Industry Approach," *Journal of Business and Industrial Marketing* 24 (3/4, 2009): 227–236.

42. Mangan and Lalwani, *Global Logistics and Supply Chain Management*, 6.

43. Karan Khurana and Marco Ricchetti, "Two Decades of Sustainable Supply Chain Management in the Fashion Business, an Appraisal," *Journal of Fashion Marketing and Management* 20, no. 1 (2016): 89–104.

44. https://www.ilo.org/global/topics/geip/WCMS_614394/lang—en/index.htm.

45. Eviatar Zerubavel, *Time Maps: Collective Memory and the Social Shape of the Past* (Chicago: University of Chicago Press, 2004).

46. Guilherme F. Frederico et al., "Supply Chain 4.0: Concepts, Maturity and Research Agenda," *Supply Chain Management* 25, no. 2 (2020): Figure 8, p. 276.

47. Frederico et al., "Supply Chain 4.0," 277.

48. Martina K. Linnenluecke, "Resilience in Business and Management Research: A Review of Influential Publications and a Research Agenda," *International Journal of Management Reviews* 19, no. 1 (2017): 4–30.

49. A full review of the relevant literature may be warranted, but is outside the scope of this essay. Noteworthy texts in the field include: Victoria de Grazia, "Changing Consumption Regimes in Europe, 1930–1970: Comparative Perspectives on the Distribution Problem," in *Getting and Spending: European and American Consumer Societies in the Twentieth Century*, ed. Susan Strasser, Charles F. McGovern, and Matthias Judt (Cambridge: Cambridge University Press, 1998), 59–83; Richard P. Tucker, *Insatiable Appetite: The United States and the Ecological Degradation of the Tropical World* (Berkeley: University of California Press, 2000); John Soluri, *Banana Cultures: Agriculture, Consumption, and Environmental Change in Honduras and the United States* (Austin: University of Texas Press, 2005); Nelson Lichtenstein, ed., *Wal-Mart: The Face of Twenty-First-Century Capitalism* (New York: New Press, 2006); Marc Levinson, *The Box: How the Shipping Container Made the World Smaller and the World Economy Bigger* (Princeton: Princeton University Press, 2006); Shane Hamilton, *Trucking Country: The Road to America›s Wal-Mart Economy* (Princeton: Princeton University Press, 2008); Nelson Lichtenstein, *The Retail Revolution: How Wal-Mart Created a Brave New World of Business* (New York: Metropolitan Books, 2009); Richard Vahrenkamp, *The Logistic Revolution: The Rise of Logistics in a Mass Consumption Society* (Cologne: Josef Eul Verlag, 2012); Bartow J. Elmore, *Citizen Coke: The Making of Coca-Cola Capitalism* (New York: W. W. Norton, 2014); Orenstein, *Out of Stock*; Helen Tangires, *Movable Markets: Food Wholesaling in the Twentieth-Century City* (Baltimore: Johns Hopkins University Press, 2019).

50. Susan Helper and Mari Sako, "Management Innovation in Supply Chain: Appreciating Chandler in the Twenty-First Century," *Industrial and Corporate Change* 19, no. 2 (2010): 399–429.

51. Nelson Lichtenstein, "Two Cheers for Vertical Integration: Corporate Governance in a World of Global Supply Chains," in *Corporations and American Democracy*, ed. Naomi Lamoreaux and William J. Novak (Cambridge, MA: Harvard University Press, 2017), 329–358.

52. Damon Yarnell, "Ford Motor Company's Lost Chapter: Purchasing Routine and the Advent of Mass Production," in *The Emergence of Routines: Entrepreneurship, Organization, and Business History*, ed. Daniel M. G. Raff and Philip Scranton (New York: Oxford University Press, 2017), 139–170.

53. Daniel M. G. Raff, "Superstores and the Evolution of Firm Capabilities in American Bookselling," *Strategic Management Journal* 21 (October 2000): 1043–1059.

54. Shane Hamilton and Andrew C. Godley, "Structure and Meaning in Strategic Paradoxes: Exploring Historical Context in the Emergence of Agrifood Standards," *Business History*, 67:2 (2025): 608–628.

55. William Millberg, "Shifting Sources and Uses of Profits: Sustaining US Financialization with Global Value Chains," *Economy and Society* 37 (August 2008): 420–451; Gerald F. Davis and Suntae Kim, "Financialization of the Economy," *Annual Review of Sociology* 41, no. 1 (2015): 203–221.

56. On the longer history of financialization, see Per H. Hansen, "From Finance Capital to Financialization: A Cultural and Narrative Perspective on 150 Years of Financial History," *Enterprise & Society* 15 (Dec. 2014): 605–642; Jonathan Levy, "Accounting for Profit and the History of Capital," *Critical Historical Studies* 1, no. 2 (2014): 171–214. On nineteenth-century multinationals as asset-lean companies, including so-called "free-standing corporations," see especially Mira Wilkins, "The Free-Standing Company, 1870–1914: An Important Type of British Foreign Direct Investment," *Economic History Review* 41 (May 1988): 259–282; Simon Mollan, "The Free-Standing Company: A 'Zombie' Theory of International Business History?" *Journal of Management History* 24, no. 2 (2018): 156–173.

57. Stefan Link, "The Charismatic Corporation: Finance, Administration, and Shop Floor Management Under Henry Ford," *Business History Review* 92, no. 1 (2018): 85–115; Link, *Forging Global Fordism: Nazi Germany, Soviet Russia, and the Contest over the Industrial Order* (Princeton: Princeton University Press, 2020), chapter 1.

58. Wouter Ronsijn and Eric Vanhaute, "From the Hungry 1840s to the Dear 1850s: The Case of Belgium's Food Price Crisis, 1853–56," *Agricultural History Review* 66, no. 2 (2018): 238–260.

59. Thomas Spain and David A. Turner, "Food for Thought: Transport Within the Food Supply Chain," *Journal of Transport History* 43, no. 2 (2022): 194–213.

60. Lichtenstein, *Retail Revolution.*

61. Nelson Lichtenstein, "Wal-Mart: A Template for Twenty-First-Century Capitalism," in *Wal-Mart: The Face of Twenty-First-Century Capitalism*, ed. Nelson Lichtenstein (New York: New Press, 2006), 3–30; Lichtenstein, "Two Cheers," 331.

62. Lichtenstein, "Preface," in *Wal-Mart*, ed. Lichtenstein, vii.

63. Pavida Pananond, Gary Gereffi, and Torben Pedersen, "An Integrative Typology of Global Strategy and Global Value Chains: The Management and Organization of Cross-Border Activities," *Global Strategy Journal* 10, no. 3 (2020): 421–443.

64. Michael Billeaux-Martinez, "Struggles on the Supply Chain," *Labor: Studies in Working-Class History of the Americas* 21, no. 2 (2024): 7–17.

65. Michael G. Jacobides, Carmelo Cennamo, and Annabelle Gawer, "Towards a Theory of Ecosystems," *Strategic Management Journal* 39, no. 8 (2018): 2260.

66. Eloisa Betti and Eileen Boris, "Feminised Work After Fordism: The New Precarity," in *The Routledge Handbook of the Gig Economy*, ed. Immanuel Ness (London: Routledge, 2022), ch. 9.

67. Susanne Freidberg, "Big Food and Little Data: The Slow Harvest of Corporate Food Supply Chain Sustainability Initiatives," *Annals of the Association of American Geographers* 107, no. 6 (2017): 1389–1406; Ximena Rueda, Rachael D. Garrett, and Eric F. Lambin, "Corporate Investments in Supply Chain Sustainability: Selecting Instruments in the Agri-Food Industry," *Journal of Cleaner Production* 142, no. 4 (2017): 2480–2492.

68. Forum for the Future, "The Future of Tea: A Hero Crop for 2030," 2014, accessed June 26, 2019, https://www.forumforthefuture.org/tea-2030. On the CIW, see Susan L. Marquis, *I Am Not a Tractor! How Florida Farmworkers Took on the Fast Food Giants and Won* (Ithaca: Cornell University Press, 2017).

69. Lichtenstein, "Two Cheers," 354–356.

70. On industrial democracy, see Steve Fraser, *Labor Will Rule: Sidney Hillman and the Rise of American Labor* (New York: Free Press, 1991); Nelson Lichtenstein and Howell John Harris, eds., *Industrial Democracy in America: The Ambiguous Promise* (Cambridge: Cambridge University Press, 1996). On the limited voice for workers or consumers in MSI governance structures, see: Doris Fuchs, Agni Kalfagianni, and Tetty Havinga, "Actors in Private Food Governance: The Legitimacy of Retail Standards and Multistakeholder Initiatives with Civil Society Participation," *Agriculture and Human Values* 28, no. 3 (2011): 353–367; Rob Barlow, "Deliberation Without Democracy in Multi-Stakeholder Initiatives: A Pragmatic Way Forward," *Journal of Business Ethics* 181, no. 3 (2022): 543–561.

71. Anna Löwenhaupt Tsing, "Supply Chains and the Human Condition," *Rethinking Marxism* 21, no. 2 (2009): 150, 151.

72. Amy J. Cohen and Jason Jackson, "Governing Through Markets: Multinational Firms in the Bazaar Economy," *Regulation & Governance* 16, no. 2 (2022): 409–426; Hope C. Michelson, *Small Farmers, Big Retailers: Are New Sourcing Strategies a Path to Inclusion?* (Chicago: Chicago Council on Global Affairs, 2016).

73. Susanne Freidberg, "Assembled but Unrehearsed: Corporate Food Power and the 'Dance' of Supply Chain Sustainability," *Journal of Peasant Studies* 47, no. 2 (2020): 383–400.

74. Freidberg, "Big Food and Little Data"; Kyla Mandel, "Walmart Has a Plan to Tackle the Climate Crisis," *Guardian*, September 13, 2021.

75. Andrew Herod et al., "Global Destruction Networks, Labour and Waste," *Journal of Economic Geography* 14, no. 2 (2014): 421–441.

76. Joshua Lohnes and Bradley Wilson, "Bailing Out the Food Banks? Hunger Relief, Food Waste, and Crisis in Central Appalachia," *Environment and Planning A* 50, no. 2 (2017): 350–369.

77. Valenti Romei, Martin Arnold, and Davide Ghighlione, "Supply Chain Squeeze: First Cars, Now Chairs and Cupboards," *Financial Times*, September 7, 2021.

78. Willy C. Shih, "Are the Risks of Global Supply Chains Starting to Outweigh the Rewards?" *Harvard Business Review* (March 2022).

79. Jakob Beer, "There Is No Such Thing as Supply Chain Management: Let's Abandon the Field," 2021, accessed May 6, 2022, https://www.beer-management.de/2021/11/08/there-is-no-such-thing-as-supply-chain-management-lets-abandon-the-field/.

80. Lichtenstein, "Supply Chains, Workers' Chains," 20.

81. Gary Gereffi, Hyun-Chin Lim, and Joonkoo Lee, "Trade Policies, Firm Strategies, and Adaptive Reconfigurations of Global Value Chains," *Journal of International Business Policy* 4, no. 4 (2021): 506–522.

PART IV

Historicizing the Politics and Culture of the New Deal Order

CHAPTER 10

"A Working-Class Hero Is Something to Be": Popular Culture and the Manufacture of "Labor"

Lauren Rebecca Sklaroff

Who were the working-class heroes in summer 2023? Hollywood actors and writers were ensnared in the longest strike in the entertainment industry's history. UPS drivers almost walked off the job, and autoworkers actually did in select plants before audaciously widening the strike to include more factories. President Joe Biden even broke with historical precedent to walk picket lines that some leading Republicans respected and others denigrated. But what really made headlines that summer was Barbenheimer, the same-day release (amid the Hollywood strike) of director Christopher Nolan's biopic of scientist J. Robert Oppenheimer and director Greta Gerwig's take on Mattel's best-selling doll. There was a lot of talk about how both films were "so different." Some viewers even embraced the challenge of seeing both in one day.[1]

Oppenheimer, *Barbie*, and the deluge of commentary about them did not seem all that concerned about the country's working-class heroes, long a fixture in American cinema. Robert Oppenheimer confronted anti-Semitism throughout his education and career in top European and American universities, and anti-Communist witch hunts cost him his government security clearance. While a central narrative of the film centered on the government's inquisition of the scientist for his association with radical activity, Oppenheimer's genius ultimately prevailed in a filmic triumph. The cost of his intellectual labor—and that of many fellow scientists who did engage in radical politics—was ultimately papered over by a presidential medal of honor in 1963.

Furthermore, the Barbenheimer phenomenon of seeing both films in one day or one weekend may have given *Barbie* a kind of transmitted historical veracity, while softening the cruel persecution of Oppenheimer into a tempered stance against authority.

Barbie seemed just as far removed from the real challenges writers, actors, truck drivers, and autoworkers faced. Barbie had already been much maligned for decades; her unrealistic proportions, materialistic lifestyle, and traditional gender expression were issues that Mattel had had to contend with almost since the creation of Barbie. Feminists, academics, and consumers had already demanded more physical, racial, and professional diversity in the Barbie world—and to a large extent, received it from Mattel. The toy giant even allowed Gerwig, an indie director, to use this best-selling doll to critique patriarchy. Mattel and Warner Brothers' *Barbie*, which far surpassed *Oppenheimer* in ticket sales, offered feminism as a fluffy, sparkly, consumer-friendly version of feminism during a moment of diminishing reproductive rights for women and homophobic, transphobic politics across the country.

Mattel, Gerwig, and actress/producer Margot Robbie profited incredibly from viewers who flooded theaters in pink outfits, sipping pink bottles of Coke, perhaps having bought Progressive insurance endorsed by *Barbie*. As Mattel and Warner Brothers de-centered the actual issues *Barbie* purported to represent in its discussion of gender inequality, they ironically made viewers feel empowered in the absence of any real change. Although many women reported crying during "real world" mom Gloria's (America Ferrera) speech about the impossibilities of being a woman in America, it still did not touch on the questions that many of the women in the audience might have faced in just getting to the theater. Could they afford the right Instagram-able outfit for the film? Did they have the money to take the kids or pay a babysitter to see a film? Could they cover the cost to also see *Oppenheimer* to appease partners who agreed to "sit through" *Barbie*? Lest we believe that this was just the summer 2023 zeitgeist, cultural commentators continue to describe the 2024 election as "Barbenheimer"—a contrast between "joy" and "darkness" in the candidacies of Kamala Harris and Donald Trump. It seems the term is here to stay.[2]

Barbenheimer was hardly the first time Americans could consume something of potentially real historical or political substance. P. T. Barnum admitted any "sucker" who could pay the price of admission, allowing Jacksonian Americans to enjoy what historian James Cooke called "the arts of deception."[3]

He and other scholars have long dissected working-class heroes in popular culture. That scholarship has important parallels and intersections to the work on labor politics and organizing discussed in the first and final sections of this volume. But this chapter aims to chart some examples of the work on working-class heroes in popular culture, illustrating themes of authenticity, the deliberations of the culture industry, and the fact that most prominent, beloved working-class heroes were White, male, and straight. Unlike other groups that have also demonstrated sustained resistance to all forms of repression—African Americans, LGBTQ individuals, and other marginalized groups—the White working-class hero has achieved a unique and elevated iconography. There are many examples of Black working-class heroes such as Bessie Smith, Ma Rainey, Big Mama Thornton, and Little Richard who had incredible meaning for Black working-class communities; however, these individuals were commonly marginalized, segregated, or appropriated by White artists. They were pushed outside of the cultural apparatus that provided a "palatable" White male working-class hero.

Thus, it is important to consider why the harmful stereotypes and dehumanizing portrayals that have depicted so many other groups over the course of the nineteenth and twentieth centuries did not pervade American culture to the same degree when White working-class men could be advantageously featured to offer the values of stoicism, Main Street universality, or admirable rebellion. Even some women, such as performer Sophie Tucker, publicly shrouded themselves in these marketable values and drew audiences into their working-class hero personae. Dripping in diamonds, famously coiffed, Tucker still could not avoid tales of her working-class background and early struggles to earn a living.

This chapter also turns to more recent examples of working-class heroes in the more polarized political landscape described in the previous section of this volume. This contribution charts the ways since the 1990s that a historically White working-class straight hero may have been more complicated. Examples from film and television illustrate the pervasiveness of many themes first put forth in the nineteenth century, but also new formulations that address new liberal, racially inclusive priorities among tastemakers that reflected the changing gender and immigration politics discussed in Leandra Zarnow's and Carl Bon Tempo's respective chapters. The working-class hero is still a staple in American popular culture, but this chapter questions whether he performs the same triumphant utility that he had offered in the past.

The Making of a (White) Working-Class Hero

Representations of various groups, whether women, people of color, or the working class have dramatically differed from actual political realities. The popular depiction of the working class, or those with working-class origins, historically has featured a level of self-congratulation and mass distortion that anticipates the *Barbie* phenomenon but is even more pervasive. As Michael Denning has argued, dime novels flooded the working-class imagination during the mid to late nineteenth century, as tales of outlaws, tramps, Molly Maguires, and other celebrated populist heroes filled "cheap sensational fiction." Improved printing and writing technology, rapid circulation, and a growing industrial, reading public deeply enabled the mechanisms for popular representations. While workers consumed dime novels at a rapid rate, their popularity among a wider swath of the American public—perhaps reading dime novels more secretly due to their lurid reputation—suggests a wider digestion of working-class tropes, ensnared in mythic figures who battled the establishment. As Denning writes, "This working-class culture is not completely autonomous. Not only is it intertwined with a commercial culture that is not the self-creation of workers, but it is always subject to the influence and power of the dominant public." While many of these novels were inspired by acts of government repression of often striking workers, they were a means for authors and publishers to imagine narratives of empowerment, escape, and re-creation. These contested texts were both engines of a capitalist machine and also, as Denning argues, representative of "different class accents with which they are inflected." The working class could enjoy fictional tales of their own agency and strike against companies that left them with little power—the Pullman Strike, Homestead Strike, or other examples of massive resistance—and perhaps there was a reciprocal relationship between formal politics and informal culture.[4]

Existing alongside dime novels, other nineteenth-century working-class heroes have similarly been amorphous figures, ranging from cowboys, to Twainian protagonists, to those who merely come from perceived humble origins. Some examples include the work of Paul Johnson, who details the art of daredevil jumper Sam Patch, whose displays of physical impossibility emboldened frustrated workers amid increasing industrialization and standardization in Rochester, New York. Joy Kasson writes about the lure of Buffalo Bill Cody, whose Wild West Shows offered an escapism and romanticism of the West at the moment of the frontier's closing. Elliot Gorn's work on bare-knuckle prizefighting highlights particular tropes of masculinity embraced by the White working class, feeling more powerless amid the rise of capitalism. These heroes, along with the perhaps lesser known figures who occupied the dance halls, vaudeville theaters, saloons, amusement parks, and other sites of working-class socialization, demonstrated both an irreverence and often a narrative of social mobility that became increasingly commercially attractive to producers.[5]

This scholarship on commercial representation is not to undermine the broad literature pioneered in the late 1970s and 1980s by Roy Rosenzweig, Kathy Peiss, John Kasson, and so many others who carefully demarcate working-class spaces and their role in the making of working-class activism.[6] That research developed in tandem with the work on labor activism parsed in Meg Jacobs's chapter. But those who write about working-class culture deftly chart the role that these genres had in working-class communities to speak against systems of power. However, not only is the mass marketing of working-class heroes quite different from the cultural products of laboring people, but often out of reach of those very communities. Representations of the White working class provided middle-class consumers with their own cultural capital and self-identification. Music scholar Nadine Hubbs argues, "In media, institutional and professional contexts, members of the middle class speak of and for the working class, acting, officially and with authority, as interpreters of the class other."[7] More than just representation, the cultural industry often isolates the working class from its heroes—the price of concert tickets for Jason Aldean will most likely frustrate the fan base.

Deliberate, manufactured working-class imagery was not always positive, but it was quite different from that of other groups when it was redeemable. For those who study identity politics—race, gender, and sexuality most adeptly—personal identity cannot be divorced from "official" enforcements of stereotypes, caricatures, and the economic engine of representation. It is worth asking why representations of White, heteronormative male workers, even with a history of collective subversion and persistent government repression—often rise to a heroic stature, while African Americans, LGBTQ+ individuals, and other marginalized groups do not.

As many have argued, racial stereotypes became cemented during this period in all forms of mass media, to the extreme detriment of African Americans who also demonstrated consistent levels of activism. Grace Hale and many other scholars forward a large scholarship on the formation of White identity, where the affirmation of whiteness depended on stock caricatures of blackness and an erasure of Black agency and humanity.[8] From the minstrel stage, to the proliferation of sheet music, to a host of consumer products, a commercially distorted and degraded imagery of blackness became the predominant means of digesting African American culture, which arguably still remains a fixture. Film scholar Thomas Cripps illuminates the persistence of minstrel images in film through the mid-twentieth century until more tokenistic, "message movies"—largely featuring Sidney Poitier—took hold. As Cripps indicates, "Poitier's work teetered on the edge, half leading it, but always in a cooled-down mode increasingly defined by the keepers of his image whose fiscal duties included husbanding a star too valuable to risk on flights of radical daring."[9] In contrast, the working-class hero, unlike Poitier's tepid assimilationist, proof of hope for racial cooperation characters, took on a deliberately anti-authoritarian messaging.

Women were also denied the kind of empowering iconography embodied in the male working-class hero for most of the twentieth century. As Susan Douglas poignantly argues in her study of the relationship between women and the mass media in postwar America, reservations about feminism were largely due to negative or even ridiculous images of women in popular culture. Viewing reaction to this media as "schizophrenic," Douglas explains how, in denigrating women in television and film, but also in news coverage of activism, the media "may have turned *feminism* into a dirty word, but they made feminism inevitable."[10] This stood in stark contrast to the postwar culture of men who were "dedicated rebels, the counterculture leaders, the ones who made history." Female-centered media was "fleeting, superficial, trivial."[11]

These negative portrayals were even more severe for LGBTQ+ individuals. As the pioneering documentary *The Celluloid Closet* advances, filmic representations of gays and lesbians presented characters as freaks, serial killers, and condemned figures who often end in community ostracization or death/suicide. The film *Disclosure* further emphasizes the negativity toward transgender characters; they provoke strong physical displays of disgust when straight characters learn they are trans, and cross dressing is a vehicle for comedy, ridicule, or hijinks.[12] The concrete, negative values around other groups remain rather fixed, while the White male working-class hero is protean, highlighting possibilities for "acceptable" rebellion, social mobility, or an authenticity that industry heads market to "common folk."

The making of an aurally distinctive working-class hero becomes evident in the literature on early recordings. Karl Miller's scholarship on the deliberate efforts to segregate sound in the making of Southern recorded music highlights the cultural import of old-timey, hillbilly records. Despite the wide listening tastes of Southerners, record executives created a national market of Southern sound—either race records performed by African Americans or the folkloric genre attached to White artists. As Miller maintains, race records continued to employ negative minstrel stereotypes while old-time records were "upstanding and serious folklore." Romanticized notions of authentic Southern working-class life parallel a marketplace of equally romanticized, authentic Black life; however, "hillbilly humor confirmed caricatures of white rural culture while assuring white southern audiences that they were in on the joke." Even after the hillbilly billboard rebranding as country and western in the 1950s, stereotypes of backwardness undoubtedly still remained, especially for those outside the region; however, the maintenance of the "musical color line" firmly depended on the commercial and marketing strategies to separate these genres, and the submission of Black artists depended on the elevation of their White counterparts. Miller's work charts the dangerous racial implications of an artificial working-class hero. Echoing Miller's argument, Benjamin Filene's work on folklorists' search for an authentic musical culture asserts, "The most significant effect of the white ballad singer was to help block African American folk music from gaining a central place in the canon of America's musical heritage."[13]

Among those who have studied LGBTQ+ history, there are serious implications to the connectivity between the working class and homophobic bigotry. Much of the literature points to queer fluidity in the first half of the twentieth century in contrast to more rigid middle-class mores. George Chauncey's seminal *Gay New York* speaks to the public spaces that allowed working-class gays to meet and engage intimately, providing a kind of "privacy in public" that was less common among middle-class men. Other scholars such as John Howard and Colin Johnson push Chauncey's thesis further by demonstrating vibrant gay life in rural spaces, even while repressive surveillance loomed.[14]

While touching on various aspects that connect to the making of a working-class hero, the larger fields of labor history and capitalism studies have arguably prevented a more holistic understanding. The frequent separation or subfielding of gender, sexuality, and culture limit more extensive conversations. Here, it is worth considering historian John D'Emilio's 1979 influential article, "Capitalism and Gay Identity," a Marxist critique of a system that simultaneously enabled and oppressed queer Americans. Like many of his New Social History contemporaries who called for systemic economic transformation, D'Emilio points to the failure of liberalism, the exploitation of wage work, and the problematic decline of the family. A student of New Deal historian William Leuchtenberg at Columbia University, D'Emilio's work unsurprisingly aligns with that of many historians born in the early post–World War II period, inspired by the social movements of the 1960s, engaged in Marxist reading groups, and propelled into activism. D'Emilio's personal and political investment in the uneven relationship between capitalism and gay identity could have likely situated the article squarely within the more prominent histories of those who labor circulating in the late 1970s and 1980s.

As much as D'Emilio could have been a budding labor historian, he was after something else entirely, as the absence of E. P. Thompson or other foundational texts on social movements indicate. D'Emilio centrally claims, "It has been the historical development of capitalism—more specifically the free labor system—that has allowed large numbers of men and women in the late twentieth century to call themselves gay, to see themselves as part of a community of similar men and women, and to organize politically on the basis of that identity."[15] This is an enabling stance on capitalism in the making of identifiable queer communities, but, as D'Emilio later indicates, one wrought with limitations and complexities. Capitalism furthered group socialization, work removed from a nuclear family, mobility and migration, public visibility—all of the ingredients that would fuel modern homophobia. While many of these elements undoubtedly engendered political worries about the working class in general, they took on a very different meaning for queer Americans.

D'Emilio's wavering stance on capitalism asks, "How do we take the contradictory relationship [that capitalism generates] and use it to move towards liberation?" Admittedly, for him, capitalism has "created the material conditions for homosexual desire to express itself as a central component of some individuals' lives," but also has led to the most confining and demoralizing possibilities for many LGBTQ+ Americans, particularly those who are working class and people of color who are ignored in a neoliberal society.[16] D'Emilio's essay may have begun as a challenge to the "eternal gay" thesis often championed by liberationists and some scholars, but D'Emilio has opened the door for a much wider discussion about the schizophrenic cultural phenomenon capitalism ushers in for all who feel marginalized.

In 1979, D'Emilio could not have predicted that later the cultural turn would, in many ways, decenter actual popular culture from the study of history, but he clearly had cultural history in mind when he wrote his essay. E. P. Thompson may be missing from the footnotes, but pioneering scholars, such as Paula Fass, as well as references to lesbian novels and queer Black musicians are well represented.[17] The most vibrant expressions of queer identity and most identities of those "from below" most often exist in the cultural realm, but not without misrepresentation, appropriation, or total erasure. Capitalism and mass culture are bedfellows in the history of modern America, and like everything else, working-class life has always been dependent on this teetering relationship.

Scholars of LGBTQ+ history have also demonstrated the ways in which moments of resistance long probed by labor historians take on a new resonance through the lens of sexuality and the making of "the deviant." Here, we may see new models for a working-class hero, outside of a heteronormative framework. Aaron Lecklider's work on the Communist Party posits that the homophobia traditionally associated with the CP did not necessarily prevent queer expression or relationships. For Lecklider, "cultural works . . . reveal unique aspects of the Left that were central to participants but not necessarily found in the official records of the Communist Party."[18] Like Michael Denning, Lecklider encourages scholars to probe the "cultural front," but with additionally empowering findings for queer, working-class individuals. In addition, if resistance has a longer historical record among some groups and a more marginalized coverage among those labeled "deviant," the categories of those who oppose producing classes may often be skewed. As Stuart Hall indicates, "As political minorities increasingly cross the line from legal demonstration to illegal forms of protest, and as deviants cross the line from privatized deviancy to a public protest, so the 'traditional right to dissent,' for both groups becomes problematic and is contested."[19]

Overlooked Working-Class Heroes

Over the course of the twentieth century, the popular celebration of working-class heroes became most pronounced during the New Deal—what Denning calls the "laboring of American culture"—and took hold in literature, film, government programs, and music.[20] As Lary May argues, films that had, in the 1920s, featured glamour, travel, and larger spectacle gave way during the Depression to films featuring "the fall of the old order and the rise of marginal characters."[21] With second-generation Jewish immigrants at the helm of most major studios, narratives of working-class heroes proliferated, whether in the gangsters of *Scarface* (1932), *Public Enemy* (1931), or *Little*

Caesar (1930), exposing corruption at the top. Women, such as Greta Garbo, and African Americans, such as Paul Robeson, occupied new spaces in these films as those who wrestled with authority, challenging more conventional imagery; however, White working-class men remained front and center in the most popular motion pictures. Yet, as Neal Gabler explains, the working-class heroes depicted in so many motion pictures were far from the lives of the "eastern aristocracy" studio heads who lived in a manner "to emulate rich gentiles in the hope of becoming them."[22] May details how "outsider" films made during the Depression appealed to an engaged, growing audience who felt that the films reflected their own anger and distrust of economic and political institutions. Yet, the gap between producers and consumers couldn't have been wider. For the studio heads who opened the filmic space in green-lighting semi-autobiographical marginalized characters, the fame and wealth surrounding their industry was a way for them to distance themselves from the poor, ethnic, working class of their parents.

While cultural offerings of working-class heroes largely centered around men, there were some women who understood the artifice of the working-class hero and manipulated it for their own purposes in ways not dissimilar to the Jewish studio heads in Hollywood. The popular vaudevillian and singer Sophie Tucker is one example of a woman who consciously romanticized her working-class origins while often also fighting for the rights of those who labored. Born to Jewish immigrants in 1886, who began their lives in America by opening a kosher deli in Hartford, Connecticut, Tucker had married and given birth to a son by her late teens, yet made the decision to abandon her family and move to New York to make a career as a singer. Moving into show business was at first difficult for the overweight, outspoken Tucker, whose physicality did not align with industry expectations for slimmer headliners. In New York, she lived quite humbly among others struggling to secure work and like many second-generation Jewish immigrants, struggled deeply with her family's Orthodox background and her own embrace of American values. Reaching fame on the vaudeville circuit by the 1910s, Tucker often incorporated her rags to riches story into her comedy routines between songs: One of her most famous jokes is, "I've been rich and I've been poor—rich is better."

Like many other Jewish performers in the early twentieth century, Tucker's career started in blackface, largely because it lent comedic license to a woman who otherwise could not be marketed as traditionally beautiful. As David Roediger and Eric Lott have argued, blackface had a particular resonance among the White working class in the early nineteenth century, allowing White workers to cherish a visually demarcated racial status.[23] While blackface was a fixture enjoyed by all White audiences in burlesque, vaudeville, and early films by the time of Tucker's rise in fame, its use by women had a unique potency by providing them with racial superiority but also increased gender fluidity. An "unattractive" woman like Tucker, masked into a stereotype, could gain entry to the stage through the quality of her singing voice or the clip of her jokes. As Michael Rogin argues, many Jewish entertainers used blackface to assimilate; however, Tucker's particular brand facilitated her frequent persona as a working-class hero.[24]

As much as she enjoyed glamorous gowns, extravagant hairstyles, and first-class travel, she conveyed a kind of populism to her audiences that only intensified her fame. Tucker romanticized her working-class origins by fixating on the rags to riches story, as well as her romantic mishaps. Images of Tucker may have most often featured her draped in jewels, perfectly coiffed; yet, the performance so often centered on the failed aspirations and struggles that made success remarkable. Tucker's own sense of imposter syndrome was not only rooted in her looks, but also her upbringing. Until later in her career, she largely rejected her Orthodox, working-class family, while capitalizing on their American narrative in her live shows.

Tucker's interviews, autobiography, and fan mail suggest the power of her populist messaging. She emphasized her humble beginnings while also drawing attention to gender transgressions. Tucker was both a woman in show business and more sexually candid, and her music echoed these themes. Early recordings on wax cylinders such as "My Husband's in the City" reveled in female independence away from controlling husbands, while her 1952 hit "Sophie Tucker for President" championed the rights of women to be cherished by their partners, decrying, "Instead of the Congressional Record I'll Give Them the Kinsey Report."[25] This blend of gendered narratives with folksy charm drew Tucker to the widest of audiences, while her size and branding of a "Mama" insulated her from the criticism that more conventionally beautiful starlets received.

While much of Tucker's working-class persona was performative, she was genuinely interested in the plight of her fellow performers, taking on the presidency of the American Federation of Actors in 1935—the first woman in that role. With 15,000 members across a variety of industries, from vaudeville to circuses to nightclubs, the union was central to those who were not marquee headliners. Tucker had always supported those who worked in the chorus or in minor roles, sympathizing with their challenges from her early days in New York. In general, Tucker avoided political affiliations or any kind of organizing that could jeopardize her career, yet her willingness to take on this very public and quite laborious role spoke volumes about her position on unions. As she stated, "It seemed to me that the actor who paid his dues to his union was entitled to relief from that union when he needed it."[26]

While she only remained in the position briefly, Tucker's care for those in her profession at all levels may have given her working-class identity more credibility. Tucker was incredibly savvy and self-serving, agreeing to whatever genres or arrangements would boost her fame. Yet, the combination of a constructed iconography and a real political commitment made her both aware of her privilege and also eager to speak to its fragility. Her work in blackface and her connections to Black female contemporaries are problematic at the least, and arguably fueling the segregation of sound in the way Miller discusses. Tucker appropriated the sounds of singers such as Alberta Hunter, and she was provided with opportunities due to the racism toward Black women; however, she was still able to ground herself publicly among those on the margins. The most cynical reading of Tucker's career was an artifice of empathy; her quite generous philanthropic donations to Black organizations and later advocacy for Black artists during moments of segregation and exclusion speak to a genuine interest in furthering racial equality among performers. However, becoming a sort of working-class hero was never detached from an unquenchable thirst for fame, with major implications for Black female performers who never received the kind of widespread recognition that Tucker did during their time.

This awareness among ambitious artists continued over the course of the twentieth century. In 1970, John Lennon might have meant it sardonically when he sang "A working-class hero is something to be," speaking to the cultural capital in the mantle of working-class trappings—or at the very least, an origin story. As John McMillan argues, compared with the manufactured delinquency of their more frequent musical counterparts, the Rolling Stones, the Beatles were actually "thugs who were put across as nice blokes."[27] While the two groups shared much in common before their early fame, growing up in a wartime London where resourcefulness was necessary for all, the middle-class background of the Rolling Stones' Brian Jones, Mick Jagger, and Keith Richards distinguished the South England group from their Northern counterparts. While McMillan contends that there was nothing in their background that predestined the Rolling Stones to maintain their reputation of rebellion, they were able to take on a persona that the early Beatles were never allowed to present. Due to manager Brian Epstein's insistence at the beginning of their career that the Beatles "behave, conform, perform, wear suits, be polite," they were a model of youthful aspiration, leaving room for the Stones to take on the artifice of irreverence, as well as Mick's "faux-Cockney tongue" and "deliberately" bohemian Edith Grove apartment.[28] Whether John Lennon detested Epstein's rules of behavior more than his bandmates is widely debated; however both worked knowingly and willingly within the established norms of a working-class hero to achieve unbounded success and fame. The Stones and the Beatles both embodied working-class hero trappings in "real" and performative ways; yet their authenticity seems irrelevant given the incomparable public consumption both received.

As Jack Hamilton argues, the Stones' dangerous and subversive reputation was also due to the band's fixation with Black music in a way that the musicians explicitly referenced. Hamilton indicates that in contrast to the Beatles, who expressed their debt to African American rock and roll pioneers, the Stones "were seen as curiously obsessed with Black American music and culture to degrees most American youth were not."[29] In addition, as White rock music became increasingly distanced from Black artists by the late 1960s, the Stones continued to immerse themselves in Black musical traditions and collaboration, most famously in Mary Clayton's vocals on the song "Gimme Shelter." The Stones would continue to produce what Hamilton deems "markers of violence"; still, there is a long lineage between these late twentieth-century working-class hero manifestations and those produced in dime novels a century before.

Lennon's album debuted at the start of the 1970s, a decade that historian Jefferson Cowie claimed was the last days of a working class that was implicitly White. If those in the culture industry churned out White working-class heroes over the course of much of the twentieth century, such as *Saturday Night Fever*'s Tony Manero (1977), this kind of iconography may have become less palatable over time. Writing about country music and the rejection of it by middle-class arbiters since the 1970s, Nadine Hubbs argues that a pervasive narrative of "Good, progressive, middle class whites over Bad [*sic*], bigoted, working class whites," has taken hold.[30] In a post–civil rights, politically polarized nation, pitting working-class flyover country versus coastal elites, a White working-class hero may not be irrelevant but is arguably not culturally transcendent. Furthermore, older values of humble folksiness may be replaced with an inclusionary outlook that make a hardscrabble existence more politically digestible for industry executives.

Dominant tastemakers enveloped queer people by the 1970s, whether or not their experiences aligned with changing attitudes about cosmopolitanism, liberalism, and an elite outlook some scholars blame for dethroning the White working-class history. Queer Americans' place in a changing popular culture was remarkable. By mid-century, as World War Two and the Red Scare led to frenzied public fears about sexual perversion, the working-class landscape documented by George Chauncey gave way to homophile middle-class politics. But queer Americans, especially men, had a place in pop culture in the 1970s. As Hubbs argues, "LGBTQ identity is imagined especially in terms of gay men, who in turn are linked to metropolitan, bourgeois, coastal lifestyles. In the dominant middle class perspective, rednecks and queers are thought to occupy opposite ends of various political, social and cultural spectrums."[31] Jefferson Cowie echoes this sentiment in describing the appeal of country music as "rebellious yet conservative political identity" at the very moment when "key aspects of southern culture were becoming national culture."[32] Hubbs's charge is to dismantle this paradigm and the misunderstandings that stem from those expressing an "everything but Country" preference by analyzing country music as a product of specific working-class economic realities, modes of communication, and social developments. She also charts examples of "protest and resistance"—specifically connected to women's empowerment and possible defenses of homosexuality that complicate Cowie's notion of a more static or even declining working class. Hubbs's assertation that middle-class tastemakers have long rejected the "anti bourgeoisie" strain in country music lays bare the deliberations of capitalists who fashion an other for the elevation of their own station.[33]

Working-Class Heroes for a New Millennium

Many historians now consider the 1970s to have ushered in the rise of neoliberalism, which displaced the New Deal order that gave White working-class men middle-class living standards at home. The chapters in this volume looking at the years before, what Judith Stein called the "Pivotal Decade," challenge how secure the White working-class was before the 1970s. Still, the final decades of the twentieth century were pretty bad for working people. Over the objections of the left-leaning Democrats in Daniel Geary's, Leandra Zarnow's, and Jennifer Klein's chapters, inequality increased and key New Deal reforms were formally replaced. The globalization, hyper profit-seeking, and aggressive entrepreneurialism that defined neoliberalism eroded New Deal–era laborite culture in decades when private-sector union membership plummeted and business regulations were repealed. The Clinton administration, in retrospect, exemplified how much, as Justin Vassallo argued, "corporate influence dwarfed that of organized labor" as lawmakers turned welfare into workfare, undid banking rules that safeguarded everyday borrowers, and privatized schooling.[34]

Yet 1997 was a banner year for one of the most celebrated films about the working class—*Titanic.* James Cameron's blockbuster received eleven Oscars among countless other awards, praised almost universally by critics. If the turn of the twenty-first century was showing no signs of triage for representations of country music listeners, it was, ironically, a high point for a very different iconography of the White working class. As sociologist Beverly Skeggs indicates, "aspects of working class culture can be used for a particular exchange-value. Rather than being designated as simply pathological, some parts of the working class are represented as offering the value for consumption."[35]

So how can we consider an often maligned representation of the working class in one cultural genre with a simultaneous embrace in another? Media studies scholars such as Michele Hilmes have discussed the aural creation of racial and ethnic categories, and along with scholarship on the making of hillbilly music as a category, it may be natural to assume that the difference is rooted in genres and a longer connotation between working-class, rural backwardness in music than in visual media.[36] While this is certainly part of the explanation, many images and portrayals of redneck culture pervaded vaudeville, motion pictures, and television over the course of the twentieth century—some with the kind of inside joke among Southerners that Karl Miller claims—but many as a subject of ridicule and regional ridiculing. Furthermore, as political polarization by the 1970s only strengthened distaste for country music listeners by 1997, the answer to the *Titanic* phenomenon may be more rooted in socioeconomic circumstances.

The year 1997 could be seen as the perfect time for a film like *Titanic*—a time to cheer for those 1912 steerage passengers when the real working class was struggling.[37] The hero of *Titanic* was Leonardo DiCaprio's Jack, who provides a bridge among a multiclass audience who root for his romance with Kate Winslet's Rose amid the most dire of circumstances.[38] The technological advancements *Titanic* featured no doubt added to its popularity; however, at a moment of economic inequality viewers may have embraced the possibility of Jack's triumph over Rose's aristocratic clan, as well as her decision as a

Titanic survivor to shed her elite upbringing. While there are countless films featuring cross-class romance, the historical grounding of *Titanic* may have added a realism that only bolstered the power of Jack's character, as one *New York Times* reviewer called it "a story that is perceived to be true." White, handsome, charming, and artistic, Jack had the tools for upper-class mobility, even as he convinced Rose that his carefree life was a better existence than hers. In the end, viewers could imagine Rose and Jack being successfully in love, cut short by Jack's sacrificial death. They would find a middle ground in capitalist society through their own imagination and entrepreneurship—not collective action with others in steerage and not with Rose's inheritance. In the United States but also globally, *Titanic* was a sensation, with various audiences taking in the themes that were most resonant, whether critiques of an aristocracy in Japan or the "ship's fate as punishment for the arrogance of modern technology" in Germany.[39]

The romance between Jack and Rose was tailor-made for the Clinton years, and although global audiences may have enjoyed the protean nature of the film's messaging, the class dynamics were front and center in the United States, made only more evident by the other major film to dominate the 1997 box office and awards season—*Good Will Hunting*. The film's titular protagonist (Matt Damon) is a math genius from South Boston whose difficult home life and economic challenges only permitted him to be a janitor at MIT. Solving problems written on a blackboard during his shift that were left for graduate students, Will's talents are recognized by an MIT professor, but Will's anger and resentment initially prevent him from engaging. Soon, the professor bails him out of jail after a tavern brawl. Working for the professor as a condition of his parole, Will must also see a therapist, Dr. Sean McGuire (Robin Williams), who turns out to be very much like himself—a South Boston prodigy who endured searing childhood abuse. As Will learns more about himself from his therapy sessions and also falls in love with an upper-class Harvard coed, Skye (Minnie Driver), he realizes that he can move beyond his difficult circumstances. While his closest friends from childhood keep him grounded, he can only achieve true intimacy in a relationship with Skye at the film's end, when he follows her to California where she will attend medical school.[40]

The film also delivers a working-class hero whose romance grants him the ultimate happiness, but also mobility. Although Will turns down opportunities to work for big tech think tanks, in following his girlfriend audiences can imagine him setting himself up in a comfortable position. The answer for Will is not with his lifelong Southie friends who will, as Chuckie (Ben Affleck) reminds him, never move beyond construction work. Chuckie also demands that Will's genius makes it insulting to his less gifted friends for him to remain in any working-class position. As critic Janet Maslin offers, "Whether Will sees refuge or honor in a life of bricklaying, the film captures the extent of his turmoil."[41] The film never elevates the possibilities for bricklayers; if unions were marginalized in 1997, *Good Will Hunting* provided affirmation that the working class could still prevail through ingenuity and close friendships, but not improvements gained collectively. *Good Will Hunting* delivers South Boston as both a site of enduring poverty and unbreakable male solidarity. Both Will and psychiatrist Sean McGuire were able to escape—after accepting his need to move on after his wife's death, Dr. McGuire is leaving to go abroad for years at the end of the film. Here, love and camaraderie can empower economic and social mobility, without any real attention to improving the structural circumstances that trapped so many.

The celebration of working-class mobility or community preservation through foodways is a common theme in current programming, whether in featuring Guy Fiori's *Diners, Drives, and Dives* or the contestants on competition programs such as *Chopped*. Racially diverse and often queer, this kind of working-class hero usually speaks to advancing a worthy cause, such as creating a community eatery or preserving their own heritage in opening a new restaurant. Whether the current landscape is structurally more amenable to working-class entrepreneurs is questionable; however, modern media has situated underrepresented groups at the center of creative gastronomic output in programming. Yet, as Hasia Diner and others have studied, foodways have historically been some of the most dynamic spaces of racial and ethnic expression, but also often at the expense of those communities.[42] Foodways can also serve as deliberate sites of manufactured values; in his study of Starbucks, Bryant Simon also questions the artifice of the coffee giant for liberal, middle-class professionals "and their throngs of emulators to portray themselves as they wanted to be seen." Cosmopolitan, globally conscious, seeking authenticity and community, Starbucks consumers found a venue that could seemingly symbolize a dissipating 1960s radicalism.[43]

Foodways highlight, over twenty years after *Titanic* and *Good Will Hunting*, another way the working-class hero still pervades American culture, taking on a new identity, epitomized in *The Bear*'s Carmen Berzatto (Jeremy Allen White). Urban, racially tolerant, and aspirationally sensitive to women, Carmen is struggling to run his family's business in a flailing service economy. Having left his position as head chef in a Michelin-starred restaurant following the suicide of his brother, Carmen has taken on the task of transforming his family's beloved sandwich shop into a hub of haute cuisine. Carmen and his kitchen crew represent specific working-class Chicago families, across race and gender, with critics and prestige television pundits branding this authenticity.[44]

While Carmen is from the Midwest, he is not a redneck, a bigot, a homophobe, or many of the other derogatory stereotypes ascribed to the working class, particularly in rural areas. Carmen is decidedly working class even if his Michelin restaurants previously elevated him—unlike *Saturday Night Fever*'s Tony Manero, he does not describe his community as a place of departure, as Manero declared, "They're all assholes."[45] In *The Bear*, the working class is celebrated through its racial and generational diversity, as well as the teamwork involved in opening a new restaurant. Significantly, Carmen and his crew discard his family's beloved community sandwich shop to deliver haute cuisine and achieve gastronomic recognition.

By the third season of *The Bear*, Carmen's working-class hero status becomes even more central to the essence of the show: He is haunted by his prior experiences in haute establishments and driven to a level of perfectionism that is incompatible with stable relationships. In his community, those who are exceptional, much like Will Hunting, wrestle with the discomfort of their talents among others who are satisfied with steady work. Whether Carmen, like Will, will ultimately have to leave his community to achieve personal fulfillment is still unknown at this moment in the series; however, the weight of his leadership among co-workers and family limits his functionality as a chef. The series hinges on the contradictions of success and mobility, and whether working-class heroes can ever accept their own societal roles without sacrificing unusual levels of excellence.

The contradictions of capitalism have been the main ingredients of recent popular culture, as shows like *Succession* centrally question both the artificial nature of democracy and the production of ruling-class media tropes. They also present the possibility that a working-class hero can—as in those Depression-era films that consumed the public—be triumphant in the face of disfunction and ruthlessness. Based loosely on Rupert Murdoch's empire and family dynamics, *Succession* follows the Roy family and the ineptitude of the three Roy children, all of whom hope to run their father's company. As much as *Succession* is frequently read satirically by audiences and critics, it is valid to consider the impact of election rigging or the direct line between the White House and major CEOs, both of which occur in the Roy orbit. The

Roys manufacture their version of working-class values at a Fox proxy network (Waystar Royco), naturally oblivious to anything outside of the .01 percent orbit; they are not only tastemakers but careless and flippant at best. As CEO Logan's (Brian Cox) brother Ewan (James Cronwell) quips of the family's expanding media presence, "The Logan Roy School of Journalism? What's next, the 'Jack the Ripper Health Clinic'?"[46] Viewers may hope that American capitalists possess more competence and decency than the Roy family exhibits, but the possibility of inherited, unearned control always looms. The central question *Succession* asks is whether meritocracy is, in fact, a fiction, and whether anyone outside inner sanctums can penetrate them.[47]

In the penultimate episode of the series, *Succession* leaves that question—and the possibility of a victorious working-class hero—ambivalently. Tom Wambsgans (Matthew Macfadyen), a midwestern leech who marries daughter Shiv Roy (Sarah Snook), largely serves as a punching bag for the entire series. While he ends up closest to the titular role of Logan Roy's successor in the final episode, it is tenuous at best—he works for a tech giant, Gojo, which has acquired the company. Scheming Shiv is still by his side, pregnant with his child who will carry the Roy bloodline (in a devastating scene, Roman [Kieran Culkin] reminds Kendall [Jeremy Strong] that his adopted children are outsiders). Brothers Kendall and Roman have made billions of dollars from the sale of Waystar Royco and could easily unseat Tom or other men in his position. The architecture of capitalism already has positioned them indelibly, and whether they want to be part of an American aristocracy or not, they may not have a choice.

Succession is one of many contemporary shows that exposes corporate greed, but perhaps the most stinging indictment of aristocratic ineptitude in perpetuity.[48] Unlike *The White Lotus*, *The Morning Show*, or other critiques of corporate capitalism that feature characters at varying levels of the workforce, *Succession* makes no claim to sympathize with the Waystar Royco employees. Those in the C-suite face enough abuse, and as earlier episodes featuring Roman in a management training program make clear, the family has little interest in the people who work at the company or the articulated "morons" who soak in their content. Despite the business analysis of *Succession* on popular podcasts and granular attention to corporate authenticity, the show removes the nuts and bolts of political economy by prioritizing an analysis of family disfunction and the implications of landed wealth.

The C-suite executives from *Succession* may share many of the frustrations with those working at Mattel in "real-world" *Barbie*. Paradoxically, we know way more about the sexism that the female characters in *Succession* endure—Jerri (J. Cameron Smith), Kerri (Zoe Winters), Jess (Juliana Canfield)—all who cater to the whims of the Roy family, than we do about those at Mattel, who are seemingly absent. The only employee who represents "real world" inequality is Gloria (America Ferrara), whose impassioned speech arouses the specter of impossible standards, yet provides no real attention to structural inequality, racism, or the machinery that inflicts the pain she endures. The speech is another artifice, a packaged diversion from the concerns facing those on strike in 2023, or even those sitting in the audience who worry about their own socioeconomic fragility. Gloria's speech given in Barbieland appears siloed, where divisions between women are absent, "weird Barbie" is ostracized, and the ultimate hope is for coexistence in a heteronormative setting. Audiences may see themselves in Gloria's descriptions of shamed parenting, unachievable body standards, or ambiguous behavior in the workplace, but what is the impetus for change? And how will Gloria, as a Mattel employee, combat these impositions in her own company? The answer is not to strike, as the actors did during the film's nationwide rollout.

As a working-class hero, Gloria ultimately brings about the kind of change that we see in most of popular culture—mobility. Her mentorship of Barbie ultimately leads to Barbie's transformation into a "real woman" with genitals, leaving behind the community she was integrally part of; she somehow has the health care to see a gynecologist and a terrific wardrobe to boot. Billed as a feminist film, *Barbie* never moves into the foundations of inequality, and like all of its predecessors, exists in the hopeful, proto-capitalist imaginary. We can ponder whether this aspirational working-class hero can ultimately mirror working-class lives and move beyond a vapid space.

Notes

1. Lindsay Bahr, "The Story Behind Barbenheimer, the Summer's Most Online Movie Showdown," AP, July 14, 2023. Accessed October 15, https://apnews.com/article/barbenheimer-barbie-vs-oppenheimer-61a6ec6c67359b851ddeccd6d655b5ab; Patrick Ryan, "The Barbenheimer Phenomenon: How a Weird Movie Meme Inspired the 'Crazy, Weird' Double Feature," *USA Today*, July 18, 2023. Accessed October 15, 2023, https://www.usatoday.com/story/entertainment/movies/2023/07/18/barbenheimer-barbie-oppenheimer-movie-double-feature/70421503007/; Nicholas Barber, "What Does 'Barbenheimer' Really Mean for Hollywood?" BBC, July 21, 2023. Accessed October 15, 2023, https://www.bbc.com/culture/article/20230720-what-does-barbenheimer-really-mean-for-hollywood.

2. *Barbie*, Greta Gerwig, Director (Los Angeles: Warner Brothers, 2023); *Oppenheimer*, Christopher Nolan, Director (Los Angeles: Universal Pictures, 2023); Niall Ferguson, "The Barbenheimer Election," Free Press, August 20, 2024. Free Press. Accessed August 20, https://www.thefp.com/p/niall-ferguson-barbenheimer-election.

3. James Cook, *The Arts of Deception: Playing with Fraud in the Age of Barnum* (New York: Harvard University Press, 2001).

4. Michael Denning, *Mechanic Accents: Dime Novels and Working Class Culture in America* (New York: Verso, 1998), 11, 60, 82.

5. Paul Johnson, *Sam Patch the Famous Jumper* (New York: Hill and Wang, 2004); Joy Kasson, *Buffalo Bill's Wild West: Celebrity, Memory and Popular History* (New York: Hill and Wang, 2001); Elliott Gorn, *The Manly Art: Bare Knuckle Prize Fighting in America* (New York: Cornell University Press, 2010).

6. Roy Rosenzweig, *Eight Hours for What We Will: Workers and Leisure in an Industrial City, 1870–1920* (Boston: Cambridge University Press, 1984); Kathy Peiss, *Cheap Amusements: Working Women and Leisure in Turn of the Century New York* (Philadelphia: Temple University Press, 1986); John Kasson, *Amusing the Million: Coney Island at the Turn of the Century* (New York: Hill and Wang, 1978).

7. Nadine Hubbs, *Rednecks, Queers, and Country Music* (Berkeley: University of California Press, 2014), 32. Accessed October 10, https://ebookcentral.proquest.com/lib/southcarolina/reader.action?docID=1650803&query=.

8. Grace Elizabeth Hale, *Making Whiteness: The Culture of Segregation in the South, 1890–1940* (New York: Vintage Press, 1999).

9. Thomas Cripps, *Making Movies Black: The Hollywood Message Movie from World War II to the Civil Rights Era* (New York: Oxford University Press, 1993), 289, https://ebookcentral.proquest.com/lib/southcarolina/reader.action?docID=272243.

10. Susan Douglas, *Where the Girls Are: Growing Up Female with the Mass Media* (New York: Random House, 1994), 8, 10.

11. Douglas, *Where the Girls Are*, 5.

12. *The Celluloid Closet*. Rob Epstein, Jeffrey Friedman, Directors (Los Angeles: Tristar Pictures, 1996); *Disclosure*. Sam Feder, Director (Netflix, 2020).

13. Karl Hagstrom Miller, *Segregating Sound: Inventing Folk and Pop Music in the Age of Jim Crow* (Durham: Duke University Press, 2010), 211–212; Benjamin Filene, *Romancing the Folk: Public Memory and American Roots Music* (Chapel Hill: University of North Carolina Press, 2000), 27.

14. George Chauncey, *Gay New York: Gender, Urban Culture, and the Making of the Gay Male World, 1870–1940* (New York: Basic Books, 1995); Colin Johnson, *Just Queer Folk: Gender and Sexuality in Rural America* (Philadelphia: Temple University Press, 2013); John Howard, *Men Like That: A Southern Queer History* (Chicago: University of Chicago Press, 2001).

15. John D'Emilio, "Capitalism and Gay Identity," in *The Lesbian and Gay Studies Reader*, ed. Henry Abelove, Michele Aina Barale, and David M. Halperin (New York: Routledge, 1993), 468.

16. D'Emilio, "Capitalism and Gay Identity," 474.

17. Paula Fass, *The Damned and the Beautiful: American Youth in the 1920s* (New York: Oxford University Press, 1977).

18. Aaron Lecklider, *Love's Next Meeting: The Forgotten History of Homosexuality and the Left in American Culture* (University of California Press, 2021), 7.

19. Stuart Hall, "Deviance, Politics, and the Media," in *The Lesbian and and Gay Studies Reader*, ed. Henry Abelove, Michele Aina Barale, and David M. Halperin (Routledge 1993), 64.

20. Michael Denning, *The Cultural Front: The Laboring of American Culture in the Twentieth Century* (New York: Verso, 1997).

21. Lary May, *The Big Tomorrow: Hollywood and the Politics of the American Way* (Chicago: University of Chicago Press, 2000), 65.

22. Neal Gabler, *An Empire of Their Own* (New York: Anchor Books, 1988), 240–41.

23. David Roediger, *The Wages of Whiteness: Race and the Making of the American Working Class* (New York: Verso, 1991); Eric Lott, *Love and Theft: Blackface Minstrelsy and the American Working Class* (New York: Oxford University Press, 1993).

24. Michael Rogin, *Blackface, White Noise: Jewish Immigrants in the Melting Pot* (Berkeley: University of California Press, 1996).

25. Sophie Tucker, *Origins of the Red Hot Mama, 1910–1922* (Archeophone Records, 2009); Sophie Tucker, *Sophie Tucker: The Very Best Of* (Master Classics Records, 2009).

26. Lauren Rebecca Sklaroff, *Red Hot Mama: The Life of Sophie Tucker* (Austin: University of Texas Press, 2018), 150.

27. John McMillan, *Beatles vs. Stones* (New York: Simon & Schuster, 2013), 9.

28. McMillan, *Beatles vs. Stones*, 30, 24–25.

29. Jack Hamilton, *Just Around Midnight: Rock and Roll and the Racial Imagination* (Cambridge: Harvard University Press, 2016), 257. Accessed October 2, 2024, https://web.p.ebscohost.com/ehost/ebookviewer/ebook/ZTAyNXhuYV9fMTM2NDI3MF9fQU41?sid=d28895b7-6fcb-4c8e-bdcd-f39c1c1de939@redis&vid=0&format=EB&lpid=lp_246&rid=0.

30. Hubbs, *Rednecks, Queers, and Country Music*, 2.

31. Hubbs, *Rednecks, Queers, and Country Music*, 30.

32. Jefferson Cowie, *Stayin' Alive: The 1970s and the Last Days of the Working Class* (New York: New Press, 2010), 170.

33. Hubbs, *Rednecks, Queers, and Country Music*, 137.

34. Justin Vassallo, "How Democrats Traded the New Deal for Neoliberalism," *Jacobin*, July 7, 2022. Accessed October 10, 2023, https://jacobin.com/2022/07/democratic-party-neoliberalism-dlc-clinton; Judith Stein, *A Pivotal Decade: How the United States Traded Factories for Finance in the 1970s* (New Haven: Yale University Press, 2011); Gary Gerstle, *The Rise and Fall of the Neoliberal Order: America and the World in the Free Market Era* (New York: Oxford University Press, 2023); Nelson Lichtenstein and Judith Stein, *A Fabulous Failure: The Clinton Presidency and the Transformation of American Capitalism* (Princeton: Princeton University Press, 2023).

35. Beverly Skeggs, *Class, Self, Culture* (Philadelphia: Taylor and Francis, 2003), 98. Accessed October 10, 2023, https://ebookcentral.proquest.com/lib/southcarolina/reader.action?docID=1543047.

36. Michele Hilmes, *Radio Voices: American Broadcasting, 1922–1952* (Minneapolis: University of Minnesota Press, 1997).

37. Vassallo, "How Democrats Traded the New Deal for Neoliberalism."

38. *Titanic*, James Cameron, Director (Los Angeles: Paramount Pictures, 1997).

39. Alan Riding, "Why Titanic Conquered the World: Reports from Britain to Beijing on the Blockbuster's Wide Wake," *New York Times*, April 26, 1998, AR1.

40. *Good Will Hunting*, Gus Van Sant, Director (Los Angeles: Miramax Films, 1997).

41. Janet Maslin, "Logarithms and Biorhythms Test a Young Janitor," *New York Times*, December 5, 1997, E10.

42. Hasia Diner, *Hungering for America: Italian, Irish and Jewish Foodways in the Age of Migration* (Cambridge: Harvard University Press, 2003).

43. Bryant Simon, *Everything but the Coffee: Learning About America from Starbucks* (Berkeley: University of California Press, 2009), 7.

44. *The Bear*, Christopher Storer, Creator (Hulu, 2022).

45. Cowie, *Stayin' Alive*, 316.

46. Adam Epstein, "No TV Show Has Ever Weaponized Figurative Language as Well as HBO's 'Succession,'" *Quartz*, October 15, 2019. Accessed October 11, 2023, https://qz.com/quartzy/1728395/the-best-insults-from-season-2-of-hbos-succession.

47. *Succession*, Jesse Armstrong, Creator (HBO, 2018).

48. Daniel Fienberg, "Critic's Notebook: Capitalism and TV Today: A Love/Hate Story," *Hollywood Reporter*, March 20, 2023. Accessed October 15, 2023, https://www.hollywoodreporter.com/tv/tv-reviews/succession-you-capitalism-1235362176/.

CHAPTER 11

From Labor History to Political Economy: A Reassessment of Work, Capital, and Democracy

Meg Jacobs

In September 1992, on Labor Day, the *New York Times* ran an op-ed about the centrality of the American working class to the shaping of the nation's modern history, even as, or rather just as, the fate of organized labor was unclear. Under the title "What Happened to the Working Class?" the piece ran amid Arkansas Governor Bill Clinton's challenge to sitting Republican President George H. W. Bush. If Clinton were to win, that would possibly offer a chance to bring the Reagan era to a close, returning to a time before President Ronald Reagan had fired striking air traffic controllers in his first year in office. But a progressive transformation of American politics, at a moment when the Democratic candidate used the language of the "middle class" to denote working people, was far from clear. As the piece explained, to reclaim its place as the voice and advocate of workers like the Black mother of three who sliced chicken at one of Arkansas's poultry factories, both the Democratic Party and the union movement had to once again deploy a class language that resonated with the lived reality of those whose lives hovered not much above the poverty line. For that, the opinion piece argued, we ought to look to history, a history "tested by time and trouble" in which working people had made substantial progress by mobilizing the most down and out and not just the so-called middle class, a mobilization from which all benefited. At the heart of American prosperity stood the labor movement.[1]

The essay argued we should all be thankful—on Labor Day and every day. Without the trade union movement we would not have the weekend, paid vacation, workplace rights, and more. It was clear to anyone who studied labor history then, and it is certainly clear with the benefit of three decades of hindsight, that we were at a turning point in the early 1990s, as the chapters in this volume's previous section stress. Bill Clinton would go on to win, but as Nelson Lichtenstein, the labor historian who authored that op-ed, pointed out, that would settle nothing. A pressing question remained: Would labor, in the post-Reagan world, in its most expansive version, ever again be central?

That question stood at the center of the research conducted by Lichtenstein and other scholars of his New Left generation, a group identified as the "New Labor" historians. Indeed, it is the question that should be at the center of all modern American history, especially as the power and influence of organized labor has become more and more attenuated. When he wrote that op-ed, Lichtenstein lamented that unions represented "only" 16 percent of the workforce; today that number is around 10 percent. At a time of rising inequality, ever-present political instability, and an erosion of democracy, it makes sense more than ever to reassess the institutions and ideas that have historically checked these forces. Such progressive phrases as the American Standard of Living, Eight Hours for What We Will, Industrial Democracy, Solidarity Forever, Black and White Unite—all the phrases that Lichtenstein pointed to—are all the more vital in the late twentieth and early twenty-first centuries. After all, the neoliberal moment that defined the 1990s and early 2000s has underscored the degree to which the weakness of organized labor made impossible the construction or maintenance of the social democratic tilt so characteristic of American politics in the mid-twentieth century, the era covered in this volume's second section.

To appreciate the role of labor in the nation's past, scholars need to return to a much older version of history, one that preceded the creation of the New Deal order and went by the label of political economy. That is what labor intellectuals, including Richard Ely and his student John Commons, called their research, which largely had an institutional focus.[2] Their scholarship was limited by all kinds of nineteenth-century blinders. They also would not have used terms like state and society that became popular with the appearance in the late twentieth century of the historical subfields known as American Political Development and Policy History. Yet their work—with its essential focus on institutions and institutional strength—provides an essential template if we are to understand work, capitalism, and democracy today, as the title of this volume purports.

Lichtenstein's work provides a useful lens to capture what the study of political economy looks like a century after the Wisconsin school. As Howard

Brick wrote in a review of Lichtenstein's work, "Before there was such an academic thing as 'the history of capitalism,' there was Nelson Lichtenstein's labor history." He is a particular kind of labor historian who eschews that very label, or at least what that label came to mean when scholars first adopted it. And with good reason. A graduate student in the late 1960s, he was not a part of the social history movement that took as its subject the Lowell mill girls and the Knights of Labor. But this member of Berkeley's International Socialists chapter (a left-wing anti-Stalinist organization reflecting the political zeitgeist described in Geary's chapter) was also not a practitioner of old-fashioned political history. Rather, then as now, Lichtenstein was a student of political economy, which meant that he saw working-class concerns of identity, income, and public power at the fore of modern US history—as historian Steve Fraser, an editor instrumental to the New Labor History's rise, once put it to Nelson, "Pay attention to the corridors of power."

Parsing the avenues of authority has been a part of recent histories of policy, state building, and capitalism that could all benefit, as the chapters in this volume individually and collectively aim to show, from the flavor of labor history that Lichtenstein and others helped found. After all, only by paying attention to questions of culture, capital, and the state all at once—in other words, studying political economy—can scholars appreciate the history of what Lichtenstein called "justice and dignity on the job, democracy and welfare in the larger polity."[3]

In the 1990s, as organized labor was in decline, the language of working-class empowerment seemed to be falling further out of favor among workers themselves, even as the news media started to use that term more frequently, as Robyn Muncy has carefully documented. But, as Muncy explained, there was an inverse relationship between the use of the term working class and its threat to social order—the phrase, as Lichtenstein captured, no longer meant what it once had. In the 1990s, with the end of the Cold War, the deindustrialization of the heartland, and the discovery of racism among non-college-educated Whites, the press could use the term because workers were no longer at the vanguard of a vibrant social democratic movement. The term gained currency, and retains it today, because workers were seen as "pitiful rather than powerful."[4]

Yet of course, as Lichtenstein pointed out in his 1992 op-ed, the working class was, as it has always been, still there. And here, a perhaps unexpected reading list might point the way. For anyone wanting to understand how to revive a vibrant working class, there were three books, according to Lichtenstein, that were essential reading—shortcuts, as it were, to whole schools of labor history that collectively pointed the way to recovering and restoring the role of a vibrant working-class movement, one that appreciated customs, institutions, and the role of the state in promoting progressive change. (Full disclosure: I was one such graduate student in the 1990s when, as my mentor, Lichtenstein made me read all three.) They are Thomas Bell's 1941 *Out of This Furnace*, a tale of immigrant labor in the steel factories; Harvey Swados's *On the Line*, published a decade and a half later when unions were ascendant but workers still faced a life of drudgery; and Thomas Geoghegan's 1991 *Which Side Are You On? Trying to Be for Labor When It's Flat on Its Back*, which offered the beginnings of a post-Reagan reassessment of what unions might have to offer. Let's take each in turn to see their contributions to a revamped and resurgent study of political economy.

Out of This Furnace

When Thomas Bell published his proletarian novel in 1941, *Out of This Furnace*, it came at the peak of a Popular Front celebration of work and solidarity. Telling the story of three generations of Slovakian immigrants, whose first arrival came to the United States in 1881 to settle just outside Pittsburgh, the novel shows their descent into the steel mills, their participation in strikes and other struggles, and ultimately their triumph in the formation of a union. Along the way, the central characters bemoan the hardships of life in the mills, even as they also aspire for a better future. As the narrator remarks, "They ceased to be men of skill and knowledge, ironmakers, and were degraded to the status of employees who did what they were told for a wage, whose feelings didn't matter, not even their feelings for the tools, the machines, they worked with, or for the work they did." Yet they did not give up all hope. "It takes a long time for the dead to die," remarked Bell's central character Dobie.[5]

Bell told this story in four parts, beginning with two Slovaks who migrated in the late nineteenth century and concluding in 1937 when their community in Braddock, Pennsylvania, finally finds the American Dream through the success of the CIO. Bell himself left the steel towns, seeking the life of a writer, but his imaginary alter ego was Dobie, the second-generation union organizer. Ignored by the AFL's ancient organizers in Pittsburgh, Dobie realizes that his path forward required rank-and-file mobilization. As he said to his friend, "You know what I've been thinking? It wouldn't hurt if we knew a lot more about unions than we do. I mean how they're supposed to be run and the right way to deal with the company and so on. . . . If we had the experience and knew all the ins and outs we could get a lot more done." When he finally succeeds, it is through the solidarity of the union that he finds his freedom—not just for better furniture for his wife and family, but rather for a sense of manhood and citizenship. "Made in the U.S.A., he thought, made in the First Ward. But it wasn't where you were born or how you spelled your name or where your father had come from. It was the way you thought and felt about certain things," by which he meant the right to organize. "About freedom of speech and the equality of men and the importance of having one law—the same law—for rich and poor, for the people you liked and the people you didn't like. About the right of every man to live his life as he thought best." For Dobie, as it was for Bell, the story of America was, as Bell told an interviewer, a history of how "the Slovaks with their blood and lives helped to build America."[6]

That long forgotten but then rediscovered novel speaks to the textured, nitty-gritty details of what it meant to be a member of the working classes, which animated so much of the early New Labor History. David Demarest, a professor at Carnegie Mellon who devoted his career to a celebration of working-class life, republished *Out of This Furnace* in 1976; he even offered walking tours of Braddock where the story had taken place. Soon after its republication, Lichtenstein and others were assigning the book to their undergraduates. It was readily available in college bookstores across the country. In the 1980s, as manufacturing jobs were on the decline, it was important, in the phrase that Roy Rosenzweig and his collaborators used as a textbook title, echoing Bell, to understand "who built America."[7]

If Bell's book offered but a male perspective on the rise of an immigrant industrial working class, one could look instead to Mary Antin's autobiography, *The Promised Land*. From the Russian Pale to Boston, Antin told a story of a young Jewish woman who described her wonder in a new homeland. Light was free, music was free, and above all education was free. Antin recalled a transformative experience in which she goes "uptown" to a "beautiful palace called a 'department store,'" where she and her siblings exchanged "our hateful homemade European costumes, which pointed us out as 'greenhorns' to the children on the street, for real American machine-made garments, and issued forth glorified in each other's eyes." Like Bell, Antin offered a hopeful account of possibilities ahead along with the dreary details of the daily grind of working-class life. The novel echoes the era's early twentieth-century black-and-white photographs, when Lower East Side immigrants, largely penniless, playacting as they posed for the camera, wore top hats and strings of pearls, clearly borrowed for the occasion.[8]

If Antin and Bell offered hopeful firsthand accounts, many other social histories of the 1970s and 1980s provided a far less triumphant narrative that emphasized class oppression and collective struggle. In *Immigrant Women in the Land of Dollars*, Elizabeth Ewen offered up a darker remembrance of work and class that was reflected in other black-and-white photographs from the time. Think of Lewis Hine's photographs or those of Jacob Riis, which both captured the reality of hard and tiresome employment, when immigrant children, boys and girls, labored in dank, dark, dirty, and dangerous conditions.

Ewen nonetheless celebrated the aspirations of those immigrants who posed for photographs in their borrowed costumes. The women in her book wore and fought for the big hats fashionable in that era. When 20,000 teenage garment workers went on strike in 1909 for higher wages, better working conditions, and union recognition, one of the leaders explained, "We're all human, all of us, and we're young. We like new hats as well as any other young women. Why shouldn't we?" Rose Schneiderman, who led the strike, explained, "The woman worker wants bread, but she wants roses too."[9]

It was precisely these conflicts that became the focus for social historians, writing largely about the Gilded Age and Progressive Era. Inspired by British historian E. P. Thompson's classic work about the English working class, they absorbed his dictum that classes are not the product of economic conditions alone, but rather they are "made" by the men and women who imagine them. Few did that as well as Roy Rosenzweig. In his 1985 *Eight Hours for What We Will*, Rosenzweig recounted the parks, picnics, and pubs that gave meaning to workers' lives in Worcester, Massachusetts. It was not surprising that the book received a favorable review from Yale historian David Montgomery.[10] In 1948, Montgomery had voted for Progressive Party candidate Henry Wallace and then worked as a machinist in a Minneapolis factory, reflecting not only the organizing strategy of the American Communist Party but the industrializing impulse that would later animate a generation of New Leftists, many of whom were young, committed labor historians.[11]

In the same year that Demarest reissued *Out of This Furnace*, another leading labor historian, Herbert Gutman, published a foundational text, *Work, Culture, and Society*. Gutman, like Montgomery, also worked on the Wallace campaign. The point was not to reject the New Deal, but rather to embrace its most expansive version, one that included a social democratic impulse and a cultural pluralism that put the working classes front and center in American progressive politics. Gutman, like Thompson before him, focused on the customs and traditions that immigrant workers carried with them as tools of resistance, not something to be shed, but rather as something to hold onto in the process of class formation. That insight, which could have been lifted off the pages of Bell, inspired a whole generation of labor historians.

All of their histories were so fun to read. From Bruce Nelson's West Coast dock workers to Michael Kazin's building trades to Susan Porter Benson's department store clerks, they all offered deep, rich, and textured histories that explained the vital role of workers in making the United States into the world's leading industrial economy. So, too, did the Black sharecroppers in Alabama who barely left a record but nonetheless had a story worth telling. As Robin Kelley captured them so poignantly in his 1990 *Hammer and Hoe: Alabama Communists During the Great Depression*, even the most powerless could have agency. Workers could use many tools to exercise their authority and assert their personhood, including their use of clothing, hair styles, and language, as, for example, Jacquelyn Dowd Hall made so clear in her chronicle of a courtroom trial of striking Appalachian female textile workers. As Gary Gerstle understood it, this kind of social and cultural history reflected the ways that US workers, foreign-born or native, claimed and redefined the very meaning of Americanness.[12]

These stories helped make sense of much of modern working-class life. That was the success of social history. In 1974, the winner of the National Book Award was the autobiography of Nate Shaw, a Black sharecropper, under the title *All God's Dangers*. The book beat Robert Caro's *Powerbroker* about Robert Moses, Bob Woodward and Carl Bernstein's *All the President's Men*, and also Studs Terkel's *Working*. As much as that last one gave voice to the routine trials and tribulations of how people earned their money, it was the story of a Black sharecropper that won.[13]

On the Line

If those social histories of labor captured the centrality of workers to the making of modern life, another book, *On the Line*, offered a very different sensibility. In 1990, Lichtenstein wrote the introduction to this reissued classic work by journalist and novelist Harvey Swados. Originally published in 1957, *On the Line* offered a compilation of eight short stories set in the "golden age" of American capitalism when industrial unions like the United Automobile Workers seemed so strong and stable. While many contemporary commentators were celebrating the relative peace found in the nation's factories and the market miracle of postwar production, Swados lamented the nature of the work he found in a New Jersey auto plant during a year-long stint in the mid-1950s. As one of his characters says, "They don't even know your name here, only your social security number and your time clock number."[14]

In these short, interconnected stories, Swados shows men hard at work, disappointed with the life they have achieved. When an Irish worker decides to buy a car, thinking this will give him purpose, he ends up realizing the hollowness of his ambitions. "He saw with bitter clarity that he would be chained to the line for years, chained to the drudgery, the monotony, the grinding labor," lamented the worker, who soon sold his car and moved back to Ireland. "The worst thing about the assembly line is what it does to your self-respect," said another young worker. "It's hard to keep from feeling like a fool when you know that everybody looks down on what you're doing even the men who are doing it themselves."[15] As Robyn Muncy shows, it was at this precise moment that the use and meaning of the phrase "working class" faded from language as part of the mid-century Cold War mythos holding that everyone had been absorbed into a middle-class society. Yet, Swados wanted his readers to see that the working class was still very much there.

Even more, Swados saw the collaborationist spirit of industrial unionism that emerged out of World War II as much of the culprit as anything else in explaining the dulling sensitivity (or dull stolid character) of postwar unionism. As Lichtenstein put it in the 1990 introduction to the reprint, "Manipulation therefore replaced mobilization of the membership, and bureaucracy triumphed over locally initiated activism." In the fall of 1963, Swados published a classic essay in *Dissent* under the title, "The UAW: Over the Top or Over the Hill?" The answer to him and like-minded disciples was clear. As Swados put it, "The UAW leadership no longer takes its own demands seriously." If the thrust of social history was to recapture working-class culture as an independent force, distinct from the mainstream middle classes, then the argument here was to steer clear of the state and the unions it spawned and constrained in order to preserve that independence.[16]

Nothing made that point as forcefully as Lichtenstein's own work. His 1982 *Labor's War At Home* was not a rejection of social history per se but a different strand of the literature on labor that he and his contemporaries were writing. It was also notably about the trade union movement *after* the New Deal reforms but before liberal jurists began to undermine them, as shown in Jean-Christian Vinel's chapter. Lichtenstein wrote about just the types of workers who populated Swados's stories. But the heart of this monograph, first written as a dissertation in early 1970s Berkeley, was less a celebration of authentic cultures and more a denunciation of the Faustian bargain that the newly formed CIO unions struck with the wartime state. Lichtenstein, with deep sympathies for the young leftists appearing in Geary's chapter, largely agreed with Swados's view that the mobilization for World War II necessarily limited the gains that had been achieved in the 1930s. By 1945, after five years of all-out production, the ban on strikes, and the stifling of discontent, the autoworker's world, according to Lichtenstein, looked a lot different than it had in 1941; the union at best was a collaborationist tool in a world of statist capitalism.[17]

That view had been an important part of David Montgomery's work too. There is a reason why his 1987 book's title, *The Fall of the House of Labor*, about the American Federation of Labor from the end of the Civil War through World War I, a period when membership grew, nevertheless advances a declension narrative. Once the unions got a seat at the table, their story was largely over. If in the late nineteenth century steelworkers shared an authentic culture of mutualism, one in which they cooperated to retain power over their own labor, their participation in the World War I–era National War Labor Board and other state institutions led to their cooptation.[18]

This was also the thrust of Lizabeth Cohen's 1990 *Making a New Deal* about industrial workers in Chicago. If workers used mass culture to unite in the formation of a working-class solidarity, nevertheless, by virtue of relying on and working with the New Deal state, they gave away their power and autonomy. What she calls "moral capitalism"—the working-class version of modern consumer culture—was still capitalism, and the desire for the good life led workers to rely on the false promises of prosperity offered from the New Deal state. To be sure, these stories showed how workers pursued more than bread and butter unionism, and they also rejected the view of Werner Sombart that American workers abandoned their activism in exchange for the chance at higher living standards. It was not that the pursuit of the American standard of living automatically dampened working-class militancy but rather that accommodation with the New Deal's industrial relations regime constrained union radicalism.[19] In her next book, *A Consumer's Republic*, Cohen makes the point even more sharply: After the New Deal, workers replaced a culture of solidarity with culture of individualism, and any hope of radical change went out the window.

There were no shortages of examples that offered up this view. For example, Christopher Tomlins's *The State and the Unions: Labor Relations, Law, and Organized Labor* (1985), even as it covered a large sweep of history, looked most carefully at the 1935 National Labor Relations Act and the administration of labor law under the newly formed National Labor Relations Board. As Melvyn Dubofsky wrote in a critical review, Tomlins offered a "sharp condemnation of federal labor policy for curbing the strength of labor in the interests of capital and an equally bitter denunciation of most trade union leaders for compelling their rank and file to participate in their own subjugation at work." Case by case, the courts undercut any prospect for labor radicalism. That was the insight of Tomlins, who was certainly more readable than some of the other legal works that similarly advanced a view of the state as a corrupting and confining influence. In cutting-edge law review articles, scholars Katherine Stone and Karl Klare advanced a clear thesis: The state, whether in the form of justices or labor bureaucrats, suppressed activism and agency. That was because inevitably the state served the interests of capital. As Stone remarked in her 1981 essay, "The industrial pluralist view of labor relations was based on a false assumption: that management and labor had the equal power in the workplace." That point of view culminated in the work of Colin Gordon, who went so far as to argue that capitalists themselves pushed for the Wagner Act as a stabilizing influence that muted radicalism.[20]

In this move toward state-centered analyses, scholars showed not only the class dimension of industrial pluralism but also its deep limitations by race and gender, the historic inequity that energized the feminist political strategists in Leandra Zarnow's chapter. For example, Alice Kessler-Harris, Linda Gordon, and other feminist scholars demonstrated the gendered assumptions built into the welfare state that rewarded benefits for White working men while it devalued assistance for the rest of the workforce, especially Black women in excluded categories like agriculture, domestic, and public employment. Rather than provide pensions and public assistance as a right of citizenship, the New Deal state tied these provisions to work-based contributory entitlements, reinforcing the male-centered nature of employment and the limitations of a more generous welfare state. Other scholars, such as Robert Lieberman and Ira Katznelson, documented how the New Deal state rested on the preservation of racial privilege, especially in the South. Describing the politics of that era as trapped in the "southern cage," Katznelson argued that the presence of Southern Democrats in the New Deal coalition served as a barrier to more universal benefits. As Katznelson aptly put it, this period of political reform can properly be known as the moment "when affirmative action was white." It was not simply that Black workers were largely excluded from coverage by the Social Security system, the National Labor Relations Board, and the 1938 Fair Labor Standards Act, and the educational opportunities and housing assistance provided under the 1944 GI Bill. Rather, it was that White entitlement rested on Black exclusion, an omission that had long-term consequences, increasing the Black-White wealth disparity and creating de facto segregation in housing, education, and employment. In his work on postwar Detroit, Thomas Sugrue showed exactly how narrow the window was for a multiracial New Deal social democratic state. In other words, the state itself was the source of setbacks for millions of working-class Americans.[21]

Which Side Are You On?

A slow reassessment of that line of reasoning began in the aftermath of the Reagan era when it became clear that the state itself could be, under certain circumstances, a central ingredient in democratic progress. In his 1991 book, *Which Side Are You On?*, Thomas Geoghegan, a Harvard-trained labor lawyer, wrote a memoir of his experiences defending union workers in their decades of defeat starting in the 1970s. Again and again, he relayed tales of standing up for steelworkers and miners only to have corrupt officials subvert their efforts. It was not only autocratic union leadership that undercut authentic organizing efforts, but rather the larger phenomenon of deindustrialization. With one in three jobs in heavy industry vanishing in the 1980s, so continued the offshoring and exporting of American manufacturing jobs, a process that scholars like Judith Stein and Jefferson Cowie wrote about so effectively, building on the work of political economists Barry Bluestone and Bennett Harrison. This phenomenon did not happen automatically, according to Geoghegan, who witnessed this debacle from the Chicago industrial trenches. Rather, the disappearance and decline came as the result of deliberate policies of deregulation under Presidents Jimmy Carter and Ronald Reagan and the legal constraints imposed on unionization by the judiciary and the National Labor Relations Board.[22]

And yet, writing in the shadows of the Reagan era, Geoghegan appreciates that the New Deal state was essential for building a democratic labor movement, including the role of labor lawyers like him. In 1976, the year he likely encountered *Out of This Furnace*, he recalls watching *Harlan County,*

USA, a documentary about the 1973 strike in those notorious mines. He realizes that as much as the movie highlights the heroic roles of the miners and their families who risked their lives, he himself is missing. "As I watched the movie, I thought, Where's the staff? Yes, yes, I wanted to see the miners, the wives locked up in jail, but then I noticed that *we the staff* were missing." With a self-acknowledged inflated sense of self, he says "We, the staff, had won that strike. *We* had organized the boycotts, the rate challenges, even a brief nationwide strike. . . . *We* had gone to the White House and the Labor Department to demand that they intervene."[23]

The problem in the 1990s was that bureaucrats were no longer powerful, because the labor laws were no longer powerful. As he explained, it was easy to to fire workers if they tried to unionize. "I doubt today if any group of workers can form a union if their employer is truly determined to resist." As he concludes, "I can think of nothing, no law, no civil rights act, that would radicalize this country more, democratize it more, and also revive the Democratic Party, than to make this one tiny change in the law: to let people join unions if they like, freely and without coercion, without threat of being fired." He described the change since the passage of the Wagner Act as a "civil rights movement in reverse."[24]

And yet, even as tenuous as the movement seemed, this labor lawyer, like Lichtenstein in his op-ed, appreciated that there was something different about the culture of workers. As he explained, the one thing that was absent was a sense of individualism. "Labor thinks of itself, consciously, as American as apple pie. But it is not. Go to any union hall, any union rally, and listen to the speeches. It took me years to hear it, but there is a silence, a deafening Niagara-type silence, on the subject of individualism. No one is against it, but it never comes up." As he put it, even in 1991, "The subversive thing about labor is not the strike, but the idea of solidarity." On the streets of Chicago, in the winter months, he is struck by how many steel union members walk around in their Local 65 windbreakers.[25]

As it turned out, after Reagan-Bush and the turn to neoliberalism, labor did not look so bad. And neither did the state. Instead of *On the Line* and *Out of the Furnace*, Jack Metzgar's family memoir about a long-forgotten 1959 steel strike suggested the importance to the most recent generation of labor historians, including volume contributor Samir Sonti, of reconsidering both state and unions in the new millennium. As this huge work stoppage demonstrated to hundreds of thousands of steelworkers, even the most ossified unions could still light a spark, provided the members stuck together and fought for the security that rules and regulations could guarantee for shop floor dignity and higher living standards. Metzgar's book appeared after reformer John Sweeney and his "New Voices" team won top leadership posts at the AFL-CIO. Sweeney aimed to infuse new life into the labor movement by reaching out to campus radicals, working-class feminists, and immigrants from Latin America and Asia. After Lichtenstein had published his *New York Times* op-ed and Bill Clinton won a couple of months later, even the limited reforms put forward by the Clinton administration seemed the most hopeful prospect in a generation. Because what was the alternative?[26]

That hope—that a different political regime could make a difference and so, too, could a different kind of union movement—became clear in Lichtenstein's book about Walter Reuther, *The Most Dangerous Man in Detroit*. The book is a magisterial recreation of the role of Reuther in creating the UAW as a progressive social force in the twentieth century. Was the union perfect? Was it limited? Was it at times self-serving, and did it also at other times serve the interests of some (i.e., White male workers) better than others? Sure, and Lichtenstein shows as much. But the point of the union movement was to advance a notion of collective rather than individual rights, as he effectively argued in his influential essay in Steve Fraser and Gary Gerstle's seminal 1989 collection, *The Rise and Fall of the New Deal Order* (that chapter became a blueprint of sorts for how labor historians would begin to bring scholars back to a better version of Ely and Common's political economy). When Florence Reece, the wife of a union organizer in the Kentucky coalmines, wrote her 1931 labor ballad "Which Side Are You On?," made famous as a union anthem by Pete Seeger, she captured the essence of the post–New Left perspective (or really maybe just an Old Left perspective). At the end of the day, Reuther was on the workers' side, even if, and at times precisely because, he was willing to rely on the authority of the state to legitimize the labor movement and win new rights for working people. While it was true that Reuther could become a prisoner of the institutions he created, there would be no left-leaning tilt to American political economy without them.[27]

Yet Lichtenstein's acclaimed biography was hardly a celebration. As he explained, the story was one of "devolution, missed opportunities, and structural sclerosis." That explanation came in an exchange, one that was at times deeply personal, between Lichtenstein and Herbert Hill, a longtime NAACP civil rights activist. Hill and some of his old comrades denounced Lichtenstein as a sell-out for seeing any good that came from the Reuther story. However, in the context of the post-Reagan decimation of labor, there was room, according to Lichtenstein, to revisit the role of the UAW as a progressive force that rested on and encouraged a social movement that could take on corporate power. To be sure, its opponents perceived unions as a threat. The title of Lichtenstein's Reuther biography came from George Romney of the Automobile Manufacturers Association, future governor of Michigan and father of GOP presidential hopeful Mitt. The senior Romney saw Reuther as "the most dangerous man in Detroit" because, as he put it, "No one is more skillful in bringing about the revolution without seeming to disturb the existing forms of society." If Montgomery's *Fall of the House of Labor* was a declension narrative, Lichtenstein's was not an ascension; he was not blind to the limitations that came from reliance on the state to rebalance power on the shop floor. He also did not ignore the union's opportunistic relationship to the civil rights movement. As he explained, the UAW could be complicit in upholding the racially coded nature of private employment in the United States. And yet, writing a rejoinder to Hill's critique at just the moment when John Sweeny was coming to power, Lichtenstein was willing to see unions as an important institutional force in building a modern American political economy committed, even if incompletely, to redistribution of economic and political power.[28]

Millennial Reconsiderations of Political Economy

By the time Clinton left office, there was no doubt that the world of work was shifting. The globalizing of production, in no small part from the supply chains that Shane Hamilton explores in his essay, reinforced the decimation of organized labor, not just because of the failure of unions as progressive institutions nor because of their collaboration with the state. But rather, as Lichtenstein demonstrated in his work on Wal-Mart, in the post-manufacturing world, unions had lost much of their power to help construct the "template" for the American political economy, as they had when General Motors was the nation's largest employer instead of Sam Walton's retail empire. If once the UAW-GM relationship had created a pattern imitated at many other workplaces and reinforced by a set of laws and institutions that upheld the right to organize, from the 1970s on, it was the low-wage, part-time, nonunionized pink-collar jobs of Wal-Mart's "associates" that came to typify work in America.[29]

A century ago, the experts in the field of labor history were institutional political economists. Social historians tend to think of their work as offering ossified accounts of the labor movement as a conservative force that eschewed radicalism and instead supported what became known pejoratively as business unionism. Yet in fact, under the tutelage of Richard Ely, scholars of labor like John Commons had a capacious understanding of what constituted work as well as the complex set of social and political forces that shaped the lived experience of labor. Before they could offer theories of how to bring about the kind of progressive reform they advocated, these scholars set about creating a documentary record of labor in America. Commons's eleven-volume work included not only documents and newspaper clippings related to the modern union movement but also letters and ledgers from plantations as well as accounts of the slave trade and slave conspiracies. Theirs was indeed a broader view of labor as a fundamental institution shaping the contours of American history.[30]

Today many scholars are revisiting the history of American labor through a political economy lens, one that brings together social relations, capitalism, and the state. That includes rethinking the role of World War II as a democratic moment, or at least one that held the promise of a progressive transformation of the modern American political economy. For sure, the thrust of Lichtenstein's *Labor's War at Home* was to see unions as inevitably junior partners in a corporatist arrangement. This was the moment when the rank and file, according to this New Leftist view, was "robbed of their radical heritage." Social patriotism went hand-in-hand with social quiescence. If previously the goal had been some form of industrial democracy, now the mantra was industrial relations and collective bargaining. But Lichtenstein's worldview was never that singular and a reread of this now four-decade-old book reveals that in fact there was contingency on every page. The book is full of astute observations, including, for example, the importance of wildcat strikes, which at bottom, Lichtenstein argued, were about the dignity of work and the contestation that is always present in labor's struggle. Recent work by Mark Wilson on government production, James Sparrow on fiscal citizenship, and Matthew Delmont on race also suggest that we rethink the war as the occasion for fundamental battles over work, capitalism, and democracy.[31]

The point of studying political economy is to see labor history as a story of complexities, contingencies, and an ever-shifting struggle over the distribution of power. You could see why there was a hint of hopefulness in 1992. The turn to neoliberalism was far from inevitable, as Lichtenstein shows in his most recent book, *A Fabulous Failure: The Clinton Presidency and the*

Transformation of American Capitalism (2023), about the Clinton years. If the Clinton administration facilitated a rightward turn, it was not for lack of trying to advance a progressive alternative. And that is the point. While there are certainly cycles of history, with moments of progress and retreat, we benefit more from seeing the past as an ongoing saga in the fight for workplace rights, human dignity, and a robust political democracy, with unions as a vital institution in this struggle. As Lichtenstein concluded in his op-ed, "At its core the union idea embodies a fundamental impulse toward human solidarity that transcends the rational calculation of individual gain and loss. Such a spirit is indeed subversive to the materialism and me-first individualism of these times. But those who have felt its power know, in the words of the old Wobbly song, 'We can bring to birth a new world from the ashes of the old, for the union makes us strong.' "[32]

Notes

1. Nelson Lichtenstein, "What Happened to the Working Class?" *New York Times*, September 7, 1992.

2. Meg Jacobs, "The Forgotten Left Economics Tradition," *American Prospect*, April 13, 2023.

3. Quoted Lichtenstein, "What Happened to the Working Class." For Lichtenstein's biography see: Nelson Lichtenstein, *A Contest of Ideas: Capital, Politics, and Labor* (Urbana: University of Illinois Press, 2013), 1–12; Howard Brick, "Nelson Lichtenstein's Essential Contributions to Understanding Class, Labor, Capitalism, and Democracy in the United States," *LABOR: Studies in Working Class History* 20, no. 4 (December 2023),:24–41.

4. Robyn Muncy, "The Strange Career of 'the Working Class' in US Political Culture Since the 1950s," *LABOR: Studies in Working Class History*, December 2018, 37–58.

5. Thomas Bell, *Out of This Furnace*, with an afterword by David P. Demarest (Pittsburgh: University of Pittsburgh Press, 1976).

6. David Demarest, Afterword to *Out of This Furnace*, 418.

7. Ibid.; video of Demarest's walking tour available on "Out of This Furnace: A Walking Tour of Thomas Bell's Novel," 1992, https://www.usw.org/video/out-of-this-furnace-a-walking-tour-of-thomas-bells-novel-1992-20-minutes; Roy Rosenzweig et al., *Who Built America? Working People and the Nation's History*, 3rd ed. (New York: American Social History Project, 2007).

8. Mary Antin, *The Promised Land* (Boston & New York: Houghton Mifflin, 1912), unpaginated version available online: https://digital.library.upenn.edu/women/antin/land/land.html (no pagination in e-book for quotes).

9. Elizabeth Ewen, *Immigrant Women in the Land of Dollars* (New York: Monthly Review Press, 1985).

10. Roy Rosenzweig, *Eight Hours for What We Will: Workers and Leisure in an Industrial City, 1870–1920* (Cambridge: Cambridge University Press, 1985).

11. See the biographical sketch of Montgomery in Shelton Stromquist and James R. Barrett, *A David Montgomery Reader: Essays on Capitalism and Worker Resistance* (Urbana: University of Illinois Press, 2024).

12. Bruce Nelson, *Workers on the Waterfront: Seamen, Longshoremen, and Unionism in the 1930s* (Urbana: University of Illinois Press, 1990); Michael Kazin, *Barons of Labor: The San Francisco Building Trades and Union Power in the Progressive Era* (Urbana: University of Illinois Press, 1987); Susan Porter Benson, *Counter Cultures: Saleswomen, Managers, and Customers in American Department Stores, 1890–1940* (Urbana: University of Illinois Press, 1986); Gary Gerstle, *Working-Class Americanism: The Politics of Labor in a Textile City, 1914–1960* (Cambridge: Cambridge University Press, 1989); Lizabeth Cohen, *Making a New Deal: Industrial Workers in Chicago, 1919–1939* (Cambridge: Cambridge University Press, 1990); Robin D. G. Kelley, *Hammer and Hoe: Alabama Communists During the Great Depression* (Chapel Hill: University of North Carolina Press, 1990).

13. Dwight Garner, "Lost in Literary History: A Tale of Courage in the South," *New York Times*, April 18, 2014, https://www.nytimes.com/2014/04/19/books/all-gods-dangers-a-forgotten-autobiography.html.

14. Harvey Swados, *On the Line*, with an introduction by Nelson Lichtenstein (Urbana: University of Illinois Press, 1985), 15.

15. Swados, *On the Line*, 40, 65.

16. Swados, *On the Line*; Harvey Swados, "The UAW—Over the Top or Over the Hill?" Dissent 10 (Fall 1963): 321-343.

17. Nelson Lichtenstein, *Labor's War at Home: The CIO in World War II* (Philadelphia: Temple University Press, 2003).

18. David Montgomery, *The Fall of the House of Labor: The Workplace, the State, and American Labor Activism, 1865–1925* (Cambridge: Cambridge University Press, 1989).

19. Cohen, *Making a New Deal.*

20. Christopher Tomlins, *The State and the Unions: Labor Relations, Law, and the Organized Labor Movement in America, 1880–1960* (Cambridge: Cambridge University Press, 1985); Melvyn Dubofsky, review of *The State and the Unions: Labor Relations, Law, and the Organized Labor Movement in America, 1880–1960* 4:2 (Autumn 1986): 470–473, quoted 470; Katherine Stone, "The Post-War Paradigm in American Labor Law," *Yale Law Journal* 90:7 (1981): 1509–1580; Karl Klare, "Judicial Deradicalization of the Wagner Act and the Origins of Modern Legal Consciousness, 1937–1941," *Minnesota Law Review* 62:3 (March 1978): 265–340; Colin Gordon, *New Deals: Business, Labor, and Politics in America, 1920–1935* (New York: Cambridge University Press, 1994).

21. Alice Kessler-Harris, *In Pursuit of Equity: Women, Men, and the Quest for Economic Citizenship in 20th-Century America* (New York: Oxford University Press, 2001); Linda Gordon, *Women, the State, and Welfare* (Madison: University of Wisconsin Press, 1990); Robert Lieberman, *Shifting the Color Line: Race and the American Welfare State* (Cambridge: Harvard University Press, 1998); Ira Katznelson, *When Affirmative Action Was White: An Untold Story of Racial Inequality in Twentieth-Century America* (New York: W. W. Norton, 2005); Thomas Sugrue, *Origins of the Urban Crisis: Race and Inequality in Postwar Detroit* (Princeton: Princeton University Press, 1996).

22. Thomas Geoghegan, *Which Side Are You On? Trying to Be for Labor When It's Flat on Its Back* (New York: New Press, 2004); Jefferson Cowie, *Capital Moves: RCA's Seventy-Year Quest for Cheap Labor* (New York: New Press, 2001); Judith Stein, *Running Steel, Running America:*

Race: Economic Policy and the Decline of Liberalism (Chapel Hill: University of North Carolina Press, 1998); Barry Bluestone and Bennett Harrison, *The Deindustrialization of America* (New York: Basic Books, 1982).

23. Geoghegan, *Which Side Are You On*, 23.

24. Geoghegan, *Which Side Are You On*, 252–253.

25. Geoghegan, *Which Side Are You On*, 5, 6, 124.

26. Jack Metzgar, *Striking Steel: Solidarity Remembered* (Philadelphia: Temple University Press, 2000); Kristoffer Smemo, Samir Sonti, and Gabriel Winant, "Conflict and Consensus: The Steel Strike of 1959 and the Anatomy of the New Deal Order," *Critical University Studies* 4:1 (Spring 2017), 39–73. Three decades later Lichtenstein would revisit the early Clinton years in *A Fabulous Failure: The Clinton Presidency and the Transformation of American Capitalism* (Princeton: Princeton University Press, 2023).

27. Nelson Lichtenstein, *Walter Reuther: The Most Dangerous Man in Detroit* (Urbana: University of Illinois Press, 1997); Steve Fraser and Gary Gerstle, eds., *The Rise and Fall of the New Deal Order, 1930–1980* (Princeton: Princeton University Press, 1989).

28. Herbert Hill, "Lichtenstein's Fictions: Meany, Reuther and the 1964 Civil Rights Act," *New Politics* 7:1 (Summer 1998), https://archive.newpol.org/issue25/hill25.htm; Nelson Lichtenstein, "Walter Reuther in Black and White: A Rejoinder to Herbert Hill," *New Politics* 7:2 (Winter 1999), https://archive.newpol.org/issue26/lichte26.htm; Herbert Hill, "Lichtenstein's Fictions Revisited Race and the New Labor History," *New Politics* 7:2 (Winter 1999), https://archive.newpol.org/issue26/hill26.htm.

29. Nelson Lichtenstein, *Retail Revolution: How Wal-Mart Created a Brave New World of Business* (New York: Metropolitan Books, 2009).

30. John R. Commons et al., eds., *A Documentary History of American Industrial Society* (Cleveland: Arthur H. Clark Co., 1910–1911), available online at https://onlinebooks.library.upenn.edu/webbin/book/lookupid?key=olbp44978.

31. James Sparrow, *Warfare State: World War II Americans and the Age of Big Government* (New York: Oxford University Press, 2011); Mark R. Wilson, *Destructive Creation: American Business and the Winning of World War II* (Philadelphia: University of Pennsylvania Press, 2018); Matthew Delmont, *Half American: The Epic Story of African Americans Fighting World War II at Home and Abroad* (New York: Viking Books, 2022).

32. Lichtenstein, "What Happened to the Working Class?"

Afterword

Nelson Lichtenstein

As I read the essays Elizabeth Tandy Shermer has collected in this volume, a common theme emerged that put these interventions in conversation with each other and with one of the central dilemmas of our time. How did intellectuals and activists, often isolated and marginal, leverage their ideas to influence and alter the institutions that seem so stolid and immovable in an era of capitalist stability so characteristic of the middle decades of the twentieth century? In most circumstances, radical change was not on the agenda in those decades, but liberalism held a certain vibrancy, which gave to those who sought to advance a more democratic ethos a degree of leverage and élan.

Reformers didn't seek the wholesale transformation of capitalism. They pushed forward ideas and policies directed toward specific institutions, laws, social conventions, and ideologies: a political party, a court decision, a government agency or policy, a cultural institution, or an academic line of thought. Of course, some institutions are more amenable to change than others. The Federal Reserve Board, for example, has long been powerful, autonomous, and accommodative to the most elite financial strata. Neither Congress nor the White House, much less the labor movement, has been able to apply much in the way of democratic pressure. In contrast, cultural institutions, from academia to Broadway and Hollywood, are much more porous, giving artists, writers, and intellectuals of all sorts a creatively expansive beachhead that generates new ways of thinking about the past and new ways of understanding the cultural world.

What is an institution? In this afterword we consider a set of institutions that seem to have definitive boundaries and clear geographies of power: the

Democratic Party, the AFL-CIO, a business corporation, the Federal Reserve Board, the Internal Revenue Service, Immigration and Customs Enforcement, the Supreme Court, and the National Labor Relations Board. These are all institutions, some actually part of the government, that had leaders, defined authority, and varying levels of legitimacy. Those who sought to push them in one direction or another knew what pathways to take. Success and failure were measured by the policy outcomes that were either newly generated or fell by the wayside.

But there are other "institutions" discussed in this collection that were of a more borderless character but hardly of less importance. At least four of the chapters discuss what C. Wright Mills once called "the cultural apparatus," an expansive venue stretching from the halls of academe to the world of Hollywood and beyond. Higher education, film studios, publishing houses, and various forms of news media stand at the core of this cultural apparatus, so there were gatekeepers and bosses who, in both the past and present, have policed these cultural institutions to advance a kind of aesthetic and ideological orthodoxy. In doing so they have necessarily excluded other people and ideas whose work or persona was thought to fall outside those boundaries and standards that they propagate. Still, the cultural apparatus has been relatively pluralistic. Compared to the interest rate decisions of a Federal Reserve Board, the tax determinations of the IRS, or the platform of a political party, Hollywood, academe, and publishing exercised power that was vast but hard to quantify or identify.

Let's start with the Democratic Party. Two chapters in the collection discuss efforts by a set of political activists to prod and push that institution in directions congruent with their politics and worldview. Max Shachtman and Michael Harrington traced their ideological roots to the same brand of unorthodox Trotskyism born in the late 1930s, while Bella Abzug and Mim Kelber had been schooled in a set of mid-twentieth-century popular front politics not far from the Communist orbit. By the late 1960s, however, they had all come to the same conclusion: A Democratic Party capable of passing landmark civil rights and social welfare legislation might well be a political vehicle, properly reformed and led, that could forge a path toward even more social progress.

Shachtman and Harrington wanted to "realign" the party. That meant adopting policies and programs that would ensure the departure of conservative elements, especially the Southern segregationists, so that the Democratic Party took on more of a social democratic coloration. They both wanted labor and the newly mobilized civil rights forces to play a greater role. But in the era when the Vietnam War was dividing both the Democrats and the nation, the AFL-CIO remained a Cold War bulwark supportive of the war and hostile to the "New Politics" and New Left forces who provided much support for George McGovern's successful campaign to win the Democratic Party nomination in 1972. Shachtman died in 1972 but not before he made clear his distaste for the McGovernites and his defense of the Cold War AFL-CIO. During the 1972 election, AFL-CIO President George Meany pushed the federation to declare a pro-Nixon neutrality in the presidential contest of that year. In contrast, Harrington sought a progressive party animated by a "Coalition of Conscience," heavily weighted toward liberals, civil rights advocates, and feminists. Perhaps even more important, writes Dan Geary, Shachtman proved an ideological grandfather to the neoconservatives who considered the McGovernites a new elite, even a "new class," hostile to the labor movement and the working class. That was patently false, but the idea would sustain right-wing politics in America for decades.

As Leandra Zarnow makes clear, Abzug and Kelber clearly stood on the Harrington side of this divide. They were committed to a socialist-inflected feminism that they argued, in *Gender Gap* and elsewhere, had the very real capacity to harness the power of women voters against Reaganite conservatism and welfare state austerity and on behalf of a revitalized liberalism housed within the Democratic Party. Abzug and Kelber had a much broader approach to gender issues than groups like the National Organization for Women, arguing, far earlier than many other women activists, that a feminist impulse divorced from issues of racial discrimination and class oppression was doomed to a sterile identity politics.

When it came to the Democratic Party, Harrington, Abzug, and Kelber won a pyrrhic victory. The Democrats came to fully embrace a set of coalition politics that saw ethnic, racial, gender, and religious pluralism as central to the party's ideological definition, an inclusive progress that may well have reached its apogee in Hilary Clinton's 2016 presidential campaign. But the party's failure to adopt the economic side of the Harrington/Abzug program opened the door to the kind of cosmopolitan neoliberalism identified by Gary Gerstle in his *Rise and Fall of the Neoliberal Order* (2022). In this free market global era, glass ceilings might well be broken as corporations ardently promoted an ethos of multiracial inclusion, but capitalist hierarchies remained inviolate.

Jennifer Klein's analysis of the historical context that gave rise to petrochemical domination of politics in a state still ostensibly Democratic in the

1970s and 1980s throws under a harsh light the reactionary political economy that would flourish in that neoliberal world, shaping and distorting virtually every Louisiana institution, public or private. Citizen activists appalled at the despoliation of their communities found allies among a newly energetic set of environmental regulators, both in Washington and the state itself. But when such officials sought to actually curb powerful business interests, they were quickly blocked and cast aside by the governor and other political elites beholden to the corporate polluters. "This is the price we pay [for economic growth] and we have no apologies for it," asserted the state's Democratic governor, Edwin Edwards.

Most conservative White Democrats in Louisiana and other Southern states would eventually depart the party of Franklin Roosevelt and Lyndon Johnson, fulfilling a central goal of those advocating realignment of the Democratic Party. But that too was a pyrrhic victory because the Republican capture of the White South quickly advanced the increasingly conservative character of that party without generating a counter movement to the left on the part of mainstream Democrats. As the Carter, Clinton, and Obama sojourns in the White House would demonstrate, the Democrats were careful to keep the left in check while avoiding any confrontation with the corporate world. The Biden presidency offered a partial break with such neoliberal orthodoxy, but the Democratic defeat in 2024 demonstrated just how electorally fraught was any effort to move that party to the left.

One reason that realignment bore so little fruit can be traced to two other institutions of post–World War II America that did much to thwart and distort a postwar progressivism oriented toward the material interests of the working class. These were the Supreme Court and the Federal Reserve, one a separate and formal branch of the American government and the other holding de facto autonomy just about equal to the Supreme Court and Congress. Those two institutions did much to weaken and ghettoize the power of organized workers, an eventuality that did far less to radicalize than to constrain, conservatize, and delimit the ambitions of the American trade union movement.

The 1949 Taft-Hartley Act has long been recognized as a signal defeat for the union idea in postwar America, but as Jean-Christian Vinel makes clear, the subsequent Supreme Court ratification of the state right-to-work laws made possible by Taft-Hartley constituted an equally potent legal and ideological repudiation of union power. In a capitalist society, argued lawyers from the American Federation of Labor, strong and secure unions—and this involved a measure of dues and membership coercion directed toward recalcitrant workers—were essential for the vast majority of employees who sought to exercise power in a truly democratic fashion. Led by once sterling liberals, including Hugo Black and Felix Frankfurter, the court disagreed, persuaded by the strike chaos of the immediate postwar era that the specter of "monopoly" unionism poised a greater threat to a democratic polity.

Within a decade, the civil rights and civil liberties decisions of a court led by Earl Warren would cloak the nation's highest bench with a liberal patina. But when it came to decisions that advanced union rights or curbed corporate power, even the Warren Court left much to be desired, leaving a legacy that would turn increasingly callous and dark in the next several decades. In the long history of American jurisprudence since the onset of late nineteenth-century industrial capitalism, the Supreme Court's departure from a Gilded Age understanding of labor's democratic rights and empowerment has been rare indeed.

A similarly blinkered engagement with working-class well-being can be found in the role played by the Federal Reserve, another highly autonomous institution resistant to liberal-labor influence. As Samir Sonti points out, the New Deal Fed was an institution subject to congressional and presidential influence, but the "Fed-Treasury Accord" reached in 1951 gave the Federal Reserve the autonomy it has guarded ever since. In nearly three decades before the disastrous Volcker Shock of 1979, the Fed used its independence to pursue a restrictive monetary policy inimical to the interests of organized labor and the working class more generally. Fixated on inflation control, the Fed manipulated interest rates so as to precipitate three recessions during the 1950s and 1960s, an era of labor's presumptive political and social power that nevertheless saw unemployment remain almost always above 5 percent. Although union economists and labor-liberal politicians marshaled arguments and data proposing a more targeted and progressive credit policy, the Fed rarely gave an inch. Thus, during the apogee of organized labor's power, both the Fed and the Supreme Court exercised such a high degree of institutional autonomy and ideological conservatism that they subverted not just the power of union labor but the entire thrust of the postwar New Deal.

The insulation of so many governmental agencies and bureaucracies from popular democratic control is certainly a dominant strand within recent American history; likewise the functioning of the political party system, which also tilts toward unrepresentativeness. But in an era when "populist" disdain for such institutions seems on the ascendant, Joseph Thorndike's deep dive into Richard Nixon's entanglement with the Internal Revenue Service might provide a bit of balance and ballast. Backed by a Congress armed with its own investigative capacity, the IRS effort to force a president to pay back taxes and forego lucrative use of tax deductions (on the value of his presidential papers deposited with the National Archives) seems a salutatory independence properly free from political or popular influence. Should others follow Nixon's example, then presidential malfeasance would come to pose a threat to the nation's fiscal health. But even more important, argues Thorndike, a presidential scofflaw would surely corrode the meaning of citizenship itself, "that web of reciprocal rights and responsibilities that bind individuals to the state" and vice versa. That's a bedrock principle of democratic governance. When Gerald Ford pardoned Nixon, he put a large dent in the accountability owed by high office holders to the people, a breach that has itself been increasingly become a norm in the twenty-first century.

Indeed, the American Right has become the chief critic of governmental institutionalism, not only attacking the regulatory state, an old target, but once sacrosanct agencies like the FBI, the military, the Justice Department, and the courts. Obama-era Tea Party insurgents had little in common with the left-wing activists of the 1970s and 1980s who sought to move the Democratic Party toward social democracy and gender rights. But this New Right proved highly successful in taking a set of culturally inflected grievances about big government and deploying them in a rather successful fashion to make at least one political party—the Republicans—shift policy and politics to their liking.

A touchstone issue for the Right has been advocacy for and governmental implementation of a restrictive immigration policy, especially with Mexico and the rest of Central America. Regardless of the administration in power, hostility to such immigration has been a major driver of Republican Party identity. That new prominence constituted a remarkable political inversion, because for decades beginning even before World War II, the liberalization of the nation's refugee and immigration policies seemed part and parcel of a world sustained by civil rights advocates, trade union power, Cold War competition, and a triumphant ethos that combined cultural pluralism and global economic integration. After the big immigration reform of 1965, the inclusion of new categories of immigrants, the growth of border security, and the debate over how the undocumented might become citizens took place within a relatively normal political context in which various compromises, like the 1986 Immigration Reform and Control Act, sometimes bore legislative fruit.

But in recent decades, as Carl Bon Tempo makes clear, the "sanctification of the border as some sort of securitized, tangible place" has achieved "an almost talisman-like" meaning when it comes to the definition and defense of national sovereignty. This took a giant step forward with the Tea Party eruption that linked immigration issues of both legal and undocumented individuals to the racial and cultural meaning of the imagined Americanism they sought to recapture and defend, and it has been driven forward by the rise of a MAGA racialism that seems likely to outlive Donald Trump. Bon Tempo is right to argue that just as the "labor question" once seemed an insoluble dilemma at the heart of what defined American democracy, so too has the contemporary immigration issue become thoroughly entangled with the most basic ideas and values that define the nation.

The last four essays we discuss in this afterword might seem disparate and disconnected. They consider the scholarly historiography of labor and capital during the last century, how contemporary courses on "supply chain management" are taught in business schools, what films can tell us about the search for a culturally resonant "working-class hero," and why a trio of mid-twentieth-century writers and academics turned against the New Deal. There is a lot going on here, but all the essays discuss people and ideas who occupy a slice of the capitalist economy that C. Wright Mills labeled the "cultural apparatus" more than sixty years ago. This was a realm that traded in ideas and entertainment, generating a set of cultural products that were distributed to a vast consuming public, mainly for profit, although sometimes paid for by the tax dollars that sustained public education as well as various other government activities.

This cultural apparatus was not quite as structured an institution as some of those discussed above, but it was hardly formless. There were workers, managers, owners, and others whose job was close to that of an ideological police force. There were "hacks" and "stars." And like the institutions and agencies that composed the state or gave structure to business and commerce, the cultural apparatus was tangibly potent. As Mills put it in a note to himself, "I am not at all sure, at least until it's been gone into, that the entertainment world is so powerless. At any rate, it is part of the institutional set up. Hollywood, for instance: in 1950 it was the fifth largest industry in the US, so it's an economic institution, isn't it? And as for political institutions, who is to say so quickly that the thousands of hours a year spent with TV and at the movies basking in the dim light of the entertainment elite are politically irrelevant?" About his own occupation, Mills opined, "Educational institutions produce not only cultural products and distribute them, they produce cultural workmen and maintain them."[1] In the late 1950s when Mills considered the meaning and politics of a cultural apparatus, his conceptualization struck many as radical. Today, when Hollywood, academe, publishing, and social media have become so much a part of contemporary politics, the idea of such an apparatus offers many a way to explain how ideas central to our understanding of society are created, contested, legitimized, and transmitted.

Reuel Schiller offers a set of instructive examples indicating how intellectuals can have a pervasive impact on how millions of people think about the world and the institutions that govern their relationship to their jobs, their leisure, and their government. As Kim Phillips-Fein argued in her first book, *Invisible Hands: The Businessmen's Crusade Against the New Deal* (2009), and as Lawrence Glickman demonstrated in *Free Enterprise: An American History* (2019), most American conservatives never made their peace with the New Deal and the state it created. But Schiller identifies another set of critics, ostensibly on the left, that may have done even more to undermine big government and the post–New Deal administrative apparatus responsible for economic and social regulation.

R. Buckminster Fuller, E. F. Schumacher, and Charles Reich were writers and academics sympathetic to a set of countercultural values and projects that they deployed to critique both an intrusive government bureaucracy and the sociocultural power wielded by large corporations. Their critique of postwar America came wrapped in the cloak of an antistatism rightly suspicious of the national security apparatus and the big institutions, from the university to the corporation, that sustained it. "Small is beautiful" wrote Schumacher, coining a catchphrase that lasted for generations. They favored a radical decentralization, a libertarian-inflected utopianism standing as an antidote to an administrative state that had become corrupt, oppressive, and dehumanizing. They were skeptical of expertise, "the widely read tip of an iceberg of social thought," writes Schiller, "that has a lot to tell us about the erosion of faith in government in the last three decades of the twentieth century."

Fuller, Schumacher, and Reich might well be put in the same ostensibly left-wing camp occupied by the environmental lawyers and public interest groups identified by Paul Sabin in *Public Citizens: The Attack on Big Government and the Remaking of American Liberalism* (2021). Like the ecologically minded Reich and Schumacher, environmental groups battled with a federal government that in the aftermath of Vietnam and Watergate also concealed information and programs they thought harmful to wetlands, forests, and mountain wilderness. These public interest crusaders added their moral and legal weight to a post-Sixties political culture that helped bring an end to a New Deal order characterized by federal agency discretion and ambitious deployments of technology, private investment, and public infrastructure in pursuit of economic growth.

Hollywood may well be the most potent institution of the cultural apparatus. That collection of studios, writers, actors, and audiences played a large role in shaping the discourse that came to erode the legitimacy of the world sustaining the New Deal and the leftist "cultural front" identified by historian Michael Denning.[2] That front projected a decidedly progressive, working-class sensibility that put film, folksong, music, plays, and posters at the service of an ambitious Depression-era understanding of a populist, plebian America. Of course, as Lauren Sklaroff argues, every generation rediscovers the working-class hero it finds most congruent with a larger set of ideas about what kind of society is feasible and desirable. In her essay she covers a lot of cultural and cinematographic terrain, finding a variegated set of films, performances, and people, from Sophie Tucker to the Rolling Stones, who came in one form or another to represent working-class performativity. Women and people of color have always been in short supply, but even far less present has been any genuinely realistic depiction of working-class collective action, in a union or not.

So we get a set of sympathetically portrayed working-class individuals, almost always young White men, whose triumph comes with their escape from the working class itself. In *Titanic*, the elite passengers are heartless and cowardly while the men and women in steerage dance and drink in the hours before the cold Atlantic snuffs out their merry-making. Leonardo DiCaprio introduces his shipboard love interest to the hearty joyfulness of those on the lower decks and wins her over, but then literally sacrifices his life for that upper-class woman when the ship goes down. Even more formulaic is *Good Will Hunting*, where the film's protagonist (Matt Damon) is a math genius from South Boston whom we find working as a lowly janitor at MIT. He reads Howard Zinn and solves problems left on the blackboard that even the grad students can't handle. Once he is discovered, Damon's rise is assured, but the film has nothing for his South Boston buddies, who are destined to remain in a set of dead-end blue-collar jobs. Their male solidarity offers no hint that it might be transformed into a class-based collective action. If Damon is a working-class hero, his story legitimizes hierarchy, meritocracy, and the Gilded Age values of Horatio Alger.

The late Todd Gitlin might well have thought all this a bit overwrought. Cultural criticism is one thing; state power is another. A critic of the cultural apparatus in his own right, especially the news media, Gitlin was nevertheless famous for his swipe at an inward-looking academic left: "While the Right has been busy taking the White House," he wrote in 1995, "the Left has been marching on the English department."[3] Given the American Right's fierce contemporary assault on what kind of literature and what kind of history should be taught in high school and college classrooms, the American Left, academic or otherwise, might be wise to erect a few more barricades on the campus quad while not neglecting its own effort to take a slice of governmental power.

In the essays of Meg Jacobs and Shane Hamilton, we can see why and how one particular academic discipline, history and its labor history offspring, has become consequential to the way many people outside the university think about capitalism and the degree to which some workers might use their unions or the state to win a measure of democratic power within that economic realm. There is no direct ideological conveyor belt between the professorate and the way managers or unionists or government officials think and act, but the scholars who teach and publish on a particular topic do refract and systematize more generally held sentiments, and in the process advance their own politics and perspective. Stephen Waring, a historian of management thought in the United States, once described business school professors as the "organic intellectuals of the capitalist class."[4] They organized and propagated the "best practices" so as to advance the legitimacy and power of the corporate world. No one would describe labor historians in recent decades as the kind of intellectuals from which union officials take their lead, but their students sometimes take jobs in the labor movement, reporters call them up for a contextualizing comment, while lawyers and legal scholars mine their research to advance progressive changes in the labor law. And they write books, like those published by E. P. Thompson, Mike Davis, and Jeremy Brecher, whose readership is in the millions. Moreover, there was a time during the quarter century right after World War II when industrial relations experts, a set of historically minded institutional economists that included Clark Kerr, Charles Schultze, John Dunlop, and Derek Bok, often ran the nation's top universities and frequently took the Washington-bound plane or train to offer sage advice within the corridors of power.

Meg Jacobs explains how a series of books she read as a graduate student exemplified the stages—historiographical and ideological—through which the so-called "New Labor History" evolved. Her first offerings are that of Thomas

Bell's *Out of This Furnace* and Theodore Rosengarten's *All God's Dangers: The Life of Nate Shaw*. Both were classic social history narratives, the first published in 1941, the second in 1974. While Bell's novel, rediscovered in the 1960s, celebrated the capacity of an ethnic working class to achieve New Deal citizenship, the Shaw narrative conjoined the spirit of the civil rights movement with the travails of a hyper-exploited agricultural working class, Black and rural, that the industrial relations academics had excised from their scholarship and policymaking advice. The plebian militants found in both books, true working-class heroes, were central to the New Labor History's repudiation of institutional economics. Consciousness and culture were more potent, which is why a lot of us then endorsed a march on the departments of both English and History.

A 1963 essay by Harvey Swados, rediscovered by many New Leftists a few years later, exemplified a second stage. "If the thrust of social history was to recapture working-class culture as an independent force," writes Jacobs, then many historians took from Swados a warning that unions had become self-serving bureaucracies, organizationally muscular but politically and ideologically timid. Their cooptation by the Rooseveltian state suppressed activism and agency. That was a thesis I put forward in some of my early work, aligned with the New Left critique of "big labor," during an era when the AFL-CIO defended the Vietnam war, offered but tepid support to the civil rights movement, and proved powerless when corporate globalizers decimated union ranks.

Of course, the emergence of Ronald Reagan and his conservative, anti-union successors forced a reassessment, especially when a more liberal leadership arose in some trade unions. This constituted the third stage in the evolution of New Left labor scholarship. If the first two ways of thinking about the working class in a capitalist society drove a wedge between the actually existing unions and many politically active young people, the third iteration, found in the work of Thomas Geoghegan, Jack Metzgar, and myself, saw unions as imperfect but necessary defenders of working-class livelihoods. Government regulations and procedures, derived from the 1935 Wagner Act and embodied in agencies like the National Labor Relations Board, might be inadequate, but in the hands of Democratic liberals they were hardly mendacious and might even be of assistance.

In the postpandemic years, interest in and activism on behalf of a renewed trade union movement can hardly be credited to the work of an aging generation of New Left labor historians. There were a far more important set of economic and social preconditions, ranging from the health risks confronting so many "essential" workers to the actual labor shortage found among the nation's enormous retail, restaurant, and service sector workforce. And then there was a Democratic president who actually showed up on a picket line of striking auto workers. But if few direct links can be found between the left academy and the United Auto Workers, except for the remarkable surge in union organizing on campuses, their openness to the gender fluidity and racial diversity apparent among young militants has certainly made them a better set of mentors and commentators than that embodied in the older generation of industrial relations mandarins.

Like Jacobs, Shane Hamilton is also interested in how a set of campus intellectuals think about workers and capitalists in a world where production has taken on a global configuration. But in Hamilton's case, the absolute failure of the business school professorate to even consider the historical and social context in which a set of giant supply chains have emerged speaks just as loudly as any New Left speculation about the character of working-class consciousness. While some business schools have indeed heeded calls to integrate a more humanistic, historically contextualized approach to their research and curricula, that historical turn is absent when it comes to the booming effort to codify all that is efficient and dynamic in a new subdiscipline, "supply chain management." As Hamilton puts it, "Disowning the past is a strategic and intentional process, not a simple oversight." Those who train the new generation of supply chain managers—perhaps the most strategic new post engendered by the rise of global commerce—think of their work as a product of "predetermined" technological and organizational forces, denuded of social or historical context.

This studied ignorance reminds me of the work of John R. Commons, and more especially Selig Perlman, two labor history pioneers who nevertheless sought to marginalize culture, race, and ideology in favor of an economistic "job consciousness" as the key to any understanding of worker consciousness and action. Commons sought to legitimize trade unionism by sidelining its more radical partners and collaborators, including the Populists and the Industrial Workers of the World; Perlman, writing in the aftermath of the Bolshevik Revolution, offered an even more pointed denunciation of all those who thought workers might have aspirations that transcended a bit more money in the paycheck or secure ownership of their current job.

We find the same kind of blinkered analysis in the new world of supply chain management research. E. P. Thompson once wrote of the enormous condescension the present has for the past. Then it was all so naïve and misbegotten compared to the more rational if complex world we have constructed. That is precisely the ahistorical hubris that attaches to the scholarship and proffered advice of those who study and celebrate contemporary global logistics. Of course, it is highly likely that this sort of arrogance will face a historical comeuppance. The Great Depression discredited the Commons school of labor history scholarship. Likewise, the dysfunctional cracks that have already appeared within the globalization edifice—from the soaring cost of container shipments during the pandemic to the new US-China rivalry—are certain to make clear, even to those professors and professionals seeking the most assured path toward profit maximization, that historical contingency and worker consciousness cannot be ignored in that quest.

And on an even larger canvas, the splendid essays collected in this book make clear that the institutions sustaining the capitalist world during most of the twentieth century can only be understood if we also probe their history and examine the ideas and interventions of those intellectuals and advocates who have sought to reshape them.

Notes

1. Kim Sawchuk, "The Cultural Apparatus: C. Wright Mills' Unfinished Work," *American Sociologist*, Spring 2001, vol. 32, no. 1, 35, 41.

2. Michael Denning, *The Cultural Front: The Laboring of American Culture in the Twentieth Century* (New York: Verso, 2011). This is a new edition of the book originally published in 1997.

3. Todd Gitlin, *The Twilight of Common Dreams: Why America Is Wracked by Culture Wars* (New York: Metropolitan Books, 1995), 126.

4. Stephen Waring, *Taylorism Transformed: Scientific Management Theory Since 1945* (Chapel Hill: University of North Carolina Press, 1991).

LIST OF CONTRIBUTORS

Carl J. Bon Tempo is associate professor of history at the University at Albany, State University of New York. He has published essays, chapters, and books, including *Americans at the Gate: The United States and Refugees During the Cold War* (Princeton University Press, 2008) and *Immigration: An American History* (Yale University Press, 2022), co-authored with Professor Hasia Diner.

Daniel Geary is the Mark Pigott Professor of U.S. History at Trinity College Dublin. He is the author of numerous articles, book chapters, and op-eds. He is also the author of *Radical Ambition: C. Wright Mills, the Left, and American Social Thought* (University of California Press, 2009) and *Beyond Civil Rights: The Moynihan Report and Its Legacy* (University of Pennsylvania Press, 2015).

Shane Hamilton is Reader in Strategy, Management and Society at the University of York. He has written widely on the history of food and agribusiness for leading journals and in two books, *Supermarket USA: Food and Power in the Cold War Farms Race* (Yale, 2018) and the award-winning *Trucking Country: The Road to America's Wal-Mart Economy* (Princeton, 2008).

Meg Jacobs teaches history and public affairs at Princeton University. She is the prize-winning author of several books, including *Pocketbook Politics: Economic Citizenship in Twentieth-Century America* (Princeton, 2005) and, most recently, *Panic at the Pump: The Energy Crisis and the Transformation of American Politics in the 1970s* (Hill and Wang, 2016). She is currently working on a new book about the New Deal and World War II.

Jennifer Klein is the Bradford Durfee Professor of History at Yale University. Her award-winning publications include *Caring for America: Home*

Health Workers in the Shadow of the Welfare State (Oxford, 2012), co-authored with Eileen Boris, and *For All These Rights: Business, Labor, and the Shaping of America's Public-Private Welfare State* (Princeton, 2003).

Nelson Lichtenstein is Research Professor in the Department of History at the University of California, Santa Barbara, where, for two decades, he directed the Center for the Study of Work, Labor, and Democracy. He is the author or editor of twenty books, including a biography of the labor leader Walter Reuther and *State of the Union: A Century of American Labor* (2002, 2013 revised). His reviews and opinion pieces have appeared in the *Los Angeles Times*, the *New York Times*, *Dissent*, *New Labor Forum*, *American Prospect*, and academic journals.

Reuel Schiller is the Honorable Roger J. Traynor Chair and Professor of Law at the University of California, College of the Law, San Francisco. He has written extensively about the legal history of the American administrative state and the historical development of labor law and employment discrimination law. His book *Forging Rivals: Race, Class, Law, and the Collapse of Postwar Liberalism* (Cambridge University Press, 2015) won the American Society for Legal History's John Phillip Reid Award and was an Honorable Mention for the Law and Society Association's J. Willard Hurst Award.

Elizabeth Tandy Shermer is a professor of history at the University of Georgia. She has written about labor, capitalism, and politics in op-eds, academic articles, and scholarly books, including *Sunbelt Capitalism: Phoenix and the Transformation of American Politics* (University of Pennsylvania Press, 2013) and *Indentured Students: How Government-Guaranteed Loans Left Generations Drowning in College Debt* (Harvard University Press, 2021).

Lauren Rebecca Sklaroff is Professor of History and Women's and Gender Studies at the University of South Carolina. Her work centers on how race, ethnicity, and gender inform the development of American cultural institutions and has appeared in academic journals and media outlets like the *Chicago Tribune*, the *Los Angeles Times*, and *Salon.com*. She is also the author of two books, *Black Culture and the New Deal: The Quest for Civil Rights in the Roosevelt Era* (University of North Carolina Press, 2009) and *Red Hot Mama: The Life of Sophie Tucker* (University of Texas, 2018).

Samir Sonti is an assistant professor in the City University of New York's Urban Studies and Labor Studies programs. He has published widely. The University of Pennsylvania Press will publish his first book, *The Price of Prosperity*.

Joseph J. Thorndike, director of the Tax History Project at Tax Analysts, is a nationally recognized tax historian. He is a regular columnist for Tax Analysts' publications, including *Tax Notes Federal* magazine, and a writer for the Tax Analysts blog. His writing has also appeared in the *New York Times*, the *Washington Post*, the *Wall Street Journal*, the *New York Daily News*, *Barron's*, *Bloomberg*, Time.com, Forbes.com, and numerous academic journals. A prolific author on the history of American taxation, his books include *Their Fair Share: Taxing the Rich in the Age of FDR* (Urban Institute Press, 2013).

Jean-Christian Vinel teaches US labor history at Université Paris Cité. His previous publications include *The Employee: A Political History* (2013, 2020) and *Capitalism Contested: The New Deal and Its Legacies* (2020).

Leandra Zarnow is an associate professor in the Department of History and affiliated faculty in Women's, Gender, and Sexuality Studies, Jewish Studies, the Rockwell Center for Ethics and Leadership, and the Center for Public History at the University of Houston. Her work has appeared in scholarly journals and mainstream news outlets, including *Time*, the *Washington Post*, *Axios*, and the *Houston Chronicle*. Harvard University Press published her first book, *Battling Bella: The Protest Politics of Bella Abzug*, in 2019.

INDEX

abortion rights, 143, 144
Abzug, Bella, 6–7, 133, 137–38, 280, 281; background of, 7, 140–41; hopes of, for Democratic Party, 138, 142–43, 147, 152–55, 280, 281; and Jimmy Carter, 7, 139, 142, 143, 146; in 1970s and '80s, 7, 133, 139–40, 142–55. See also *Gender Gap* (Abzug and Kelber)
Afghan refugees, 205
AFL-CIO, 119, 120–21, 198–99, 272, 289; and Federal Reserve, 47, 50–51, 53, 54; socialists and, 113, 122–23, 124, 128, 129–32, 281
African Americans: in Louisiana, 166–67, 169, 173, 176–77, 179, 180; in music, 248, 249; and the New Deal, 269–70; stereotypes of, 241–42, 246–47. *See* also civil rights movement
agricultural workers, 7, 224–25, 289
air traffic controllers' strike (1981), 9, 260
Aldean, Jason, 241
Alexander, Donald, 100–101, 106
Alger, Horatio, 151, 287
Alibaba Group, 223–24
All God's Dangers (Shaw), 266, 289
Allied Chemical Corporation, 168, 171
Amazon, 4, 223–24
American Dilemma, An (Myrdal), 26–27
American Federation of Actors, 247–48
American Federation of Labor (AFL), 16, 18, 45; and Taft-Hartley Act, 18, 19–21, 22, 23–29, 31, 34n40. *See also* AFL–CIO
American Federation of Labor v. American Sash and Door, 5, 13, 14, 21, 28
American Federation of Teachers, 122–23, 129, 132
Americans for Democratic Action (ADA), 121, 123, 124, 125, 127, 132
Anderson, Jack, 98–99
Angola State Penitentiary (Louisiana), 163, 167
Antin, Mary, 264, 265
anti-statist thought, 64–65, 80–83; and counterculture intellectuals, 5, 65–66, 73, 76–77, 80–81; flourishing of, in 1970s, 64–65, 80; and hostility to expertise, 64, 65, 68, 72, 73, 80–81, 94–95, 286
A. Philip Randolph Institute, 120, 122, 129
Arizona, 194, 203; right-to-work law in, 13, 19, 20, 21, 24, 25, 26
Arpaio, Joe, 194
automation, 69

Babbage, Charles, 214
Bair, Jennifer, 215–16
Ball, Joseph, 19
Baltimore Sun, 98
Bangladesh, 219. *See also* Rana Plaza disaster
Banking Act of 1935, 39–40
Barbie (film), 237, 238, 240, 255–56
Barnes & Noble bookstore chain, 222
Barnum, P. T., 238
Baxter, Sandra, 149
Bay of Pigs invasion (1961), 123
Bear, The (television series), 253–54
Beatles, 248–49
Bell, Daniel, 65
Bell, Thomas, 263–64, 265, 266, 288–89
Bellow, Saul, 115
Benson, Susan Porter, 266
Berkeley, Calif., 77, 79, 117, 123, 262, 268
Bernstein, Carl, 266
Biden, Joe (and Biden administration), 107–8, 154, 205, 206, 237, 282
"Bills Only" doctrine, 46–47, 51–52, 53, 54

Black Power movement, 122, 144
Black, Hugo, 13, 27–28, 30–31, 75, 283
blackface, 246–47, 248
Bluestone, Barry, 270
Boggs, Grace Lee, 115
Bok, Derek, 288
Bon Tempo, Carl, 293; chapter by, 186–210
Booz Allen Hamilton, 213
Borders bookstore chain, 218, 22–22
Boxer, Barbara, 148
Brand, Stewart, 66
Brandeis, Elizabeth, 30
Brandeis, Louis, 29, 30
Brat, Dave, 201
Brecher, Jeremy, 288
Bretton Woods regime, 52
Brewer, Jan, 194
Brick, Howard, 261–62
Brown, Anthony, 66
Brown, Jerry, 66
Buchanan, Patrick, 190, 195, 201
building trades unions, 21, 26
Burke, Yvonne, 142
Bush, George H. W., 147, 260
Bush, George W., 190, 194, 197, 199
Bush family, 196. *See also* Bush, George H. W.; Bush, George W.
Byrne, James, 95

Cable News Network (CNN), 142, 149–50
Cameron, James, 251, 256. See also *Titanic*
"Cancer Alley," 164, 180. *See also* "Chemical Corridor"
Cantor, Eric, 201
capitalism, 48–49, 125, 164, 279; counterculture intellectuals and, 5, 67, 82–83; feminist critique of, 137, 151; and immigration, 190–91, 195; intertwining of, with work and democracy, 2–4, 32, 138; and popular culture, 8, 243–45, 252, 254–56, 285; unions and, 2–3, 266–67, 268, 269, 282–83, 288, 289. *See also* supply chains
Caplin, Mortimer, 99
Carmichael, Stokely, 119
Caro, Robert, 266
Carter, Jimmy, 7, 66, 107; economic policies of, 55, 131, 270, 282; and feminists, 7, 139, 140, 142–43, 146, 148; in 1980 election, 143, 144, 146
Casey, Carol F., 147
Catholic Worker movement, 115
Celluloid Closet, The (film), 242
Central America, 192, 284
Chandler, Alfred, Jr., 223
Chauncey, George, 243, 250
"Chemical Corridor" (southeast Louisiana between New Orleans and Baton Rouge), 7, 164–65, 168, 173, 180
chemical industry (in Louisiana), 7, 164–72; hazardous waste generated by, 163, 164–65, 168–72; resistance to practices of, 172–80; state agencies and, 165, 166, 171, 172, 175, 177–80; unions and 172–73
China, 191, 192, 291
Civil Rights Act of 1964, 118, 123
civil rights movement, 116, 118–20, 124, 273, 289
Civil War, 107, 164, 166
Clark, J. M., 47
Clayton, Mary, 249
Clean Air Act (1970), 169
Clean Water Act (1970), 169
Cleaver, Eldridge, 75
Clinton, Bill, 196, 272, 273; in 1992 election. *See also* Clinton administration
Clinton, Hillary, 112, 154, 281
Clinton administration, 192, 195, 251, 272, 275
closed shops, 14, 15–16, 18–19, 20, 25, 29; AFL craft unions' special stake in, 19, 20, 26; distinction between, and union shops, 15, 29. *See also* "closed shop cases"
Clymer, Adam, 144, 145
"Coalition of Conscience," 113, 119, 121, 122, 125, 281
Coalition of Immokalie Workers, 225
Cochrane, Thad, 201
Cohen, Lizabeth, 268
Cohen, Rachel, 1
Cold War, 5, 151, 267; AFL-CIO and, 113, 281; early years of, 140, 141; end of, 4, 262
Coleman, Sarah, 196
Commentary magazine, 120, 129
Committee for a Democratic Majority (CDM), 130
Commons, John R., 5, 24, 27, 261, 274, 290, 291; on the "credit problem," 37, 55
Communist Party USA, 114, 140–41, 245, 265, 266, 280

computers, 8, 69, 70, 96
Congress of Industrial Organizations (CIO), 16, 27, 263, 268; and "closed shop cases," 16, 18, 19–20, 28, 29, 30; and federal monetary policy, 44–45, 47. *See also* AFL-CIO
Cooke, James, 238–39
Coser, Lewis, 116
Council of Economic Advisers, 42
countercultural intellectuals, 5, 65–66, 71, 81–82, 83, 165, 286; anti-statist thought of, 5, 65–66, 73, 76–77, 80–81; and individualism, 72–74, 75–76, 79, 81–83; and Vietnam War, 75, 76, 80. *See also* Fuller, R. Buckminster; Reich, Charles; Schumacher, E. F.
country music, 243, 249, 250, 251
COVID-19 pandemic, 227
Cowie, Jefferson, 249, 250, 270
Cripps, Thomas, 242
Cuban refugees, 192, 205
"cultural apparatus," 239, 280, 285–86, 287, 288
cultural pluralism, 64, 266, 280, 281, 284
Currie, Lauchlin, 39
Curtis, Carl T., 104

Dahl, Robert, 65
Dale, Edwin, 48
Daley, Richard, 124
Darwin, Charles, 67, 81
Davis, Mike, 288
Day, Dorothy, 115
"Day Without an Immigrant" protests (2006), 197–98, 203
Dean, John, 101
Deaver, Michael K., 153–54
Debs, Eugene V., 115
Deferred Action for Childhood Arrivals (DACA) program, 204. *See also* "Dreamers"
deindustrialization, 131, 262, 270
Delmont, Matthew, 274
DeMarco, Frank, Jr., 93
Demarest, David, 264, 265
D'Emilio, John, 243–45
DeMille, Cecil B., 18
Democratic Party: in 1968: socialists and, 6, 112–14, 116, 118, 119–20, 124–26, 128, 131–33; unions and, 20, 113, 123, 124, 129–30, 131, 271, 281; and Vietnam War, 113, 122, 123, 124, 280–81; women and, 6–7, 138, 139, 141, 143, 154–55, 280, 281. *See also* "New Politics" wing (of Democratic Party)
Democratic Socialist Organizing Committee (DSOC), 112, 114, 132–33
Democratic Socialists of America (DSA), 112, 133
Denning, Michael, 240, 245, 287
Department of Homeland Security, 194
Department of the Treasury, 56n19, 94; and Federal Reserve, 40, 41–42, 45, 46, 51 (*see also* "Bills Only" doctrine; Fed-Treasury Accord)
deregulation, 64, 219, 270
Derthick, Martha, 66
Dilliard, Irving, 31
Dillon, Douglas, 52
dime novels, 240, 249
Diner, Hasia, 253
Dioxin, 171–72
Disclosure (film), 242
"disowning" the past, 211–12, 216–18, 220, 223
Dissent magazine, 116, 123, 133, 267
Dole, Elizabeth, 154
Douglas, Paul, 43, 50
Douglas, Susan, 242
Dow Chemical, 168, 172
Draper, Hal, 123
"Dreamers," 188, 202, 206
Drucker, Peter, 212, 214, 217
Dubofsky, Melvyn, 269
Dunn, Betsy, 145
Dylan, Bob, 119

Eccles, Marriner, 39, 40, 41, 42, 44, 57n40
Edwards, Edwin, 179, 180, 282
Ehrlichman, John D., 98–99
Eisenhower, Dwight D., 6, 45, 47, 48
Ellul, Jacques, 75
Ely, Richard, 261, 272, 274
Employment Act of 1946, 42, 44
Environmental Protection Agency (EPA), 169; in Louisiana, 165, 173–78, 180
Epstein, Brian, 249
Equal Rights Amendment (ERA), 143, 144, 145, 149, 150
Ethical Tea Partnership, 225
Ewen, Elizabeth, 265

Fabulous Failure, A (Lichtenstein), 274–75
Fair Labor Standards Act (1938), 270
Fairtrade Foundation, 225
Fall of the House of Labor, The (Montgomery), 268, 273
Farah, Barbara, 149
Farmer, James, 122
Fass, Paula, 244–45
Federal Advisory Council (FAC), 42
Federal Reserve Act (1913), 45
Federal Reserve, 5, 37–45, 52–55, 83, 279, 282, 283; in 1950s, 37, 45–52; role of, in causing recessions, 5, 37–38, 47, 49–50, 55, 283; and Treasury Department, 40, 41–42, 45, 46, 51 (*see also* "Bills Only" doctrine; Fed-Treasury Accord); unions' critiques of, 38, 39, 44–45, 47, 50–51
Federation for American Immigration Reform (FAIR), 195, 198
FedEx, 219
Fed-Treasury Accord (1951), 43, 45, 283; unions' response to, 44–45, 47
Feinstein, Dianne, 148
Feldman, Paul, 128–29
feminism, 132–33, 138, 269, 281; differences over, among socialists, 130, 132–33; Jimmy Carter and, 7, 139, 140, 142–43; in 1970s–1980s, 142–50, 152–54 (see also *Gender Gap*)
Ferraro, Geraldine A., 153
Field, Thomas, 100
Filene, Benjamin, 243
financial crisis of 2008–2009, 37, 220. *See also* Great Recession
Financial Times, 213
Fiori, Guy, 253
fiscal citizenship, 89–90, 199, 274
Flores, Nichole M., 90
food industry, 224–25, 226
foodways, 253–54
Ford Motor Company, 221, 222, 223
Fortune, 41–42, 214
Ford, Gerald, 106, 284
Fourteenth Amendment, 22, 24, 28
Fox, Vincente, 197
Frankfurter, Felix, 13, 14, 16, 28–30, 31, 283
Frankfurt School, 75
Franklin, Benjamin, 90
Fraser, Steve, 262, 272
Freidberg, Susanne, 226
Freud, Sigmund, 81
Friedan, Betty, 141
Friedman, Milton, 83
Frost, David, 88
Fuller, R. Buckminster, 5, 65, 66, 67–70, 72–73, 286; anti-statism of, 5, 80–81, 286; popularity of, 66, 82, 84n7; on technology, 67, 68–69, 70

Gabler, Neal, 246
Galbraith, John Kenneth, 65, 117, 125, 127
Garbo, Greta, 246
Geary, Daniel, 293; chapter by, 112–36
Gender Gap (Abzug and Kelber), 137–38, 139, 140, 146–55, 281
gender gap (in voting preferences), 137, 144, 147, 149, 153, 154
General Motors, 48, 273
Geoghegan, Thomas, 263, 270–71, 289
Georgia, 194, 203
Gereffi, Gary, 215
Gerstle, Gary, 266, 272, 281
Gerwig, Greta, 237, 238
GI Bill (1945), 270
Giebelhouse, Dan, 21
Gilded Age, 3, 265, 283, 287
Gitlin, Todd, 63, 288
Glickman, Lawrence, 286
globalizing of production, 273. *See also* supply chains
Gold, Michael, 140
Goldfinger, Nat, 38, 55
Goldstein, Betty. *See* Friedan, Betty
Goldwater, Barry, 131, 143
Goodell, Charles, 78
Good Will Hunting (film), 252–53, 254, 287
Gordon, Colin, 269
Gordon, Linda, 269
Gorn, Elliott, 240–41
Graham, Lindsey, 198, 199
Great Depression, 39, 48, 63, 287, 291; movies during, 245–46, 254
Great Recession, 4, 192. *See also* financial crisis of 2008–2009
Great Society, 138
Greening of America, The (Reich), 65, 75–79
Greenspan, Alan, 83
Gutman, Herbert, 265–66

Haldeman, Bob, 101
Hall, Jacqueline Dowd, 266
Hall, Stuart, 245
Hamilton, Jack, 249
Hamilton, Shane, 293; chapter by, 211–33
Harlan County, USA (film), 270–71
Harless, Raymond F., 100
Harrington, Michael, 6, 112–14, 115–21, 123–28, 130, 132–33; background of, 115–18, 280; and Bayard Rustin, 118–19, 126, 128; difference of, with Shachtmanites, 6, 113–14, 123–29, 132, 133, 280–81; hopes of, for Democratic Party, 6, 112, 114, 116, 125,132, 280–81; *The Other America* by, 116–17, 123; and Vietnam War, 113, 124-25, 127, 128
Harris, Kamala, 154, 238
Harrison, Bennett, 270
Hartley, Fred, 19
Harvard Business Review, 227
Hayden, Tom, 117–18
Heckler, Margaret, 145
Heller, Walter, 52
Herberg, Will, 17
Herod, Andy, 226
Hill, Herbert, 272, 273
Hill, Norman, 119
hillbilly music. *See* country music
Hilmes, Michele, 251
Hine, Lewis, 265
Hoffman, Clare, 19
Horowitz, Rachelle, 118, 119, 122–23, 126, 129
House Ways and Means Committee, 97, 108
Howard, John, 243
Howe, Irving, 115, 116, 123
Hubbs, Nadine, 241, 249, 250
Humphrey, Hubert, 124, 126
Hunter, Alberta, 248
Hunter College, 140–41
Huntington, Samuel, 190

IKEA stores, 227
Illegal Immigration Reform and Immigration Responsibility Act (IIRIRA, 1996), 193, 195
immigrants, 7, 187, 197–98, 203; changing composition of, 191–92; depiction of, in books, 263–66; Jewish, 245–46. *See also* immigration policy; Mexican immigrants
Immigration and Nationality Act (1965), 7, 191, 284
immigration policy, 7–8, 186–206, 284–85; legislation on, 7, 191–92, 193, 194, 195, 197, 284; and party alignments, 188–89, 190, 195–96, 198–99, 203, 205; and refugees, 191–92, 194, 200, 205; Tea Party and, 199–201, 202, 285; unions and, 194–95
Immigration Reform and Control Act (IRCA, 1986), 193, 195, 197, 284
Independent Socialist League (ISL), 114, 115, 117
individualism, 29, 152, 154, 268, 271, 275; and counterculture intellectuals, 72–74, 75–76, 79, 81–83
industrial pluralism, 16, 269
Industrial Workers of the World, 290
inflation, 38; in late 1940s, 5, 20, 41; in late 1960s, 91, 92, 96; in 1950s, 37, 38, 39, 45–46. *See also* stagflation
interest rates, 54–55; Federal Reserve's role in, 5, 38, 40, 41–43, 45–46, 51, 53–54 (*see also* Volcker Shock); and neoliberalism, 38, 39, 55; political differences over, 41–43, 47, 51–52, 54
"intermediate technology" (Schumacher), 72
Internal Revenue Service (IRS), 88, 94–95, 96, 107–8; and Nixon tax scandal, 88, 95, 96–97, 99–101, 105, 106, 107, 284
International Labour Organization, 219
International Ladies' Garment Workers' Union (ILGWU), 17
International Socialists, 262
Isserman, Maurice, 66

Jackson, Kirtley, 174–75, 180
Jacobs, Meg, 293; chapter by, 260–75
Jagger, Mick, 248–49
James, C. L. R., 115
Jaworski, Leon, 106
Jetson juvenile prison (Louisiana), 11
Johnson, Colin, 243
Johnson, Lyndon (and Johnson administration), 93, 117, 120, 124–25, 282
Johnson, Paul, 240
Joint Committee on Internal Revenue Taxation (JCIRT), 95, 98; and Nixon tax scandal, 89, 95, 97–98, 99–100, 101–5, 106–7
Jones, Brian, 248

Kafka, Franz, 73, 80
Kahn, Tom, 118–19, 124, 129, 130, 131; and Bayard Rustin, 118–19, 121; in factional disputes among socialists, 122, 126, 127; and Max Shachtman, 113, 118, 121
Kariel, Henry, 65
Kasson, John, 241
Kasson, Joy, 240
Katznelson, Ira, 269–70
Kazin, Michael, 66, 266
Kefauver, Estes, 48; Senate subcommittee headed by, 48–50, 51–52, 53
Kelber, Mim, 6–7; background of, 6–7, 140–41; in 1970s and '80s, 7, 137–40, 142–55. See also *Gender Gap* (Abzug and Kelber)
Kelley, Robin, 266
Kemble, Penn, 128–29
Kennedy, Edward, 142, 143, 197, 198–99, 203
Kennedy, John F. (and Kennedy administration), 52–54, 117, 119, 124
Kennedy, Robert F., 63
Kerr, Clark, 288
Kesey, Ken, 75
Kessler-Harris, Alice, 269
Keyserling, Leon, 38, 43, 44, 120
King, Martin Luther, Jr., 63, 118, 119, 121
Kirkland, Lane, 129
Kirkpatrick, Jeane, 127, 153
Klammon, Joseph, 31
Klare, Karl, 269
Klein, Ethel, 149
Klein, Jennifer, 293–94; chapter by 163–85
Kobach, Kris, 202
Koch family, 199
Kolkin, Miriam. *See* Kelber, Mim
Kolko, Gabriel, 65, 66
Korean War, 43, 47, 118
Kotz, Nick, 93
Kristensen, Ella, 30
Kristol, Irving, 115, 130

Labor and Nation magazine, 17
labor history, 243, 260–61, 265, 273–74, 288–91; new understandings of, 9, 212, 245, 260–63, 265–66, 271–75, 288–89 (*see also* New Labor History)
labor laws, 1–2, 3, 271, 288. *See also* National Labor Relations Act; right-to-work laws; Taft-Hartley Act
"labor question, the," 5, 7, 14, 39, 150, 186, 285; and "immigration question," 7, 186, 189–90, 197
Labor's Economic Review, 50
Labor's War at Home (Lichtenstein), 267–68, 274
Ladner, Joyce, 119
"landfarms," 171–72, 176, 177
Lansing, Marjorie, 149
Lear, Frances, 146, 153
Lear, Norman, 146
Lecklider, Aaron, 245
Ledbetter, Brownie, 142
Lee, Amanda, 176–77
Leffingwell, Russell, 41, 43
Leiserson, William, 17
Lennon, John, 248, 249
Leuchtenberg, William, 244
Lewis, John, 119
LGBTQ people, 239, 241, 242, 243–45, 250
Lichtenstein, Nelson, 9, 186, 274–75; Afterword by, 279–91; Labor Day op-ed by (1992), 260–61, 262, 271, 272, 275; on labor history, 260–64, 266, 267–68, 271, 272–73, 274; on supply chain management, 220–21, 223, 225, 227, 273
Lieberman, Robert, 269
Limbaugh, Rush, 203
Link, Stefan, 222
Little Caesar (film), 245–46
Little Richard, 239
Long, Russell, 99
Los Angeles Citizen, 13, 31
Los Angeles Times, 98
Lott, Eric, 246–47
Louisiana, 163–180; incarceration in, 11, 163, 167–68, 169, 174, 180; industrial pollution in, 163, 164–65, 168–72; remedial efforts in, 165, 172–80. *See also* chemical industry (in Louisiana)
Louisiana Board of Commerce and Industry (BCI), 166, 172, 175, 177, 179
Louisiana Department of Environmental Quality, 165, 177–80
Louisiana Department of Natural Resources (DNR), 171, 172, 175, 177, 179
Louisiana Environmental Quality Act (1983), 177
Lowi, Theodore, 65
Lynd, Staughton, 122

Macdonald, Dwight, 65, 115
MacLaine, Shirley, 142
Mailer, Norman, 75
Making a New Deal (Cohen), 268
Makovicky, Nicolette, 90
Malthus, Thomas, 67
Mandel, Ruth B., 147, 148
March on Washington (1963), 113, 119, 120, 129
Marcuse, Herbert, 66, 75
Martin, William McChesney, 45–46, 59–50, 51–54
Marx, Karl, 67, 81
Maslin, Janet, 253
Mathewes, Charles, 90
Mattel corporation, 237, 238, 255–56
Max, Steve, 117–18
May, Lary, 245, 246
Mazey, Emil, 132
Mazzocchi, Tony, 173
McCain, John, 198–99, 202, 203, 204
McCarthy, Eugene, 124, 125
McConnell, Grant, 65
McDaniel, Chris, 201
McGovern, George, 113–14, 128–32, 133, 281
McMillan, John, 248–49
McReynolds, David, 127
Means, Gardiner, 48, 49
Meany, George, 50, 113, 119, 123, 281; and 1972 election, 128, 130, 131, 281; Shachtmanites and, 113, 122, 123, 128, 129, 130, 131
Merritt, Walter Gordon, 15, 23
Metzgar, Jack, 271, 272, 289
Mexican immigrants, 189, 191, 192, 200, 203; demeaning of, 187, 200, 284
Mid-Atlantic Association of Radical Historians, 143–44
Mikulski, Barbara, 142, 148
Miller, Karl, 242–43, 248, 251
Millet, Columbus, Jr., 174, 175
Mills, C. Wright, 17, 65, 66, 75, 280, 285–86
Mills, Wilbur, 97–98, 106–7
Mink, Patsy Takemoto, 142–43
Minutemen, 198
modern monetary theory (MMT), 38
Mondale, Walter, 153
monetary policy, 5, 37–55, 283; and fiscal policy, 39–40, 44 (*see also* Fed-Treasury Accord); unions' efforts to influence, 38–39, 44–45, 47, 50–53, 54. *See also* Federal Reserve; interest rates
Montgomery, David, 265, 268, 273
Montgomery, Donald, 38, 39, 44, 47
Montgomery bus boycott (1956), 118
Moore, Jason W., 164
Moore, Mary Tyler, 145
"moral capitalism," 268
Morgan, Edward L., 98–99, 103, 106
Moses, Robert, 266
movies, 237–38, 242, 245–46, 270–71, 287. See also *Barbie*; *Oppenheimer*
Ms. magazine, 140
"multi-stakeholder initiatives" (MSIs), 224–25
Muncy, Robyn, 262, 267
Munro, Rolland, 217
music, 242–43, 247–49, 250, 251, 287
Myrdal, Gunnar, 26–27

Nader, Ralph, 66
Nation, The, 153
National Advisory Committee for Women (NACW), 139, 143, 149
National Council of La Raza (NCLR), 203–4
National Labor Relations Act (Wagner Act, 1935), 4–5, 31, 269, 271, 289; ambiguity of, on union security agreements, 15–16; and industrial democracy, 25; Supreme Court and, 22, 23, 30. *See also* National Labor Relations Board
National Labor Relations Board (NLRB), 1, 20, 141, 269, 270, 289; and union security clauses, 15–16, 17
National Lawyers Guild, 141
National Security Entry-Exit Registration System (NSEERS), 194
National Women's Conference (Houston, 1977), 142–43, 148
National Women's Political Caucus (NWPC), 142, 143
Nebraska right-to-work law, 13, 21
Nelson, Bruce, 266
neoconservatism, 6, 113, 129, 130–31, 281
neoliberalism, 2, 190, 244, 261, 271, 274–75, 281; economic changes brought by, 133, 190, 250–51, 261, 282; historians on, 80, 137, 250; and interest rate increases, 38, 39, 55

"new class," 113, 125–26, 129, 130–31, 281
New Deal, 3, 6, 245, 268–70; critiques of, by counterculture intellectuals, 76, 285, 286, 287; and Federal Reserve, 5, 37, 39, 283; limits of, 7, 14, 22, 27, 30, 31–32, 268, 269–70. *See also* National Labor Relations Act
New Deal order, 261; end of, 38, 250, 287; historians' new understandings of, 8, 14, 38; and unions, 4–5, 14, 22–23
New Labor History, 261, 262, 264, 288–89
"New Politics" wing (of Democratic Party), 126, 131, 132, 138, 139, 281; Michael Harrington and, 113–14, 126, 132; Shachtmanites' opposition to, 113–14, 126, 129, 281
Newspaper Guild, 141
New Yorker magazine, 75
New York Times, 13, 49, 144, 252; bestseller list of, 65, 75; on Nixon tax issues, 96, 97, 98, 104; opinion columns in, 48, 96, 97, 153, 154, 260–61, 272
Nicaragua, 139
Nike corporation, 219
9/11 attacks (2001), 194, 196, 197, 220
Nixon, Richard M., 48, 49–50, 127, 132; in 1968 election, 63, 114, 128, 131, 281. *See also* Nixon tax scandal
Nixon tax scandal, 6, 88–89, 92–108; congressional investigation of, 89, 95, 97–98, 99–100, 101–5, 106–7; and "I am not a crook" quote, 88; IRS and, 88, 95, 96–97, 99–101, 105, 106, 107, 284; pardon for, 106; and Watergate scandal, 88, 93, 99, 106
Nolan Christopher, 237
North Carolina, 203; right-to-work law in, 13, 19, 21, 203
Norton, Patricia, 177–80

Obama, Barack, 190, 282; and immigration, 201–2, 203–4; right-wing opposition to, 199, 201–2
Ocasio-Cortez, Alexandria, 112
Occupational Safety and Health Act (1970), 173
Occupational Safety and Health Administration (OSHA), 173, 174, 175, 180
offshoring, 8, 227, 270
Oil, Chemical and Atomic Workers Union (OCAW), 172–73, 180
O'Neill, Thomas P. "Tip," 145
On the Line (Swados), 263, 266–67, 268
Oppenheimer (film), 237–38
Orenstein, Dana, 217
Other America, The (Harrington), 116–17, 123
Out of This Furnace (Bell), 263–65, 271, 289

Padway, Joseph, 18, 22, 23, 24; and "closed-shop cases," 20, 22–24, 25, 27, 32n4, 34n40
Pate, E. W., 178
Patman, Wright, 43
Patriot Act (2001), 195–96
Pegler, Westbrook, 18
Peiss, Kathy, 241
People magazine, 106–7
Perlman, Selig, 23
Poitier, Sidney, 242
political economy, 255, 261–62, 272–75
popular culture, 8, 84n7; queer identity in, 244, 250. *See also* movies; music; television shows; "working-class heroes"
Popular Front, 6–7, 129, 150, 263, 280; Bella Abzug and Mim Kelber in, 6–7, 138, 140, 141, 150, 280
Populists, 121, 290
Porter, Michael, 214–15
price controls, 41, 42, 96
Proctor, Barbara, 151
Progressive Era, 15, 29, 265
Promised Land (Antin), 264–65
Proposition 187 (California, 1994), 194, 195–96
Providence Journal-Bulletin, 96, 97
public debt, 4, 42, 51
Public Enemy (film), 245–46

Quirk, Paul, 66

racial segregation, 26, 173, 248, 270
Raff, Daniel, 221–22
Railway Labor Act (1925), 25
Rainey, Ma, 239
Rainforest Alliance, 225
Rana Plaza disaster (Bangladesh, 2013), 219, 227

Randolph, A. Philip, 119, 120, 121. *See also* A. Philip Randolph Institute
Reagan, Ronald, 83, 143–44, 150–51; in 1984 election, 144–45, 147, 149–50, 153–54. *See also* Reagan administration
Reagan administration, 131, 138, 150–51, 152, 154; and unions, 9, 131, 289
recessions, 5, 37–38, 47, 49–50; Federal Reserve's role in causing, 5, 37–38, 47, 49–50, 55, 283. *See also* Great Recession
Redbook magazine, 140
Reece, Florence, 272
Reeve, Gianna, 1
Refugee Act of 1980, 191–92, 194
Reich, Charles, 5, 65, 66, 74–79, 81–82, 84n8, 86n72, 286; anti-statism of, 5, 65, 66, 76–77, 80; background of, 65; on "Consciousness III," 77–79, 81, 82; *Greening of America* by, 65, 75–79; popularity of, 65, 82, 84n7
Reisman, David, 75
Resource Conservation and Recovery Act (1976), 173, 176
Reuss, Henry, 52
Reuther, Victor, 132
Reuther, Walter, 47, 48, 272–73; and progressive wing of labor leadership, 119, 122, 129, 272–73
Reynolds, James, 15
Richards, Ann, 148
Richards, Keith, 248
Richardson, Samuel, 30
Richberg, Donald, 25–26
right-to-work laws, 14–15, 18; liberals and, 25, 26–29, 31–32; referenda on, 5, 18, 19, 31–32; Supreme Court and 14, 22–29; Taft-Hartley Act and, 14, 19, 31; unions and, 19–25
Riis, Jacob, 265
Rise and Fall of the Neoliberal Order (Gerstle), 281
Rise and Fall of the New Deal Order, The (Fraser and Gerstle), 272, 281
Robbie, Margot, 238
Roediger, David, 246–47
Rogin, Michael, 247
Rolling Stones, 248–49, 287
Rollins corporation, 169–72, 175, 176–80
Romer, Christina, 46
Romer, David, 46
Romney, George, 273
Romney, Mitt, 188, 202
Ronsijn, Wouter, 222
Roosevelt, Franklin D., 13, 15, 31, 39, 138; administration of, 4, 6–7, 18, 24, 39, 91 (*see also* New Deal). *See also* Roosevelt era
Roosevelt era, 2, 3, 5, 14, 89, 138
Rosengarten, Theodore, 289
Rosenzweig, Roy, 241, 264, 265
Rossi, Alice, 148
Rubio, Marco, 204
Rustin, Bayard, 113, 118–21, 131; and AFL-CIO, 10, 122, 129; and civil rights movement, 113, 119, 120, 122, 125; and Michael Harrington, 118–19, 126, 128; and Vietnam War, 123
Rutledge, Wiley, 31
Ruttenberg, Stanley, 38, 47, 50

Sabin, Paul, 286
sacrifice zones, 164, 181n3. *See also* "Chemical Corridor"
Saint Louis Post-Dispatch, 31
Samuelson, Paul, 53
Sanders, Bernie, 112, 117, 133
Saturday Night Fever (film), 249, 254
Savitzky, Bella. *See* Abzug, Bella
Scarface (film), 245–46
Schiller, Reuel, 294; chapter by, 63–87
Schlafly, Phyllis, 143
Schlesinger, Arthur, Jr., 127, 189–90
Schneiderman, Rose, 265
Schroeder, Patricia, 148, 153
Schultze, Charles, 288
Schumacher, E. F., 5, 65–66, 71–74, 79, 81, 82, 286; anti-statism of, 5, 73, 80, 286; background of, 71; on entrepreneurship, 72–73, 74, 82–83; popularity of, 66, 82; *Small Is Beautiful* by, 66, 71–74, 286
Seeger, Pete, 272
Selden, David, 132
Senn v. Tile (1937), 22, 24, 35n5
Sensenbrenner, James, 196, 197
Service Employees International Union (SEIU), 1, 198
Sessions, Jeff, 204
Sexton, Brendan, 132

Shachtman, Max, 112–13, 118; and AFL-CIO, 113, 120, 122–23, 131; background of, 114; in conflicts within Socialist Party, 113–14, 123, 124, 126–29, 131; realignment strategy of, 114, 116, 120;
Shachtmanites, 6, 113–15, 122–23, 126–33; differences of, with Michael Harrington, 6, 113–14, 123–29, 132, 133, 280–81; and Vietnam War, 6, 123, 124, 127. *See also* Shachtman, Max
Shanker, Albert, 132
Shaw, Nate, 266, 289
Shermer, Elizabeth Tandy, 279, 294; Introduction by, 1-9
Shishkin, Boris, 45
Shultz, George, 100
"Silent Majority," 91–92
Simpson, Alan, 204
Sinclair, Upton, 140, 226
"Sixties, the," 63–64
Skeggs, Beverly, 251
Sklaroff, Lauren Rebecca, 294; chapter by, 237–59
Skocpol, Theda, 200
Slaiman, Don, 122, 123
Small Is Beautiful (Schumacher), 66, 71–74, 286
Smeal, Eleanor, 145, 150
Smith, Bessie, 239
Smith, Robin, 90
Snyder, John, 41–42
Socialist Party (SP), 115–16, 117, 119–20, 126, 128
Socialist Youth League, 115, 117
social mobility, 190, 241, 252–53, 254, 256
Social Security, 91, 145, 270
Sombart, Werner, 268
Sonti, Samir, 295; chapter by, 37–58
Soviet Union, 114, 129. *See also* Cold War
Spain, Thomas, 233
Sparrow, James, 274
Sproul, Allan, 41, 43, 51
St. Gabriel Prison Camp (Louisiana), 163, 167, 168, 169, 174, 180
stagflation, 37, 38, 54
Stalin, Joseph, 114
Stanton, Elizabeth Cady, 149
Starbucks, 253; unionizing at, 1, 2, 4
State Industrial School for Colored Youth (SISCY, Louisiana), 167–68, 180
steel strike of 1959, 271
Stein, Judith, 250, 270
Steinem, Gloria, 132–33, 142, 145
stereotypes, 239, 241–43, 247, 254; gender, 242; racial, 241–42, 243
Stone, I. F., 119
Stone, Katherine, 269
strike waves, 2, 41, 48
Student Nonviolent Coordinating Committee (SNCC), 119, 122
Students for a Democratic Society (SDS), 63, 117–18
Succession (television series), 254–56
Sugrue, Thomas, 270
supply chains, 8, 213–16, 273, 285, 290–91; ahistorical studies of, 8, 211–12, 216–20; historians and, 212, 220–28; "value chains" in, 215–16, 223; Wal-Mart and, 212, 214, 218–19, 220–21, 223, 225–26
supply-side economics, 138
Swados, Harvey, 263, 266–67, 268, 289
Sweeney, John, 131, 272

Taft-Hartley Act (1947), 14, 19, 20, 30, 41; as a major defeat for unions, 32n4, 282; and state right-to-work laws, 14, 19, 31; unions' efforts to repeal, 22, 121
Tannenbaum, Ira, 94–95
Tax Analysts and Advocates, 95–95, 100, 104
taxes, 6, 89–92, 94–95; and fiscal citizenship, 89–90, 199, 274. *See also* Nixon tax scandal
Tax Reform Act of 1969, 93, 102
Tea Party, 188, 199–202, 209n48, 284, 285
technology, 67, 68, 70, 71, 73, 252; "intermediate," 72
television shows, 242, 253–56
Terkel, Studs, 266
Thatcher, Margaret, 153
"third camp" politics, 114, 123
Thomas, Norman, 115–16
Thomas, Woodlief, 49
Thompson, E. P., 244–45, 265, 266, 288, 290
Thorndike, Joseph J., 283–84; chapter by, 88–111
Thornhill v. Alabama (1940), 22, 24

Thornton, Big Mama, 239
Thornton, Mary, 153
Tichenor, Daniel, 194
Titanic (film), 251–52, 253, 287
Tomlins, Christopher, 269
Treen, David, 177, 179
Trotsky, Leon, 114
Truman, David, 65
Truman, Harry S. (and Truman administration), 19, 22; and Federal Reserve, 41–42, 43, 45–46, 52, 57n40
Trump, Donald, 107–8, 132, 154, 155, 201, 238; and immigration, 187, 190, 192, 202, 205, 285
Tsing, Anna Löwenhaupt, 225–26
Tucker, Sophie, 239, 246–48, 287, 287
Turner, David, 223
Turner, Fred, 70

unemployment, 47, 49, 52, 283
unions: in building trades, 21, 26; and capitalism, 2–3, 266–67, 268, 269, 282–83, 288, 289; and Democratic Party, 20, 113, 123, 124, 129–30, 131, 271, 281; and federal monetary policy, 38–39, 44–45, 47, 50–53, 54; and immigration, 7, 194–95; and right-to-work laws, 19–25 (*see also* "closed shop cases"); and Starbucks, 1, 2, 4; and Vietnam War, 6, 123, 132, 289. *See also specific unions and federations*
union shops, 14–15, 18, 27, 29. *See also* "closed shop cases"
United Automobile Workers (UAW), 132, 267, 272–73; and AFL-CIO, 119, 129; and civil rights movement, 119; Shachtmanites and, 114, 122; strikes by, 2, 48. *See also* Montgomery, Donald; Reuther, Walter
University of Chicago, 43, 117
U.S. Supreme Court, 3–4, 282–83; and "closed shop cases," 13–14, 16–17, 22–25, 27–31

Vanhaute, Eric, 222
Vassallo, Justin, 251
vertical integration, 215, 221, 222, 223
Vietnam War, 141, 172; counterculture intellectuals and, 75, 76, 80; Democratic Party fractures over, 113, 122, 123, 124, 280–81; socialists' debates over, 6, 123–24, 127–28, 280–81; unions and, 6, 123, 132, 289
Vinel, Jean-Christian, 295; chapter by, 13–32
Vinson, Fred, 41–42
Volcker Shock, 38, 55, 283
Voting Rights Act of 1965, 3, 119, 167

Wagner Act. *See* National Labor Relations Act
Wagner, Robert, 5, 15. *See also* National Labor Relations Act
Wallace, Henry, 129, 265
Wallerstein, Immanuel, 215
Wall Street Journal, 100
Wal-Mart, 212, 214, 218–19, 220–21, 223, 225–26, 273
Walters, William D., 99–100
Walton, Sam, 273. *See also* Wal-Mart
Waring, Stephen, 288
Warren, Earl, 283
Washington Post, 49, 153; on Nixon tax scandal, 93, 96, 104, 105–6
Waste Alert!, 176
Watergate scandal, 6, 80, 93, 286; and Nixon tax scandal, 88, 93, 99, 106
Wattenberg, Ben, 130
Weinberg, Nat, 132
Which Side Are You On? (Geoghegan), 263, 270–71
Whitaker, James, 21
White House Coordinating Council on Women, 154
whiteness, 241–42
wildcat strikes, 274
Williams, Herbert, 19
Williams, John, 93
Williamson, Vanessa, 200
Wilson, Mark, 274
Wilson, Pete, 196
Wilson, Woodrow, 96
Women's Presidential Project, 153
Women Strike for Peace (WSP), 141, 143
Women USA, 142, 144–45, 146, 147, 149
Woodward, Bob, 266
Work, Culture, and Society (Gutman), 265–66
Workers Party, 14
Workers United, 1

"working class" (term), 130, 262
"working-class heroes," 237–56, 285, 287, 289; in dime novels, 240, 249; and gender, 242, 246–48; in movies, 245–46, 251–53, 256, 287; in music, 242–43, 247–49, 250, 251; and race, 8, 239–43; in television shows, 253–56
World War I, 19, 268
World War II, 68, 91, 151, 165, 250, 274; Federal Reserve in, 40–41, 46; labor issues during, 5, 17, 18, 19, 31, 33n20, 268; race relations in, 26–27

Yard, Molly, 145
Yarnell, Damon, 221
Young People's Socialist League (YPSL), 117, 119, 131

Zarnow, Leandra, 295; chapter by, 137–59
Zinn, Howard, 287

ACKNOWLEDGMENTS

A lot of people helped this book finally get published. I got the idea in 2019 when Nelson Lichtenstein announced that he would be retiring the very next year. Since earning his PhD at Berkeley in 1974, he had spent decades as an advisor, mentor, and friend to many students and scholars, young, old, and middle aged. But he did not want a festschrift. He also recoiled at the idea of a retirement conference where attendees would recount everything that he had published since the beginning of his career. Better, he insisted, was a volume dedicated to new work, featuring younger scholars who had already transformed the field of American history or were poised to do so. The papers would be due in spring 2020.

COVID-19 pushed that deadline back two years. But the University of California, Santa Barbara's College of Letters and Science, Graduate Division, History Department, Interdisciplinary Humanities Center, and Center for the Study of Work, Labor, and Democracy remained committed to this project. Their combined support helped pay two graduate students invaluable to this drawn-out endeavor, Doug Genens and Emma John. Many faculty and administrators also remained encouraging, including Rich Appelbaum, Adrienne Edgar, Dick Flacks, Mary Furner, Mary Hancock, Laura Kalman, Stephan Miescher, Alice O'Connor, Erika Rappaport, David Stein, and Chancellor Henry Yang. Scholars far from Santa Barbara also appreciated the need for a project emphasizing the historic intersections between work, capitalism, and democracy, including Andrew Wender Cohen, Nick Cohen, George Cotkin, Colleen Doody, Andrew Elrod, Masha Federova, Serge Ferrari, Gary Gerstle, Jesse Halverson, Toby Higbie, Jill Jensen, Neil Johnson, Michael Kazin, Lizzie Lamoree, Henry Marr, John Munro, Marta Peluso, Kit Smemo, Doug Smith, Cody Stephens, Tom Sugrue, and Hugh Wolford.

The University of Pennsylvania Press's Bob Lockhart never faltered in his support for this project. Bob had been an editor of books and collections coming out of UCSB's Center for the Study of Work, Labor, and Democracy for years. Once again, as this project came into fruition, he offered sharp, thoughtful criticism that made this book better before the manuscript went out to reviewers, who also provided helpful feedback. I also need to thank copy editor Sheryl Rose and indexer Jim O'Brien, who expertly shepherded this book through the final stages of the production process.

The manuscript never would have been ready for submission without the unyielding support of Eileen Boris. Some of that help came out of the funds tied to her endowed chair. But I cannot put a price tag on the advice she gave as a scholar, friend, and confidant. I have been lucky to have her as a wellspring of inspiration and guidance since my first year in graduate school, when she hired me to help her plan the 2005 Berkshire Conference of Women Historians. For more than twenty years, we have joked that I may have worked *with* Nelson but I really worked *for* Eileen.

Kolibri 360 GmbH
Ferdinand-Jühlke-Straße 7
99095 Erfurt, Deutschland
produktsicherheit@kolibri360.de